Praise for
## TO THE LAST MAN

"Macdonald is particularly skilled at presenting war from the standpoint of those directly involved in its bloody business…. [Her] uncompromising narrative brings the bloody dawn of the century into vivid, human relief." —*Publishers Weekly* (starred review)

"Beautifully written, spectacularly researched…. Macdonald weaves together the forgotten voices of the war to create a comprehensive picture that offers a perspective unlike the ones provided by such contemporary historians as John Keegan and Niall Ferguson…. The ultimate account of the end of the Great War."
—*Kirkus Reviews* (starred review)

"Through the thoughtful, sensitive marshaling of information from letters and interviews, Macdonald has not only conjured up the horrific sights and sounds of the First World War but has captured the heartfelt feelings of the participants as well."
—*Houston Chronicle*

"Macdonald's narrative, constructed around a succession of remarkable and fresh firsthand accounts, is both compelling and vivid." —*Times Literary Supplement*

"She is a considerable scholar of war…. One of Lyn Macdonald's achievements…has been to give a voice to those whose memory of these events is on the point of disappearing. It is for this aspect of her work that she will always be remembered and admired."
—Sebastian Faulks, *Literary Review*

"Superb…. [Macdonald] conveys vividly what they did, who they were, and what it was like to be there." —*Financial Times*

"Macdonald successfully shows us the suffering of soldiers and civilians on all sides. Recommended for academic and public libraries as well as special collections." —*Library Journal*

# LYN MACDONALD

# TO THE LAST MAN

## SPRING 1918

CARROLL & GRAF PUBLISHERS, INC.
NEW YORK

First Carroll & Graf cloth edition 1999
First Carroll & Graf trade paperback edition 2001

Carroll & Graf Publishers, Inc.
A Division of Avalon Publishing Group
19 West 21st Street
New York, NY 10010-6805

Library of Congress Cataloging-in-Publication Data is available.
ISBN: 0-7867-0797-6

Manufactured in the United States of America

# Contents

# List of Illustrations

# List of Maps

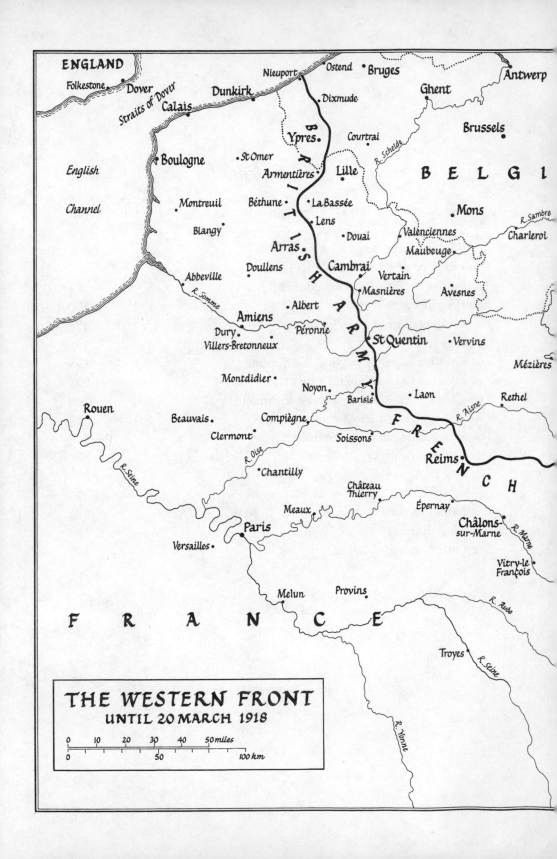

THE WESTERN FRONT
UNTIL 20 MARCH 1918

0   10   20   30   40   50 miles

0            50            100 km

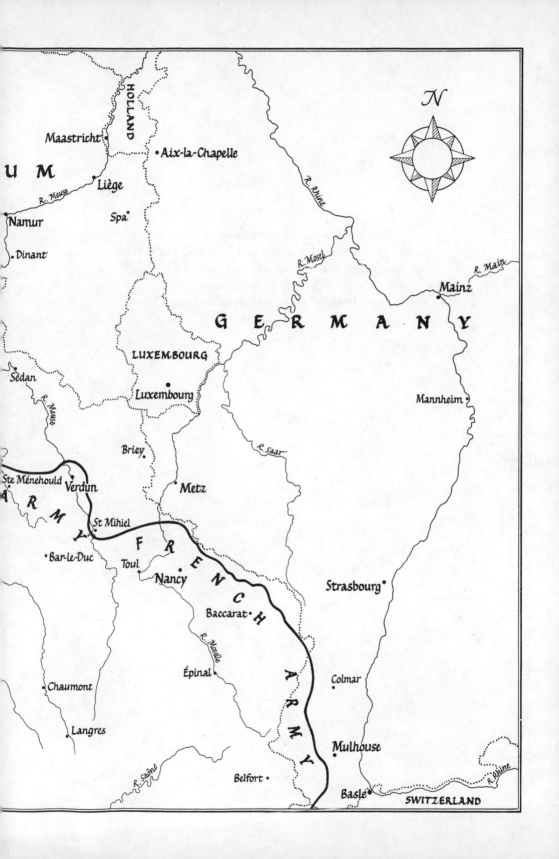

This book is for my own beloved boys,
Benjamin and Daniel and Saul and Paul and Thomas,
who are not so very different from the
boys of that earlier generation,
whose histories are part of their heritage.

'. . . there is only one degree of resistance and that is to the last round and the last man.'

LIEUTENANT-COLONEL W. ELSTOB
16th Battalion,
The Manchester Regiment

# Author's Foreword and Acknowledgements

The word 'horror' has become inseparable from contemporary judgement of the First World War, but it is too glib an appraisal. In many years of conversing with former soldiers I can say with perfect honesty that I have never heard the word 'horror' on their lips, though many of the experiences they spoke of were indeed horrific. A distinguished military historian, Sir John Fortescue, who was also librarian at Windsor Castle and author of the monumental *History of the British Army*, wrote as early as 1914, 'We are too much inclined to think of war as a matter of combats, demanding above all things physical courage. It is really a matter of fasting and thirsting; of toiling and waking; of lacking and enduring; which demands above all things moral courage.' Four years later, despite the ghastly effects of modern weaponry in the first industrialized war, of stultifying battles which dragged on for weeks or months, of the nightmare casualties in a war of attrition, his words still held good, and few soldiers returning from the war would have disagreed with them.

A poem which seems to me to sum up the experience of the 'ordinary soldier' was written by Second Lieutenant Jim Aldous, whose story appears in this book:

> The endless road moves to a darkening sky,
> A road where withered trees and shadows sigh
> Across the years, where memories lie
> With friends long-dead in Picardy.

> The tide ran in, that day, so deep
> The sun was drowned; yet friendship flows
> Deeper, from springs which childhood knows,
> Mirrored in ageing memory.

> It wasn't much.
> A scramble up a bank, a foot or two;
> A hundred yards as if you said
> 'Look, post a letter for me, will you?'

*Just fifty years ago. A summer's day,*
*Not screaming as the poets like to say,*
*Because shock numbs, and anyway it's rare;*
*But frightened, naturally, and tense,*
*And, until the end, rather enjoying it.*

*Thus came the end of a beginning.*
*No poet-prince fought in Picardy,*
*No golden voice of immortality*
*Sang Crispin's day; but old men in their dreams*
*Will sometimes ramble with their youthful friends*
*And mingle shadow with reality.*
*In five years' time, or ten at most,*
*They will be gone.*
*It matters not – so long as not in vain*
*The ghosts of far-off friends should die.*
*For though the poplars dream beside the road,*
*Yet through their dreams, the silver bombers fly.*

Jim Aldous wrote these lines on the fiftieth anniversary of the Battle of the Somme, when he was living in retirement in East Anglia, where American airbases were active in the 1960s, the 'Cold War' was more than a slogan, nuclear war seemed a real possibility, and newspaper headlines on the war in Vietnam were growing larger by the day. Jim Aldous's poem is a powerful plea for peace, and who has a better right to make it than a man who fought in the Great War?

*To the Last Man: Spring 1918* is not an oral history of the events it describes but, like my earlier books on the First World War, it is strongly based on the contemporary accounts and recollections of the soldiers. As always, my aim (and in a sense my obligation) has been to stand in their boots – regardless of rank, position or nationality – and, although their experiences are set in the wider context of situations and events of which they could have known nothing, to see things through their eyes, to try to understand, and above all not to be judgemental.

In recent years I have listened in the company of war veterans to speeches which were kindly meant and expressed with real sincerity but whose sentiments have caused them pain. They keep their thoughts to themselves, for they learned self-control in a hard school and they realized long ago how difficult it can be to explain the concepts of service and loyalty, as *they* understood them, to a more liberal, less reverent and perhaps more self-indulgent generation. Moreover, they themselves have not been impervious to the bombardment of scathing criticism of 'the Generals', the analysis of the conduct of the war, the re-evaluation of its worth, and the shift in perception of the ordinary soldier from brave hero to pitiful victim. They never saw themselves as heroes, nor even as particularly brave, for they were scared stiff most of the time, but they had some sense of achievement in what they had endured and they decidedly did not regard themselves as victims. Now many are half-convinced that they were and, worse, are half-ashamed of it.

It is hard to stand in a war cemetery among those serried headstones with their homely, poignant inscriptions and fail to be moved to sadness, to pity, sometimes to anger, and even to conclude that such a sacrifice was futile. Looking back on the threshold of a new century as the Great War recedes into history, it is easy to believe that it was, but the generation who fought that war were neither fools nor dupes, nor sheep led bleating to the slaughter, and to pity them as such is to do them a deep injustice. Only a handful of survivors are still alive to tell the tale, and they are very old, but they represent the legions of young men who did not survive, and surely we owe all of them the courtesy of trying to understand their world, the principles which inspired them and the context in which they fought that 'war to end wars'. Many of the men whose experiences appear in this book have not lived to see them in print. But I hope that it does them honour, for they were a remarkable generation.

In any record of 1918 it is impossible to avoid mention of the politics. Even after eighty years they can still rouse passions and revive old arguments. The situations and relationships were so complicated, aims and attitudes – both personal and national – so different, and human nature, then as now, so unpredictable that it is no easy task to distinguish opinion from fact, accurate observation from gossip, even the official standpoint from reality, without taking into account the rivalries in high places and between the personalities involved. Nor can one discount the personal considerations which must have carried weight with those who were writing in retrospect of events which took place behind closed doors. The waters are muddy – and mud sticks. But I have done my best to stick to indisputable facts, and I hope that I have been fair.

As always, I owe a huge debt to other people who, with great kindness and usually unsolicited, have made available valuable original material in the form of diaries, memoirs and letters. My first thanks, of course, must go to the old soldiers whose names are listed separately at the end of the book. It has given me huge satisfaction to be able to include more first-hand accounts of German soldiers than I have been able to do in the past. People often enquire why I have never attempted to record the Germans' experiences like those of the British, but the time and cost of such an exercise would be prohibitive, besides which my knowledge of spoken German is far too limited even to contemplate attempting in-depth interviews with German veterans. But someone else has. Richard Baumgartner is a third-generation American of German descent, and some years ago, in pursuit of his interest in the Great War, he traced almost 300 German veterans, very few of whom were living in the USA. To quote him:

> I placed adverts in a variety of German newspapers and was astounded by the response – not just the number but the quality of the responses. I was very nearly overwhelmed with correspondence, which led to a month-long sojourn in Germany in 1981 when I visited a goodly number of these gentlemen, researched at several military history archives and spent more than a few pfennig in antiquarian bookstores. I returned to the States with a treasure trove of material which would fill several volumes if only there was time.

Richard is a publisher, and his interest has moved on, but with breathtaking generosity he has made much of this 'treasure trove' available to me. Mere thanks are hardly sufficient to express my gratitude for this and other acts of kindness – including his permission to quote from Fritz Nagel's memoirs, which he published, and, of course, for the translations. The stories of some of those German boys are mirror images of those of their British counterparts – some of whom, indeed, must have been literally within yards of them.

Among other American contributors I must thank Mrs Margaret Barr for the letters written by General Alexander, 41st US Division, to her step-mother, who was his half-sister. In France, thanks are due to Mme Blanche de la Place for the memoirs of her grandfather, Capitaine Désiré Wavrin; to M. Jack Thorpe for a wealth of papers and much-appreciated hospitality and assistance; to M. Jules Notteau for his kindness in giving me volumes of valuable information on the French Army; to M. Antoine Caulliez for his interest and for copies of the sketches of the fighting at Grivesnes; and to M. Claude Dubois, mayor of Grivesnes, for his enthusiastic welcome and a mass of precious documentation unavailable elsewhere.

I am grateful to Colonel J. G. Aldous, OBE, for the papers of his father, Second Lieutenant Jim Aldous, and for permission to reprint his father's splendid poem (which received a mere 'commended' from the Suffolk Poetry Society!); to Major A. W. Howitt for the memoirs and letters of his father, Brigade-Major Harold Howitt; and to Mr R. J. O. Ward for the memoirs of his father, Major Ronald Ward. Michael Wilson not only supplied additional information on his father, Second Lieutenant 'Peter' Wilson, RFC, an old friend and contributor, but also an illuminating interview with his father-in-law, Dick Gammell. Lesley Kemp kindly made available the diaries of her father, Private Stanley Sutcliffe, AIF, and in New Zealand Dr

D. A. Purdie not only interviewed but also transcribed hours of colourful conversation with Private George McKay of the New Zealand Rifle Brigade. My warm thanks to them all, and to the many other people who have assisted in different ways, not least with interviewing old soldiers in parts of the country which were too distant to be easily accessible to me.

My military researcher, John Woodroff, has been my unfailing support for more than twenty years, always available to discuss problems (sometimes knotty), to research the answers to difficult queries, and to check titles, ranks, honours and a host of regimental and divisional details. He is a mine of knowledge, a stern critic, a staunch colleague and an indispensable ally.

Over the years my husband, Ian Ross, has been a great support, despite his own demanding commitments. I have much appreciated his company on working trips to France – not only for doing the driving but for assistance with the photographs, and for sharing my pleasure when, by the merest fluke, we stumbled on the old keeper's cottage at Rouez and recognized it eighty years on. My assistant, Sandra Layson, has also come on forays to the battlefields and kept track of a thousand details along the way. Her interest and enthusiasm never flag, she cheerfully relieves me of a host of routine chores, and I value her cool judgement, her work and her encouragement rather more, I suspect, than she realizes. Of the many people who have had a hand in the production of this book, none has played a more important role than hers.

Lyn Macdonald
London, May 1998

# Prologue

By 1 January 1918 the Great War had been grinding on for 1,245 days. In the vigorous early years of dash and determination they had called it 'the War to end Wars', but the dash and the vigour were long gone, the determination was grimmer, and the only thing that seemed to be endless was the war itself. *Punch*'s parody of the old schoolboy riddle summed up the mood and raised an occasional wry smile:

> *Absolute evidence have I none,*
> *But my Aunt's charwoman's sister's son*
> *Heard a policeman on his beat*
> *Say to a housemaid in Downing Street*
> *That he had an uncle who had a friend*
> *Who knew for a fact when the war would end.*

Europe was caught in the grip of a cruel winter. In Paris, where the Seine was frozen over for the first time in 120 years, people crowded into bars and cafés in search of light and warmth. Wood (when it could be found) fetched astronomical prices and, with much of the country in the industrial north overrun by the Germans, coal supplies in this fourth winter of the war were more meagre than ever and there was precious little fuel to spare for civilians. A quarter of France was in enemy hands, locked behind the wasteland where the big guns thundered and the armies of the Kaiser and the armies of the Allies lived a troglodyte existence in trenches and dugouts gouged from the freezing earth.

The snow did nothing to improve the lot of a soldier shivering in the trenches, sleeping in a ramshackle barn, or on the march, splashing through slush or hunched against a blizzard on the roads behind the lines. But it laid a gentle hand on the battlefield, where the snow drifted into fire-blackened shell-holes, softened the tortuous outlines of splintered trees, buried the clumsy hulks of abandoned tanks, glistened delicately on the barbs of the deadly wire, shrouded the bodies of the quiet, unburied dead.

At Passchendaele in low-lying Belgium, where the ground had turned to a soupy morass under the weight of 10 million shells and months of heavy fighting, the bitter weather came as a relief. The ground hardened underfoot, the fetid water froze in the labyrinth of shell-holes, and the troops slithering on their way to the line were obliged to pull sandbags over their boots to keep their footing on the icy duckboards. But it was better than floundering in a sea of mud.

In front of a trace of rubble that had once been Passchendaele village the line was little more than linked up shell-holes. Here at the tip of the infamous Ypres salient, won at the cost of many lives, a few dugouts and pillboxes captured from the enemy provided the only shelter. It had taken the Army more than three months to slog through the slough and up the ridges to capture Passchendaele in the teeth of the November wind and rains. Many of the 100,000 men who died had simply disappeared in the mud. The long lists of dead and missing soldiers had cast a blight over the closing months of a miserable year.

In the British Isles, food supplies were running seriously low. Basic commodities had all but disappeared from the shops, and the Government was putting the finishing touches to a general rationing scheme that would come into force before the end of the month. They had already issued ration cards that would entitle each person to half a pound of sugar a week. At least it would ensure fair shares for all.

The well-to-do, who were able to pay high prices and buy large quantities, had suffered least from the shortages, and it was painfully obvious that the long queues outside food shops were confined to the poorer areas. The excuse that middle-class people were queuing *inside* the spacious stores where *they* shopped was a lame one. It was offered at a public meeting by Sir Arthur Yapp, director of the food economy campaign, but it failed to pacify angry hecklers. The scandal of the moment was the case of Miss Marie Corelli, a popular author of sensational romances. She appeared in court on 2 January accused of obtaining no less than 183 pounds of sugar and forty-three pounds of tea from various suppliers. The goods were confiscated and she was fined fifty pounds.

There was a move to start communal kitchens to provide wholesome, if unexciting, meals − pease pudding and gravy for a penny, and sausage pudding or lentil savoury for twopence. Even the serious newspapers turned their august attention to the food problem, and obliged their readers with recipes for vegetable mousse in the guise of galantine, for cutlets concocted from nuts and macaroni, and for cakes baked with potato flour. From 1 January the manufacture of ice cream was banned, and in many parts of the country there was neither butter nor margarine to be had. Butchers were forced to close for several days a week because they had no meat to sell, and fish-and-chip shops were closed for lack of fat. The shortage of meat early in the New Year was said to be due to heavy demand over the Christmas season, when large numbers of soldiers had been home on leave. Now, until fresh supplies arrived from across the Atlantic, beleaguered by marauding U-boats, there was little or no meat to be had.

It was immeasurably worse in German towns, where townspeople queued for hours for carp – the traditional centrepiece of the New Year's feast. They queued ankle-deep in slush – for there was no manpower to clear the streets – and they queued in shoes with soles of wood and uppers of thick paper – for leather was scarce and the soldiers must be shod. And often they queued in vain – for the Army had swallowed up so many men that there were few left in the countryside who knew how to crack the ice on the frozen ponds and entice the sleeping carp from the mud below. The few fish that did reach the towns fetched such enormous prices that they were beyond the means of all but the wealthiest households.

There was not much else to sustain life, let alone to cook a celebration meal. The British naval blockade of the seaways prevented supplies of essentials reaching Germany's ports and cut her off from her African colonies and from the world markets. Traditional sources of supply had dried up. Before the war the average daily consumption of calories had been 2,280 for every German citizen. By 1917 he could count on less than 1,000. Chestnut flour and clover meal were standing in for traditional foods, and acorns, even pine kernels, were added as a matter of course to 'stews'. There was no fat, no milk, no eggs, no sugar. Such vast quantities of meat were required to feed the Army that little more than bone and gristle fell to the share of the civilians, and horsemeat was a rare, luxurious treat. The bread was coarse and unpalatable, the ingredients were suspect, and potatoes – which were the staple diet that winter – rotted in the frozen ground and collapsed when they were cooked to a foul-tasting greenish pulp which could be made palatable only by dousing it with ersatz sauce. The sauce was tasty enough, but it contained quantities of sand that crunched unpleasantly between the teeth and left a gritty deposit on the plate. It had not been much of a Christmas on any of the home fronts.

Even Uncle Sam had been forced to tighten his belt and, although the United States was richly nourished by comparison with her European allies, the Government had decreed one 'wheatless' and two meatless days a week.

At the battlefront in Flanders, where Christmas was a movable feast to be celebrated when convenient regardless of the date, it was not until the evening of 2 January that the officers of the 13th Rifle Brigade were free to enjoy their Christmas dinner. It was the first time for many months that they had all sat down together, and in the battered village of Locre it had not been easy to find an undamaged venue large enough to accommodate them. Three days previously they had hauled themselves out of the glutinous trenches at Klein Zillebeke and marched back through the snow to thaw out, to rest and clean up, to count their casualties – thirty-one on that last stint up the line. The previous evening the riflemen and the corporals had feasted on turkeys paid for from Battalion funds, with enough beer and wine to float a battleship and enough plum pudding to sink one. There were fruit and nuts and sweets paid for by the officers, and a packet of cigarettes per man sent out by the officers' wives. Now it was the turn of the officers themselves, and it promised to be worth waiting for.

The mess cart had made no less than three journeys to Bailleul, where trade still thrived and some delicacies were occasionally on sale. Captain Nothard, as mess president, was delighted with his haul, the mess cooks had risen nobly to the occasion, and the dinner was sumptuous. Bill Nothard drew up the menu, Sergeant Rowlands in the orderly room typed it on stiff card, and a copy was propped against the battery of glasses that flanked each officer's place.

*Hors d'Oeuvres Variés Hannescamps*
*Bouillon d'Ovillers*
*Truites à l'Ancre*
*Ris de Porc Hulluch*
*Dindon Roti Monchy-le-Preux*
*Pommes de Terre et Petits Pois Verts*
*Plum Pudding au Rhum Gavrelle*
*Champignons Route de Menin*
*Glaces Basseville Beek*
*Dessert*
*Coffee*

Nothard had taken the trouble to name the dishes in a style appropriate to the Battalion. Hulluch – where they had held the line after the Battle of Loos. Hannescamps – the so-called quiet sector where they had spent Christmas 1915, their first in France. Ovillers in 1916, in the aftermath of the first day of the Somme, and the long slog through to the Battle of the Ancre at the close of the campaign in November. By the end of that year, of 1,100 original members the Battalion had lost 815, killed, wounded and missing. They had lost many more in the Battle of Arras, attacking through a snowstorm on Easter Monday against the bastion of Monchy-le-Preux. Gavrelle came later – and then the Menin Road.

The succession of dishes added up to a fairly accurate record of their progress in the war. By the time the officers reached *Champignons Route de Menin* a large quantity of wine had been consumed, and the idea of anyone picking mushrooms anywhere along the Menin Road struck them as not only unlikely, but hilarious. Not even a blade of grass was growing within miles of it.

The 13th Rifle Brigade had been at the front for two and a half years. Of the officers who had brought the Battalion to France, only Captain Pughe, the transport officer, remained.

The 149th Field Artillery Brigade of the United States Army had been in France for less than two months. They had arrived at St Nazaire on 31 October, so full of vigour and enthusiasm that they had fully expected to be eating Christmas dinner in Berlin. The fact that they were still in a training camp in the wintry wilds of Brittany had not dampened their enjoyment of the Christmas season. Their chilly tarpaulin huts gave little protection from biting winds, but holly and mistletoe scoured from the Forest of Merlin provided a homely touch, the cooks had succeeded in making the turkey edible, and there was an ample supply of beer and French wine. There were doughnuts and there was pie, and after weeks of subsisting on Army rations of 'hard tack and corned willie' the Doughboys considered it to be a feast.

A mountain of mail and parcels from the USA arrived on Christmas Eve, and they were welcome, although in some cases the homefolks' idea of appropriate gifts for their boys overseas was rather wide of the mark. Scores of letters home pointed out that electric toasters could not be powered by candles, that cuff-links and necktie racks were redundant on active service, and that in future 'smokes' would be more welcome than hymn books. One soldier, whose admiring family sent him an officers' Sam Browne belt, made the best of it and traded it with his lieutenant for a safety razor and a pass into Rennes. George Daugherty was not so lucky. His loving relatives sent him six large cans of the same corned beef which had been his outfit's unvarying diet for more than a month. George was livid, and the ribbing of his comrades did nothing to assuage his feelings.

That Christmas, London was full of troops from overseas – Australians, New Zealanders, Canadians on leave from France, and America's Doughboys on Christmas leave from training camps in England. Thousands of Londoners took part in a hospitality scheme to give the boys a good time, entertaining them in their own homes or escorting them on tours of the sights. Even the King cut short the traditional New Year shoot at Sandringham and returned to London on 2 January to confer with his ministers and to hold the first investiture of 1918. Sergeant Arnold Loosemore of the 8th Battalion, the Duke of Wellington's Regiment, was one of over 350 soldiers, many straight from the trenches, who went to Buckingham Palace to be decorated by the King. Sinking into the deep carpets, treading gingerly up the grand staircase in their army boots, listening bemused to the strains of the string orchestra as they waited their turn to march up to the King, it was hard to believe that they had not been transported to some celestial sphere. It seemed a million miles from the mud and stench of Flanders and the roaring of the guns. Loosemore was one of eight to receive the Victoria Cross.[1]

Later, in a private interview, the King had another duty to perform. He presented Sir Douglas Haig with his field-marshal's baton, chatted at some length on the progress of the war, and enquired solicitously about the health of the Field-Marshal's wife, who was expecting her third child. Before her marriage Lady Haig had been maid-of-honour to the King's mother, Queen Alexandra, and she was still on intimate terms with the Royal Family. 'Give our love to Doris,' said the King as Sir Douglas took his leave. This evidence of the monarch's affection and friendship was balm to the Field-Marshal's soul, for he was beset by difficulties. Like several thousands of his men, the Commander-in-Chief was at home over the festive season, but even during his leave there were many weighty matters on his mind, and many meetings to attend. But he did set aside one afternoon to take his wife and children to the pantomime at the Theatre Royal, Drury Lane.

'If ever there was a time when we wanted to laugh and to forget all about the trials and tribulations of the present day,' remarked the theatre critic of the *Daily Telegraph*, 'it is surely now!' But, it was the topical wartime jokes that were relished most, and they were worked into the most unlikely fairy tales. At the Kennington Theatre, Dick Whittington, falling asleep on Highgate Hill, as tradition demanded, dreamed the legendary dream of being Lord Mayor of London – but a Lord Mayor on a great white horse, reciting couplets in praise of the Mother Country while reviewing a procession of the Empire's gallant allies bearing flags of all the nations. In a hilarious production of *The Babes in the Wood* the jokes leaned heavily on the new food regulations, and at the King's Theatre, Hammersmith, in a fairly free

---

1. The others were Sub Lieutenant Wilfred Malleson, RN; Brigadier-General Clifford Coffin; Brigadier-General Bernard Freyberg; Lieutenant-Colonel Lewis Evans, Black Watch attached to Lincolnshire Regiment; Sergeant Fred Greaves, Sherwood Foresters; Sergeant Alfred Knight, London Rifle Brigade; Private Albert Halton, Royal Lancaster Regiment. 15805 Sergeant A. Loosemore's citation read: 'For most conspicuous bravery and initiative during the attack on a strongly held enemy position. His platoon having been checked by heavy machine-gun fire, he crawled through partially cut wire dragging his Lewis gun after him and single-handed dealt with a strong party of the enemy, killing about twenty of them, and thus covering the consolidation of the position taken up by his platoon. Immediately afterwards his Lewis gun was blown up by a bomb, and three of the enemy rushed for him, but he shot them all with his revolver. Later, he shot several enemy snipers, exposing himself to heavy fire each time. On returning to the original post he also brought back a wounded comrade under heavy fire at the risk of his life. He displayed throughout an utter disregard of danger.'

adaptation of *Little Red Riding Hood*, the wolf sported a German helmet and the enchantment of the witch's castle was broken by – a tank! It brought the house down.

At Drury Lane, where Sir Douglas Haig and his family were in the audience, the pantomime was *Aladdin*, and it was sheer magic from the moment the curtains swept aside to reveal a flowery lawn, where two mandarins, magnificently robed and bearded, began the prologue, to the final moment when true love triumphed. Madge Titheradge, as Aladdin, cut a splendid figure in tights and naturally won the heart of the Princess ('Aladdin a lad in a thousand!' she trilled). Stanley Lupino was hilarious as the washerwoman Widow Twankey, and if 'she' occasionally forgot to wash the clothes before ironing them it only added to the fun. Abanazar was as evil and spine-chilling as a good panto demanded, and Caleb, the slave of the lamp, as magnificent as a pantomime audience could desire.

Haig might have given a good deal for a magic lamp and the power to summon up a genie to resolve the many difficulties that faced him both in London and across the Channel in France. He was still smarting from the row that had erupted three weeks ago and forced him (much against his will) to part with his Director of Military Intelligence and right-hand man, Brigadier-General John Charteris.

In certain political and military circles, the names of the great offensives had become a litany of failures smoothed over as setbacks, of partial successes bruited as great victories, of minuscule advances hailed as breakthroughs, and of small victories gained at a price which the Prime Minister, Lloyd George, feared would be too much for the nation to stomach for much longer. Lloyd George was inclined to agree with the opinion of King Pyrrhus after the ancient battle of Asculum: 'One more such victory and we are lost.' But if the Commander-in-Chief had had any such feeling after Arras or Passchendaele or Cambrai, the complacent bulletins emanating from his headquarters had given no hint of it. The official communiqués published daily in the press, as well as informal disclosures from GHQ passed on in good faith by war correspondents, were so complacent, so optimistic and, as it now seemed, so far from the truth that they were seriously misleading. It had become glaringly obvious that sneering assessments of the enemy's prowess and morale, exuberant predictions of easy success and airy dismissal of obstacles were seldom vindicated by results. Information had recently come to light that laid the blame on the shoulders of Brigadier-General Charteris.

Charteris was not only Sir Douglas Haig's right-hand man, he was also a close friend, and Haig had implicit trust in his judgement. Charteris was an urbane man – as loquacious as Haig was taciturn, as cordial in his relations as Haig was reserved, a *bon vivant* where Haig was a puritan. He ran the

Intelligence Department with breezy aplomb; he was solicitous of his Chief's interests, ever ready with advice and ever anxious to smooth his path and ease the burden of his manifold responsibilities. It was not surprising that his influence on the Commander-in-Chief was considerable. If his old friend General Charteris had a fault it was not apparent to Sir Douglas Haig, but, as time went on, it became all too apparent to his Staff. Charteris was a clever man, but he was so sure of his opinions that he was seldom swayed by anything so mundane as facts. The world seen through General Charteris' eyes existed as he supposed it to exist, despite any evidence to the contrary. He was a delightful companion, an accomplished raconteur, and the most amusing member of the mess.

There were worse places to be on the Western Front than on the Staff at General Headquarters in the picturesque hilltop town of Montreuil-sur-Mer. The whole town had been taken over by the British Army, and no more suitable place for a headquarters could have been found in the whole of France. It could be entered only by easily guarded gateways in the ramparts, communications were excellent, there were frequent boats to England from Boulogne less than twenty miles away, and the railway line to Paris was at the foot of the hill. A dispatch rider setting off from a divisional headquarters anywhere between Arras and Amiens could scorch to GHQ in less than an hour, and a complex network of telephone lines linked GHQ with London, with Paris and with every part of the long front.

The intelligence branch was installed in the École Militaire, and the Department of Military Operations in the Hôtel Dieu. Churches, schools, every possible building was commandeered by the Army, for in the web of narrow streets within the ramparts there was no room for expansion. But a Church of Scotland hut had been erected on a patch of grass in front of the Citadel, and in the dry moat below there had been just sufficient room to build a tennis court – much appreciated in summer by officers off duty. Otherwise, situated as Montreuil was, it was difficult to take exercise, other than a brisk twenty-minute walk round the ramparts or an occasional ride in the surrounding country. But the town had other charms. It had more than its share of cafés, inns and restaurants (some with excellent cellars) where a civilized evening could be passed in good company. In a private room in one such *estaminet* four majors of the intelligence staff were in the habit of meeting once a week, with the object not only of partaking of an excellent dinner but of relaxing away from their own official mess presided over by Brigadier-General Charteris. He was an entertaining companion, and occasionally he let slip a titbit of interesting gossip, but he dominated the conversation and it was not easy to have an informed discussion or for another officer to venture an opinion which did not coincide with the General's views without being genially pooh-poohed for his pains.

Edward Jack, Jimmy Marshall-Cornwall, John Dunnington-Jefferson and Stuart Menzies were excellent friends, although in Army terms they came from widely differing backgrounds. Jack, an officer of the Royal Engineers, was head of the Field Survey and Map Department, Dunnington-Jefferson, of the Intelligence Department, was a Royal Fusilier, Menzies was a Guards officer, and Marshall-Cornwall was a gunner.

It was not surprising that Marshall-Cornwall had been co-opted into the intelligence staff early in the war, for he was a sharp young man with a flair for languages and, as an amateur of military history, for exploring the battlefields of Europe. In the seven peacetime years after he had been commissioned he had indulged both hobbies during his two-month annual leave and, assisted by language grants from the War Office, had travelled extensively in Europe. In 1913 he had passed the examinations to qualify as First Class Interpreter in German, French, Norwegian, Dutch and Italian. In 1914 three weeks' Easter leave had not been quite long enough to give him a similar qualification in Spanish, but, although he only managed the Second Class Certificate with a 60 per cent pass, he had fully intended to spend the summer vacation in Spain and Portugal perfecting his Spanish and exploring the battlefields of the Peninsular War. He had got as far as Oporto when the outbreak of the present war had claimed more immediate attention.

For the past two years Marshall-Cornwall had been at GHQ, where his knowledge of Europe and European languages was invaluable. It was his task to collect and collate the intelligence information from a multitude of sources and, working closely with his counterpart at the headquarters of the French, to compute as accurately as possible the strength and disposition of the enemy forces. It was an arduous job, and even with the help of several junior staff officers it took a good twelve hours a day to get through the avalanche of papers that descended on GHQ. There were reports of interrogations of captured prisoners (a job which Marshall-Cornwall himself had done earlier in the war), there were reports of information gleaned on raids and patrols, and there was the 'pigeon post', Marshall-Cornwall's own brainchild. The pigeons were dropped behind the German lines in baskets which also contained a polite invitation to any patriotic Frenchman who found them to report on the movements of the German Army in his area. Many did so, at considerable risk, but information which arrived in this way was particularly tricky to assess: while much of it was genuine, the Germans themselves occasionally took advantage of the 'pigeon post' to send misleading information. But, in the main, the pigeons that flew across the lines and intermittently fluttered into the GHQ lofts brought news which, at the very least, confirmed intelligence gathered from other sources.

And, of course, there was the Dame Blanche – the organization of agents that grew from a single cell in Liège in Belgium to cover occupied France from Metz to the sea. It had over 1,000 members, of whom fifty-one were signalmen on the railways. Others were priests, monks, even nuns; 140 were university lecturers, 278 were women, and some were even men from Alsace or Poland who were reluctant conscripts in the German Army. The Dame Blanche was organized like a military operation, with a second line of reserve 'troops' in case the first line was wiped out.[1]

The organization had been started by Walthère Dewé, director of telephone and telegraphic communications in the Liège area. The information on German troop movements, construction of fortifications and many other matters of importance travelled with astonishing speed across the formidable border to neutral Holland and on via Paris and London to the headquarters of the British and French armies. Wallowing in an avalanche of paper in the long watches of the night, it occurred to Jimmy Marshall-Cornwall that he knew a great deal more about the German Army than he did about his own. It was his job to report the result of his work to his immediate chief, General Charteris, and it was Charteris' job to report to the Commander-in-Chief and to put him in possession of the information.

In April 1917, during the Battle of Arras, Marshall-Cornwall began to suspect that all was not well. General Charteris had succumbed to a bout of pneumonia, and during his illness and convalescent leave Marshall-Cornwall reported direct to Sir Douglas Haig with the daily intelligence summary. He was astonished to find that the Commander-in-Chief appeared to take an extraordinarily roseate view of the situation and of the fighting capacity of the German Army. In the course of their brief discussions, Haig's comments, given with courteous reserve, were so much at odds with the situation as Marshall-Cornwall knew it, and bore so little relation to the intelligence which had been so conscientiously gathered and punctiliously analysed, as to make Marshall-Cornwall wonder if they were discussing the same war. Not that it could be described as a discussion: the Commander-in-Chief merely expressed his view. Marshall-Cornwall was left with the uneasy feeling that Haig, on whose shoulders lay the responsibility for the conduct of the war in France, was being misled. If he were, it could only be by General Charteris, in whom, as Sir Douglas had made it quite clear, he had complete trust.

It was an awkward situation. It was no more than a suspicion. There was no proof – or at least none sufficient on which to take action. All that Jimmy

1. Only forty-four of its members were ever caught by the German authorities, of whom only two were shot. The organization was reconstituted under the code-name 'Clarence' under the same director, Walthère Dewé, in 1939, with many of its original members as well as a new generation of young patriots, and did valuable service throughout the Second World War. M. Dewé died in 1971.

Marshall-Cornwall could do was to keep his mouth shut and his eyes open, and if he ventured to hint at his suspicions – perhaps in the relaxed atmosphere and privacy of the Friday-night sessions with the 'Dining Club' – it was with the utmost discretion.

The summer passed. In June the Army swept over the Messines Ridge and, advancing over a mile, captured it from the enemy. On 31 July the Passchendaele offensive was launched. Of course the original objective was not merely Passchendaele – that was part of a greater plan to wrest the Belgian ports from the enemy's hands. But it had not worked like that. The Ypres salient was a tough nut to crack, the bad weather set in, the ground turned to mud, the troops inched up the salient, the summer died into the autumn, and, as autumn turned to winter in the gales of November, the troops ground to a halt on the topmost ridge. It had cost more than 100,000 lives to get there. The advantage gained was small.

Even before the campaign was over they were planning the attack on Cambrai to breach the formidable Hindenburg Line beyond. It did make sense to hit at another part of the line where the Germans least expected it and while they were still reeling from the losses sustained at Ypres, for they had suffered as much as the British. They would hardly expect an offensive so late in the season, and would certainly not expect it at Cambrai. The British Army would be able to attack with 500 tanks, not piecemeal as on the Somme a year before, but in force, with the infantry following triumphantly behind. It would be the Army's last throw of 1917 – the vindication of all that had gone before, and a heartening conclusion to a disappointing year. It was true that the Army was short of troops, for, even apart from the Passchendaele losses and the sparsity of reinforcements, Haig had been reluctantly forced by the Government to send five of his divisions to assist the Italians. But the Germans too had suffered great losses, although Russia was on the point of collapse and the Germans would soon be able to move their troops from the disintegrating Eastern Front to Flanders. Haig believed, on the basis of Charteris' information, that it was all the more important to strike soon, before these reinforcements arrived.

Many of them were there already, and Jimmy Marshall-Cornwall knew it. But it was another matter to convince his boss.

*General Sir James Marshall-Cornwall, KCB, CBE, DSO, MC, Royal Artillery*

It really let the side down, because Charteris had told the Chief that there were no German reserves behind, and I gave him *proof* that three new divisions had arrived from the Russian front, just before the battle. He said, 'I don't believe it. It's a bluff on the part of the German

General Staff to frighten us off the attack, and I'm not going to spoil the morale of my Commander-in-Chief by giving him false information.' It was wicked! He got this fixed idea in his mind that the German casualties were greater than they had actually been, and that if he could only keep Douglas Haig's determination going we would sweep through. He built that up in his own mind, and I suppose he felt it was his mission to put his view across. But it was fatal. It nearly wrecked Douglas Haig's reputation, and it cost us a great many casualties.

He even went so far as to take the Commander-in-Chief up to a German prisoner-of-war cage, having removed the best-looking men, the men with the best physique, and showed him the runts that were left and said, 'These are the sort of people we've got to fight against now. Nothing compared with our own troops.' And of course he had removed the sturdy ones beforehand! Completely misleading! I was horrified at the way Haig had been misled about the morale and condition of the German troops. Charteris had been staff captain to Douglas Haig out in India when Haig was Chief of the General Staff, and he had got a sort of almost hypnotic influence on Haig. And Haig wouldn't listen, even to his *own* Chief of Staff, General Kiggell, and he took all the advice from Charteris. Unfortunately!

When it came to a head in the Battle of Cambrai in November 1917, when I couldn't stand it any more, I went to the Director of Operations, 'Tavish' Davidson, and told him the position. I told him I didn't want to go on working here any more. I wanted to go back to my battery. He said, 'No! Stay where you are. But let *me* know the truth.' And very soon afterwards Charteris was sacked.

The Commander-in-Chief had no choice but to sack Charteris, for not only the War Office but also the Cabinet was arraigned against him. 'A Case for Inquiry', thundered *The Times*:

... the truth is slowly leaking through the correspondents' tales of heroism. We have said little by way of comment on the tremendous struggle which broke out to the south of the new Cambrai salient on the morning of November 30th and raged during the two successive days. The official communiqués were more than usually laconic. The correspondents have so far been limited almost entirely to details of amazing individual gallantry ... we can no longer rest satisfied with the fatuous estimates, e.g. of German losses in men and morale, which have inspired too many of the published messages from France ... the published and censored version is being amplified every day by innumerable and most disquieting first-hand accounts from officers and men who took part in the actual fighting. It is high time . . . that the charges of blundering should be sifted and that the blame, if and where it is due, should take shape in the prompt removal of every blunderer . . . The merest breath of criticism on any military operation is far too often dismissed as an 'intrigue' against the Commander-in-Chief . . . but Sir Douglas Haig's position cannot but depend in large measure on his choice of subordinates. His weakness, if it be a weakness, is his inveterate devotion to those who have served him longest – some of them perhaps too long, or at least too long without a rest.

Hitherto the columns of *The Times* had, if anything, been unctuously supportive of the Commander-in-Chief, and it came as a bitter blow that his one-time ally Lord Northcliffe had now turned against him. The polemic burst on the public on 12 December. It was aimed at Haig's Chief of Staff, General Kiggell, as well as at Charteris, and it had clearly been inspired by a leak in high places. The source was not far to seek, for the Prime Minister and Haig were at loggerheads. In Haig's opinion Lloyd George was a vulgar upstart, and Lloyd George regarded the Commander-in-Chief as a disdainful snob.

The stolid Scot and the volatile Welshman had little in common. The Prime Minister was deeply suspicious of Haig's obduracy and his unshakeable view that the war could be won only by battering away on the Western Front. Even more infuriating, in Lloyd's George's view, was the fact that all the senior generals up to Sir William Robertson, the Chief of the Imperial General Staff, backed Haig. It was therefore impossible, it seemed to him, to get objective advice from any other quarter, and any proposal or suggestion that the war could be won other than by continuing the battering-ram strategy in the west met with short shrift at the hands of the powerful military lobby. The unanimity of this Sandhurst-trained élite was, in Sir Maurice Hankey's opinion, 'remarkable'.

Desperate for views and advice from other quarters, Lloyd George had mooted and pushed through the creation of a Supreme War Council, on which all the Allies would be represented. General Sir Henry Wilson was the military representative for Great Britain, with General Foch for the French, General Cadorna for the Italians and General Bliss for the USA. Although the brief of the Supreme War Council was 'to watch over the general conduct of the war', there was now a forum to which fresh ideas and suggestions could be submitted for consideration. The first official session of the Council after its inauguration took place at Versailles on 1 December.

It had not been a good month for the Commander-in-Chief. Before it was out he had been forced to part with both his Chief of Staff and his

Director of Intelligence. Kiggell was removed on the grounds of ill health. Charteris was not really removed at all, for Haig was determined that his old friend should not be humiliated; he was found another post at GHQ, and he continued to have the ear of the Commander-in-Chief. Before the end of January Brigadier-General Edgar Cox had been sent to Montreuil as Director of Military Intelligence and Jimmy Marshall-Cornwall returned to London to replace General Cox as head of MI3. It was a considerable promotion, for MI3 cast a wide international net in its task of evaluating the strength and the movements of the enemy.

The changes in the topmost echelons of the Army, the political machinations and the creation of the Supreme War Council were of little interest to the soldier at the front, whose main concern in the bleak winter days and nights was keeping warm in the bitter chill.

# Part 1

# The Eve of Armageddon

*God heard the embattled nations sing and shout:*
*'Gott strafe England' – 'God save the King' –*
*'God this' – 'God that' – and 'God the other thing.'*
*'My God', said God, 'I've got my work cut out.'*

J. C. SQUIRE

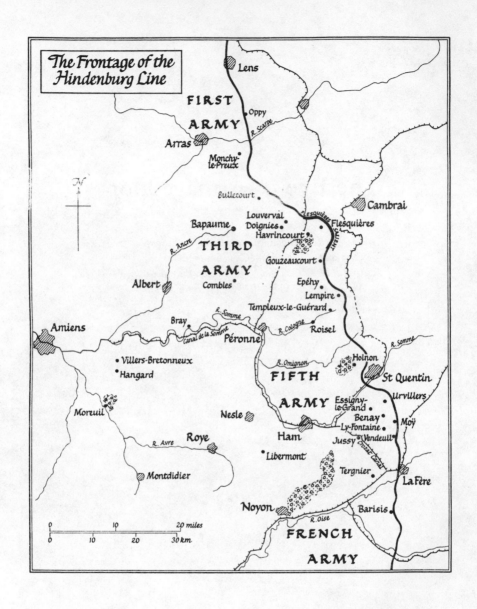

The Frontage of the Hindenburg Line

FIRST
ARMY

Lens
Oppy
R. Scarpe
Arras
Monchy-le-Preux

Bullecourt

Cambrai
Louverval
Flesquières
Bapaume
Doignies
FLESQUIÈRES SALIENT
Havrincourt
THIRD
Gouzeaucourt
ARMY
R. Ancre
Epéhy
Albert
Combles
Lempire
Templeux-le-Guérard
Bray
R. Somme
R. Cologne
Roisel
Amiens
Canal de la Somme
R. Somme
Péronne
Villers-Bretonneux
R. Omignon
Holnon
Hangard
FIFTH
St Quentin
Urvillers
Essigny-le-Grand
Moreuil
ARMY
Benay
Moÿ
Nesle
Ly-Fontaine
Roye
Ham
Jussy
Vendeuil
R. Avre
Libermont
Crozat Canal
Montdidier
Tergnier
La Fère
Noyon
Barisis
R. Oise
FRENCH

0        10        20 miles
0    10    20    30 km

ARMY

# Chapter 1

Throughout the month of January the shelling was desultory, but the impact of the shells on frozen ground was doubly dangerous and even Tommies well out of the immediate range of an explosion could be maimed or knocked unconscious by flying lumps of frozen mud. Nothing short of high explosive could penetrate the rock-hard surface, and the picks and shovels that the long-suffering infantry were obliged to carry into the line for 'trench improvements' were seldom used. The clang of implements on the frozen earth merely signalled to the enemy that fatigue parties were out and about and provoked streams of bullets from machine-guns sited too close for comfort.

The enemy soldiers were in the same boat, occupying the same kind of outposts not many yards distant, in the same tundra of frozen shell-holes. At night small sounds ringing sharp and clear in the frosty air came as strangely personal reminders of their presence – the stamp of half-frozen feet on a duckboard, the rasp of a cough, the click of a rifle-bolt, the thud of a mallet, the ping of barbed wire – with always the scurry of scavenger rats that preyed across the terrible sprawl of the battlefield. Even quite far behind the front line the shallow-buried dead of the autumn battles had been disturbed by shell-fire, and until the thaw came it would be impossible to rebury them. As for the living, so long as the freeze continued the front-line soldiers of both sides were content to leave the war to the gunners, and there was a tacit agreement to live and let live unless they were positively provoked.

Bill Lockey had spent three winters at the front, and he had never experienced cold like it. The 1st Sherwood Foresters went out of the line in a snowstorm on Christmas Day, and the boys of No. 5 Platoon discovered to their disgust that they were not much warmer in their rest billet than they had been in the trenches.

*71938 Private William Lockey, 1st Bn., The Sherwood Foresters (Notts. & Derbyshire Regt.), 8th Division*

The road leading down to Spree Farm was made of large battens of timber for the use of the transport and taking up the guns, and when we were relieved we trudged down like a battalion of cripples. Some of the chaps' feet were that swollen they couldn't walk without help! Trudging on and on we at last arrived at Vlamertinghe. When we went in the door of the Nissen hut we found the opposite end conspicuous by its absence! It had been blown out by some of Fritz's iron works, and the snow was drifting in! That night, or rather morning, when I got under the blankets and got warmed up my feet started to ache and I got very little sleep that night. It was torture – and some chaps' feet were in such a state that the worst cases who reported sick were sent off to hospital. The M O's quarters that morning put me in mind of the queue that gathered outside the grocers' shops for the half-pound of Maggie-Ann, butter or whatever was in stock.

Going into the line on the 7th the ground was covered by a white mantle of snow and it was that cold we hardly knew we had any feet on – wearing two pairs of socks at that! We went in to the left of Passchendaele and we occupied anything to afford a bit of shelter – not what one would call trenches. Here we passed the following two days, not daring to show ourselves during the daytime.

On the night of the 9th a battalion of the Northamptonshire Regiment took over our positions, while we took over their positions in the support lines. Two men of the Northants, each carrying a rum jar, happened to set them down while the changeover was in progress, and as we were leaving one of our chaps got his eye on the rum jars and picked one up and lugged it back to the supports. The line was only sections of trench here and there, with about a dozen or sixteen men in each, and the chap who had stolen the rum jar was occupying the section on our left. He and his companions – about a dozen of them – set to work on the rum, and before long strains of 'Tipperary' and other ditties rent the air. When they'd got well warmed up, some of them even got out on top and stood shaking their fists towards the enemy line and started shouting what they would do to the bloody squareheads.

Next night Fritz didn't half forget to strafe us! For three solid hours he bombarded our positions. We had a ground-sheet stretched across one end of our post and here we sat, all huddled together. One shell fell near the parapet and almost buried us. Four of the lads had put their packs down at the far end, and the packs were blown to smithereens! When the bombardment stopped we all shook hands with each other. It seemed to us a miracle that none of us had been hit. It had simply *rained* shells.

On the whole it was safer in the front line, where the opposing lines were too close for the guns of either side to risk shelling them. The bitter cold was hardest on the men who had been on leave enjoying the comforts of home. And there was another reason to dread the return from leave, as Burt Eccles — hardened soldier though he was — was disconcerted to discover.

*203694 Rifleman Burt Eccles, 7th Bn., The Rifle Brigade, 14th Division*

It was upsetting coming back. I was scared stiff. I was, honestly, I was frightened. It was the only time I had nerves, I think, and I know what the cause of that was. I'd been on leave and slept in a comfortable bed and seen how people lived — and then I looked on the skyline and saw the flashes and heard the guns firing, and I thought, 'What am I doing here? I wish to hell I'd never been on leave.'

We were on working parties, going up the line with rations and all sorts of stuff. Beyond the Passchendaele Ridge there were no trenches. They were all in shell-holes — eight or nine fellows in a shell-hole here, then another lot in a shell-hole there. That was the line! Company HQ was further back, near a pillbox. What puzzled me was that Jerry could have broken through there quite easily with nothing to stop him. We were so near we could hear him talking. We could hear him coughing. We daren't put any earthworks up, because the new earthworks would have shown where we were, and they didn't know exactly.

Anyway, after two or three days they sent me down the line as a guide. 'Go back, find your way in the dark, then bring up a company of Worcesters' — which I did. It started to freeze like mad — *and* snow. I was delighted, and everybody else was too. You couldn't fall into a pond, you couldn't drown, because the ground was real hard. The only trouble was the snow obliterated a lot of landmarks that I knew.

We paraded about ten o'clock at night. There was a foot of snow on the ground, and it was a clear night with the moon almost full. You could read a newspaper! I didn't like the look of it at all. A platoon of fifty men came up with a guide, and away they went. The next lot came — my lot! I said to one of the officers, 'This is a crackpot idea!' I told him straight, 'You can see for miles in this light.' He said, 'It's nothing to do with me. I can't alter things!' You can imagine what happened! We got up to the last ridge and of course Jerry spotted us — he was bound to spot us! He opened up with his machine-guns — and we had the lot! We lost a lot of men. The platoon behind me lost their guide, and they shouted to me, 'Can you do anything for us?' So I gave *my* lot to another chap and took on that lot. Well, we went forward practically on our hands and knees from one shell-hole to

another, but there were so many of us that we must have looked like
an attack!

The German SOS went up – parachute flares: red, green, red. The
Jerry artillery opened up – and, by God, they *did* open up, and how
the Dickens we weren't all wiped out I don't know! I lay with a fellow
called Ravenhill in a shell-hole, pressed to the ground. Shells were
dropping everywhere except just on top of us. I said to him, 'What
about trying to get to a pillbox? The further we get forward the safer
we are.' (The front line was so near them that they wouldn't fire on
their own men.) 'Stay where you are and chance your luck,' he said.
When it eased up a bit and we decided to go forward he was hit and
badly wounded. He died in hospital.

We knew they wouldn't be much good, the Worcesters, because
they'd lost so many men. Anyhow, I said to an officer, 'I got my men
up – as many as I could.' He said, 'All right then, grease out of it!' So
we set off. It must have been two and a half miles. We came out of
the shell-fire and there was a lovely canteen at the side of the road –
hot tea with lashings of rum in it and cigarettes handed out. Then we
carried on for another mile to a place where there were all bell-tents,
and in spite of the fact that it was the middle of winter we just went
in, lay down, and were asleep in five minutes! We hadn't had any sleep
for days.

The soldiers who were killed and wounded that moonlit night on Passchendaele Ridge could ill be spared. After the losses of the Flanders offensive
and the disastrous effect of the German counter-attack at Cambrai the Army
was dangerously short of men, and this was a further bone of contention
between Field-Marshal Haig and his political masters. The Field-Marshal
believed he had every right to feel aggrieved. Five divisions had been
peremptorily removed from his command and transferred to Italy, and after
the autumn fighting his remaining divisions were seriously under strength.
Some battalions had been reduced almost to skeletons, and drafts of reinforcements were far fewer than the Commander-in-Chief desired. Furthermore, he was being asked to take over many more miles of line from the
French, whose losses had been even more severe than his own and who were
holding more than three-quarters of the labyrinthine trenchline that
straggled from the North Sea across the face of France to the mountains of
the Vosges.

Now that Russia had collapsed, the German soldiers who had won victory
for the Kaiser on the Eastern Front could be released to serve in the west,
and it would only be a matter of time before the Germans launched a major
assault in France. There was no secret about it: no less an authority than the

Kaiser had said so in a Christmas message to his troops. Indeed, if the Kaiser was to be believed, God Himself had said so:

The year 1917, with its great battles, has proved that the German people has in the Lord of Creation above an unconditional and avowed Ally, on Whom it can absolutely rely. Without Him all would have been in vain. The great success and victories of the recent time, the great days of battle in Flanders and before Cambrai, where the first crushing offensive blow delivered by the arrogant British showed Him that, despite three years of war sufferings, the old offensive spirit was still in our troops, have their effect on the entire Fatherland and on the enemy. We do not know what is still in store for us, but you have seen how in this last of four years of war God's hand has visibly prevailed, punished treachery, and rewarded heroic perseverance. From this we can gain firm confidence that, in the future also, the Lord will be with us. God's blessing rested on our arms in 1917. He will in 1918 lead our righteous cause to a good end.

The view of the *Frankfurter Zeitung* was a touch less florid and emotional, but its message was clear:

The burden of all the crises in the next six months will fall exclusively on the Entente. The Central Powers have a strategical superiority and will be able to concentrate all their force on the Western Front, while the hope of the Western Powers that troops will be forthcoming from America can in no case be realized. Never again, and certainly not in the next half-year, will Great Britain and France have such favourable opportunities for a general offensive as they had in 1915, 1916 and 1917, as strong forces will be released to another position and can be moved at will by our military leaders. Thus every hope of the Western Powers of success in a new offensive on the Western Front will be frustrated. Moreover, our High Command has declared that it is possible to strike a death blow against France. The strategical conditions on the Western Front are completely reversed, and the war will be directed against France. If there is a French crisis, it may well be a military one next time and the last of the present world war.

To anyone with a scrap of strategical reasoning it was perfectly obvious that Germany must and would strike in the west – and strike soon, before the full might of American wealth and manpower could be ranged against her. Now that America stood with the Allies it was clear that Germany could not hope for a wholly triumphant conclusion to the war but, after her

successes in Russia, a substantial victory in the west would vastly improve
her chances of making peace on advantageous terms.

A quarter of a million soldiers of the American Expeditionary Force were
already in France, and several times as many, still stuck in training camps
across the USA, were impatiently waiting to join them. On Long Island,
at Camp Upton alone there were 40,000 recently enlisted Doughboys and,
as Lieutenant Phelps Harding observed, this was seven times the population
of his home town, Saranac Lake. The nickname 'Doughboy' had been
earned during the Mexican War in the arid heat of the Rio Grande, where
the uniforms of an earlier generation of infantrymen had become stiff with
the white dust of adobe soil. 'Dobies' had long since become 'Doughboys'
on the lips of Americans, and not many of the boys in Camp Upton gave
much thought to the word's derivation. It was a harsh winter and, as they
trudged out day after day to dig trenches in the frozen ground, the opinion
of the luckless Doughboys was that 'Snowboys' would have been a better
description. Having joined the Army at the behest of Uncle Sam with the
sole object of licking the Germans as bloodily and as speedily as possible,
they failed to see how such unheroic labour thousands of miles from the
fighting line could be of the slightest assistance to the Allied cause. The
temperatures were sub-zero, and conditions were no less arduous for the
officers.

*Lieutenant J. Phelps Harding, 3rd Bn., 154th Infantry, 42nd [US] Division,
American Expeditionary Force*

Just imagine taking 700 men somewhere up the State Road and saying,
'Well, boys, our line of trenches will be built where you see these
strings' – and then set them to work. In the first place, the ground,
which has about six inches of snow on it, is frozen about two and a
half feet deep – and frozen hard! When you strike it with a pick, little
pieces fly into your face and sting like little whips, and your wrist feels
as if you had batted a home run. The first day we just scratched the
surface a little and it was pretty chilly work – but the second day took
the brown derby.

When we started for the trenches Wednesday at 7.10 a.m. it was
mighty cold, and there was a hard wind blowing. Most of us had warm
helmets, so with our sheepskin coats and high collars we got along
pretty well. Some of the fellows had no helmets, or were too proud
to wear them, and before we had marched ten minutes several men
had been sent back with frozen ears. Then some froze their noses, and
they too were returned by the officer in command. After a half-hour
march we reached the trench, threw up a shelter of trees for our

hospital unit, and went to work. I never had such a cold proposition to face before! Our hands and feet were soon cold, and the strong wind just sailed into us. By 10 a.m. several men had had their feet or fingers treated by the hospital corps – one man is still limping around the barracks with a sore foot from having it pretty badly chilled.

Our march home was fierce, for we had to go right into the wind. I put a wristlet over my nose, under the helmet, and even so I chilled one side of it, but considered myself lucky that I didn't freeze a cheek. That finished our trench digging for the day, for it was too cold for the work to be practical. In the evening when we assembled for a conference, every here and there a piece of adhesive plaster, stuck over an ear or nose or chin, reminded us of our day's experience – but not many of us need the reminder!

Every day this week has found us digging trenches. One day we will be in water, mud and ice, the next day we will skate, almost, and work a couple of hours to make up for the depth the ground froze in the preceding night. It does not have to be very cold to make soldiering an unpleasant task. Cold fingers and toes soon realize that they are no longer beside the family hearth.

This morning we passed groups of wireless men doing field work, signal men using smoke signals, regular infantry in open-order work, and, to make it all more realistic, from the range we could hear the machine-guns pounding away like riveting machines. They have an ominous sound, those machine-guns, and I have a very wholesome respect for them.

Like Kitchener's Army raised by Great Britain more than three years earlier, the United States' new National Army, although impressively large, was woefully deficient in the arts of war, and no amount of Yankee enthusiasm could disguise the fact. Training was a major problem. Some officers had been seconded from the French Army and sent across the Atlantic to help, and some American officers who had sailed with the 42nd and 26th Divisions had been sent back to the States as instructors almost as soon as they had landed in France. The main difficulty was the lack of experienced officers to command the new divisions and battalions and take them to the war. But although the peacetime army had been small it had seen plenty of action, and the few officers who could be spared to take charge of the embryo troops were tough and battle-hardened.

Colonel Rob Alexander had served in the Philippines and in Cuba, and had commanded his regiment on General Pershing's expedition to Mexico. For the last three months of the campaign he had served on the General's staff, but the task of preparing the 77th US Division for the war was as hard

as any he had encountered in his long military career. Writing wearily from
Fort McPherson, Georgia, to his sister Florence he made no bones about it.

*Colonel Robert Alexander, 41st [US] Division, American Expeditionary Force*

My dear Florence,

I feel heartily ashamed of myself when I looked at the date of your
letter, nearly two months ago and I am just starting to answer it. If it's
any excuse I can say in all sober earnestness that I have been pretty
busy here lately. We are all of us trying to get a respectable force in
something like condition to face Frightful Fritz some time or other in
the reasonably near future and believe me it is some job. Of course the
Regular Army, as it existed last March for instance, is scattered to
the four winds and we are now trying to build up something as good
as it was on a mighty slim foundation of experienced instructed officers
and men. It looks like a pretty long road to success but we are making
some progress – enough to be reasonably encouraging. But the work
required is pretty strenuous, however if we can get results it will be
well worth while.

To give you an idea of how we are fixed, I have here a brigade of
the 17th. My senior officer was appointed from civil life last November,
and the majority of the non-commissioned officers have enlisted since
last January. So you see we have to build pretty much from the ground
up. In addition to all that the literature of the profession has increased
so enormously as the result of this trench warfare that one has to do a
tremendous amount of reading to keep up with it, even approximately.

I am a colonel now – permanent appointment in the Regular Army.
I was confirmed by the Senate a week ago but so far haven't any new
orders and I don't expect any for a couple of weeks more, as I know
the War Department is just swamped with work. Of course, like
everyone else, I'm hoping for a regiment in France but large numbers
of patriots are looking for those jobs and my chance isn't any better
than that of any one of about fifty other colonels. Of course I would
like to get my chance over there now, but I'm not worrying much.

If we really and actually are in this war to a finish everybody will
get plenty of chance before it's over.

Personally I think that unless we have a patched-up peace we
are in for two years more of war. Nor do I see how it's possible
now to fix up any proposition which would be acceptable to both
England and Germany. So I reckon we will all get a chance sooner
or later.

The British Commander-in-Chief fervently hoped to see a large force of Americans sooner rather than later. For months now he had been urging the gravity of the manpower situation and pleading for reinforcements. He was supported by the Chief of the Imperial General Staff, Sir William Robertson, but, seen from the War Cabinet's point of view, the situation was more complicated. It was not simply a question of putting every available man into khaki and sending him to France. With 4 million men already under arms, resources were diminishing and, as the war-machine ground on and gained momentum, demand was increasing in other quarters. The Government was at its wits' end to know how to supply it. Every shell and bullet fired in France had to be replaced fourfold to meet demand. The American Government had placed huge orders with British and French armaments suppliers, for Uncle Sam's formidable muscle would be useless without the thrust of sufficient arms behind it. A whole army of women was working in factories and workshops, but there was a huge and growing demand for skilled men. They needed lathe-turners, engineers, fitters and tradesmen, for heavy industry and shipbuilding. They needed men to build aeroplanes for the rapidly growing Royal Flying Corps (soon to become the Royal Air Force), and they needed men to fly them – not merely to replace the casualties among the bold young men whose flimsy aircraft had spiralled out of the skies, but to man the new fighters and the long-range aircraft that would bomb enemy towns and defences far behind the German lines.

The new Tank Corps also required more men. And, above all, more tanks – and faster tanks – were needed by the score, by the hundred. Tanks had proved their worth in the first euphoric success at Cambrai, battering through the previously impregnable Hindenburg Line and smashing a huge hole in the enemy's defences. Despite the unhappy reverse of fortune that followed, it seemed obvious that a few thousand more might tilt the balance and go a long way towards winning the war.

That meant more iron, more steel and yet more men in the steel mills, more miners to hew coal for the furnaces, and still more workers to produce rolling-stock, lorries and wagons, and to build ships to replace vessels which had been sunk. In the last six months alone more than 3 million tons of British and Allied shipping had been lost by enemy action.

And the population had to be fed. Although all but the smallest farms boasted at least one land-girl, daringly attired in breeches and tunic smock, women could not entirely replace the experienced farm workers which the agricultural economy badly needed. When food stocks grew dangerously low, 2,000 skilled ploughmen were winkled out of the Army and returned to the land. The Army's needs were great, but in the view of the Government they were not paramount, for the Merchant Marine as well as the Royal Navy was crying out for recruits, and such meagre resources as there were had to be spread effectively, if thinly. It was fair to say that they were scraping the bottom of the barrel.

The days were long past when recruiting sergeants had turned away enthusiastic youngsters below the military age of nineteen. Now youngsters were called up for training at eighteen and sent to France when they reached their nineteenth birthday. Mostly they were glad to go.

*304723 Rifleman Charles Ruck, 1/28th (County of London) Bn. (The Artists' Rifles), The London Regt., 63rd Division*

A lot of that training consisted in building us up, because we were very young and puny-looking youngsters, and of course the whole thing about military training in those days was fitness, particularly marching. Everything was done on the foot, all the exercises in the field, even night exercises, and we were encouraged in cross-country running as well as other sports, so after twelve months we were quite a tough little crowd in spite of the fact that we were only nineteen. But the curious thing was that the sort of musketry instruction we were given really harked back to the Boer War, when the rifle was *the* weapon. Machine-guns were very much in their infancy in those days, and the fire-power was a section or a platoon of very highly trained, very accurate exponents of the art of rifle fire. There was a thing called ten rounds rapid fire concentrated by, say, twenty men, at very long ranges. It was very effective, though they had to be very highly trained and accurate in their shooting. But, of course, when you went to France and saw the conditions there, that was a complete waste of time, because you hadn't a target, and controlling fire with small groups of men was completely out of the question in the conditions of trench warfare.

We were tuned up to reach the peak of our training by our nineteenth birthday. The first thing that happened was that we were all sent home on our draft leave, and when we came back we were all issued with brand-new clothing – everything down to the last pair of socks. We went by train to London and down to Southampton, and it was all quite uninteresting. So many people were in uniform at that time that a body of youngsters fully equipped to go overseas was no news. It didn't create any sort of excitement – much to our disappointment. We duly embarked with crowds of other drafts on one of the old cross-Channel steamers, and we set out for Le Havre. I was a pretty good sailor, as I thought, but on board that ship there were only about two who weren't violently ill, and by the time we got into Le Havre we were a pretty sorry sight.

We marched from the docks in Le Havre up to the base camp at

Harfleur – this was in January, of course – and we found that the base camp was under canvas and it had started to snow. It wasn't a frosty snow, it was a wet snow, and we were under canvas in ordinary old-fashioned bell-tents and, believe it or not, they put us in twelve to a tent, with all our beautiful new equipment and new clothing, in there with the snow and the mud. If you could ever imagine twelve people with their feet towards the centre pole with all the accoutrements and equipment you can imagine the sort of absolute chaos and mess we were all in.

We stayed at this camp for two or three days, ploughing through the mud. We all got plastered with mud! We were issued with rifles and ammunition and the various final little bits and pieces, and then, at long last, we were put on a train to go in search of our battalion. It was to have been the 2nd Battalion, the London Rifle Brigade. We were very glad to get away, because we were all young and it was an adventure and we all enjoyed it. The spirit amongst the youngsters, the morale, was extraordinarily high. Oh yes, we were excited about it. The war had gone on so long and any self-respecting youngster couldn't wait to join the Army, and particularly the Rifle Brigade. But I must say that all these long, long, weary journeys and the experiences at the base camp all rather tended to lower the initial enthusiasm and the excitement of the thing.

We went trundling along and trundling along. I don't think these Army trains did more than at the most twenty miles an hour. To get up to the Cambrai salient, which was eventually our destination, we had to detrain two or three times and spend a night or two at other places and then join other trains, and we eventually joined the 2nd Battalion at some point to the west of Havrincourt Wood, and from that point it was a long trek over the duckboards. We got up into Havrincourt Wood and we discovered then for the first time that we were no longer LRB, we were Artists' Rifles!

You had to be taken up by guides, particularly in a deep area like the Cambrai salient. You wouldn't have found your way if you hadn't had a guide. There were no positive landmarks to follow, and naturally the whole thing was done at night. What was more impressive was the noise, the sound, the roar of the guns, and it was that that caused a sinking feeling in your stomach – the noise of the guns and the whizz of the shells going over. It didn't stop. It went on the whole time, whether from our side or theirs, the flashes of the guns. It took a couple of days to get used to it.

Eventually we got to the second line to discover it was the old Hindenburg Line, which had been captured the year before. The

Hindenburg Line was deep – it must have been fifteen feet deep, like
a sunken road, so to speak. The dugouts were all wrong for us, because
they were built for the Germans in the forward side of the trenches,
but of course we had to use them, and the experience of a dugout was
something quite extraordinary. I mean, the smell and the general
squalor was quite revolting, but that was one of the things we had to
get used to. In the daytime we had a very good view. We could see
the front for miles and miles, and from that point we could see the
tanks which had been used the autumn before for the breakthrough
to Cambrai. Ditched tanks lying all over the place.

The idea of mounting an attack with the assistance of the new 'wonder
weapons' had been almost irresistible – not least to 'Boney' Fuller, senior staff
officer of the newly formed Tank Corps, and to his chief, Sir John Elles. It also
appealed strongly to Sir Julian Byng, in command of the Third Army, which
was holding the front north and south of Cambrai. It was virgin country of
gentle hills and valleys unviolated by battle, as far removed from the waterlogged wasteland of Ypres as it was possible to imagine and a world apart from
the devastated battlefield of the Somme less than eight miles away.

During the final stages of the Battle of the Somme the Germans had set
about constructing a formidable new line well behind the battlefronts. Early
in 1917 they had fallen back on the new position, retiring slowly and
methodically in a fighting retreat, with the British and French armies following in their wake. The Hindenburg Line had been built and fortified in five
months. It comprised a network of deep trenches guarded by a forest of
barbed-wire defences sixty feet wide which no infantry and still less cavalry
could hope to penetrate. But tanks could, and at last there were enough of
them to mount a mass attack in ideal terrain, where the going would be easy
across the firm, chalky downland. There were copses for concealment, and
thrusting its nose right into the German line was the great bulk of Havrincourt
Wood, where the tanks and the infantry could assemble in secrecy.

Sir Douglas Haig was easily persuaded. A demonstrable victory at the end
of the year would lift morale all round and do a good deal to atone for the
disappointments of 1917. Almost 400 tanks were available. 'Impregnable'
though it was, according to Intelligence – or, at least, according to General
Charteris' interpretation of intelligence reports – the Hindenburg Line was
lightly held, few German reserves were available, and such reserves as there
were could not possibly reach the battlefield in time to affect the outcome.
There were enough British troops – just – to mount a major attack, but
there were none to spare. On 26 October, the very day on which General
Byng laid out his plans before his corps commanders at Third Army Headquarters, the Commander-in-Chief had a nasty surprise. It was then that he

was warned that two of his divisions must be sent immediately to the Italian front. Three more would shortly be required to follow.

But the preparations began, and nothing was left to chance. Damaged tanks were reclaimed from the bogs of Flanders and overhauled. They built colossal sledges, light enough to be hauled by supply tanks, strong enough to carry seven tons of tools, ammunition, rations and water. And there were stranger contrivances. Aerial photographs clearly showed that the width of some trenches in the Hindenburg system was as much as twelve feet – wider than a tank could possibly cross – so fascines were constructed, huge compressed bundles of wood that could be carried on top of the assaulting tanks and tipped into the trenches to bridge them and help the tank across. Four hundred tons of faggots were cut and shipped to France, and all England was scoured for the 12,000 feet of chain that would compress them into solid cylinders weighing almost four tons apiece. To complete the element of surprise, there would be no preliminary bombardment before the tanks began to roll forward through the mist with the massed infantry following behind. Only then would the guns roar out and start to pound the German lines.

On the morning of 20 November it had all worked like a dream. By that afternoon the Hindenburg Line had been well and truly pierced and the troops had advanced four miles along a six-mile front. Although Cambrai was still well out of reach, by the 29th they had captured Flesquières, Noyelles, Marcoing, Masnières.

But the attack had run out of steam. Almost half the tanks had been lost – some broken down, some ditched, some shelled and disabled. The hard fighting had cost many casualties, and there were few reserves to replace them and to relieve the exhausted troops. When the Germans hit back in strength with fresh troops, the Third Army was outnumbered and over-whelmed. They were not quite back where they started, but the strip of ground that remained in British hands had been dearly bought.

Now the fighting had died down, and the drafts of youngsters who had come to reinforce the battalions in the line were being blooded in the 'normal' conditions of active service.

*Rifleman Charles Ruck*

If you weren't fool enough to get on the top and walk about in the daylight, you had a reasonably peaceful time. We spent four days and nights in the second line, and then of course we were due to go up to the front line. To our surprise we found the front line wasn't a trench at all. We were just put into holes in the ground. Oddly enough, the nearer one got to the enemy, the more sort of adventurous the whole thing became, particularly as we had a lot of old friends there – chaps who'd gone out on earlier drafts.

I volunteered to go out on wiring parties in No Man's Land and some other exercises, the idea being to try and capture a prisoner if one could, and bring him back. Well, we never even stumbled across a German during the time I was there, because the No Man's Land was very wide and it was smothered in wire – there were gaps in the wire which we were sent out to repair. But there was a kind of exhilaration in being there in No Man's Land with the enemy not very far away. It was rather fun. You felt that at last you were doing something purposeful. I'd spent four years of the war as a boy, and there I was, for the very first time after all these years, within a few yards of the enemy, and although it was only wiring and very small things one felt that one was really doing something.

Another youthful soldier was also 'doing something' – but he was doing it on the other side of the line, and he was doing it, reluctantly, for the Germans. Frank Caulton had been captured at Masnières, now back once more behind the German line but not so very far away from the No Man's Land which young Charles Ruck found so exhilarating. In the previous seven weeks he had experienced a gamut of moods and emotions, but exhilaration was not one of them. Fear, fury, indignation, dejection and humiliation were nearer the mark, topped off by cold and hunger.

For the ten days before his capture Frank Caulton had been in the thick of it, advancing with the 29th Division and enjoying the fruits of victory – not least in Noyelles, where he and his section of scouts and signallers were fortunate enough to go into a house which had been used by the Germans as a store. They made a good haul, including some excellent Mauser pistols, which they pocketed as 'souvenirs', and a collection of brass-band instruments, which afforded them some innocent entertainment until they had to move on. For several days now Battalion Headquarters had been on the western outskirts of Masnières, where the signals section had found an excellent billet.

*66020 Private Frank Caulton, 2nd (City of London) Bn. (Royal Fusiliers), The London Regt., 29th Division*

Most of the houses in Masnières were still standing. We stayed at a very large house and made ourselves quite comfortable with the bedding the Germans had left behind in their hurried retreat. At the back was a stable and a garage, and in the garage was one of the Germans' field cookers, and in the stable was a calf. You can guess what happened!

Fortunately one of our men had been a butcher, so we called on him to kill the calf and cooked it bit by bit in the field cooker. We ate it over the next few days while we stayed there having a well-deserved rest.

Masnières was not given up without a struggle. The Royal Guernsey Light Infantry and the 2nd Royal Fusiliers were spread in a thin line round the outskirts of the village. Since his place was at Battalion Headquarters, Frank should have got away when the retirement came. But things happened fast, and by the time he was sent forward to give the Guernseys the order to retire he found that they had already gone. He also found that the Germans were coming down the street. There were a few troops still sheltering at the Guernseys' HQ, and he joined them in the cellar. There was no possibility of escape, for a tank had plunged through the bridge on the main road. Frank had clambered with difficulty across the few remaining girders, but he could hardly repeat this exploit in full view of the Germans, so, since they were obviously surrounded, he and the others simply stayed where they were. There had been no time to distribute the Guernseys' mail, and it was piled in a corner of the cellar. As the Germans drew nearer and the Tommies realized that the game would soon be up, they opened the most likely-looking parcels and filled their pockets with as much foodstuff as they could carry. They had a fair idea that they would soon be needing it, and that precious little food would come their way as prisoners. A little later, when they were searched by German soldiers, the food disappeared into the pockets of their captors.

Frank was still at the front, working in contravention of the Geneva Convention, maintaining and building railway lines for the enemy. He amused himself by placing stones on the rails whenever he had the chance, and on one occasion at least he had the satisfaction of derailing an inspection truck. It was not much, but it was at least something.

Frank Caulton was one of more than 1,200 men posted missing in the 29th Division alone. The grand total of missing men was more than 10,000, and the total casualties in the eighteen days until 8 December were 2,390 officers and 41,817 men. The last desperate gamble of 1917 had cost the Army dear. Nineteen divisions were thrown into the battle at Cambrai – a quarter of the British Army's total strength on the Western Front. Now the Army was weaker and more debilitated than ever.

The great and tantalizing hope on the horizon was the American force – but most of the Americans were likely to remain on the horizon unless more ships could be found or built to bring them across the Atlantic. Late in January 1918, after earnest conclaves, the Supreme War Council gave its considered opinion that the war could be won fifteen or nineteen months hence, in 1919, but certainly not before. Meanwhile they must mark time, contain the war, and keep the Germans at bay until the Americans arrived. The question was, How was it to be done? Sir Douglas Haig made clear his view that it could not be done without more men, and Lloyd George made it equally clear that more men would not be forthcoming. He believed they were not really necessary. If the British, with their superior strength, had not succeeded in breaking the German line in three years of all-out warfare, was it not equally logical that, even if the situation were reversed, the Germans would not be able to break through the British? If the Germans were planning a major assault, the forces on the Western Front must simply be reorganized to meet it.

The Supreme War Council proposed that each army should withdraw seven divisions to form a general reserve which could be rapidly dispatched to meet an emergency anywhere on the entire front. Field-Marshal Haig was appalled at the very idea. He and General Pétain, the French Commander-in-Chief, already had a private agreement to support each other in case of need, and such matters, he believed, should be left to the discretion of professional commanders on the spot and not be subject to the decision of a committee. Cambrai had already eaten up two of the divisions which had been earmarked to take over part of the French line, and the question of reserves was worrying. Since no large bodies of reinforcements would be forthcoming, he reluctantly accepted that the only way to bring battalions up to strength was to amalgamate some and disband others, dispersing the ranks as reinforcements. It meant a full-scale reorganization. Each brigade of four battalions would be reduced to three – but they would be three stronger, fitter battalions, better able to mount attacks and withstand assaults.

If the reorganization caused grief to the Commander-in-Chief, it caused even more heartache to the soldiers whose battalions were selected for disbandment. Returning from a magnificent leave, whose delights included being decorated by the King and fêted by his home town, Sheffield, Corporal Arnold Loosemore, V C, was disgusted to find that his battalion was about to be broken up. It was the 8th Service Battalion, the Duke of Wellington's (West Riding Regiment), and the fact that it was a service battalion, as opposed to a mere Territorial or even Regular battalion of the Regiment, was something that its members considered to be a mark of distinction. It was true that they had been reinforced many times and had absorbed numerous drafts, but the heart of the Battalion was still the band of volunteers who had joined up to form its nucleus in August 1914. They were 'K 1 men' – men of Kitchener's First Army – and no laggards. They had trained together and fought together at Suvla Bay, on the Somme, at Passchendaele; now they were to be broken up and dispatched piecemeal to other units. It was at least some comfort that they were being sent to other battalions of their own regiment.

The disbandment of a long-established battalion like the 8th Dukes was not a simple process. There were a thousand loose ends to tie up, from inter-company football fixtures to be played off to the presentation of medal-ribbons – the DCM to the quartermaster of Y Company for devotion to duty at Ypres, and the Belgian Croix de Guerre to Privates Padgett and Watmough for their service with the Brigade trench mortars in the same offensive. There were kit inspections, which induced near apoplexy in company quartermasters, for hardly a man had a full complement of kit and equipment and the deficiencies had to be supplied before the troops marched off. There were hundreds of indents to draw up, excuses for lost items to be detailed, and hundreds of hours of pen-pushing for the unfortunate quartermasters' clerks. 'Lost by enemy action' was the most popular excuse, and with mountains of paperwork to get through it was easiest to turn a blind eye and accept it. And there was a final spit and polish for the farewell parade at Beuvry. The Battalion was drawn up on three sides of a square, the Divisional General stood on a dais on the fourth side, and behind him detachments from the remaining three battalions of the 32nd Brigade were on parade to honour the departing Dukes. The General's speech was as fulsome and gratifying as any soldier could desire. The Battalion replied with three cheers for the General, and the General reciprocated by calling on the Brigade (as represented by the detachments of their sister battalions) to give three cheers for the 8th Dukes. The officers' farewell dinner went on until the early hours of the morning.

Over the next few days the Battalion slowly trickled away, but Headquarters staff still had plenty to do. There were Battalion records to be collected and collated, mobilization stores to be handed in, the surplus of men who had not been posted to be sent to reinforcement camp. The string orchestra, which was the Colonel's pride and joy, had been sent at his request to the 2nd Battalion, and almost the last piece of paper filed by the orderly-room clerk was a letter of thanks from that battalion's Colonel.

Dear Colonel

Your string band arrived yesterday. It will be a great boon to us and we are all very grateful to you for sending the men and presenting the instruments to us. It is very hard on you being broken up but great luck for us to get such a fine draft.

Yours,
J. Walker,
2nd Duke of Wellington's Regiment.

The 10th Battalion the York and Lancaster Regiment was fortunate enough to have a full-scale brass band, and the Colonel made sure that it was the last to go, so that each departing body of troops would have a good send-off.

*Private J. Mortimer, MM, 10th Bn., The York and Lancaster Regt., 37th Division*

We were inspected by the divisional commander. We worked hard to look smart for this parade. Normally we had to buy our own cleaning kit, but on this occasion we were issued – free, gratis – with Blanco, boot polish, Pinko for button-polishing etc. I polished my leather equipment until you could see your face reflected in the holster that held my revolver. (Numbers 1 and 2 on the Lewis-gun had a Webley revolver, not a rifle.) After this parade the Lewis-guns were cleaned, greased, and packed in their boxes. All Lewis-gunners with revolvers handed them in and got a rifle. We were told officially that two companies were going to the 6th Battalion and two companies to the 2nd Battalion.

Then came the day. The commanding officer, Colonel Ostler, MC, addressed us. He said he had every confidence in us that we would keep up the tradition of the Regiment no matter what battalion we were going to serve in – or words to that effect. He wished us all the best of luck. Then we marched to the station and boarded the trucks. The band was lined up and as we moved slowly out of the siding the band played 'Auld Lang Syne'. The Colonel stood there saluting until all the trucks had passed him, and that was my last memory of him, standing in the distance and the faint strains of 'Auld Lang Syne' dying away. It was very impressive, but it was sad too.

At Bapaume, C Company and D Company left the train. We were taken to a camp with a number of huts. I was posted to No. 4 Platoon, A Company, 2nd Battalion, York and Lancaster Regiment. And that was the end of the 'Old Tenth'.

In every brigade and every division similar scenes were taking place. In future there would be not four but three battalions to a brigade, but they would be battalions at full strength. The Army was being tightened up and stiffened to withstand the German onslaught when it came.

# Chapter 2

The Army was short of soldiers. It was even more short of officers and NCOs to lead them, for such men were at the forefront of the action and the casualties among officers and NCOs had been proportionately greater than casualties among the troops. In recent months the ranks had been combed through again and again, not only for skilled tradesmen, but for men of experience and education who might be worthy of being elevated to the status of 'temporary gentleman'. In the 8th Duke of Wellington's, as in many other disbanded battalions, the quartermaster and two company sergeant-majors were sent directly to officer-cadet battalions in England, where those who had begun officer training several months earlier were sweating over the final exam papers. For most infantrymen the practical side was a walkover. The paper on military law and military organization required more thought:

> You are temporarily in command of a company on active service and the following cases are brought before you for investigation and disposal at your Company Orderly Room: –
> (1.) Private A. Being half-an-hour late for company parade.
> (2.) Private B. Dirty and improperly dressed on parade.
> (3.) Corporal C. Neglect of duty when i/c of a ration party.
> (4.) Private D. Using insubordinate language to company sergeant-major.
> (a.) State which of the above offences you think you could dispose of yourself and which would be remanded for the Commanding Officer.
> (b.) What entries would be made in the Minor Offence Report in **each** case?
> (c.) Where would a record be made of the punishment awarded to each man?
>
> (15 marks)

Even when an embryo officer had not studied so assiduously as he might have done, experience and common sense went a long way towards supplying the answers, but there was one apparently straightforward question which was not so easy as it looked:

As a 2nd Lieutenant you are in charge of a draft of 4 non-commissioned officers and 36 men under orders to proceed by train. On arriving at the station, half-an-hour before the train is due, you are informed that one first-class and five third-class compartments have been reserved for your party. The train will only stop for five minutes. What action do you take?

(15 marks)

This caused much furrowing of the brow among young men whose soldiering until now had been done in the democratic ranks. Should the officer choose to occupy the first-class carriage in solitary splendour and cram the men and NCOs into the rest? Should he invite the NCOs to join him? Should he allocate one NCO to each of four third-class compartments, or should they have a carriage to themselves? There were endless permutations, and it was not easy to guess which would most happily combine discipline and respect for the King's Commission, as personified by the officer, with practical good sense and the comfort of the men. Given the choice, most of the would-be officers would have felt more at home deploying a platoon for action on the battlefield.

Reg Lloyd was terrified that he would not pass the examination, for his six months' training had been blissful by comparison with the previous two years as a reluctant infantryman in the trenches. When the chance came to get out of them, he had seized it.

*Second Lieutenant Reg Lloyd, A Bty., Royal Horse Artillery, 41st Division*

I was in the trenches by Armentières, and I had to go to Divisional Headquarters at Bailleul to go before General Bainbridge, who was the GOC of the Division. He said to me, 'You have been recommended by your colonel to be a commissioned officer,' and he asked me a lot of questions.

I said, 'If I'm lucky enough to go for my commission, Sir, could I go to the gunners, Sir?'

He said, 'The gunners? You don't know anything about the gunners. You're an infantryman!'

I said, 'Well, I know quite a bit about horses, Sir. I was in the Cheshire Yeomanry.'

'Were you, by George!' he said, just like that. 'Who was your colonel?'

'The Duke of Westminster, Sir.'

'My God! How long were you trained as a cavalryman?'

'About two years, Sir.'

He didn't say any more to me. He just said to the sergeant-major, 'See that this man gets some tea.'

So I had a drop of tea from the cookhouse next door, and then I got a wagon to take me back up the line. An order came through a few days after that: 'You will report to Number 3 Royal Horse Artillery Equitation Training School at Weedon.' Well! I'm a horseman again! Wearing spurs again! Six horses to a gun, six mules to a gun-wagon, so I'm right in my element. I loved it, because it was exactly what I wanted, and I worked damned hard, because I didn't want to fail. If I failed it would be RTU – return to unit. Back in France again, or maybe a second chance at an Infantry Cadet School.

It was a long course. First of all there was a month in what they called the kindergarten, which was a sort of trial. Then you had to get up to three different grades – C, B and A – and, if you got through that, a final month at Larkhill, shooting on the range. Then at the end, when you're waiting for the results of the exams to come through – in the cadets' mess, you know – what an anxious time! We spent hours chewing over the papers, comparing what we'd written. We had to dress for dinner, wear a bow tie – it was always done properly. It was very pukka. Then a notice appeared one day: 'The following cadets will be gazetted and will report to . . .' I hardly dared look down the list, and when I came to 'L' and saw my name there I thought 'Thank God for that!' We'd just had weekend leave, and I'd been walking round Chester as an officer-cadet with a white band round my hat. Very smart. I thought, 'My God, if I'd to go back to those trenches!' But I didn't, of course.

*39181 Private W. Luff, 1st Bn., The Queen's (Royal West Surrey Regt.), 33rd Division*

There was an outcry about youngsters going to the front and, being under age, they put me on what they called A3, which was training for the officers. We were drilled with two men with toggles and ropes representing platoons and battalions, and in charge was our old regimental sergeant-major, Chokey Sullivan. He used to stand there with about half a dozen subalterns, and he would say, 'Mister So-and-So!' Mister So-and-So would come out, and he would say, 'Back! Step off your left foot with your cane in your right arm, bring your cane up and slap it on your left arm and walk smartly.' And he would make them do it again.

'Now,' he'd say, 'you've got your battalion facing south in column of route. Now get them facing east in open order.' Just like that. *We* knew all this battalion drill, but we had to do just as the officer ordered us, not what *we* knew was the right thing to do, and of course some of those young subalterns tied us up in knots! And Chokey would say, '*Well*, Mister So-and-So –' he always addressed them as Mister So-and-So – '*now* what have you done?' They got us in all sorts of knots.

It was the 3rd Training Battalion, and it included us recruits and two companies of old sweats who had been wounded and were there training before they were sent back again. Chokey used to drill in front of them with a pace-stick, and he'd stand there and he'd slap the old stick like that – *Bang!* And one of these old sweats was a cheeky old so-and-so – he thought he would get away with it – and he said, 'You can do that with that stick, but can you do it with this rifle?' Chokey said, 'Stand at ease! Now that man, six paces forward, march!' He said, 'Give me the rifle!' He gave him his rifle, and Chokey went through all of it. All the blasted drill there was – slope arms, present arms, the lot. 'Now,' he said, 'let's see if *you* can do it.' And he put the poor blighter through it for half an hour, up and down, up and down the parade ground. Oh, he was tough old codger – and he was just as tough on these rookie subalterns as he was on us.

The Royal Military Academies at Sandhurst and at Woolwich were still turning out 'permanent gentlemen' who would be commissioned into the Regular Army. Even in wartime, even with the desperate shortage of officers, the standards of entry and training were as rigorous as they had always been. Young Lieutenant Baines had recently been commissioned from the RMA at Woolwich – known colloquially as 'the Shop' – where they trained the sappers and gunners who would serve with the Royal Engineers or the Royal Artillery. Michael Baines had worked extremely hard to get there, but it was not the glamour of wartime that attracted him to a career in the army.

*Lieutenant Michael Baines, 55 Bty., Royal Field Artillery, 8th Division*

There was a long Army tradition in our family. In fact I was born in India when my father was serving as a captain with the York and Lancasters. I'd been sent to school at Cheltenham, and it was a pretty high-level Army school. I was there until 1915, and then I went to

Woolwich. All my mother's family were sappers – in fact my mother's great-grandfather was Lord Raglan, who made a bit of a muck of it at Balaclava – but I didn't want to be a sapper, because you had to be jolly good at mathematics, and I couldn't stand mathematics. I wanted to be with horses and guns. Fortunately in the entrance examination I didn't get quite enough marks to be a sapper, so I was a gunner.

They fairly put us through the hoop! It was very good for you. It hardened you off to be a decent officer.

I had to mark time until I was nineteen, but eventually I *did* manage to get to France. This was engineered by a family friend called Bill Duncan, who happened to command a Regular battery. It was the 55th Battery, quite an illustrious one – started the war at Mons and finished at Mons. Anyway, Bill Duncan had heard I was coming over and I suppose a few strings had been pulled. He made one stipulation. He said, 'If this young man joins us he's got to get his riding breeches made at Huntsman's.' I ask you! In those days riding breeches cost eleven pounds at Huntsman's in Bond Street. A huge sum! So I had to have a pair of riding breeches made by Huntsman, but I didn't wear my Huntsman breeches – good gracious no! I got a pair from the quartermaster ordnance, which didn't fit anywhere. Luckily, because I got a bullet through the seat! They were very baggy – lots of folds and creases – and I got a machine-gun bullet through the folds. Four to be exact.

Having enjoyed a period of sick leave, which he had contrived to stretch over Christmas and into the New Year, Michael Baines arrived back in Flanders as it began to thaw. The icy cold had bitten hard and driven deep, and the thaw began slowly. First the crackle of splintering ice beneath the heel of a heavy boot; opaque sheets of ice gradually turning translucent and floating in dimpled shards on the surface of flooded shell-holes; duckboards tilting and sinking a little as a shivering soldier stamped his chilly feet. The slow ooze of mud across the white landscape. The trickle of water as snow melted, swelling to a flood when it started to rain, turning every trench into a torrent, every track into a cascade, every camp into a seat of mud, and the Ypres salient into a waterlogged morass.

Further south, where the unfortunate Aussies of the 24th Battalion were in the line, the River Douve broke its banks. Trenches fell in, dugouts collapsed under the weight of water, and, since the German soldiers across the way were in the same plight, the fighting died down. Pumps chugged on both sides of No Man's Land and, rather than wade through the flooded trenches, some daring souls took their chance in the open and ploughed through the mud on top. The risk was small, for, as Lieutenant Gordon

Beith bitterly remarked as he contemplated their watery domain, they ran more risk of being attacked by the enemy's U-boats than by the enemy's infantry. The general verdict was that they would be better off with torpedoes than with the heavy boxes of small-arms ammunition that their brawniest efforts could hardly prevent from disappearing into the mud.

Since the capture of Passchendaele two months previously it had at least been possible to build a light railway track as far as the gun-line, to relieve the burden of the troops and ease the difficulty of hauling rations and supplies through the worst of the slough. Michael Baines' first job on his return from leave was to deliver two guns to the battery at the top of the salient.

*Lieutenant Michael Baines*

We had to get them up by rail and then through the mud and stuff to the batteries about 150 yards away. So I went up with the two guns and we got them off-loaded, and I met another cheerful subaltern with a few chaps, and we had to drag these guns through the mud. Awful job! We had to get them along what they call gun skids – long wooden troughs. You wheel the guns along them and then move the troughs at the back to the front again until you get the guns about fifty yards away from the railway line on to platforms – rafts actually! – on the mud. And we got *covered* in mud. We were in the open on Passchendaele Ridge, and we had to try and get this finished before daylight, or we'd have been shot at. We flogged away, and I busted my braces buttons and the only way I could keep my trousers up was by bending down, so I bent down. And when I eventually stood up the Germans' line was about 100 yards away and dawn was breaking, I might say.

Along came a very highly polished body of troops and a fellow with a flag. Well, that meant the divisional commander.[1] However, we didn't take any notice of him – we were just getting on with getting these ghastly guns into position – and a very highly polished staff officer came over covered in red tabs. He was only a subaltern, but he said, 'Stand to attention when I speak to you!' So I looked at this bloody man and said, 'I can't.' And he said, 'Why not?' And I said, 'Because my trousers will fall down.' He then walked over to the other subaltern, and this man had turned his back on him and was going on camouflaging the guns! Well, we got the guns camouflaged, and over came the 5.9 shells, and needless to say all the staff pushed off as soon as *they* started. But we thought we'd better report it to Brigade. So we went down the line, and at Brigade HQ good old Colonel Wheeler said, 'Yes, I

1. Major-General W. C. G. Heneker.

heard about this. You two young men, *you* were flippant and frivolous, and *you* were insolent and insubordinate. What have you got to say?' 'Nothing, Sir.' And he said, 'Come in and have a drink, my boys.' So we went into the pillbox and had a very good drink. Didn't hear any more about it. You see, it was the attitude of some of the staff – only some of them. Mostly they were young ADCs who'd made it to the staff. And the Colonel didn't like it any more than we did.

But appointment to the staff was no longer the prerogative of the exclusive few whose entries in the Army List were distinguished by the addition of the letters PSC.[1] In these days of ultra-rapid promotion even temporary gentlemen, and even temporary gentlemen who had been commissioned from the ranks, might easily, with luck and application, be given a job on the staff of a brigade or a division. Such appointments were not to be sneezed at, for they were often accompanied by promotion, and since most wartime officers were without private means the extra pay was more than welcome. Although in Army terms an officer's upward progress was as slow as it had been in peacetime, and substantive promotion arrived in due season and not before, in the exigencies of war, advancement in regimental terms could come at a dizzy rate. There were battalions commanded by twenty-five-year-old officers whose regimental rank was that of lieutenant-colonel but who were still captains or even mere lieutenants in the eyes of the Army. There were even brigadier-generals whose Army rank was only that of major.

A correspondence course, widely advertised in the newspapers and magazines which circulated at the front, had recently had a considerable vogue among men desirous of a commission and among officers ambitious for promotion. It was a method of training the memory and increasing mental power, and it arrived in weekly parts in a series of small grey books which fitted conveniently into a tunic pocket. It seemed that half the Army had taken it up. While many were embarrassed when found surreptitiously studying and claimed that they had merely found it 'lying around', others were loud in their praise of Pelmanism and perfectly willing to swear to its effectiveness. It was particularly popular in the 9th (Scottish) Division, and at one divisional dinner, when the subject came up in conversation, an illustrious brigadier-general, and holder of the Victoria Cross, modestly disclaiming any personal credit, admitted not only that he had been given command of a battalion shortly after beginning the course, but that before he completed it five months later he was given command of a brigade.[2] One

1. PSC = Passed Staff College.
2. Brigadier-General Frank Maxwell, VC, who had won the Victoria Cross at Thiepval on the Somme.

junior officer emboldened by a generous intake of wine and brandy presumed to cap the General's story. 'I did better than that, Sir,' said Captain Will Darling. 'I had no sooner written for a prospectus than I was given a job on the Staff!'

Will Darling was a colourful character who was not afraid to speak his mind, but he could get away with murder for he was excellent company and an accomplished storyteller. Darling had plenty of stories to tell, for he had knocked around Australia working as a journalist and dabbling in politics before returning home at the start of the war to join the 9th Black Watch as a private soldier. By the time he was wounded at Loos he had risen to the rank of company quartermaster sergeant. Darling was a good soldier, a born leader and a bit of a fire-eater. It was indifferent health rather than the power of Pelmanism which had caused him to be transferred to the staff from the 11th Royal Scots, where he had been in command of A Company. Each company was distinguished by a coloured shoulder flash, and since A Company's was red it pleased Captain Darling's ghoulish sense of humour to christen it 'Blood Company'. By the time young Alex Jamieson joined the battalion in a draft of newly fledged soldiers Captain Darling had been gone for some time, but stories of his daring and prowess were still doing the rounds.

*42821 Private Alex Jamieson, MM, 11th Bn., The Royal Scots (Lothian Regt.), 9th (Scottish) Division*

He was transferred to Brigade as brigade-major, and when I was sent to Brigade HQ as a runner between there and the battalions in the line I met him for the first time at the rum issue. The sergeant was pouring out far more than I had ever seen! I held out my mug and he just poured it in, and I should think it might have been half-full. So I said, 'Stop.' Darling looked at me with a steely glare and said, 'What! A man of Blood Company says stop? Carry on, sergeant.' It must have been half a pint! Whether I took it all or not is another matter. This, of course, confirmed the view of the troops that the rum jars were well sampled on their way up the line and by the time they got to the line there was only a medicinal dose left.

Whether or not the Tommies' suspicions were justified, it was a fact that the officers had access to greater supplies of alcohol, and there were certain advantages in undertaking duties which brought a soldier into close contact with the officers' mess. Ted Organ was one such soldier. He had landed on his feet since arriving in France in 1914 with the Queen's Own Oxfordshire Hussars. 'Queer Objects On Horses' they had been rudely called, but it was many moons since they had been required for cavalry duties. Ted did not regret the loss of his steed, for he had a mode of transport that suited him far better. It was a large Sunbeam motor, which he drove for Major Watson of the Tank Corps. By a strange coincidence he had driven Major Watson before the war, when Watson was an undergraduate at Balliol College, Oxford, and long before he ever dreamed of being a major.

*1745 Corporal Ted Organ, A Squadron, Queen's Own Oxfordshire Hussars and Tank Corps*

I went to this nunnery to fetch an officer who'd just come out from England, and I picked him and his servant up and a load of his luggage and put it in his car. The servant sat on top of this luggage and the officer got in front with me. Directly I saw him I recognized him. He was nearly seven feet tall, this man, and thin as a lath. I saw him looking at me, and he said, 'What's your name, driver?' He seemed a bit puzzled.

I said, 'Organ, sir. And this isn't the first time I've driven you. Do you remember when you were at Balliol College you used to hire my taxi off Broad Street rank?'

'Yes, of course,' he said – 'you used to take my bicycle on the roof of your car.'

I said, 'That's right.' I used to take him to the station with his bicycle and his luggage and bring him back again.

Major Watson was delighted enough to pull a number of strings and to commandeer the Sunbeam plus the services of Organ for his personal use. The vehicle appeared on the list of the company's transport as 'the reconnaissance car'. No one ever queried it, and Ted had now passed many enjoyable months in Major Watson's service. But driving the staff car in winter was no sinecure. A soft hood sheltered the passengers, but the driver's seat was open to the sky with no protection whatever from the weather. A driver could muffle himself in layers of clothing against the cold, but when the thaw came, and with it the rain, it was another matter. The night Ted was obliged to drive from Tank Corps HQ in Blangy to Boulogne it was teeming with rain, and Major Watson was genuinely sorry to have to send him out in it.

*Corporal Ted Organ*

I had to meet Colonel Kingdon coming back off leave on the old *Victoria* at midnight and bring him back to Blangy. Major Watson said, 'Will you have a drink before you go?' I said, 'Thank you very much.'

So he poured me out a big lemonade tumbler, and it was half whisky and half champagne. Well, I was quite young, you know – just over twenty – and I wasn't a drinker at all. I was only used to that very weak French beer, which was more like water, but I drank it down and off I went.

I got about six miles and came to a level crossing when the gates closed and there was a lot of flat, open trucks going up towards the line carrying tanks and I had to wait there until the road was clear and the gates opened. Well, this was about nine o'clock at night, I suppose – it was dark anyway. The next thing I remember was a military policeman shaking me on the shoulder. He said, 'Hey, son, your headlights are on.' I came to. I said, 'What time is it?' He said, 'Eight o'clock.' Eight o'clock the next morning, this was! I should have met the Colonel at midnight! So I thought, 'My God! I'm in for it now.' All the way to Boulogne – about sixty-odd miles – I thought, 'Now how can I fake an accident so I can prove that I was delayed and have a reason for being late?' And I thought, 'Well, if I run into the bank and I bend the steering a bit, get it a bit wobbly, that'll be a good excuse.' But every time I came to a quiet place something came round the corner and I couldn't do it. So I eventually got to Boulogne about midday, I suppose.

I went along to the quayside and stopped at the hotel and went in and reported that I'd arrived, and I said, 'Is Colonel Kingdon here?' So the sergeant there said, 'Nobody of that name came over on the *Victoria* last night and all officers have to report at this hotel.' So I thought to myself, 'Thank God!' So I passed a few hours in Boulogne and went back to the quayside, knowing I'd have about six hours to wait. The *Victoria* came in at midnight, and the first man down the gangway was Colonel Kingdon, and I was the first car. 'Oh,' he said, 'I'm glad you're here, Organ. I was delayed last night. There was an air raid at Folkestone and the train was delayed. Go straight along to the Louvre Hotel. I won't keep you long.'

It was pouring with rain again. It was absolutely teeming down. The drivers in a limousine had no shelter like they've got in cars now. It was open. There was a car screen for the people in the back, and a windscreen, but the driver's sides had no doors and nothing to stop the wind and rain coming in. So I pulled up at the Louvre Hotel, coat collar up right round over my neck, waterproof cape over, and cap comforter down over my ears. There was a canopy over the pavement and several steps up to the entrance of this big hotel. So he went up there, and after a few minutes he came down and opened the door and I heard the door slam and off I went back the sixty miles to Blangy.

When I got back there I was frozen stiff and absolutely soaked to the skin. I got out. Opened the passenger door. No Colonel! His briefcase was there, and his stick, but there was no sign of him. Well, I couldn't think what the devil had happened. I hadn't stopped on the way – I knew that. So I went round to the orderly room – it was then about four o'clock in the morning – and knocked the sergeant-major up. He wondered what the hell I was up to at that time in the morning. I told him, 'I picked the Colonel up,' I said, 'I've come home and he's not in the car. His briefcase is there and his stick, but he's not in there.' The sergeant-major wasn't best pleased. He said, 'You'd better report it in the morning.' But in the morning when I went round, there was the Colonel sitting behind his desk! 'I'd forgotten something,' he said. 'I went back for my gloves after I put my briefcase and other belongings into the car. It's a good job Major Haskett-Smith had a car,' he said, 'or I don't know what I'd have done. He drove me home.' He took it in good part, luckily.

Staff cars were not for the likes of Reg Lloyd, returning to France as the proud possessor of the King's commission, clad a touch self-consciously in a new uniform of fine barathea and whipcord breeches which, although they had not been tailor-made at Huntsman of Bond Street, were a considerable improvement on the coarse khaki of a private soldier. Setting off to board the train that would take him to join his unit, Reg was happy in the knowledge that his newly acquired status would entitle him to travel in a carriage rather than on the floor of a cattle truck.

His complacency was short-lived. The train took fifteen interminable hours to complete a journey that should have lasted seven at most. It was bitterly cold. A penetrating wind whistled through the broken windows of the dilapidated carriages, and there was neither light nor heat in the train. If the authorities had set out to devise a system calculated to make the troops almost glad to reach the firing line they could hardly have improved on it. The train finally crawled into the station at La Gorgue, but it was by no means the end of the journey. Passes and travel warrants were stamped with the time of arrival, but after that it was up to the officers and men who had alighted to find their units as best they could. Sometimes it took them days.

*Second Lieutenant Reg Lloyd*

I had to link up with the 41st Divisional Artillery somewhere on the Arras front. It was quite a job tracking it down. Eventually I got to a certain point where a guide took me up the line to the battery in the

gun-pits, and I went in to report and Major Harrigan was there. I said,
'My name's Lloyd, Sir, and I have to report to you for duty.' (They'd
already got my papers.) He said, 'By George! We're pleased to see
you. We're having a hell of a lot of casualties here.' I thought, 'That's
a bloody nice start!' They were short of officers like everybody else
was. I shall never forget standing there in that dugout. There was a
packing-case with a candle or two on it, and Major Harrigan was
sitting on the other side of it and he said, 'Have a drink.' He pushed
a bottle of Scotch towards me and he said, 'Have a big one. You'll
find you'll want it here!' There was a barrage going on at the time and
the whole place was shaking and these candles flickering. They'd lost
a lot of men. Even in quiet times there were a lot of casualties.

Despite the lack of manpower, and despite Sir Douglas Haig's reluctance, a
bargain was a bargain and the British front had to be extended as far as the
River Oise to relieve the French Sixth Army. It was far short of French
demands, and it was understood that, at a later date, the British would take
over the French line as far as Reims. But that was in the future. The
immediate situation to be faced was how best to defend a longer front with
too few troops, many with no experience of battle. There was no question
of a continuous system of trenches, revetted, sandbagged, thickly wired, well
manned and well organized for defence, for even if there had been sufficient
manpower the Germans could hardly be expected to sit back and wait until
it was built. They were already drawing up plans for an offensive against the
British in the west, and Colonel Wetzell of the German General Staff had
made an interesting assessment of their adversary. It was not entirely without
foundation. 'We have in front of us', he said, 'a strategically clumsy, tactically
rigid, but tough enemy.'

This time, against the full weight of Germany's resources, it was doubtful
if toughness would be enough.

The British Army had last stood on the defensive in November 1914, and
generations of soldiers had lived and died since then. To the few originals
who remembered, aeons seemed to have passed since those long-gone days
of mobile warfare, before men went to ground in the burrows of the trenches,
and before the 'trench mentality' took hold. The Germans were more
experienced in the tactics of defence. Of the forty-four months since they
had invaded France, forty had been spent defending their positions on the
Western Front against a series of Allied offensives. They had developed a
system of defence in depth, relying on an outpost line, on redoubts skilfully
sited to command and protect their main line of defence, with a third system
of redoubts and defences beyond that. It was highly effective, and had proved
so costly to the British at the Somme and at Ypres that it had added

significantly to the length of the campaigns and had led, in both cases, to stalemate.

Now, if the positions were reversed, with the Germans poised to attack, it was high time to take a leaf out of their book.

# Chapter 3

The new system was mapped out and the troops were put to work. The outpost line was to consist of well-wired machine-gun posts sited to cover each other and command a good field of fire, with the intervening spaces connected by shallow trenches and blocked with wire in such a manner that they would funnel attacking troops into the very mouth of the machine-guns. The front line was not intended to be held. It was meant to hold up the enemy, to delay his advance and to inflict such damage that his attack would falter and be weakened. It was meant to buy time. The battle zone, the main line of resistance, would be further back, and here, it was hoped, the enemy would be stopped. Even if he were not, even if a certain amount of ground had to be sacrificed, there would be another line a mile or so beyond it. If all else failed, that would surely be the final insurance.

Up and down the front, from the trenches in Flanders to the marshland that bordered the Oise, every available man who was not actually on duty in the line was rounded up into a working party. There was no possibility that the defence system as envisaged by GHQ could be completed in less than six months, but, urged on to ever greater efforts, the men did their best. Their best, in the immortal tradition of the infantry, consisted of as much as was required and as little as they could get away with. There were no medals for endlessly digging trenches, humping tons of iron pickets, erecting miles of barricades, filling mountains of sandbags, and there were few commendations for soldiers who bore arms of picks and shovels. There were no wound stripes for aching muscles and barked shins, and no time off to compensate for sleepless nights of labour, returning at daybreak for a few hours' rest in some ramshackle billet, mustering at nightfall to start all over again. It was not soldiering as they had envisaged it during their training, but they took things as they came.

The Australians were a good deal less philosophical and were not entirely content to take things as they came. They were second to none in toughness and endurance, they had no equal in a fight, and, now that the cream of the British Army had gone, they were taller, stronger, fitter on the whole than most of the Tommies. With not a conscript among them, they were the pick of the bunch – and they knew it. They approached life with a breezy bonhomie that was not always appreciated by authority, and if, in the Aussies' opinion, authority was occasionally unreasonable in its demands they had a habit of adjusting orders to suit themselves.

*Private Stanley Sutcliffe, 51st Bn., 4th [Australian] Division, AIF*

We were camped in Nissen huts in Scottish Wood. Each day we went up the line on working parties, making strongpoints and barbed-wiring. At night we did patrol work and wiring. The Germans evidently heard us, for their machine-guns kept chattering away all the time. We were in among a lot of charred stumps of trees where at some time there had been a wood. As morning drew near and we were tired and cold after being standing in the mud observing all night, we used to imagine many tree stumps to be Germans.

The German machine-gun posts were only 150 yards away from us, and they seemed to have plenty of them. Two nights we were there, and I along with two other men went barbed-wiring. We could manage to get out there quietly enough, creeping through shell-holes full of mud and water, but when we started to work and happened to make a slight noise two or three machine-guns would open up and then we had to get our heads down until they had stopped. When we went back and the corporal put his report in he said he had found some very bad places in the wire and had run it all out. But the true state of affairs was that we dumped the whole lot into shell-holes full of water!

In the flatlands of Flanders the terrain itself was a barrier, and it was unlikely that the Germans would contemplate attempting an advance for many months to come. The experience of Passchendaele was too recent and too raw in their minds, for Passchendaele had been a martyrdom for both sides. Further south, especially where the line had been extended and new ground had been taken over, the situation was less determinate. A front of over 100 miles was held by thirty-three divisions, and far too many of the troops were young and inexperienced. Field-Marshal Haig would have liked half as many again to secure his front, but they were not forthcoming. The solution of the Supreme War Council (to form a General Reserve which would be able to move quickly to any endangered section of the French or British front) was not welcomed by Haig, for he himself would be obliged to withdraw seven divisions from the line to commit them to the General Reserve. With perfect logic, he put it to Lloyd George that, having disposed every available man in the line – and spread them all too thinly at that – having reorganized his divisions to stiffen them and make them more effective, it would cause a complete upheaval of his plans and take up precious time if he were forced to reorganize again. It simply did not make sense. Furthermore, he pointed out, he had already come to an agreement with General Pétain that each would send troops to support the other in case of need.

Sir William Robertson supported the Commander-in-Chief. As Chief of the Imperial General Staff, Robertson was implacably opposed to the idea of power being vested in the newly created Supreme War Council. He believed there might be a devious plot afoot to turn it into the *de facto* High Command of the Allied armies and a threat to his own position of authority. He was also disinclined to be impressed by an idea which had come from Sir Henry Wilson. Nor was Robertson mollified by Lloyd George's suggestion that he himself might replace Sir Henry Wilson as Britain's military representative on the Council, along with Generals Foch for France, Bliss for the USA and Cadorna for Italy.

Sir William Robertson – affectionately known as 'Wully' in the higher echelons of the Army – was the only soldier of Queen Victoria's Army who had risen from the rank of private to that of field-marshal, and the strength of character which had guided his brilliant career made him an obdurate adversary. He would have nothing to do with the Supreme War Council unless he could also continue as CIGS – but he also wished it to be known that he would not continue as CIGS if he were to be subject to the dictates of Versailles. Robertson was a well-known soldier, as popular with the Army as he was with the public. He could not be sacked outright without a scandal and without causing bad feeling among many people whom the Prime Minister knew it would be unwise to alienate.

Lloyd George had a certain adroitness in his dealings which, in the view of his enemies, occasionally verged on the machiavellian, as he had recently demonstrated in the wake of the Italian debacle. After General Cadorna's defeat at Caporetto, which had all but resulted in a rout, it was obvious that Cadorna would have to go. But, despite the arrival of a substantial British force to assist the Italian Army, it was equally obvious that the British Prime Minister was in no position to impose his views either on the Italian Government or on the Italian military authorities. He was, however, in a position to propose that Italy's military representative on the newly formed Supreme War Council should be none other than General Cadorna. As Lloyd George had rightly calculated, the General was flattered and accepted without making the slightest objection to being replaced as commander-in-chief of the Italian Army.

This ploy had worked to the satisfaction of all concerned, and Lloyd George doubtless entertained the hope that it would work again with Sir William Robertson. But 'Wully' was a tougher nut to crack. The powers he enjoyed as CIGS were exceptional. They had been conferred on him by Asquith, Lloyd George's predecessor, who had wished to curb the power and influence of Lord Kitchener (then Secretary of State for War), and indeed Sir William had insisted on these powers before accepting the post. But he had not exercised them with a heavy hand, for he and Haig had been very much at one in their views, and the present Secretary of State for War, Lord Derby, had backed the CIGS to the hilt. Now, since the creation of the Supreme War Council, it would clearly be undesirable if a British Chief of Staff could issue orders that were at variance with the consensus of its Allied representatives. The British Government therefore proposed to reduce the authority of the CIGS to its previous status, thus placing Sir William Robertson in what he deemed to be an untenable position.

Before February was out he had resigned and was appointed to the Home Forces as head of Eastern Command. Sir Henry Rawlinson went to Versailles, and Sir Henry Wilson replaced Robertson as Chief of the Imperial General Staff. There were those who suspected that this was exactly what Lloyd George had intended – or, at the very least, that he was far from displeased by the outcome.

It was not surprising that the ebullient Wilson appealed to Lloyd George's mercurial temperament. Wilson had a methodical, incisive mind, but it was concealed by a jocular manner, and the flippancy he adopted when discussing weighty matters sometimes disconcerted his colleagues. He had imagination and he also possessed a capacity for original thought – a quality which Lloyd George believed to be woefully lacking in the higher ranks of the Army. All in all, the Prime Minister found Wilson a refreshing change after his dealings with the two determined taciturn Scots, Robertson and Haig, and he was particularly entranced by Wilson's current enthusiasm. He and his Staff had worked out a war game and, on the basis of logic plus certain mathematical calculations, Sir Henry believed that it was possible to predict when and where the German attack would take place and, by extension, its likely outcome. The game was played by two of Wilson's staff officers at a meeting of the Allies at Versailles, and it was a great success. The American general, Bliss, was delighted and, as a result, he succeeded in persuading General Pershing that it would be better to send his troops to Europe piecemeal, and even untrained, rather than waiting until they could operate as an independent army. Lloyd George was no less impressed, the French were interested, and only Sir Douglas Haig was not bowled over by the demonstration, saying little in public but in private treating it with scorn – 'The whole position would be laughable but for the seriousness of it.'

Haig doubted Wilson's motives, and it was true that Sir Henry himself was no stranger to intrigue. Furthermore, both Robertson and Haig resented the fact that Lloyd George had sought advice from Sir Henry Wilson and from Haig's own predecessor, Sir John French, above their heads, and it was only natural that Haig should be wary. Within a matter of weeks, he had been forced to part with his trusted Chief of Intelligence, with his Chief of Staff and with his Quartermaster-General, General Maxwell, and now his friend and ally Sir William Robertson was under threat. Lloyd George's dislike of Haig was such that Sir Douglas himself had come within an ace of losing his job and being transferred to command the forces in Italy. But other considerations had prevailed, not least the feeling that it might be injudicious to change horses in midstream – especially since the stream showed every sign of turning into a torrent.

No one doubted that the Germans would shortly launch an attack in the west. Only two questions remained to be answered: Where would it fall and how was it to be met?

Exactly where the offensive should take place had also puzzled the enemy. After their victory on the Eastern Front, German strategists were agreed that the moment was ripe to strike in the west, and to strike hard enough to end the war. Their object was not outright victory. They wanted peace – and they wanted it in circumstances that would enable Germany to drive a hard bargain. Naturally she would retain her African colonies and keep her Navy and her Army intact. There would be no question of indemnities, and no nonsense about the return of Alsace and Lorraine, annexed by Germany at the end of a previous war with France. Indeed, with one eye on the first round of a future conflict, Germany wished to 'improve' her frontiers by holding on to at least some of the territory she had conquered in this one. Germany wanted Belgium.

The German Army was at its strongest. Troops had been brought back from the Eastern Front and also from the Dolomites, where they had assisted the Austrian Army in smashing Cadorna's army at Caporetto. Their British and French opponents, on the other hand, had been obliged to diminish their forces by sending men and materials to help the Italians. There would never be a better time to attack. But where? There were more than 400 miles of front to choose from.

From Ypres to La Bassée, in muddy Flanders, where the so-called ridges were little more than folds in the endless swamp, the ground would not dry out before April – and, if the war was to be won before the Americans arrived in strength, April might be too late. Verdun had taught the hard lesson that a limited objective could result at best in limited success and a catch-as-catch-can struggle, both long-drawn-out and costly. A powerful strike further west was given serious consideration. To hammer at the gates of Paris, to raise the spectre of the siege that had won the Franco-Prussian War and fifty years on still haunted France, would so demoralize the French that they would surely force their allies, Great Britain and America, to sue for peace.

But if France collapsed, would the British fight on? Some thought that they might, and in that case, as General Ludendorff remarked at one strategic meeting, he would have a second Battle of Flanders on his hands. There were other considerations. Like the Germans, the French had a vast hinterland of virgin countryside behind their lines, and a good network of communications. The British, on the other hand, with most of their line squeezed into the narrow coastal strip, had nothing at their backs but the sea. The conclusion of the German Supreme Command was a simple one: 'We must beat the British.'[1] They must beat them, moreover, before the Americans were strong enough to intervene.

President Wilson's *Fourteen Points for Peace*, presented to Congress early in January, had been drawn up without consultation with his allies, and they were far from pleased. 'Fourteen points!' scoffed the French Prime Minister, Georges Clemenceau. 'Mon Dieu! Even Almighty God only has ten.' But on the German side Wilson's *Points* gave Ludendorff and others the impression that America was more interested in pursuing a speedy negotiated settlement than in making a serious effort to end the war by dispatching her young men en masse to the actual conflict. Nevertheless, even the arrival of a comparatively small number at the front might tip the balance in favour of the Allies. There was nothing to be gained and possibly a great deal to lose by waiting. The Germans were aware that three US divisions were in France, but, since only one was yet in action, Ludendorff was inclined to agree with Grand Admiral von Tirpitz that 'America's military help is and remains a phantom.' There were nevertheless some fairly substantial ghosts flitting around on various fronts.

The Yanks attached to the French Army had the benefit of interpreters, and this went a long way towards avoiding confusion, although officers in transit occasionally spent much time and frustration endeavouring to find Dubonnet on a map before discovering that this was an advertisement for a popular drink and not the name of an unfamiliar station. Those attached to

1. At the conclusion of the conference, Ludendorff summed up: 'The situation in Russia and Italy will, as far as can be seen, make it possible to deliver a blow on the Western Front in the new year. The strength of the two sides will be approximately equal. About thirty-five divisions and one thousand heavy guns can be made available for an offensive. That will suffice for one offensive; a second great simultaneous offensive, say as a diversion, will not be possible.

'Our general situation requires that we should strike at the earliest moment, if possible at the end of February or beginning of March, before the Americans can throw strong forces into the scale.

'We must beat the British.'

the British were naturally assumed to speak the same tongue, but the language of the British Army baffled the Americans.

The arcane but universal use of the signallers' code, devised for clarity in messages transmitted by telephone, was as clear as mud to the Americans. What was Joe Doakes to make of a garrulous Tommy announcing that he was with the Tock Emmas or the Emma Gees, or that he must be at the O Pip at 7 Ack Emma? How could the uninitiated be expected to translate Tock Emma as trench mortar and Emma Gee as machine-gun – still less to grasp an order to report to the observation post at 7 a.m.? Even the habit of referring to British officers only by initials drove American officers to distraction. MO and CO were all very well, but how was a man to know that CRA was Commander Royal Artillery, that the officer familiarly referred to as DADOS was the Deputy Assistant Director Ordnance Service, or that DADMS – to an American ear sounding ridiculously like 'Diddums' – was the Deputy Assistant Director Medical Services?

Like the Australians, American soldiers had a relaxed attitude to their senior officers which was not appreciated by their starchier British counterparts. One brigadier, incensed when his staff car was forced to an abrupt halt by a horse careering across the road, did not hesitate to give the rider a piece of his mind. The rider happened to be an American officer, and the brigadier was not mollified by his indignant reply: 'Take it easy, Buster. Your vehicle's got a brake. Mine hasn't!'

The Americans were refreshingly keen and enthusiastic. They demanded nothing more than to get to grips with the enemy, and the armies in France could have done with many, many more of them. But, although America's National Army was training hard, it was quite another matter to arm and equip it. The United States had placed huge orders with French and British firms for guns, ammunition, rifles, steel helmets, even bandages and surgical instruments, and for many months factories had been working flat out to fulfil them. But it all took time, and it was natural that the USA did not wish the flower of her young manhood to be used merely as reinforcements and to be thrown into the fight willy-nilly merely to replace casualties on the battlefield. Wilson had promised a million men, but they wanted to fight as an army, marching under their own colours to pulverize the enemy and marching back again victorious. But such an army would first have to be armed and assembled in France, and there were simply not enough ships to transport a million men across the ocean. By February barely a quarter of that number had arrived, and it was obvious that their comrades, still languishing on the far side of the Atlantic, would not be able to reach Europe and complete their training in time to turn the tide. The assault, when it came, would have to be met with such resources as there already were.

★

Alternative plans for a large-scale German offensive in the west had been laid for years, and so long as the Allies remained in the dark about the precise intentions of the enemy the better his chances of success.

Both French and British airmen, flying dangerously low above the German lines in widely disparate sectors of the front, brought back similar and puzzling reports. Along most of their line the Germans were strengthening their front – constructing more trenches and strongpoints, adding depth to their barriers of wire – as if it were their intention to stand on the defensive. But there were also signs along most of the line that they were preparing to attack – tell-tale tracks to new gun positions, mushrooming supply dumps, new aerodromes and hospital tents, new roads, and even new bridges over rivers and canals. Day after day, when the weather permitted, the flimsy aircraft made dangerous forays behind the German lines, snapping aerial shots by the thousand.

It took a good deal of skill and considerable nerve to take to the skies in a contraption consisting of a few slats of wood, paper-thin wings, and a solitary engine which a single random shot could put out of action. It took daring to throw a plane round the sky in dogfights, and cool courage to fly a steady pre-planned course with anti-aircraft shells bursting all round. The flyers contemptuously called them 'Archie' – and their nickname for the shells was as familiar to the man in the sky as 'Tommy' and 'Jerry' were to the man in the trenches.

Most of the newly fledged pilots and observers had started off in the infantry, and they were glad to be out of it. As a Territorial, Second Lieutenant Peter Wilson had been serving since the first day of the war. He had done his stint as a humble corporal at the Battle of Aubers Ridge, where his best friend had been blown to pieces at his side, and later, as a newly commissioned officer, he had been badly wounded at Thiepval during the Battle of the Somme. A signalling course after convalescence had led him to the Royal Flying Corps and a job as an observer. It was all a far cry from his peacetime role as a bank clerk, and not a bad curriculum vitae for a young man who had not yet reached his twenty-fourth birthday when he joined No. 7 Squadron in November 1917. The reputation of the RFC was notorious, and Peter had been prepared for a certain amount of levity, but the high jinks on his first evening were an eye-opener.

*Second Lieutenant A. ('Peter') Wilson, 7 Squadron, Royal Flying Corps (diary extract)*

I arrive mid-evening and find a special dinner celebration is on for new CO, Major B. E. Sutton, DSO, MC, of the Cumberland Yeomanry. There is much merriment and many guests in for dinner

– about fifty or sixty diners and many 'shot away' before the meal. *Much* alcohol dispensed and there appears to be a very ample supply of whisky. The dinner is very noisy and is followed by typical RFC games like 'Stiff Man', blind boxing, and glass throwing, which is a wild affair. Two take part, and one partner throws the glass at the hand of the other stretched out against the wall. (Awful destruction of drinking glasses!) Happily, aiming is poor and no broken glass strikes a naked hand. Then followed blind boxing. This is a fierce affair with much heavy punching and very wild combat. By 10 p.m. several young hearties are down and out and I help to carry victims to their huts. Much rowdiness! My batman fixes me up for the night in a B-flight hut with Pilot-Officer R. V. Facey, Lieutenant Ian Johnson-Gilbert (Royal Scots) and Lieutenant Watson – all pilots. All are very tight and Facey is quite OUT! By midnight all is quiet. The guests have departed and very soon I am fast asleep in my flea bag and blankets. My batman brings early morning tea at 7 a.m. and I join my friends for breakfast.

This party was a tame affair – a mere Mark IV on the Squadron's scale of festivities and not to be compared with the Mark I reserved for really special occasions. Wilson was one of several replacements, for the Squadron had taken a hammering and had seen too many comrades, and even the command-ing officer, plunge out of the sky. Losses that might be less noticeable in a battalion of 800 men were glaringly obvious in an intimate unit of fifty. Statistics were against survival, and it was best not to think of them. Their byword was 'Eat, drink and be merry . . .' Even if the unspoken rider hung in the air, bravado was a bulwark against emotion, and alcohol guaranteed some hours of oblivion before the next trembling dawn. Frenetic merriment relieved nerves taut-strung with the tension of several flights a day, the see-sawing of elation and terror, when the pilot or observer who relaxed vigilance for one moment might be a dead man the next.

Young Gerard Robin, who had joined up as an air mechanic at the age of seventeen, had wangled his way to a commission and a pilot's wings four months before his nineteenth birthday. He had been in France for just three weeks, flying an SE5, when his number almost came up. Writing home to his young lady, Rhoda Marriott, he spared her none of the dramatic details.

*Second Lieutenant Gerard Robin, 41 Squadron, Royal Flying Corps*

Three of us went up on a patrol and we came across six Huns, which we dived on, and of course they gave us a rainstorm of bullets and belted off east. We were too far over the lines to follow them. Immediately after this the Hun Archie spotted us and opened fire and gave us Jericho for five minutes – the best shooting I have seen so far! Soon after this I lost the other two and I wandered about looking for a friend, which I soon found – one of our own lads who came over just to see what he could find. He immediately began to get into formation behind me. Now, I was lost to the world, and of course I wanted him to show *me* the way. I tried to make him understand this, but there was nothing doing. So I resolved to fire a Very light. I loaded my pistol, and on doing so it went off, hit my fingers a terrible rap, and went down inside the machine, burning like fury. Of course I had terrible wind up and got into a spin by mistake. I realized if I didn't get the nasty thing out I would go down in a spinning nose-dive in flames! So in abject terror I undid my belt and slid down into the cockpit, and managed to move this flaring ball into the metal groove and then I got back and pulled the bus out of the spin and side-slipped until the beastly thing went out.

I was at 13,000 feet when I began this stunt and at 5,000 feet when I pulled her out. I didn't know if any other part of the machine was on fire, so I dived due west, but I had no idea where I was, so when I came to an aerodrome I landed. This was at 5.30, and it was horribly dark. When I found my position I made for home and arrived back in the dark. You should have seen the fine firework display of flares along the landing field when I got back!

Well, I made the best landing I have ever made – wasn't it luck, especially as all the air mechanics and officers were watching! When I got out of my machine, I was pretty shaky, and I was covered with sulphur dust from the burning light, and very white. Everybody thought I had been wounded. It was the nearest thing to death I ever want to be. I only got to sleep at three o'clock this morning, and every time I shut my eyes I began to come down in flames! Horrible nightmares!

This morning our Archie battery reported that a machine came down last night out of control, and presumably on fire owing to the amount of smoke seen. But for once they were wrong!

The monotony of routine, so often the bane of the infantry in the trenches, was seldom complained of in the Royal Flying Corps. There was counter-battery work, spotting for the artillery and signalling by wireless to the ground. There were bombing raids on targets well behind the enemy lines. There were reconnaissance flights, searching for enemy troops on the march, or trains or transport on the move. And there were the camera sorties on which the map-makers and collators of intelligence depended. The job of the fighters on contact patrols was to intercept enemy planes bent on similar missions above the British lines.

But the Royal Flying Corps could not easily capture prisoners, and prisoners were a valuable source of information. It was up to the infantry to supply them. Along the length of the line from Passchendaele to Verdun, there was hardly a night when raiding parties from one side or the other were not out stalking No Man's Land and not infrequently meeting on the way. The fracas that ensued were every bit as hair-raising as the dogfights in the sky.

# Chapter 4

As soon as darkness fell across the long and straggling front, men were on the move, and roads on which hardly a mouse would stir by day were suddenly alive with the rumble of wheels and the rattle of wagons. Deep in rural France, where motor cars were seldom seen in peacetime, all but the arterial roads were narrow tracks strung between farms and villages, trodden into being by generations of plodding horses and country clogs. The transportation of supplies to the line posed a thousand problems for friend and foe alike, for the guns of both sides had the roads perfectly registered. At intervals military police laboured to control the traffic, halting vehicles to allow a working party or an ambulance to pass, shifting a weary bunch of soldiers to the roadside while a string of ammunition lorries lurched by, clearing the miserable debacle of men and vehicles when a lucky shell smashed into a convoy, organizing a repair gang to fill in the crater it gouged from the surface.

The roads, clearly delineated on pre-war ordnance maps, were easy targets for the guns, and, knowing that wheeled traffic was obliged to use them, both sides frequently shelled them after dark, confident of hitting some target and disrupting the lifeline to a gun-line or supply dump. The dumps were close to the trenches – though not always close enough for the liking of the carrying parties groping their way for a mile or more to their battalion's ration dump and back again across broken duckboards to their company in the trenches. It took a long time in the dark, and even with a runner to guide them it was quite possible to get lost.

In some places where there were no communication trenches and the front line was only a system of outposts, everyone was on the alert, and even a company runner, fumbling and stumbling as he went about his lawful business, could run into trouble.

*39181 Private W. Luff, 1st Bn., The Queen's (Royal West Surrey Regt.), 33rd Division*

At Passchendaele we didn't have trenches; we had outposts with just a machine-gun here and there. There was one big dugout at a place called Crest Farm, and you go from there up on to Passchendaele

Ridge. There was one heap of rubble there which they called 'the Doctor's house', and another heap that was the church. That had a right-angled turn, and the company runner used to have to take his relief up there to show him the way around, and there was only two trees to give you a clue. Not big, tall trees, because the tall trees were knocked down and this was brushwood. Tucked in there was an eighteen-pounder, which they said was the sacrifice gun.

You went along all these posts and at the last post a unit on the left overlapped us, but they were slightly in front. I went along there with my relief one night and *Bang!* They fired and *we* yelled! Well, the password we had was 'A Company' or 'B Company', or whatever you were, but, naturally, when somebody let rip like that we didn't say anything about 'A Company'! We just went through the alphabet with all the swear words we knew!

A string of English curses delivered vehemently in the accents of far-off Surrey was unorthodox, but probably as effective as the nightly password which every man who ventured near the line or beyond it had to know. Nerves were on edge, and a raiding party or a patrol scattered by skirmishing, or simply mistaking direction, could easily stray and return to the line on an unfamiliar part of the brigade front into the sights of a nervous sentry posted by another battalion.

There were two unfortunate incidents at Lempire in the Fifth Army sector, where the 6th Connaught Rangers were in the line. The defences were being strengthened, and jumpy sentries, thinking there was nothing but empty darkness between them and the Germans, inadvertently fired on parties of pioneers who were wiring gaps between the outposts. Fortunately no one was injured, but the commanding officer of the Pioneer Battalion complained vociferously to the brigadier. Brigadier-General Gregorie was furious. He laid the blame squarely on the shoulders of the sentries, and made his feelings known in no uncertain terms. This was the news that greeted the Connaughts' CO, Colonel Feilding, when he returned from leave. Fearing that the sentries might in future be overcautious, Feilding was of the opinion that the General's reprimand had been a big mistake.

With no continuous trenchline, it was a difficult part of the front to defend, and the weakest point was a sunken road which ran from behind the German line across No Man's Land and on through the British lines. The road was blocked by a rampart of sandbags with a Lewis-gun mounted on top of it, and Colonel Feilding had ordered that it must never be guarded by fewer than two men. It was a moonless, misty night and the sentries could see nothing, but they heard a flurry of movement in the darkness in front of them. With the General's admonition ringing in their ears, they held their fire and called out, 'Who goes there?' The reply was a shower of hand-grenades.

*Lieutenant-Colonel R. Feilding, DSO, 6th Bn., The Connaught Rangers, 16th Division*

Private Mayne, who had charge of the Lewis-gun, was hit in many parts, including the stomach. His left arm was reduced to pulp. Nevertheless, he struggled up and, leaning against the parapet, with his uninjured hand he discharged a full magazine (forty-seven rounds) into the enemy, who broke – not a man reaching our trench. Then he collapsed and fell insensible across his gun. The second sentry's foot was so badly shattered that it had to be amputated in the trench.

Words cannot express my feelings of admiration for Private Mayne's magnificent act of gallantry, which I consider well worthy of the V C. It is, however, improbable that he will live to enjoy any decoration that may be conferred upon him.

The incident so filled me with pride of the Battalion that I confess I have been aghast at receiving – instead of any acknowledgement of the successful and heroic repulse of the German raiders by Private Mayne and his companion – the following memorandum, which had been circulated in the Division.

*Another instance has occurred of an enemy patrol reaching within bombing distance of our line. This must not occur again. Our patrols must meet the enemy patrols boldly in No Man's Land.*

How simple and how grand it sounds! I think I can see the writer, with his scarlet tabs, seated in his nice office seven or eight miles behind the line penning this pompous admonition.[1]

It was hardly fair. The staffs of divisional and brigade headquarters carried heavy responsibilities, but officers and men who were closer to the fighting had no time for the staff, and the bold spirits who prowled round No Man's Land at the behest of intelligence officers demanding prisoners despised them most of all. In the weeks before the battle, officers of high degree were dispatched on morale-raising tours of the rest areas to inspect the troops and stiffen them with fiery talks on the theme of do-or-die, with the emphasis on holding-on-at-all-costs and fighting-to-the-last-man. But the scheme misfired badly and merely reinforced the belief that GHQ was 'windy'. As far from the line as brigade headquarters, the report 'Patrols report all clear'

1. Private Mayne died and received a posthumous mention in dispatches.

could evoke a muttered aside, 'Good, now GHQ can stand down!' The
sarcasm was understandable. It was hard to imagine some corpulent Colonel
Blimp crawling across No Man's Land, dodging bullets, freezing beneath
the soaring Very lights, grappling hand to hand with the enemy. Such
adventures required a special kind of man with a special kind of nerve. In
principle members of raiding parties were volunteers. In practice they were
mainly picked men. George Hull of the Queen's went raiding on Passchendaele Ridge.

*Private George Hull, The Queen's (Royal West Surrey Regt.)*

We were excused all other duties, and while we prepared for the raid
we were quartered in a big underground sap which had been captured
from the Germans at a place known as Crest Farm in our support lines.
The entrance was by steps cut into the earth and reinforced with
timber, and the sap itself was quite spacious, with a number of rooms
and also wash-places and toilets. There were rough tables, chairs and
sleeping bunks, and water and facilities for cooking.

On our first day underground we were briefed and instructed on
how we were to make the raid. We were to carry rifles and bayonets
with fifty rounds of ammunition and two Mills hand-grenades, one in
each bottom tunic pocket. Steel helmets would be too awkward to
wear crawling across No Man's Land, so we would wear our woollen
caps instead. An hour or so before we were ready to start we blacked
our hands and faces with burnt cork, and at about eight o'clock we
made our way, single file, up to the front line – just a series of shell-holes,
deepened and lined with sandbags filled with earth with emplacements
for firing Lewis-guns and rifles. We got a final briefing from the officer,
and started across No Man's Land crawling on our hands and knees.
The enemy's front line was about 200 yards from ours at this point, so
it took quite some time to crawl that far. Our own troops had been
ordered not to fire any Very lights, but the Germans sent up their usual
liberal supply of star-shells, and each time one of these lighted up the
landscape we froze in whatever position we happened to be. Directly
in front of us a German machine-gunner kept firing bursts of bullets,
not necessarily because he could see us but probably as a matter of
routine, and also to deter any raiders like ourselves. Most of the
bullets went over our heads, though some of them seemed to come
uncomfortably close. We were spread out roughly fanwise, with the
officer in the centre.

Then Private Sutton, who was just behind me, called out to me in a stage whisper that he was going to be sick. Some distance back I'd noticed a really large shell-hole, and I told him to crawl back in a straight line and get into it. Couldn't risk taking him any further. He was a new lad.

We crawled on until we were about twenty yards from the enemy front. We could hear the noise of picks and shovels, and it sounded as though they were digging a trench. The officer gathered us into a group behind a small hillock. He whispered to the senior corporal to stay there with half the party, and this included me. He was going to move over some way to the left with the others, and when we heard two blasts on the officer's whistle we were to rush to the enemy's front line, grab hold of the first German we saw, and frog-march him back to our own line. The officer disappeared into the darkness and we waited.

Then, before he could possibly have got into position, some fool back at our own front line sent up the SOS signal for artillery support, and to our horror the batteries on our front started barrage fire. Dozens of Very lights went up on our side *and* star-shells on the German side, so that No Man's Land was almost as light as day. We saw the German soldiers grab their rifles and shovels and make a beeline for their support trenches. We couldn't follow them. If we had we would have been running into our own barrage, and of course by this time the German guns were retaliating and pouring shells down on No Man's Land and on our front-line positions.

We started dodging back through a positive storm of explosions and flying splinters of steel. Then suddenly in all the noise and confusion we heard Sutton calling up from the bomb crater, and you can be sure we lost no time in jumping into it. We stayed there crouching as low as we could, until the shell-fire got a bit less and we could creep back to our front line.

There were fourteen of us, and not one had got a scratch. It was a miraculous escape!

After more than two years' soldiering, George Hull was still a private. He did not hanker after promotion, for he knew perfectly well that even the humble distinction of a lance-corporal's stripe would never come his way, and he also knew why. Although he had joined the Army as a volunteer, George had spent the first few months of his service on the run, and the remarkable truth was that he was a double deserter, for he had also joined the Navy and deserted yet again. All this took place within the space of six weeks. It was not normal behaviour, but George had not been normal at the time. He had been literally suicidal. 'I joined up because I wanted to die. Get to France, get a bullet, and finish it.' That had been the idea.

In a more enlightened age he might have been diagnosed as suffering from depression. Only a few months earlier his father had killed himself, the family broke up, and George, who had recently left school, moved into lodgings. On an under-gardener's meagre pay of eleven shillings a week it took him all his time to pay for them. He was the thirteenth of fourteen children, and well used to knocks. He had been disliked by his father, and from the age of seven, after his mother's death, he had been unkindly treated by a shiftless housekeeper. It was not much of a life, and at the end of 1915, when he had just turned eighteen, George joined the Army.

At the headquarters of the 10th Queen's at the Town Hall in Battersea he was issued with kit and uniform, allotted a civilian billet with a Mrs Bourne in Sugden Road, and given a forty-eight-hour pass. He returned to Woking to spend the weekend at his aunt's house, convinced that he was not cut out for soldiering. He did not think of applying for release, though he was under military age, and he did not think of consulting a doctor about the blinding headaches and insomnia that plagued him. He could think of nothing but escape. He borrowed thirty shillings from a brother, picked up some clothes from his old lodgings, changed into them on Purford Common, dumped his uniform, and walked to Weybridge station to catch a train for London. It was Christmas Eve.

*Private George Hull*

I didn't dare go to Woking Station, because I would have been recognized there, and I paid for a single ticket, because I didn't dare use my Army travel pass. I decided to go to London, because I could easily lose myself there and I reckoned the police would come looking for me in Surrey, but when I got to Waterloo Station I had no idea what to do next. I walked down into Lower Marsh, then into Kennington Road, and hired a room at the Surrey Commercial Hotel for a shilling a night. All next day I walked around. Being Christmas Day there was nobody about, and I had my Christmas dinner in the only café that was open – hot pie and beans for threepence.

I stayed at the Surrey Commercial for several days. It wasn't far from the police station, and every night I made up my mind I'd go to the police station and give myself up, but every morning the prospect didn't look so enticing and I always put it off for another day. I didn't know what the Army did to people like me. I imagined that I'd be taken to the Tower of London and court-martialled and shot. I knew

I'd done wrong, and my principal concern was to have courage enough not to show the white feather but to be able to stand up and take my punishment. It didn't worry me. I thought then, at least, my troubles would be over. But walking round London and thinking things over I got the idea that it would be better to enlist again rather than give myself up, and going along the Strand I saw a recruiting office for the Royal Naval Division, so I went in there and enlisted giving the name of Frank Green.

They took me and two other new recruits to Ludgate Hill Station to entrain for HMS Crystal Palace, and there we were fitted out with naval uniforms and had to sleep in hammocks. The discipline, if anything, was stricter than in the Army, and I didn't like it there. We were paid on Friday, and I made up my mind to abscond on the Saturday evening. I got permission to take my civilian clothes home, so I made my way to Waterloo Station, took a single-fare ticket to Woking, and went to my aunt's place in Walton Road. I got a very mixed reception! My uncle was extremely alarmed, because the police had been there looking for me and told them there was a warrant out for my arrest. But my aunt took me in against my uncle's wishes, and I stayed there for a week. Then she lent me some money and I went back to London in civvies. That was the safest place.

But now I was in a real jam. As well as being a deserter from the Army I was also adrift from the Navy, and I couldn't get a job of course. So I decided that the best thing to do was to join the Army *again*, under a false name. There was a scheme for enlistment known as the Derby scheme, and if I joined giving my correct age of eighteen I wouldn't be called up until I was nineteen the following October. So I duly presented myself at the recruiting office. This time I gave the name of George Hull and a false address in York Road, Lambeth, and after an embarrassing question about my registration card and saying I'd left it at home I managed to get as far as the medical examination. Then another problem arose. I had six vaccination marks. Four had been done in childhood, but the two that were done in the Queen's and the Royal Naval Division still had the scabs on them and naturally I had to explain them. So I said I'd been working for a firm of builders in Byfleet in Surrey and that there had been an outbreak of smallpox and all the employees had had to be vaccinated. There were two doctors, one sitting at a desk and writing down the details called out by the doctor who was doing the physical examination. The one who was writing got impatient and called out, 'Oh, never mind about details. How many marks?' The other one answered, 'Six,' and that was that. I was saved again. I got dressed and was given a khaki

armlet and a warrant card entitling me to wear it. Of course it was in
my false name.[1]

The Derby scheme was the precursor of conscription and a way of
anticipating the call-up. A man would still be called up as required, but, by
previously pledging himself for service, he was able to choose the regiment
in which he wished to serve when the time came. Meanwhile the armlet
proclaimed to the world that he was no shirker and was merely waiting to
do his bit. It was useful protection against the assiduous attentions of certain
ladies who considered it their patriotic duty to accost young men in civilian
clothes and demand to know why they were not in uniform. In George's
case it would also protect him from the attentions of the police on the
lookout for deserters. He might have got away with it indefinitely, but,
although he meant to find a job, he was short of ready cash and it struck
him that his best suit, still at his first billet in Battersea, could fetch a few
shillings to tide him over. Without a thought for the consequences, he
scribbled a note to Mrs Bourne asking when it would be convenient to call,
and he received a reply by return of post suggesting the following day at
6.30 in the evening. It was Saturday 4 March. A less naive young man might
have foreseen the outcome.

At the police station, after his arrest, the Derby armband caused the desk
sergeant some amusement. 'Well,' he jeered, '*you* certainly must like the
Army, seeing as you've joined it twice!' George was not in the mood to see
the joke. He was steeling himself and summoning up courage for whatever
lay ahead.

He was not taken to the Tower and he was not shot, but in due course
he was court-martialled and sentenced to three months in the notorious
Detention Barracks at Aldershot. They called it 'the Glasshouse', and a
prisoner was made to realize that it was no joke from the moment he entered
his cell. It was completely bare but for an iron bedstead, a narrow wooden
bed-board with a raised end in place of a pillow, two bed-sheets of rough
canvas, and three Army blankets. A pannikin of water stood on one of two

---

1. This is the only soldier who appears under a pseudonym in this or any other
of the author's histories of the First World War, and the reason will be readily
understood. It was only on the promise of anonymity that 'George' was persuaded
to repeat the story he had told in private conversation and consent to its publication.
This was not necessarily because he was ashamed of his behaviour in his muddled
youth, but because he was proud of his subsequent service as a soldier and preferred
to be remembered for that. For the same reason his original battalion and Army
number are omitted. He appears elsewhere (though not in this book) under his own
name.

small corner shelves, with a Bible on the other. A chamber pot completed the furnishings. Through the thick opaque glass of a small window high on the wall a streak of murky daylight edged into the cell.

*Private George Hull*

There were six remission marks a day, and if you kept your nose clean and didn't lose any you got a mattress after a fortnight – three sections of horsehair mattress they called 'biscuits' and a straw palliasse for a pillow. In the morning you had to lean the bed-board at a certain angle against the wall and fold the blankets into an exact square and pile them, not just neatly, oh no, they had to be precise – one blanket on the bottom, then a sheet, blanket, sheet, and the third blanket wrapped round in a certain way, no raw edges showing, and the whole bundle an exact size. Of course you have to do that for kit inspections in normal Army life, but getting it right in the Glasshouse was life and death, or you would lose points. You could lose points for anything, and if you lost a certain number that was your remission gone.

Reveille was at 5.30. The lights would be switched on, and you had to spring up, put on your trousers (you slept in your shirt), arrange your bedding, and brush out your cell – you had a dustpan and a sweeping brush without a handle. Then the order was shouted, '*Shirts off!*' and you pulled your shirt off and doubled to the washroom, braces tied round your trousers to keep them up. It was all done by clockwork – two minutes to wash, two minutes to shave, one minute to empty the toilet pot. Five minutes and you had to be in and out. You had to double to get a razor – cut-throat razors of course, and they were kept in a case and handed out – and you doubled to the washroom. In there it was like animals, all done by orders, but of course there were only eighteen washbasins for seventy-two men so rush wasn't the word for it. You had to wash thoroughly, stripped to the waist, and then you had to empty the basin and wipe it clean for the man behind, all in the two minutes.

You were watched with an eagle eye, and the NCOs would try to catch you out. If they saw a section getting lathered up, ready for a shave, they'd change the order and make you wash first. I was all right shaving, because being youthful I didn't have much to shave, but some of the older men with dark hair and tough beards went through purgatory. They'd cut themselves to pieces with these cut-throat razors trying to shave in the time, because it had to be a proper close shave and if it wasn't that would be another remission mark gone. Then you had to double back to your cell and you had another five minutes to dry yourself and dress before you doubled out to parade for work on an empty stomach.

The first two weeks they gave you the worst jobs. Chopping wood, or picking coir, which is even worse. It's coconut fibre, and it comes in great lumps and you have to shred it apart. It wears the skin off the top of your fingers. Then I struck lucky with a good job in the workshop – sewing the bottom of horses' nosebags. Some men had to sew up sandbags, and of course you could do nosebags much quicker than the same number of sandbags, and they had the same quota to do. This was the morning task, as they called it, and at 7.45 you were marched back to your cell and the order came, 'Diets Up', and the orderly men brought round breakfast.

The food was just sufficient to live on. Breakfast was ten ounces of bread and a pint of skilly, which was a thin oatmeal porridge, and tea. Dinner was a pint of stew with not much in the way of meat – just a few bits of fatty meat – five ounces of potatoes cooked in their jackets and five ounces of bread. Tea was ten ounces of bread and a pint of cocoa. That was all, except that on Tuesdays and Friday you got two ounces of cheese, and on Sunday you got a two-ounce lump of suet pudding in your stew. These meals were dished up in mess tins made of very inferior metal and they rusted as soon as you looked at them. As soon as your food was finished you had to wipe them out with a rag and polish them like silver, and woe betide you if you didn't hand them back clean. The tiniest spot of rust and you'd be put on report, and 'on report' could mean three days on bread and water *and* automatic loss of remission marks.

After breakfast you had to scrub out your cell, and Monday, Thursday and Saturday you got dressed in musketry order and you did drill and gymnastics all morning. Tuesday, Wednesday and Friday it was full marching order – packs and all – and you had to march round and round and round the parade ground until very often you felt as if your legs had dropped off and you were marching on the stumps. Then it was back to your cell for dinner, change into fatigue dress, and back to the workshop for the afternoon. All at the double. Everything at the double. Then you'd double back to your cell for Diets Up at teatime, and after that you worked in your cell for two hours. Then you had to clean and polish your kit – because you'd be on report if *that* wasn't perfect – and then you could read until lights out. All you had to read for the first two weeks was the Bible; after that you were allowed one library book a week. Other than that there was no recreation. You weren't even allowed to speak to anyone else. That's what nearly landed me in trouble.

I'd done everything by the book, because I knew perfectly well that the better I behaved the quicker I'd get out, and on the way there one of the escorts had told me that when you'd done half your sentence you could apply for your release. I'd done nearly six weeks and I was living for the day, when one afternoon in the workshop the man next to me spoke to me and nudged me to answer. He spoke without moving his lips – probably he'd done time in a civil prison and learned the technique, because a lot of these chaps had been jailbirds in civvy life. Anyway, I didn't reply, and he spoke and nudged me again. The third time he did it I answered, and of course the NCO saw me, and he called me out. Name, number, regiment – he wrote it all in a notebook and said, 'Right, you'll be on report in the morning.' Well, I doubled back to my place, and I must have been looking pretty crestfallen, holding back the tears, because I'd been living for the day, and I thought that was my remission gone. Anyway, he called me out again and took out his notebook and crossed it out, and he said, 'I'll give you a warning this time, but don't be such a fool again.' He was a very fair man – strict, but fair. So I thanked him and told him how grateful I was, because I'd wanted to apply for release. He was really decent; he said he'd arrange for me to have an interview with the commandant.

Two days later I was called to the commandant's office, at the double, and the sergeant marched me in at the double to see him. He said, 'This man wants to apply for release, Sir.' The commandant said, 'On what grounds?' I told him because I'd done half my sentence, and he roared at me, 'Oh, so you think that's enough, do you?' Well, I had to do a bit of quick thinking, and I said, 'I'm willing to soldier, Sir.' He looked at me for a minute, and then he said, 'Very well. I'll consider it.' And my release came through three days later.

The Colonel had made a remarkable decision, because George had been misinformed. Only a third of a man's sentence could be remitted for good behaviour, and remission of as much as half was unheard of. But the circumstances were exceptional. Besides the Glasshouse at Aldershot there were military wings in prisons throughout the country, but now, in May 1916, just weeks after the Easter Rising, when hundreds of arrests had been made in Dublin, space in the civil prisons was at a premium and even the military capacity had been pressed into service. The whole system was under severe strain. To release even one man would help, and if that man would make a useful soldier so much the better.

George was released to an escort of the Queen's and returned to his regiment. The irony was that he found that he liked soldiering. He knew that he was a good soldier, but, as George himself acknowledged, 'If a man isn't a soldier when he goes into the Glasshouse, he will be when he comes out!'

But, good soldier or not, after the first abortive effort on Passchendaele Ridge it took every ounce of soldierly courage and discipline to set out for the second time to raid the enemy's trenches – and with no weapons to speak of. The officer in charge had vetoed the use of rifles.

*Private George Hull*

He said he had noticed that the bayonets fitting loosely on the bosses of the rifles had made quite an amount of noise the previous night while we were crawling across No Man's Land. He was carrying a brown-paper parcel, and as he proceeded to unwrap it he said, 'I've got some good weapons for you, boys.' I expected to see revolvers or automatic pistols, and I was amazed when he produced small *hatchets* – like Red Indian tomahawks. There were only eight of us this time, and armed with those things and with only one firearm in the party (namely *his* own revolver) I didn't think much of our chances against Germans with rifles and bayonets. All of us, including the NCOs, were nonplussed, but being good disciplinarians none of us said anything.

By nightfall a mist had come up, and by the time we arrived at the front line it had developed into quite a thick fog. Most of us thought that it would be foolhardy to make the attempt that night, but that officer wouldn't be deterred, and he said he'd go on his own if no one else would come. Well, that was unthinkable, so naturally the NCOs said they would go too, and so there was no alternative but for we three privates to say the same. We started off towards the enemy lines, and, speaking for myself, with strong misgivings.

Visibility was now very bad. We advanced cautiously in the direction, we *hoped*, of the enemy lines, and we'd gone about fifty yards when we saw a small group of men crouched down in the fog just ahead of us. Our party all ducked down and concealed ourselves as well as we could. *They* did the same, so there were both lots lying down wondering what to do! Of course, all we had to protect us, apart from a few Mills bombs, were these ridiculous tomahawks. One bright spark on our side wanted to lob a few Mills bombs at them, but the officer stopped him. He rose to his feet, pointed his revolver, and called out 'Who are you?' – and were we relieved when the reply came in English! 'No. 4 Lewis-Gun Post, 1st Queen's. Who are you?' Our officer answered, 'Raiding party, C Company, 1st Queen's.' We were told to advance to be recognized, and when we did we saw that their

Lewis-gun had been trained on us ready to open fire. What had happened was that we'd lost our way in the fog and wandered round in a semicircle which had brought us face to face with our *own troops*. Eventually we were allowed to pass through the lines and make our way back to the sap at Crest Farm for a wash and something to eat. Next day we were sent back to our own platoons for ordinary duties. And that was the end of that.

The clinging mist that hung above the battlefields made for atrocious flying weather, and the aircrews kicked their heels waiting for even the slightest change that would enable them to make another of the photographic flights so anxiously desired by GHQ. Late in February a football match was abruptly interrupted when a wind blew up, the mist lifted, and the sun blinked out of a promising patch of blue. Racing back from the pitch in response to a klaxon sounding the alert, Peter Wilson was obliged to take to the air in muddy jersey and football shorts. It was not a pleasant flight. He was frozen stiff without the protection of flying gear, the sight of his bare knees was strangely disconcerting, and, for the first time, he felt unaccountably 'windy' as the R8 flew through bursts of 'Archie'. He was quite certain that the next burst would send him skimming down to earth into the arms of the Germans, and the indignity of being killed or captured dressed for a football match was too monstrous to contemplate. But all went well and Wilson returned safely to base, almost petrified with cold, and with nothing more exciting to report than the sight of Belgian civilians skating on a frozen pond and 'Huns in tramcars'.

But reports were proliferating that there were unmistakable signs that the enemy was planning a major offensive. The widespread preparations were meant to be seen, for they were part of the Germans' plan to mislead and confuse. Reports about them came from many sources other than the air, but the trouble was that they were coming from every sector of the front. Even the information obtained from prisoners was not infallible. After the strain and terror of his capture, faced with a skilled and seemingly sympathetic interrogator, given a cigarette and even a drink, a soldier was naturally thankful to be alive and might even feel grateful to his captors. In such circumstances, despite orders to divulge nothing, a prisoner frequently spilled the beans. The Germans understood this very well, and by carefully nurtured rumours and craftily worded orders they made sure that every regiment, and consequently every fighting soldier, firmly believed that the Push would take place in his own sector and that his own unit would be in the vanguard of the assault. Prisoners captured in many different areas were telling the same tale.

Weighing up the mass of contradictory evidence, intelligence officers deduced that it was a deliberate attempt to confuse them. They were quite correct. The Germans intended to muddy the waters so that no one could predict on which part of the long front the blow would fall and, if there was more than one attack, which attacks were feints and which was the main offensive. But there were also more subtle attempts to mislead the Allies and force them to spread their thinning resources over long distances. Knowing that gossip was bound to reach the ears of local spies, the Germans issued billeting requisition orders in occupied areas as far apart as Tournai in Belgium and Beaumont in the Argonne, and gave householders notice to quit. In certain places they actually cleared whole villages many miles from where an attack was intended and erected camps around them as if to mass large numbers of troops for an assault.

The troops were indeed being massed, if not always where the Germans wished it to be thought. With the advantage of their huge hinterland and good communications, the Kaiser's armies could be concentrated and trained many miles behind the front and spread across great distances. When the time was ripe and all was ready, they could be moved forward without delay.

# Chapter 5

When firm information finally reached the intelligence service it came not from the air, not from raiders on the ground, but by an indirect route from a small town in southern Germany. In late January fighter planes of the German Army Air Service took off from an airfield behind St Quentin to intercept an RFC patrol, and a young German pilot, shot through the chest, crashed behind the lines of General Gough's Fifth Army and died in a British casualty clearing station. He was given a military funeral. Four officers of the Royal Flying Corps carried his coffin, and four of its ground crew fired a volley over his grave.

When a prisoner died in captivity it was usual to notify the German authorities through the International Red Cross – a long and tortuous process which could mean months of suspense for the anxious relatives of missing men. But the fraternity of the air made up their own rules, which owed nothing to the Geneva Convention, and they had their own means of communication. Braving the barrage of anti-aircraft shells, swooping low at the last minute with a conciliatory wag of its wings, an aircraft of the RFC dropped a weighted message bag on the German base. It contained the dead pilot's personal effects and confirmed, with regret, that he had died of wounds and had been buried with full military honours.

The news of her son's death reached his widowed mother in Baden long before the official notification, and she also received a letter of sympathy which spoke of her son's sacrifice in glowingly heroic terms. It was written to a standard formula, but she could not have known that, and she was deeply impressed by the fact that it was signed by an officer of high rank – her son's Army Commander himself. The signature was certainly a facsimile, and the letter was one of many, but it was a comfort to the bereaved mother and she proudly passed it on to the local newspaper.

German newspapers were freely available in neutral Switzerland, and this particular copy of a Baden news-sheet was read with some interest by a French intelligence officer. It was his task to scrutinize German and Austrian newspapers, and he paid particular attention to provincial publications from obscure country districts where the censorship was likely to be less vigilant. He had picked up nuggets of useful information in this way before, but this time he had a greater scoop than even he realized. The letter, tucked away on the obituary page of a humble local rag, was signed by General von Hutier. The information travelled to Paris and on to General Pétain's headquarters, where its significance was speedily grasped.

General von Hutier was held in high esteem. He had risen rapidly from command of a Guards' Division in 1914, to the command first of a corps and finally of the Kaiser's Eighteenth Army. He was the architect of the Austrian victory which had routed Cadorna at Caporetto; he was the victor of the Battle of Riga, which had sealed the fate of the Russians on the Eastern Front. It was his first appearance on the Western Front since he had been a lowly divisional commander in 1914. Now he was back, trailing clouds of glory, and he was standing opposite the British on the Fifth Army front – not replacing but in addition to the two armies which were already there. The conclusion was inescapable and, when it was passed to him by French Headquarters, it did not escape General Humbert, now in command of the French Third Army.

When the Fifth Army was obliged to extend southward, it took over General Humbert's line running south to the Oise. It was unfamiliar ground, and when the two generals met they spent a long time poring over maps. General Gough received several unpleasant surprises. The area north of the river, which cartographers had so liberally spiked with symbols denoting marshland, was no longer anything of the kind. It had almost completely dried out in the course of a remarkably dry winter. Even the River Oise was unusually low, and the barrier which might have impeded an attack in this sector no longer existed. Worse, the French, thinking themselves secure, had constructed only the sketchiest of defences, and the all-important rear line, the fail-safe that would finally halt a breakthrough, had not even been pencilled in on the map. The very place where the attack was thought to be most unlikely was now the most vulnerable of Gough's overstretched line and, with the unwelcome news of von Hutier's presence, it seemed a virtual certainty that the German plan was to attack on his front. General Humbert made no bones about it. Tracing the line south of St Quentin, he said, 'They can deal you a nasty blow here!'[1]

'A nasty blow' was an understatement. Later, when Gough visited French General Headquarters at Compiègne, General Anthoine spelt it out. Von Hutier's victories had been studied, and his tactics had a similarity which could not be dismissed as coincidence. He banked heavily on the element of surprise. Not for him the classic preparation for battle – the days, even weeks, of slow bombardment of enemy defences which gave ample and

---

1. His words, as General Gough reported them, were '*On peut vous donner un vilain coup.*'

unmistakable notice of an impending attack. And not for him the massing of assault troops and reserves close to the line, where they could be
bombed and shelled by the enemy. It was von Hutier's practice to fan out
his troops in a great arc that swung over many miles, as if round the rim
of a wheel, with pre-planned routes along the spokes which would con-
verge on the narrow battlefront and set his troops at the hub of the action
on the very eve of battle. Reinforcements kept three marches away and,
moving forward according to a strict timetable, would be fed in just when
they were needed to pursue the advance. And von Hutier fully intended
that there should be an advance. His policy was to maintain a skeleton
force – of guns as well as men, for the batteries too would pull into position
only at the eleventh hour, and for a mere five or six hours before the assault
would fire a hurricane bombardment of such force that resistance as well as
obstacles could not help but be smashed before the troops surged forward
sweeping all before them. It had worked before. He had no doubt that it
would work again.

Even if he had had a sufficient number of men and reserves, unlike General
von Hutier General Gough would not have been able to dispose them over
a wide area well behind the line. It was true that some seventy-five miles
lay between his line and the coast, but it was far from virgin countryside.
The British line now ran across ground which had been vacated by the
Germans not quite a year earlier, in the aftermath of the Battle of the Somme,
when they had withdrawn to the Hindenburg Line. This had naturally been
construed as a victory for the Allies, but it was nevertheless a clever move,
for the Germans had killed several birds with one stone. They had escaped
from the ravaged Somme battlefield and vastly improved their position. By
shortening their line they had saved much needed manpower, and by
reducing the huge salient which swooped round from Arras to Soissons they
had dislocated the Allies' spring offensive, whose objective was to attack this
salient from two sides.

The retirement had been anything but haphazard, and the rearguards were
not the exhausted remnants of a defeated army. They were fresh, efficient
troops who fought brisk actions to delay the Tommies or the *poilus* as they
filtered forward on their heels. They were fighting for time, most often at
places of their choosing, while at their backs the bulk of their own army
retired, slowly and methodically, to its new position.

They left devastation in their wake. Whole villages were dynamited,
young crops destroyed, animals slaughtered and left to putrefy, orchards
devastated, trees chopped down, telegraph poles uprooted, railway tracks
torn up, bridges destroyed, buildings booby-trapped with delayed-action
explosives, roads mined and cratered to block the passage of troops and
transport. The Germans were determined to leave nothing behind that could

be of any possible use to an army in pursuit – not a shelter that might serve
as a billet, not a road or a bridge that would afford them passage, not a blade
of grass or a wisp of hay that would feed the horses. It was vandalism on a
gargantuan scale, and it was a monumental task to repair the damage. In a
little under a year the British had done the best they could to restore
communications, to patch up the roads, to build camps to shelter troops in
reserve or behind the battle zone. All this in addition to constructing some
sort of defensive line to face the enemy in his new and formidable position.
But even with sufficient labour and manpower five years would hardly have
been long enough to complete the task.

North of General Gough's line, where General Byng's Third Army held
the sector north of Gouzeaucourt to Arras, the conditions, and the difficulties,
were similar, and behind the devastated country lay the turmoil of shattered
ground where they had fought the Battle of the Somme. Only three years
ago it had been a smiling countryside of gentle hills and rolling farmland,
scattered with woods and copses, with quiet villages in hidden valleys where
the water ran clear and the fish were plentiful. Now it was hard to credit
that it was part of the same planet. More than four months' bitter fighting
through the dust and heat of summer to the first snows of winter had changed
the Somme to a desolate wilderness, mutilated by miles of abandoned
trenches, pitted by mine-craters and ravaged by shell-holes, which in some
places touched lip to lip. Houses, farms and villages had all but vanished,
and mangled tree stumps were all that remained of the pleasant woodlands.
Since the German retirement the land had lain fallow but for crops of
wooden crosses slowly growing as the Army Graves Service moved across
the battleground gathering in the dead. Already the casualties were legendary.
Some bodies had disappeared and would never be recovered; some had been
buried by shell-fire deep in the chalk or mud; and in the northern sector,
where successive attacks had failed, the bodies of many soldiers killed on the
first day of the battle had been exposed to the elements under continuous
bombardment until the enemy had abandoned his line in the spring. Not
many of them could be identified.

Now that the Germans were fifteen miles east of Bapaume, communications
of a kind had been restored. The main roads had been mended, and a local
train even ran from Amiens to the ruined town of Albert behind the old
British front line, and civilians who pressed hard enough for a pass were
allowed to travel on it to rummage for lost possessions in their ruined homes.
The Graves Registration Department had set up its local headquarters in
one of the least damaged buildings, and on 12 March it had an unexpected
visit from Brigadier-General Ludlow.

The General was not on official business. He had strictly speaking no right to be there, or indeed to be in France at all, for he was close to seventy years of age. It was more than forty years since he had joined the 1st Volunteer Battalion of the old 6th Foot – the Royal Warwickshire Regiment – which he eventually rose to command. When the Territorial Force was formed from the old Volunteers and Militia six years before the war began, their commanding officer (then Lieutenant-Colonel) was given command of the newly formed 1/8th Territorial Battalion, the Royal Warwickshire Regiment. He was immensely proud of his command, and after he had reluctantly retired it pleased him hugely that his son, Stratford, was carrying on the family tradition as an officer of the 1/8th Warwicks.

He had anxiously followed the fortunes of his son's battalion since it had left for France, and he always had news first-hand, for the old Colonel, like many another retired officer, had been 'dug out' in 1914 and sent on regimental duties to the Royal Warwicks' depot. A short time ago he had been promoted to Brigadier-General, and there was no doubt that the red tabs on his tunic collar had eased the difficulties of reaching France in wartime, and smoothed the path of officialdom once he arrived. By pulling a few regimental strings, he had booked accommodation in Amiens, obtained a pass, and engaged an interpreter. That morning, at an unearthly early hour, they boarded the solitary civilian train that rattled once a day to Albert. The General was going in search of his son's grave.

Captain Stratford Ludlow had been 'Missing believed killed' since the first day of the Battle of the Somme. Even before the official telegram reached his home, the first casualty list had come through to the depot. The 1/6th and the 1/8th Royal Warwicks had attacked together. Only one officer of two battalions had survived unhurt, and, of the 600 men who had gone over with the 1/8th Royal Warwicks, 573 had been killed, or wounded, or captured.

In the agonizing months that followed the battle the General had incessantly searched for information. He toured local hospitals to meet wounded survivors, talked to officers and men who came home to convalesce, and more than a year later he was still seeking out the men of the reserve company who had witnessed the slaughter from the support trench and were now home on leave. Some survivors of Captain Ludlow's company remembered seeing him go down as they went forward to the fourth German trench, and had even produced a rough sketch of the spot. The General brought it with him, carefully folded in an envelope, and an officer of the Graves Registration Department pinpointed the place on a large wall map.

*Brigadier-General W. R. Ludlow, CB, VD, 1/8th Bn., The Royal War-*
*wickshire Regt.*

Through the kindness of the Graves Registration Department, a motor
and a guide were placed at our disposal, and after a few miles we got
beyond to the old battlefield of Beaumont Hamel, Serre, Auchonvillers,
Hébuterne, Foncquevillers and Gommecourt. These were only names
upon the map, as there is nothing to denote that they have ever been
occupied as human habitations. Having located the village of Serre,
we worked our way back along the road to the point where the old
British line of 1916 crossed. Beyond this village, of which only the
outside walls of a few houses remained standing, the country was a
complete waste, a series of rolling plains covered with thick, coarse,
brown grass. Every tree, hedge and pollard had disappeared, and only
mounds covered with grass showed where villages had been. A few
cabbages or broccoli struggled through the matted surface, and stumps
of apple trees denoted what had once been gardens and flourishing
orchards. The trenches were grown over or had fallen in, or filled with
water in places, while the whole area was a mass of old shell-holes. It
was here that the 8th Battalion consolidated the fourth-line German
trench. Several of the officers, including my son, were seen shouting
out to their men 'That's our objective', smoking cigarettes, and waving
them on.

In the subsequent fighting and the German retreat from Serre, the
whole country has been so badly shelled that it was extremely difficult
to get about the area. This part of the field had not been fully explored,
and here and there one came across piles of equipment, coats and
tunics, rusty rifles, bayonets, bully-beef tins not opened, shells, hand-
grenades, and boxes of Mills bombs unopened – all the usual debris of
the battlefield. Along the line occupied by the 11th Brigade there were
the remains of skulls, and bones, and shrapnel helmets, in all directions.
A number of officers' tin hats were lying about, and one grave, with
a cross upon it and no inscription, had a tin hat attached to it. Another
grave was marked by a harrow, but the majority of them were hidden
by the tall, rank grass or were destroyed by subsequent shell-fire.

Within the old German lines is the Serre Road Cemetery No. 1, a
little square of about one acre, crowded with graves of our gallant
regiments. A great number of these were nameless and inscribed to
'An unknown British officer' or 'An unknown British soldier', but
there were a great many names of old friends in the rank and file,
although I could find very few officers.

As this part of the battlefield has not been thoroughly examined or cleared, there were only approximately one-tenth of the number who fell in that battle who had been identified and buried within the area of these cemeteries.[1] The many hours I was on the battlefield I never saw a single sign of life of any kind or description, or traffic, nor were there any signs of large bodies of troops anywhere within the immediate neighbourhood.

I sat on the edge of a shell-hole opposite to the German position in No Man's Land, and I wondered how it was possible that any troops in the world could attack such a position in broad daylight on a lovely July morning.

It seemed inconceivable that any army would attempt a breakthrough in a region which not only included the devastated zone but also encompassed on its northern stretch such a difficult obstacle as the old Somme battlefield, which the enemy had gone to such trouble to quit. For a long time few but General Gough believed that this was the Germans' plan. He wrote to GHQ, giving a long, detailed and sober assessment of the situation on his front, pointing out that three German armies now faced him where one had stood before. He reminded GHQ of the paucity of his own forces, of his line so thinly manned, of his defensive positions as yet so incomplete. He sketched out von Hutier's tactics and the danger of a sudden pounce that would take his army by surprise. He stressed that he needed men – soldiers certainly, but also large numbers of labourers, and above all sappers of the Royal Engineers to plan and supervise the construction of defences. Stores would be needed, and there was a desperate need of raw materials: railway sleepers and road metal, pickets, barbed wire, corrugated iron.

The reply from GHQ laid more emphasis on the need for a considered plan of withdrawal, in the event of an attack, rather than on facilitating a spirited defence. The memorandum was drawn up by Major-General 'Tavish' Davidson. 'From what has been said,' he wrote, 'it would appear that the whole question is one of communications . . .' Since they simply did not have the means to improve them to any great degree, he implied that a withdrawal to the line of the Somme would make sense. The memorandum stated baldly:

> The principles on which the defences of the Fifth Army front should be conducted should, it is considered, be similar to those laid down for the other Armies. That is, we should be prepared to fight for the Battle and Rear Zones. It may, however, at any period of the defensive

1. Captain Ludlow's body was found and identified after the war and buried in Serre Road No. 2 Cemetery, Plot 39, Row 1, Grave 12.

battle become inadvisable to employ large reserves to re-establish either of these zones, in which case a withdrawal to the line Crozat Canal–Somme–Péronne bridge-head – or even to the line Crozat Canal–Somme–Tortille – should be carried out. The possibility of having to execute a withdrawal should receive the careful consideration of the Fifth Army, and detailed plans should be worked out.[1]

It was not an order, but it was a strong hint that not much assistance would be forthcoming.

What was to be forthcoming, however, was labour – up to the middle of March the number of labourers almost doubled, but there were still not enough to complete the defences of the battle zone, still less carry out the construction of the bridgehead to protect Péronne on the River Somme as GHQ required. All in all this bridgehead amounted to fifty miles of fortifications along the banks of the River Somme and of the River Tortille, which ran into it from the north.

But it was not a bad plan. They would be able to abandon the difficult terrain that lay between the line and the rivers behind. Given the time and the circumstances in which to prepare a strong defensive position, it would be a good place to make a stand, and, despite the fact that the old Somme battlefield would lie directly to the rear, there was no doubt that the all-important question of communications would be eased. But General Gough was not a happy man. 'When it is remembered that the Hindenburg Line was about seventy miles and the Germans took some six months to construct it, under what might comparatively be called peace conditions and with a vast army of civilian labour, it was not possible for these defences to be in a forward state in the time at our disposal.'[2] By the middle of March it had been possible to do no more than mark out the site of the fortifications.

On the question of manpower, GHQ itself was in a dilemma. Haig's pressing demands for reinforcements had fallen on stony ground, and he could not conjure soldiers from thin air. The Staff were agreed that such reserves as there were must be sent further north, where the British line ran nearer the coast, and where the lifeline to England through the vital Channel ports would be in real peril if the Germans broke through. Sir Julian Byng's Third Army front was clearly threatened, but it was reasonably safe, for it had almost as many troops as General Gough to defend a front of only half the length. But, it was felt, Gough had rather more room to manoeuvre,

1. Quoted from *The March Retreat*, by General Sir Hubert Gough, GCMG, KCB, KCVO (Cassell, 1934).

2. Quoted from *The March Retreat*, by General Sir Hubert Gough, GCMG, KCB, KCVO (Cassell, 1934).

and, although the Versailles plan for a large mobile reserve had come to nothing, Field-Marshal Haig and General Pétain still had their private agreement to support each other in case of need. Sir Douglas took the trouble to visit the Fifth Army front to remind General Gough that, if the need arose, he could draw on seven French divisions as reserves. Meanwhile a few more batteries could be spared to strengthen Gough's artillery, and another squadron of aeroplanes would be sent to assist with observations. No one was satisfied, but it was the best that could be done. The French were on Gough's right, not far away, and if the Germans attacked they would hasten to his support.

By mid-March the Germans had 192 divisions on the Western Front – thirty more than the British and French combined. They added up to a grand total of more than 3½ million men, and the officers alone outnumbered the entire British Expeditionary Force of 1914. But the old professional armies which had served both Great Britain and Germany in 1914 were no more, and the new German Army was, in Ludendorff's own words, 'more of a militia – but experienced in war'. Sixty-three divisions were earmarked for the assault and, so far as it was possible at this late stage in the war, they were handpicked troops. All men over thirty-five had been left behind on the quiescent Eastern Front, and men of the same category had been taken out of divisions in the west, or from home garrisons, and sent east to reinforce them. Eleven additional divisions were sent in to hold the line while the shock troops were withdrawn to train for the assault.

The training was all-important, for the success of the campaign, and perhaps the outcome of the war itself, would depend on it. It was hard and intensive, and a little too realistic for some tastes. In the latter stages only live ammunition was used, and the infantry did not much enjoy running across rough ground not far behind a screen of bursting shells while gunners perfected the technique of firing a creeping barrage. They also practised limbering up and rolling forward fast, advancing across fields of shell-holes created by their own efforts.

But these were mere mechanics. Much more arduous was the work required by another part of the plan. It had been devised by Colonel Bruchmüller, in command of the Eighteenth Army artillery, who had brilliantly orchestrated the artillery programme that smashed resistance in the east. Now guns as well as men had been released from the Eastern Front, and batteries had been withdrawn from other sectors in order to play a part in the coming battle. They would take up position only at the eleventh hour, and it was obvious that the weapons would have no opportunity of ranging on their targets before joining in the hurricane bombardment that would ring up the curtain on the great day.

In normal circumstances it would have taken days to range each individual gun on the field of battle, and the concerted firing of so many would have given the Allies ample notice that the Germans were on their way. Instead, the skeleton batteries dug in along the front had to register the ranges for them all, and they had been doing so for weeks, under the guise of desultory firing or short, sharp bombardments followed by long periods of reassuring tranquillity. The snag was that no two guns were the same, and after years of hard service and wear and tear of the bores and even the mountings of guns, many – even most – were inaccurate. Bruchmüller had decreed that every gun must be tested over fixed distances for its own errors and idiosyncrasies, and that an individual table of adjustment must be drawn up for each of them. In this way, working from artillery maps which Bruchmüller insisted should be faultless, it would be possible to tell exactly how much to add or subtract from the elevation of any given gun in order to pinpoint a target. It sounded simple, but it involved the gunners, and particularly the officers, in an immense amount of work, and some battery majors complained wearily of lack of sleep.

By comparison the machine-gunners got off lightly, although their training schedule was punishing enough. They had to travel fast, humping their gun and its ammunition, sweating and panting in their clammy gas masks. All the time they were learning new tactics, training for open warfare and the breakthrough that would bring the trench-bound stalemate to an end.

Despite the tough training, young Reinhold Spengler was enjoying himself. He was proud of his new rank of *Leutnant*, which dated only from 1 March, and proud of his position as commander of a light-machine-gun platoon. He was twenty years old. The countryside around the training area near Vervins was lovely and reminded him with pleasant nostalgia of his home in upper Bavaria. His company were billeted in private houses in the sizeable village of Prisches, now cleared of its inhabitants, and sleeping like kings on feather beds. It would be a long while before they would be able to enjoy such luxury again.

*Leutnant Reinhold Spengler, 2nd Coy., 1st Bavarian Infantry Regt., 1st Bavarian Division*

The 1st Bavarian Division was part of General von Hutier's Eighteenth Army and we were assigned to be in the first line as a storm division. On 17 March we left Vervins and headed again towards the front and the greatest battle in history. Our destination was St Quentin. Endless columns of light and heavy artillery pieces, as well as ammunition wagons, passed alongside us on their way to the front. They were drawn mostly by teams of four or six horses. All of these guns were concealed from the enemy until the last moment. This display of military power made us hope that the long depressing years of war would soon come to a swift and victorious end. Perhaps now we would have the upper hand! But all of us were in great suspense, uncertain of the outcome. To avoid the enemy observing our movements, we always marched at night, but even at night enemy fliers flew above the roads, and every so often they would drop magnesium parachute flares to illuminate the countryside.

General Ludendorff with his Headquarters Staff was also on the move. Early in March they had moved from Kreuznach to new headquarters in the Belgian town of Spa, where the administrative offices were housed in the spacious premises of the Hôtel Britannique. It was the second time the hotel had been taken over by the Germans, and Ludendorff himself had been billeted there when the German Army was marching through Belgium in the autumn of 1914. He was struck by the coincidence, and regarded it as a good omen. Spa was closer to the front than Kreuznach, but Ludendorff was a man who liked to keep his finger on the pulse of events and see things for himself. The day after the Eighteenth Army began its long march to battle he moved forward to Avesnes with his operations branch and into the old Eighteenth Army Headquarters. Telephone communications were already in place, so Avesnes was a convenient location, but that was the only thing in its favour, and the billets occupied by General von Hutier and his staff did not suit General Ludendorff and his. They were cramped and spartan and unpleasant – good enough for soldiers, but certainly not good enough for illustrious company - and the Kaiser was on his way. By the time he arrived, on the following day, Avesnes had been scoured for more agreeable premises and a small chateau had been commandeered on the outskirts of the town. It was not luxurious and the furnishings were shabby, but that was easily put right. A message was flashed to Spa, and within hours a lavish collection of elegant furniture, removed from the Hôtel Britannique, was rolling towards Avesnes, together with a generous supply of linen, fine glassware and silver from the same source. Ludendorff was delighted. Next day he was on the platform to greet the Kaiser when the Imperial train steamed in, and, although the Kaiser and his court would live on board, he had the pleasure of receiving him for dinner that evening in his lavishly appointed mess. It was 19 March.

General Gough was well aware that the German Army was on the move and converging on his front. Open railway stations had been canopied over to conceal the movements of troop trains, and large bodies of troops were not allowed to show themselves in daylight. But, although the troops marched by night and were forbidden to sing when passing through villages, night fliers could see the tell-tale signs. They spotted fires behind the line, the glowing exhausts of a line of tanks or supply lorries shining faintly like fireflies in the dark, the faint, bobbing progress of half-dimmed lanterns swinging behind wagons when a line of transport was on the move, a sudden trail of sparks from the chimney of a field kitchen trundling in front of a company of soldiers. Raiding parties were sent off to rush the German outposts in search of prisoners, and shortly after midnight, as the Kaiser was retiring for the night after his excellent evening with General Ludendorff's Staff, two of his soldiers were being persuaded by British officers to divulge the time and place of the attack. As early as 18 February it had been fixed for 21 March.

There was a real possibility, even at this late date, that the attack might have to be called off, and in his fine bed, purloined from the Hôtel Britannique, General Ludendorff did not enjoy a restful night. The weather was not favourable for the bombardment. As well as using high explosives to shatter the British defences, it was intended to fire a large proportion of gas-shells to knock out the men behind them, and for the gas to be effective they needed a good strong breeze blowing in the right direction. For days past the wind had obstinately refused to oblige, and light breezes fluttering steadily from west to east towards the German lines showed no sign of changing direction. And there was the fog. As Ludendorff's meteorologist, Leutnant Dr Schaum, had explained, warm spring days followed by frosty nights invariably resulted in foggy mornings. In the half-light of dawn, from Ludendorff's bedroom window, the mist seemed thicker than ever.

Although there were a thousand matters to attend to, the waiting seemed interminable as the clock ticked towards mid-morning. Promptly at eleven o'clock Dr Schaum arrived with the morning weather report and forecast. It was not entirely good, but it was not all bad and it seemed that an attack would be possible. Just possible.

General Ludendorff called a meeting of his staff officers. The possibility of fog was the main problem, for without visibility the advance of the troops would be difficult, and without observation their leaders would be unable to direct them. But a few of them thought that a concealing fog might possibly be an advantage. Ludendorff was in a quandary. Already the assaulting troops were uncomfortably squeezed together behind the line and in the trenches themselves. Finally he made up his mind, and at twelve noon a message was sent to the Army Group Headquarters to inform them that the attack would take place as planned.

*Leutnant Reinhold Spengler*

On 20 March between 8 and 10 p.m. the regiment moved to Itancourt, a few kilometres south-east of St Quentin. There we readied ourselves for the attack. Just behind us the guns of the 1st Bavarian Field Artillery Regiment were in position and a number of mortars were set up in the trench. Each gun and mortar was spaced some ten to fifteen metres apart – and this on a total front of seventy-five kilometres!

The decision was made. The die was cast – and there could be no turning back.

# Part 2

# Der Tag!

*It had come at last! his own stupendous hour,*
*Long waited, dreaded, almost hoped-for too,*
*When all else seemed the foolery of power;*
*It had come at last! and suddenly the world*
*Was sharply cut in two . . .*

LIEUTENANT MAX PLOWMAN,
10th West Yorkshire Regt. (1914–1918)

## Chapter 6

The Fifth Army Infantry Training School was near the village of Caix, only twelve miles east of Amiens and a comfortable thirty miles from the line where the 36th (Ulster) Division faced the southern suburbs of St Quentin. It was a tricky frontage. Not long before the Division moved in, the Germans had launched a local attack and captured a stretch of line from the French. Consequently, although No Man's Land here was wide, it was inconveniently traversed by old saps and communication trenches which led straight to the enemy's wire and into his trenchline. It was a simple matter for patrols and raiders of both sides to close in without warning, and a tour in this sector was invariably marked by a succession of alarms and excursions which gave a whole new meaning to the term 'relief' when a battalion's stint was over.

The 2nd Royal Irish Rifles had been thankful to hand the trenches over to their 15th Battalion and move back to the village of Grand Séraucourt in time to celebrate St Patrick's Day as genially as conditions on active service would allow. They were also reasonably comfortable, for Grand Séraucourt was a large village – too large to have been completely devastated by the Germans' scorched-earth policy of the year before. The interior of the roofless sugar-beet factory that had once supported the local economy was a jumble of mangled machinery, and the largest of the houses had been blown up, but there were enough comparatively undamaged buildings in Grand Séraucourt, and in the neighbouring hamlet of Le Hamel, to put some sort of covering over the heads of most of the Battalion. Next morning three of the junior officers were delighted to be detailed to attend a platoon commanders' course at Caix. It was a five-day course and so, including travelling time, Lieutenant Tom Witherow calculated that the jaunt would last at least a week. The mild headache induced by the St Patrick's Night festivities rapidly dissipated at the prospect.

Witherow and two other junior officers, Marshall and Crawford, hitched a lift in a lorry as far as Ham. The town of Ham had escaped the fate of other towns in the path of the Germans' retreat, for they had used it as a collecting point for women and children evacuated from the forward areas, and the town still retained much of its peacetime aspect. Some shops were open and, since XVIII Corps Headquarters had been set up in the town, cafés and restaurants continued to do good business. The streets bustled with orderlies, with NCOs, with staff officers, and also with birds of passage, for Ham was the railhead for the line. Unlike troops proceeding on leave, who hung around the station with natural impatience, Witherow and his friends were not in the least disturbed by the discovery that no train was due to leave for Nesle and Amiens for several hours. They enjoyed a leisurely lunch washed down by a quantity of indifferent wine, and took a post-prandial stroll in search of the officers' clothing store, where Witherow purchased a new tunic. He was sorely in need of it, for his old one had seen service on the Somme, to say nothing of Passchendaele and Cambrai, and it was hardly fit to be seen. The new tunic cost five pounds, which was a tidy sum to a subaltern whose pay was a mere ten shillings and sixpence a day, out of which he was obliged to pay his mess bill. But there had been nothing to spend money on since his return from New Year leave in Belfast, so Witherow paid up with a good grace, and the corporal-storeman wrapped the tunic with as much care as if it had been purchased in Savile Row. It was 19 March. A few days later, when the battle began and soldiers were hurrying back through the streets of Ham, the same man would be flinging tunics free to anyone who would take them.

Stretched across two miles of front, the 10th Essex had moved into support positions in the battle zone, and they were quite aware that there were few reserves behind them. The tension in the air was almost palpable; the Germans were inconsiderate enough to shell Ly-Fontaine, and it was an unwelcome contrast to the peaceful fortnight they had just spent in the front line, where everything had been extraordinarily quiet. The weather had been fine and warm, the shelling had been minimal, and they had escaped the irksome duties that fell to the lot of support troops toiling to dig trenches in the battle zone and, by way of light relief, interminably rehearsing the march to battle positions. By comparison the front line was a picnic, and, apart from keeping an eye open for any suspicious movement on the part of the enemy over the way, the Essex had been pretty well on holiday. The River Oise spread into miniature lakes between the outposts in the swampy scrub, the stunted trees and bushes were festooned with trails and puffballs of Old Man's Beard, the first wild flowers were in bloom, and the sun was often warm enough to tempt an early dragonfly to perform its iridescent dance above a patch of water. Last summer both French and German soldiers on either side of the same waterscape had been driven near-demented by plagues of mosquitoes, but in springtime there were no such pests to spoil the idyll and only the thud of an occasional importunate shell disturbed the peace. The officers even sent back to Battalion HQ for their valises (which doubled as sleeping-bags), so that they could slumber in comfort, and relays of men had taken baths in the brewery behind Moÿ, which was actually in the front line. There was one bit of excitement. A man lying on his back on a firestep, the better to survey a dogfight high above the trench, was hit on the nose by a spent bullet dropping from the sky. He was the only casualty of their two-week stint in the line.

Now the Essex hardly needed to be told that they were for it.

A German aeroplane was brought down not far from Battalion HQ in Ly-Fontaine, and the pilot and observer – both miraculously unhurt – were sent back to Brigade Headquarters. There, under interrogation, they disclosed the very hour of the attack. It was due to begin at 4.40 Berlin time the following morning.[1]

Colonel Frizell was on leave, and Major Tween was in temporary command of the Battalion. Scattered as they were, it took him hours to go round the four companies, to make sure that every detail had been attended to, and that every officer and man knew where he should be and what he must do when the enemy attacked. He warned them that tomorrow was likely to be a trying day, and advised them to turn in early and get what sleep they could. And he wished them luck.

After he had gone, and after they had inspected rifles and seen the men settled, the officers quietly packed their gear, checked their revolvers, and changed into their shabbiest uniforms before lying down to rest, and to sleep if they could.

As wave after wave of assault troops made their way towards the line, it seemed to the German soldiers that their whole army was on the move. Hans Schetter was not marching with the rest of his company, because he had been given a special assignment on the team of regimental observers. It was a responsible job, and a great deal would depend on it, for their task would be to send back information on the progress of the troops, and not only the ranging of the field guns and trench mortars but the orchestration of the battle itself would depend on this vital intelligence. But the privilege of supplying it was not an unmixed blessing. After dark his company would move up to take its place in the front line, but Schetter had set off with Leutnant Mack many hours earlier. Arrayed in full equipment, carrying a heavy telescope was warm work. He worked up a fine sweat, and the telescope seemed to grow heavier with every mile. The British guns were paying special attention to the roads that led to the line, and a shell occasionally fell too close for comfort. Nevertheless he was fascinated by what he saw.

1. Berlin time was one hour ahead of British time.

*Musketier Hans Schetter, 3rd Coy., 231st Reserve Infantry Regt., 50th [German] Reserve Division*

We walk through Le Catelet, a French town that is almost completely destroyed. On the roadside immense quantities of ammunition are piled high and covered with branches and hay for camouflage. After Le Catelet we reach the Schelde Canal, where a large distillation station for drinking water has been built for our troops. We smell gas and hear shells flying over our heads. A German ammunition supply column is smashed to pieces by the English artillery, and dead soldiers and horses are scattered among the wrecked vehicles. After reporting to Staff Headquarters, we finally find space in a Red Cross dugout about 200 metres behind the front line. We are welcomed by Bavarian troops who think we come from Württemberg because our lieutenant has a blue and red cockade on his cap, for Oldenburg.

At 4.40 a.m. the big cannonade will start. We are watching the time and go to the entrance of the dugout to watch the passing troops and vehicles.

On the other side of the line, on the extreme right of the 14th Division, young Jim Brady was also in a field-ambulance dugout, on the outskirts of Essigny. With two four-man stretcher squads and two ambulance drivers squeezed into it, it was cramped and extremely stuffy behind the heavy gas-curtains at the foot of the entrance stairs, and only Captain Duncan, the medical officer, had some degree of privacy in his tiny cubbyhole at the end of a timbered passage. The atmosphere was getting thicker by the minute, and Jim and his friend Andy Chapman were glad to get outside for a breath of air. It was a dark, misty night. The merest crescent of the old moon hung hazily in the sky, and it was almost eerily quiet.

*101264 Private Jim Brady, 43rd Field Ambulance, Royal Army Medical Corps., 14th Division*

We scrambled to the summit of a bluff overlooking a wide stretch of the flat French countryside and gazed into the blackness. It hung like a canopy over the front lines just over a mile away. Now and again there was the dazzling glare of a Very light or the yellow flash of a light gun and an occasional thud as the Germans slung over a couple of whizz-bangs. But mostly the guns were still, and in the distance we could quite clearly hear the rumble of enemy transport – doubtless trundling eager young Bavarians up to their front-line jump-off positions, ready for the attack.

It was not a comfortable thought. The two boys raced down the hill and back to the cosy fug of the dugout. Not far ahead, beyond the concealing darkness, Reinhold Spengler was already in the line.

*Leutnant Reinhold Spengler, 2nd Coy., 1st Bavarian Infantry Regt., 1st Bavarian Division*

A little before midnight the Company Commanders were told by Rittmeister Nüsslein, Commander of the 1st Battalion, that the following morning was set for the attack. He said that our infantry attack was to be preceded by a four-and-a-half-hour bombardment, and the enemy trenches and battery positions would get the full brunt of it. At 9.15 a.m. we were to go over the top with assault packs and fixed bayonets, and every five minutes the rolling barrage ahead of us would move forward. We synchronized our watches and, holding my pocket watch in my hand, I saw that my palms had begun to sweat in anticipation. I passed on the information to my section leaders and NCOs, and they told the men.

*Private Jim Brady*

I went along the passage to see Captain Duncan, and said, 'Would you like a mug of tea, Sir? I'm just going to make some.' The Doc looked up from his book and said, 'I wouldn't say no, Brady.' The brew – no milk, no sugar – wasn't exactly 'sergeant-major's tea', but it was wet and warm and better than nothing. I took him a hunk of bread and jam, but he said he didn't feel like anything to eat. Then he did a strange thing. He fumbled in his pocket and took out his wallet and thrust a wad of French francs into my hand. He said, 'I seem to have more than I need, Brady. You'd better have some.' There were eighty francs altogether! So I thanked him, and he said, 'I expect we'll be called early tomorrow, Brady. I'd like a drink of something if you can manage it.' I said, 'All right, Sir, I'll see you get a cuppa.' I felt distinctly miserable as I made my way back along the dark passage.

That would be about midnight, and most of the others were sleeping. I clambered up into my bunk, which had a headroom of barely two feet. Upstairs everything seemed quiet – a good deal too quiet!

Tom Witherow and his companions were strolling back to their quarters after an excellent evening spent in convivial company. The food in the mess at Caix was a considerable improvement on the indifferent fare they were forced to endure at the front, and after dinner they had gone to a concert, which they all agreed had been first class. There was a good deal of talent among the Army troops based there, and Witherow had especially enjoyed musical selections given by a section of the excellent band. The platoon commanders' course had begun well and was an interesting change from the platoon officer's usual occupation of dodging bullets in the line, or supervising a dozen or so reluctant navvies constructing defences behind it.

It was a clear starry night, and it promised to be a fine day tomorrow. As he undressed in his hut and hung up his smart new tunic, Witherow was looking forward to it.

Fifty miles to the west the mist was gathering and thickening across the marshland of the Oise.

*Leutnant der Reserve Otto Porath, 271st Field Artillery, 240th [German] Division*

All battery officers were summoned to a meeting with the group artillery commander. Being pitch black, it was not a comfortable walk, owing to the many shell-holes everywhere. In the group commander's dugout we received a large number of written orders, as well as the plans and objectives of our attack. Our watches were synchronized. All of us rushed back to our batteries, because only a short time was left to do a lot of work that night. All targets were mapped on our maps, but there was no time to obtain the correct ranging distances to the various targets. That was a risk we had to accept. We also did not know what the weather would be like in the morning, nor what the temperatures would be. We were through with our calculations at 2 a.m., and my head steamed! At 2.30 all members of the gun-crews were told of what was planned, and everybody knew what types of ammunition to use and what the distances were.

A little time was left to snatch a few winks of sleep. Outside everything was quiet. It was the calm before the storm.

In the assault trenches the forward troops were packed as tight as herrings in a barrel, for the shelters and tunnels had been built to hold less than half as many, and the air was heavy with the stench of sweat and the none too sweet breath of the men squeezed into it. There was no room to stretch out, and barely enough for card-players to squat on the concrete floor for a game of skat or *Doppelkopf* to pass the time and occupy the mind. But morale was high. An order telephoned through from Eighteenth Army Group had been distributed early in the evening, and senior NCOs were given the job of reading it aloud to their platoons:

After years of defensive action on the Western Front, Germany is moving to the attack; the hour eagerly awaited by every soldier is approaching. I am certain that your regiment, true to its history, will enhance its reputation in the days which lie ahead.

This great objective will call for sacrifices, and we shall bear with them for the Fatherland, and for our loved ones at home.

Then forward, into action! With God for King and Fatherland!

It was well received. But that was not all. Just before the battle started, official word was passed along the line that the Kaiser himself, accompanied by no less a personage than Field-Marshal von Hindenburg, had arrived at the front to direct the battle in person. In Waldemar Schmielau's dugout this information was greeted with a disrespectful guffaw from Gefreiter Fritze, squatting on the cold floor in a dark damp corner. '*Ja, ja,*' he quipped, 'and he'll be doing it lying in a warm comfortable bed in his nice chateau.'

Four hours later a single white rocket soared into the air above St Quentin and, as if it were a signal for the whole German line, the bombardment began.

More than 6,000 guns took part, and there had never been a bombardment like it. The earth trembled. Even the air shook. The noise numbed the senses.

*Musketier Alwin Hitzeroth, Minenwerfer Coy., 463rd Infantry Regt., 238th [German] Division*

At exactly 4.40 a.m. the bombardment began − a rumbling, shaking, terrible noise. Some of our guns were firing Blue Cross gas-shells, and the wind brought a gust of gas back into our trenches. A few of the men were overcome as we struggled to get our masks on. For five hours we were forced to sit this way, sweating in our dugout. It was naturally quite unpleasant, but to take off our masks would have meant certain death. I thought about the hellish noise outside and what our guns must be doing to the English over on the other side.

For the British infantry sheltering in dugouts, the clangour of the bombardment in the early stages was partly muffled. The enemy was searching far behind the lines, sending huge projectiles roaring through the night to shatter a crossroads or wipe out wagon lines or camps far in the rear. The gas-shells that whistled past the outpost zone and the high explosives that shook the ground were intended to knock out the guns before the time came for the German assault troops to advance.

At first, in spite of the meticulous German calculations, the shooting was still inaccurate and, although the guns were firing at known battery positions, in many places they were firing short. The British gunners were out in the inferno, firing back in retaliation, half blinded in the suffocating damp of steamy gas-masks, working flat out to feed the guns. The flashes as each shell streaked from the barrel could just be seen in the gloom, and with the boom of each enemy shell another cloud of smoke and dust and gas exploded into the mist, until it lay thick and clammy and airless like a curtain across the night.

The dawn, when it came, was hardly perceptible, but gradually the blackness turned to grey, and gradually too the German guns shortened their range and began to pour shells on the British infantry in the outpost line and the battle zone behind it. There was nothing for the British to do but shelter as best they could, each hoping against hope with the crump of every explosion that the next one would not have his number on it and that Jerry would not be outside waiting when he and his mates emerged from the dugout in the morning.

*Captain Geoffrey Lawrence, 1st South African Bn., 9th (Scottish) Division*

First a shell blew one door in and then the other near me. The candles went out, and we groped for our gas-helmets in the dark. Splinters of metal were making sparks as they fell through just above us, and the din was quite indescribable. Soon amongst the high-explosive shells falling all around we heard the unmistakable plop, plop as gas-shells fell mixed with the others, and the burnt-potato or onion smell warned us it was time to put on our gas-helmets.

One poor chap couldn't find his helmet; another had his torn across his face by a flying piece of shrapnel. We waited apprehensively for a direct hit any moment, but luckily none came and the barrage lifted back to the front line and also to the artillery lines. We then all staggered out to find our battle positions, trying as best we could to see through helmet eyepieces and the dense fog.

We were making very slow progress when Sergeant-Major Alex Smith did a very brave thing. He pulled off his gas-helmet, fully aware of the grave risk, and led us through the thick gas to our allotted posts. I was quite aghast at Smith's selfless act, deliberately inviting a cruel death. We had witnessed it graphically in our reserve line – the terrible sight of gassed men caught by the mixed gas and high-explosive shell-fire. They were carried past on stretchers in what seemed an endless procession, each man frothing at the mouth and blowing bubbles. It was a frightful and unnerving sight.

When we reached the front line our men were holding firm in spite of heavy shelling.

The German bombardment was going as well as General Ludendorff had hoped and Colonel Bruchmüller intended, and very soon now the German infantry would find out if it had done its work. The long-range guns were still blasting the British rear positions, the carefully plotted command posts, the rearward villages where reserves might be assembling, the heavy-gun positions behind the line. Of course they were shooting 'off the map', but the maps had been drawn up with painstaking application. Even if the distant targets could not be pinpointed with 100 per cent precision, the crews who served the guns, troops at rest in billets, the unfortunate beasts in the horse lines would be drenched and disabled by gas. For the first two hours of the bombardment the deadly combination of gas and high explosive rained down without a moment's pause.

In the forward posts and battle zones the infantry also received a share, and, though the gas-shells gradually diminished (the fumes must have time to disperse before German soldiers arrived to take possession of the ground), there was worse to come.

*Private Jim Brady*

The barrage fell on us like thunder and lightning, causing the dugout to shiver and quake and stout beams to groan under the shock of direct hits and the waves of blast which roared down the stairway.

There was a lot of cursing – which was understandable – and I remember Jock McBarron yelling, 'Will nobody light a sodding candle?' Next minute there was a shattering explosion at the dugout entrance, scattering debris and fumes all around. My legs lost their strength; I was trembling. This, I thought, must be my moment of truth I'd heard people talk about but never understood – the moment when, in a time of emergency, one had to make a decision (in this case to condition oneself to the possibility of sudden death – and a messy one at that!), when one had to steel oneself to take the strain or crack. You might say it's the difference between courage and cowardice – but the reaction has to be instantaneous. I must have opted to survive.

Two hours to the minute after the opening shots, the second stage began and the massed weight of all but the heaviest German guns began to pound the infantry. From the enemy's standpoint the results were disappointing. The guns that would fire the creeping barrage when the assault troops went across at zero had been dragged up close to the line. The murky gloom that crept imperceptibly out of the night could hardly be described as daylight, and the mist that hung thicker than ever put paid to Bruchmüller's intention of ranging the field guns squarely on the British trenches and strongpoints in the forward zones. But the guns kept firing anyway.

### Private Jim Brady

One thing was quite certain: we were trapped by a ring of flying steel with little or no hope of escape until the barrage lifted. Suddenly a redcap – a military policeman – clattered downstairs with his right hand gushing blood. He said he was looking for battle stragglers, which gave us all a good laugh. I gave him a cup of tea and tied up his shattered hand.

It was quite evident Jerry meant to blow us to smithereens before unleashing his gallant storm troopers on us. My watch showed eight o'clock – by a miracle we had survived the strafe for close on five hours. The point was, How long would it go on and how long would our weakening dugout withstand the strain? It was a thought I didn't care to dwell on.

Brady made tea all round and, mindful of his promise, took a mug along to Captain Duncan. He also took him a sandwich concocted from fried bread and the last of the streaky bacon in the ration cupboard. It was mostly fat, and the doctor eyed the greasy offering with distaste. 'Just a cup of tea will suit me, Brady, thanks,' he said. 'And if there's a drop of hot water I'd like a shave before the casualties arrive.'

But, as time went on and the shelling continued, they began to wonder why there was no sign of stretcher-bearers bringing wounded men from the forward aid post on the far side of Essigny, where Joe Beech, Sandy McKay, Tug Wilson and Andy McNab were on duty. Not even walking wounded appeared. They tried in vain to telephone, but the line was cut and there was nothing to do but to go on waiting. They were not to know that a shell had landed squarely on the stretcher post and that the bearers had been blown to bits.

It was a cold, unpleasant dawn, and in the German lines the soldiers who had not been fortunate enough to find a place in the dubious comfort of a shelter pressed themselves into shallow crevices in the walls of the assembly trenches and draped bivouac sheets in front of them, doubled for extra warmth. Their last hot meal had been many hours before, and all they could expect by way of breakfast was a lump of sausage or cooked meat with a piece of black bread washed down by ersatz coffee brought up in canisters several hours before. It was thin stuff at the best of times, and when lukewarm it was worse. Leutnant Hermann Wedekind did better, for his extra water-bottle contained some vintage Burgundy presented to him by the mess steward at the chateau near Pronville where he had been so comfortably lodged. 'Here you are, Sir,' he'd said, presenting Wedekind with three fine bottles. 'I'd rather a soldier had them than the good-for-nothing skulkers who'll be moving in when you've gone.' It was extremely civil of him, considering that he was a Frenchman, and Wedekind had appreciated the gesture almost as much as the wine. One bottle was a godsend on the long march to the line, and another – sipped discreetly throughout the night – had kept his spirits high and the chill factor reasonably low. The third, now in his spare water-bottle, would provide sustenance in the battle. Crouched flinching beneath the thundering guns, Wedekind was excited rather than fearful. But the relentless vibration gnawed at the nerves and, as the time crawled slowly towards zero, tension mounted all along the line.

The culmination of the five-hour bombardment would be concentrated drumfire on the British front positions, when the massed field guns, and even the short-range trench mortars, would join in the overture to the battle. But, considering the force of the long bombardment, a disconcerting number of heavy British shells were still coming the other way, whistling across the German assembly trenches, and the soldiers had been warned that, for all the thundering of the guns, the British defence would only have been dislocated. It would not have been annihilated. Therefore they must take full advantage of the barrage that would lead them on to the assault, and keep up close behind it 'regardless of shell splinters'; only thus would the Kaiser's soldiers be victorious. As their orders had explicitly pointed out, 'A single enemy machine-gun which survives the bombardment does more harm than any number of our own shell splinters.' This did not perhaps instil the confidence that the German Staff intended.

The drumfire mounted. The minutes ticked towards zero. Alwin Hitzeroth and his comrades of the *Minenwerfer* company ducked out of the crowded shelter and ran back to the trench mortars they had left outside. Quickly checking to see that they were still in good order, they hooked them to the poles and belts with which they would carry them forward. The order came almost immediately, and Feldwebel Bandmann roared above the bombardment, '*Roll assault packs and get ready to attack!*' Knees buckling under the weight, they heaved the poles to their shoulders. They were as thick as tree-trunks, and the whole paraphernalia weighed a sixth of a ton!

Hermann Wedekind had mustered his company, and with five minutes to go they were waiting in the trench. Somewhere on his left someone began to sing their national anthem – '*Deutschland, Deutschland über alles . . .*' It was the voice of Major Scherer, the Battalion Commander. In a moment his adjutant joined in, and then the men who were nearby took up the ragged chorus. It was a reminder that the Kaiser himself was said to have dubbed this venture 'The Kaiserschlacht'.

> *Deutschland, Deutschland über alles,*
> *Über alles in die Welt . . .*

Germany before everything! All for Germany! For Emperor and Fatherland. It struck a chord, and, as Wedekind later remembered, it also did a good deal to calm their nerves.

All along the line a thousand officers stood, eyes glued to pocket watches. As the second hand touched zero they gave the order: '*Protzen heran.*' The bugles sounded, and the Kaiser's Army scrambled from the safety of the impregnable Hindenburg Line to fight the Kaiser's Battle.

# Chapter 7

Since there were no targets to be seen through the enveloping mist, they travelled light, with rifles slung, relying on stick bombs held high at the ready to deal with strongpoints in the forward zone. Advancing with his light-machine-gun section from the trenches at Itancourt, Reinhold Spengler could barely see twenty feet ahead. Even here, where the line ran away from the course of the canal and the wetlands by the river, the fog lay thick, but he had seen the ground often enough to be perfectly familiar with the flat, open country stretching from the German trenches at Itancourt to the village of Urvillers, blanketed behind the flimsy British defences. In the course of frequent raids and constant observation from the air, the strongpoints and redoubts had been scrupulously plotted, and it would have been possible to attack them head-on. But times had changed since the days when German soldiers advanced with roars of '*Hoch!*' and '*Huzza!*' in a banner-waving phalanx, and the British defences might have been designed to accommodate their new tactics. The first wave were to slip like phantoms through the mist, to infiltrate the gaps between the redoubts and to sweep past them, spreading out beyond and leaving the second wave to surround and mop up each isolated post as it was cut off from the rear. Everything depended on advancing far and fast while the Tommies' heads were still reeling from the bombardment.

Spengler had never thought it would be easy to keep a measured distance behind a wall of bursting shells, and in the pall of mist and smoke it was even more difficult than he had feared. He tried to take direction from the whine of the flying shells, listening to the explosions ahead, trying to time the progress of the barrage for fear that his men would run into it, peering intently into the fog, as if by gazing hard enough he could pierce it, and glancing back now and again to check that the platoon was keeping up. Jogging erratically across the broken ground, it was rough going.

*Leutnant Reinhold Spengler, 2nd Coy., 1st Bavarian Infantry Regt., 1st Bavarian Division*

It became more difficult to hear as we moved forward, because of the increasing noise of battle. After 500 metres a group of figures wearing flat steel helmets appeared in front of us through the fog. At first we did not know who they were, but soon they proved to be Englishmen. They carried no weapons and had raised their arms in the air as a sign of surrender. Coming closer, I could see by the expressions on their faces that they had experienced a terrifying time during the last few hours of our bombardment. I felt very sorry for them. One of them was wounded, and I ordered a medic to bandage him. Then I pointed them towards our lines and watched them trudge along into the fog without an escort.

*Leutnant Hermann Wedekind, 11th Coy. Commander, 79th Infantry Regt., 20th [German] Division*

Five or ten Englishmen without weapons and with strange expressions came towards us. They had not quite reached us when their own artillery dropped some shells between them and us. Several of them fell down, and the rest ran past us. We ran over to the first, shot-up English trench. As far as we could see, the enemy was not putting up any resistance at all and had evacuated his positions. We quickly pushed on. There were no Englishmen in the second trench either. We were in an empty field.

From their positions in deep-dug saps in the German trenches the heavy *Minenwerfers* of the 463rd Infantry Regiment had joined in the hurricane bombardment, firing at short range and hurling monster mortar bombs that weighed some 200 pounds apiece. Even when these missed their mark, they landed with a deafening explosion that shook the ground and rattled a man's wits. For the moment the work of the heavies was done, but the task of the light-*Minenwerfer* section was to follow the assault troops and to knock out any trench or strongpoint whose disobliging garrison refused to surrender. Until the advance was consolidated and the field guns could be brought forward, the role of the *Minenwerfers* would be vital.

There were four light *Minenwerfers* in an infantry battalion – one for each company – and, in the opinion of Alwin Hitzeroth's section, the description 'light' could hardly have been further from the truth. A *Minenwerfer* closely resembled a squat iron cannon of some museum-piece war, but the cannon could at least have been trundled on wheels: the *Minenwerfer*, with its heavy base-plate, had to be transported by brute force. It took six men to carry it into action, and four more to hump two heavy wooden boxes of ten-pound shells. But it was a long time before they were needed.

Here on the south-west outskirts of St Quentin, where the opposing lines encircled the town, the British defences in the outpost zone were far less scanty than those further south, where the crossing of the river and the canal might possibly delay the enemy's advance. It was true that at St Quentin the posts in the front line were 300 yards apart, but a strong line of resistance had been constructed a mile beyond them. It comprised fourteen large entrenched redoubts with field guns positioned to protect the gaps, and the troops in the forward posts were instructed to fall back to this position in the event of an attack. But the unfortunate soldiers in the isolated posts had no chance of escape. The German infantry advanced like a tidal bore on the heels of the devastating bombardment, and the posts disappeared beneath the onslaught like castles on a sandy beach. The only difficulties Hitzeroth's section encountered were in heaving their unwieldy weapon across the battered remnants of the captured redoubts, and the only British they saw were prisoners, wild-eyed, dishevelled, dazed by their ordeal beneath the merciless pounding of the German guns. Hitzeroth watched them go with mixed feelings. Although he felt sorry for the unfortunate Tommies, there were worse sights among the ravaged trenches, where dead and mutilated wounded men were scattered in such a litter of carnage that the *Musketiers* were sickened at the sight.

From the southern suburbs of St Quentin they were pushing on towards Grugies on the flank of the 36th (Ulster) Division, along the valley which had provided the Irish troops with much-appreciated cover when plodding to and from the outpost line. Now, as they approached unobserved in the fog, it made an ideal passage for the Germans, and it seemed in that first exultant hour that the attack had gone like clockwork.

The field guns were already on the move, and the supporting troops were poised to follow up and maintain the momentum of the advance, but a short distance away, on the northern outskirts of St Quentin, Hauptmann Walter Bloem was faced with the daunting task of leading his battalion blind to a fixed position, and he was none too sure of its whereabouts.

*Hauptmann Walter Bloem, 12th (Brandenburg) Bn., [German] Grenadier Regt.*

Exactly parallel to our position, there extended a marshy depression of about two to three kilometres, through the middle of which flowed a drainage canal. In order to make it possible for the dense second

wave to cross this unwholesome tract with the least delay, it had been
bridged in the last few days with a great many narrow footbridges,
which had been accurately marked on our maps and allotted among
the supporting battalions. It was therefore a question of leading the
battalion exactly to the footbridge allotted to me (it had been given
the romantic name of 'Kate's Walk'), which would have been a feat
to accomplish even in usual circumstances in this hilly waste of ruins.
During the night an almost impenetrably thick mist had enveloped the
entire battlefield. The vapour had absorbed the fumes from the guns
and held them fast – no doubt also the gas concentrations fired by
either side. Should I order the gas masks to be put on? But how then
would I get the battalion to its destination and keep it together through
this labyrinth of shell-holes? But with the help of the compass the
improbable occurred. I suddenly stood in front of a noticeboard. *Kate's
Walk!* I staggered over the frozen plank, and the battalion followed in
single file behind.

On the other side of the tract of marsh our first wounded were
streaming back, the earliest news from our front. The English first
position had been easily taken, nearly all gas casualties. A stubborn
resistance in the second position, which was to be broken down by
assault.

Beyond Grugies the redoubt line had not been taken without a fight, but
the outpost line had been so swiftly overwhelmed that fewer than one in
every four of the men who survived the bombardment succeeded in making
his way back to augment the force defending the line of redoubts. The plan
for defending it had depended on the help of the outpost troops, and without
it, and without the assistance of the artillery to defend the gaps between the
redoubts, the line of redoubts buckled, then gave way. The guns had been
ranged and barrage tables had been drawn up, but it was a long time before
word got back, and well past noon before the alert was given and the guns
began to fire. By that time it was far too late. The defence was already
crumbling.

The *Musketiers* of the *Minenwerfer* team had rested at Grugies, sweating
profusely from their efforts, thankfully laying down their burdens to mop
their brows and gulp cold coffee. It was coffee in name only, and owed
more to the humble acorn than to the coffee bean, but after their exertions
of the morning it was nectar. They also found time to explore some British
dugouts, which had clearly been vacated in a hurry, and they found with
glee that they had struck lucky. There was bacon, there was bully beef, there
was tea and even butter. They only had time to open a tin or two and
indulge in a few tantalizing mouthfuls, but they took along as much as they

could carry. They arrived at the redoubt line just as the British guns opened up, and it was the first time they had come under direct fire.

*Musketier Alwin Hitzeroth, Minenwerfer Coy., 463rd Infantry Regt., 238th [German] Division*

We joined up with the infantry again and continued forward over a flat field, then down into a slightly sloping valley. Here we came under enemy artillery fire and scrambled for cover. Although the shelling soon stopped, we lost one man dead and three wounded. As soon as it did, the Regiment's 1st and 3rd Battalions attacked and, after fierce hand-to-hand fighting, broke through the English position. It seemed that the enemy's resistance was broken here, and again we pushed forward, capturing all sorts of guns and ammunition and supplies. The supplies were especially welcomed by us lowly privates – milk, cigarettes, white bread and real coffee! Our bread-bags soon were stuffed full.

The British posts were enveloped in mist. The telephone wires were in shreds. There was no possibility of contact by semaphore or of calling for artillery support, for neither the flash of a signal lamp nor the magnesium blaze of an SOS flare could penetrate the fog, and runners who survived the pounding shell-fire to reach battalion headquarters were often killed or injured or lost in the choking mist when they tried to retrace their steps. When the range of the guns lengthened and the barrage lifted, the half-dazed soldiers in the battle zone braced themselves to meet the enemy. But, standing to in battle positions, aiming across the wire from the parapets of sketchy trenches, they could find no targets to fire on, and machine-gunners poised to sweep the open ground between redoubts could barely see fifty yards, let alone 500. In the aftermath of the shelling the fumes were slow to disperse, and the swirls of smoke that erupted with each explosion were still drifting and mingling with the fog. Peering through smarting red-rimmed eyes, expecting every trailing shadow to mutate into the solid forms of German soldiers, the Tommies waited.

When the enemy soldiers did materialize, as often as not they came from behind, attacking at close quarters, and when it was clear that a post was encircled there seemed very little point in resisting.

Reinhold Spengler's company was making for Essigny, where D Company of the 7th Battalion, the Rifle Brigade, were at the outer edge of the battle zone, just outside the village. The communications were dead, and for a long time now nothing had been heard from the King's Royal Rifle Corps manning the forward post half a mile ahead. The fog was thinning, but there was still nothing to be seen to the right or left of them and it was some time since the German barrage had lifted. Ted Gale had been in the war since the beginning, and he knew full well that an enemy attack should have swiftly followed. But nothing happened.

*3774 Corporal Ted Gale, 7th Bn., The Rifle Brigade, 14th Division*

We were holding this part of the line. There was three companies up there, and A Company was back behind alongside Essigny-le-Grand. I was in D Company. They'd been bombarding all night long, and talk about a London fog! We couldn't see the next sentry next door to us standing in the trench. We honestly couldn't see each other, it was that thick with the German guns and the fog. The bombardment was moving on and it was full daylight, but there was no Germans coming over or anything.

Well, we stand to for hours in our battle positions! Then the Captain of the company comes along the line. He said, 'Funny thing going on. It's very unusual. There's no sign of an attack. You'd better all go down in the dugouts and have something to eat, something to drink. Leave a couple of sentries up here.' So we left a couple of sentries on top and went down into the dugouts.

*101264 Private Jim Brady, 43rd Field Ambulance, Royal Army Medical Corps., 14th Division*

The bombardment stopped as if it had been switched off by a giant hand. The silence was deafening. Bob Stevens, one of the ambulance drivers, ventured upstairs and hurried down to say that things were deathly quiet. The village of Essigny was completely flattened, he said; there were one or two bodies about, and the mist had almost gone. Some of the chaps started to clear the debris at the entrance to the dugout.

In the distance we could hear the barrage start up again, dropping a mile or so down the road towards Montescourt. We settled down to wait, and McBarron, Ackroyd, Andy and I started a game of solo whist. It took us a hand or two to steady our nerves.

*203694 Rifleman Burt Eccles, 7th Bn., The Rifle Brigade, 14th Division*

With being a company runner I'd got to be at Company Headquarters a bit further back. It was in a long dugout in a sunken road, and it was a well-made thing. There were steps down at each end. Well, the first thing we knew about the Germans being on top of us was a stick bomb thrown down one entrance. Fortunately I was sitting on the bottom step of the other entrance, so I rushed up like mad with my rifle. When I got outside there must have been at least fifty Jerries looking at me with their guns. I couldn't understand it!

*Corporal Ted Gale*

We got a brew going but, damn it, we hadn't been in the dugout for more than about ten minutes when the Captain popped his head in the dugout door. He said, 'You can all come up. You won't want your rifles.' He said it quite calm, like. Anyway, we came walking up the dugout steps, and there was all these Jerries round us!

Of course, we realized what had happened. Jerry had broken through on the right and left of us. This was a mopping-up party coming. They'd never attempted a frontal attack. That was the strategy, you see: they went through on the right and left.

Our whole battalion was caught. A Company was back in Essigny-le-Grand. They were just cooking their breakfast for the Company, because they hadn't had a chance to have any, and Jerry walked in just as they were starting to dish up breakfast for the troops. Fried bacon and bread.

*Private Jim Brady*

I'd just got an unbeatable hand, and I stood to win five francs, when someone fired a pistol down the dugout steps and a bullet smacked into the ground at my feet, and there were two Jerry soldiers in field-grey uniforms and bucket-helmets gazing down at us. One shouted, 'Come up, Tommy! *Los! Los!*' And he shot another bullet, *splat*, into the side of the stairway.

We filed upstairs, scared stiff, with our hands above our heads, hoping the Germans would recognize that most of us were non-combatants, but at that precise moment there was a burst of machine-gun fire from our rear. Some RBs in reserve had spotted the Germans. All hell was let loose! Andy slumped to the ground with blood gushing from beneath his tunic, and when I bent down to attend to him a brawny German thumped me in the ribs with the butt-end of his rifle.

*Corporal Ted Gale*

They gathered us all together – on the road – and some German started opening machine-gun fire on us. And we were prisoners and all! One of the fellows was hit – a lance-corporal: I think he lived in Stepney. He was a conscript. He didn't get killed, but he got half his arm shot up. Nobody got killed. They stopped them too soon for it, but I think they *would* have if an officer hadn't come along and stopped them.

*Rifleman Burt Eccles*

One of our fellows got bayoneted – a German officer came up to me, he took hold of my arm, he said, '*Est-ce que vous parlez français?*' I said, '*Oui, monsieur – un peu.*' And he started to talk to me in French – not that I could tell him anything. I wouldn't have done anyhow! What he wanted to know was whether I was carrying any dispatches or orders or anything. Well, while that was happening the Germans couldn't touch me, because I was too near their own officer. I never put my hands up!

*Corporal Ted Gale*

There was a Jerry – he come from Saxony I think – and he said, 'The war's finished for you, ain't it?' He said it just like that. '*Ain't it?*' he said, Cockney-like. I looked at him, and I said, 'You speak good English, don't you?' He said, 'Yes, I was a barber in London.' Half of them could speak English.

Of course you lost everything. Rifles naturally, but everything else as well. In my haversack I had tobacco and cigarette papers in there. *That* went. All they left you was your gas mask. Then they started walking us back.

*Rifleman Burt Eccles*

My pal and I had our signaller with us, wounded badly. You could tell it was bad because I was on one side of him and from my chest to my feet was covered with his blood. He said, 'Leave me, chum, leave me. I can't go on.' So we left him. We *had* to leave him, just hoping the German stretcher-bearers would pick him up later on.

Anyhow, two or three German Red Cross men came up to me. They thought I was badly wounded. I tried to make them understand

1. Private Alex Jamieson, 11th Royal Scots, (*right*) photographed with a friend. Within weeks of his arrival in France he was in the forefront of the fighting. 'That was the first moment that I was frightened, really frightened, because the orders came along, "This position must be held at all costs until the last man."'

2. *Left*: Reinhold Spengler as an infantryman of the 2nd Company, 1st Bavarian Infantry Regiment, in February 1917 (Photo: Richard A. Baumgartner).

3. *Below*: Reinhold Spengler as a newly commissioned officer in 1918 (Photo: Richard A. Baumgartner).

4. *Below*: Traces of the Hindenburg Line still scar the ground near Urvillers. From this spot, or very close to it, Leutnant Reinhold Spengler led his platoon to the assault.

5. *Right*: The remains of the mighty Hindenburg Line along the Oise Canal near Vendeuil and Moÿ.

6. *Below*: The defensive posts of the Hindenburg Line ran all along the eastern bank of the Oise Canal, and the trenches behind them can still be distinguished on the ground.

7. *Below*: The formidable concrete shelters were impervious to shell-fire.

8. Looking north from Ly-Fontaine towards Benay. The clump of trees in the middle distance is roughly where the last gun of C83 Battery kept firing to the last and Gunner Charlie Stone won the VC. The Germans were advancing across the open country on the right.

9. 'Our infantry stormed on towards a railway embankment, driving the English in front ... We were lying on one side of the embankment, the English on the other ... our ammunition was dwindling down to almost nothing ...' Georg Maier, 1st Bavarian Division. 'When we saw the enemy retreating, we put our machine-guns on the top of the embankment and fired at them streaming across a large field between Flavy-le-Martel and Faillouel' Leutnant Reinhold Spengler.

10. *Above*: The chateau at Rouez village where the 10th Essex were surprised by the pursuing enemy, photographed on another misty morning eighty years later.

11. *Left*: The 10th Essex at Rouez and the keeper's cottage in an artist's impression. 'There was a gamekeeper's cottage right on the edge of the wood, and the Huns had a machine-gun at every window ...' Captain R. Chell.

12. *Right*: A modern view of the same spot.

13. The keeper's cottage today. On the walls, memorial plaques commemorate the French regiment who arrived to help the 10th Essex hold up the enemy advance on 23 March 1918.

14. The graves of German soldiers killed in the fight at Rouez. They lie in a cemetery just beyond the keeper's cottage, on the site of the line the Essex took up when they rushed to the attack from the wood in the background.

15. Gauche Wood, where the South Africans made their gallant stand in the outpost line south of Gouzeaucourt. Captain Garnet Green's redoubt was roughly on the site of the field which is white-sheeted to protect early crops.

16. Men of the Royal Naval Division still lie just behind the old front line at Villers-Plouich, just north of Gouzeaucourt in the Flesquières salient. On modern French ordnance maps the ground is still marked 'Champs de Bataille'.

18. *Below*: Second Lieutenant Gerard Robin, RFC, snapped on his arrival at 41 Squadron. Within days he narrowly escaped death when his burning aircraft went into a spin. 'Of course I had terrible wind up . . . I was at 13,000 feet when I began this stunt and at 5,000 feet when I pulled her out.'

17. *Above*: When Second Lieutenant Peter Wilson, MC, was transferred from the West Yorkshire Regiment he had the impression that the wild parties of the Royal Flying Corps were almost as dangerous as war in the trenches or in the air.

19. *Below*: The temporary bridge at Masnières erected by the Germans above the wreck of the original bridge, collapsed under the weight of a tank. Frank Caulton scrambled with difficulty across the shattered girders in November 1917 and was subsequently captured.

it was '*mein Kamerad*'. I felt like going back to find him, but I shouldn't have found him.

A little over a mile beyond the rear line of the battle zone the 8th Rifle Brigade clearly heard the machine-guns firing at Essigny, where the remnants of their sister battalion were being rounded up. But without orders they could not go forward to help, and without information there could be no orders. Since the start of the bombardment many hours before, they had not heard a single word from the 7th RB, but the sound of the firing was ominous. The village of Clastres had been well and truly flattened during the bombardment, and there had been many casualties in the two companies of the 8th which were in Brigade reserve, but Colonel Prideaux-Brune ordered every man who could to stand to. Then he personally collected the headquarters details and ushered them into a hastily wired stretch of rudimentary trench. His command consisted of the signals officer, the adjutant and a hotchpotch of signallers, servants and cooks. There was not a marksman among them, but, if they had little hope of halting the Germans' advance, they could at least slow them down and give them pause for thought. But already the machine-gun had stuttered into silence. They waited. Time passed. Nothing.

Despite their flying start, the Germans were not having it all their own way and the mist had not been entirely to their advantage, for they had overlooked some British posts where it was thickest, and even in the forward zone several isolated outposts were still holding out and were harrying them with rifle and machine-gun fire. There had been other irritating delays. The gas had been slow to dissipate, and hours after they should have dispersed the fumes were still hanging thick in the grip of the fog when the unwitting German soldiers stumbled into them. And stumble they did, for the ground which their own shells had so liberally spattered with craters was treacherous and difficult to negotiate.

Coming hard on the heels of the storm troops, the pioneers had the task of bridging the captured trenches and the worst of the shell-holes. But it was slow going to drag materials forward when even the sturdiest of wheeled carts made heavy weather of the rough ground. As more and more troops and guns moved up, congestion mounted behind the German line, and the multitude of prisoners, of walking wounded and stretcher-bearers moving back through the German lines made matters worse. Reports were local and incoherent, and even regimental officers found it hard to make sense of what was happening on their own particular front. In airfields close to the line, pilots studied ground maps, waited impatiently for the signal to take off, and wondered for the umpteenth time when the mist would lift.

Observation teams in the infantry were still kicking their heels in the trenches, waiting for the weather to improve, and Hans Schetter had been observing British prisoners with interest as they were escorted to the rear. He coveted their good leather boots, and was even more envious of the long rubber waders worn by a few unfortunate soldiers. They were far from suitable footwear for the slog that lay ahead, but it was a long time since the ill-shod German soldiers had seen anything but synthetic rubber, and they were much impressed.

Shortly after midday, as if a curtain were being rung up, the mist began to thin and then to clear rapidly. Officers moved to staff observation posts, and Schetter's observation team got the signal to move forward. Gradually landmarks loomed out of the mist, the sun began to shine, and it turned into a fine spring day.

*Hauptmann Walter Bloem*

A stupendous sight! The limitless plain, churned up with shell-holes, is covered everywhere with advancing columns of infantry and artillery, while pioneer companies are busy filling up the new shell-holes with fascines. Nevertheless, the horses are in great difficulties, and the gasping gun-crews heave to get their guns going again. And all the time a constant backward stream of limping wounded, all cheery and of good heart. We are going forward! But here at last comes the roaring of the first English shells, sometimes nearer, sometimes further away. They strike into the panting masses as they advance, and where they strike they reap a rich harvest. And so we walk wearily forward for hours across the ground between us and our front line.

Now comes the command to take cover until further orders – obviously because we have been held up in front. Through the never-ending raging of the artillery duel, the cracking of rifles and machine-guns is audible. No mistake! The English second line is being hotly contested, and the enemy artillery is also now intervening more effectively. Barrages of medium and heavy shells rain down – whoever gets into them will be blown to atoms. Still nobody crawls into the dugouts, but we all stand up in the trench and absorb with all our senses the overpowering spectacle of the battle pounding slowly forward.

Another spectator was equally impressed. In a well-protected observation post of the Eighteenth Army, where a group of German staff officers had been waiting with mounting frustration for the fog to lift, stood the man in whose name the battle had been launched. The post was some way behind the line, but large telescopes had been set up which brought the battle almost to their feet. Gazing through a powerful lens at the scene laid out like a diorama before him, marking the position of his troops as they advanced towards the battle zone, the Kaiser was ecstatic. But some distance ahead and a good deal nearer the battle, Hans Schetter and his comrades endeavouring to set up their telescope in a captured British trench were working under difficulties. The British guns were no longer firing blind; shells were dropping uncomfortably close to them, and as soon as the tall pole of the telescope was hoisted aloft the blast of an explosion knocked it askew. They had been there for some time now, and, although in Schetter's opinion the construction of the trench was of poor quality and the dugouts were vastly inferior to their own, after several men had been hit the rest were glad to shelter in them until things quietened down.

In the Headquarters' trench beyond Clastres, Colonel Prideaux-Brune had taken upon himself the duties of sentry and had been staring through his binoculars until his eyes watered. Although the sun was now shining on the high ground, the mist at ground level was painfully slow to clear. When it finally did he was appalled by what he saw. To the right of Essigny a trickle of British troops was coming back across country. The trickle swelled even as he watched, and he needed no message to tell him that the line had broken and the right flank of the 14th Division had been turned.

Some two and a half miles to the south-east, and far further forward than Essigny, where the line had given way, Walter Lugg was in a gun position outside the village of Benay. Strictly speaking it was not a 'position' in the normal sense. The six guns of C Battery had been disposed in twos south-east and east of the village, with the second pair dug in roughly 400 yards behind the first, and the third the same distance behind the second, but it was many hours since Captain Heybittel had ordered the forward section to drag the guns from the pits, which might have been registered by the enemy, to unprotected open ground some yards away. It was a wise precaution, and throughout the fearsome bombardment very few shells had fallen close to the guns and by some miracle there had been no casualties. C83 Battery had been firing incessantly since dawn, probing into the mist, aiming at fixed targets beyond the old German line, but, apart from the obvious conclusion that the Germans had broken through, they had only the vaguest idea of what was happening. They had begun to suspect that things were going badly wrong, but they did not yet realize that they were now in the front line. The guns in the outpost zone had been overrun and captured, the Germans had penetrated almost a mile behind them, and the flank of their own 18th Division was unprotected, swinging wildly in the air.

Half a mile ahead, Guingette Farm on the St Quentin road was Battalion

HQ of the Berkshires, who had been manning the defences at Moÿ, where the 10th Essex had recently enjoyed such an easy stint in the line. Now the line at Moÿ was no more, and the handful of men who fought their way back to the farm battled on to defend it until they were almost surrounded. Only then did Colonel Dewing give the signal to retire, and only then did they slip away, a handful at a time, while the few who remained kept firing to hold off the enemy. When the last Lewis-gun fell silent, the Germans surged forward and a barrage from their machine-guns followed the Berks as they ducked and wavered, seeking out the dead ground where the land sloped down from Benay. A few of them, passing close to the guns, waved and gesticulated a warning that the Germans were on their heels.

*Gunner Walter Lugg, MM, C 83 Bty., Royal Field Artillery*

We had this chap Charlie Drake, and he was a good friend of mine. (Both my mates were called Charlie – the other was Charlie Stone.) Charlie Drake had very good eyesight, marvellous eyesight, and he was looking over, and all of a sudden he shouted to our captain, who by this time was standing on top of the gun-pit, because we'd pulled our guns into the open, and he shouted to him, 'Here they are! Hordes of them!' So I looked through my telescope sight and all of a sudden I saw the blooming Germans three hundred yards away from us. Well, we didn't have to be told! We started letting fly at them, firing at short range. We had a .2 fuse on her, and they had a muzzle velocity of 1,610 feet a second, so you can work out as soon as we fired they were exploding. Point blank over open sights.

It was the first time that most of the gunners had seen Germans in the flesh, and it was a curious sensation. During their three years in France the enemy had been personified by technical niceties – a grid location on a map, the digits on a rangefinder – or by a covey of disarmed prisoners trailing disconsolately past the guns when the infantry made a successful attack. Now they were a great grey host, advancing in a mass, closing in on the guns, and half a mile beyond the first wave a second multitude was coming on fast. But the gunners were firing now with every ounce of energy, and the advancing lines of the enemy were faltering under canopies of shrapnel.

*Gunner Walter Lugg, MM*

There were 365 of these shrapnel bullets in one shell, and of course they splayed out all over the place. You fire at them and you can see them duck. Well, we kept firing and firing. Our skipper shouted,

'Hey! You're getting too enthusiastic. You'd better ease up a bit.' He was afraid that we'd run out of ammo, but fortunately we had plenty of ammo. We fired no end of shells that day – hundreds, literally hundreds. We did a lot of damage, and we definitely slowed them down, but still they're getting nearer and nearer.

To be quite honest I didn't feel windy somehow. It was a new kind of action and it was very exciting. It really was.

But two guns could not indefinitely hold off what appeared to be half the German Army advancing from more than one direction. The guns were quite exposed on the open ground, the enemy was well provided with machine-guns, and bullets were spitting unpleasantly close to the crews. By long military tradition, a gunner's ultimate dishonour was to allow his gun to be captured by a gloating enemy. The cry of 'Save the guns!' rang through a hundred tales of noble deeds, and a thousand prints or paintings on the walls of Army messes from Lucknow to Larkhill depicted guns being galloped out of action in some epic battle, in a frenzy of flying hooves and a slashing of hostile sabres. But the mist had lifted so quickly, and the enemy had appeared so suddenly on top of them, that there was not the faintest chance of saving the guns, for, even if the wires had not been destroyed by the shelling, the horses and drivers could not have arrived from the transport lines in time to drag them away. Nevertheless, even if he were forced to abandon his guns, Heybittel intended to make quite sure that they would be of no service to the enemy.

The routine means of disabling a gun was to remove the breech-block – the heavy steel device slammed into place after a shell is loaded, to plug the open end of the bore. Without it the gun would be of as much use as a pea-shooter. It was a risky manoeuvre with the enemy in full view, ready – and doubtless waiting – to rush the guns as soon as it was realized they had stopped firing. It was vital to hold them off, not merely for long enough to remove the vital mechanism – a thirty-pound weight of blistering hot steel – but to give the gun-crews time to dispose of it and get back safely to the second position 400 yards down the valley.

*Gunner Walter Lugg, MM*

The chaps who weren't handling the guns lay out with rifles to hold the Jerries off when we stopped firing. I was handling one of the guns, so I had to help to get the breech-block out, take the No. 7 sights away. Most of us managed to get back all right, creeping away in ones and twos. Captain Heybittel didn't go until nearly the end, because he wanted to see everyone away. We all got away except for Lieutenant

Patterson and three other chaps. They were on the other gun, and possibly they'd had more of a struggle with their breech-block, but they were a bit behind and to our right as we were moving back. Next thing, I heard Captain Heybittel give a shout and he was standing pointing his revolver. When I looked over my shoulder, it must have been fifty or more yards away, Lieutenant Patterson was being marched away with two or three other chaps – marched away by a bunch of Germans who must have worked round the side of us. The skipper just pointed his revolver and fired. They say he hit one of them.

The rest of us got back to the next position all right, where there were another two guns, so we helped them and kept firing, and the lads who had rifles kept firing. They were glad to have us, I can tell you. When we got back there we buried the breech-blocks we'd carried back.

It wasn't long before the Jerries started advancing on the left of us, so we had to go back again. That's where Charlie Stone came into his own. He was a great chap, a marvellous chap, and a great friend of mine. The Germans weren't just walking towards us, you know. No! They had machine-guns, and they were firing these machine-guns as they came forward. So, while we were trying to get back, old Charlie Stone lay out there, right out in front, no more than a hundred yards from the Germans, and he shot them down like a marksman. That was only one of the things he did that day. He ended up winning the Victoria Cross!

They fell back to a sunken road well ahead of the last of the Battery's guns, but Heybittel was banking on killing several birds with a single stone. From this advanced position he could spot the movements of the enemy and direct the fire of his remaining guns in the dead ground behind. He could also help to protect the flanks of the hard-pressed infantry, inching their way back on either side and fighting as they came. There were barely fifty yards to cross before the gunners reached the cover of the road behind, but two of them were killed before they reached it. They also lost their solitary machine-gun. But with their six remaining rifles they held their ground. They held it for more than an hour. It was ample time for Heybittel to work his way back to the last two guns and to direct their fire to such effect that the Germans on their front hesitated, wavered, and stopped long enough to allow the infantry to retire; long enough also for Heybittel to gather the infantry under his wing and form a strongpoint close to the guns, and long enough for the surviving gunners to reach them.

*Gunner Walter Lugg, MM*

That was the final position, so we knew we had to stay there! There were two of our guns there, and one of them went out of action because the gun had got so darned hot it jammed. When they got that hot you didn't have enough physical force to open the breech-lever. You had to get a pickaxe and lever it out with that. A pickaxe. Can you imagine! It was a case of sort of levering it by putting it behind the breech-block and pulling on the wooden handle. Then the breech-lever broke, so *that* was out of action. So we only had one left, and then a part on the *other* gun broke, but we were able to take out part of the trigger mechanism from the one gun and shove it in the other one, so we were able to continue firing, but the gun got so hot that the shell-case couldn't be ejected. So we had to get a long pole, go round, and poke the pole down the front of it and knock the case out. Of course, all the time the Germans are getting closer.

After a while one of these Red Baron aeroplanes started buzzing around and he came low down, right over the top of us, and we thought, 'Now, we're for it!' But he was spotting. We could see him with his goggles on, and we could see him look over the side at us and he waved to us. I could see him waving.

The gunners were not entirely sure if the German pilot was waving in admiration of their efforts, or if he was encouraging them to surrender. A few waved back. But several others put their fingers to their noses in a lewd gesture which they hoped would be correctly interpreted and convey to the Germans that they had no intention of giving in. The pilot replied by waggling his wings in an almost friendly manner.

## Chapter 8

As the German plane banked and flew off, a few of the Tommies in the strongpoints near the guns spared a moment to speed it on its way with a volley of rifle fire. But their more immediate concern was holding off a substantial force of enemy infantry which was pressing in from the slope to the north. With the help of Heybittel's guns and another of B Battery, which was covering the approach to Caponne Farm, they were succeeding admirably. Although he prudently increased his altitude, the pilot could see enough of the fighting below to judge that it was more than a little confused. There were no clear-cut battle lines, no chequerboard pattern of troops advancing in orderly columns, and no movement on the roads behind the battle zone which would suggest that the British were demoralized or in flight. From such a height it was hardly possible to distinguish the sombre grey of the German uniforms from the dingy khaki of the Tommies, but it was plain to see that there was still spasmodic firing in places close to the original front line where the fighting should have died down long ago.

It was now mid-afternoon and, although German troops had penetrated deep into the line just a mile or so to the north, the battle zone south of Caponne Farm had not been breached. To the annoyance of the Germans, it now seemed that even the flimsy outpost line had not been completely cleared. The German generals wished to know why, and the aeroplane circling overhead was expected to come back with the answer. This small area of resistance was seriously impeding their advance and, furthermore, preventing a full-scale attack on the 58th Division to the south of it. According to the well-laid German plan, the line should have been almost rolled up by now.

The ground south of Caponne Farm comprised most of the 53rd Brigade sector and, seen from a height of a thousand feet, it formed a rough trapezium. From Ly-Fontaine it ran eastward to the river, from the redoubt in the battle zone at its top left, to the village of Vendeuil in the outpost line at the bottom right. The main road to St Quentin bisected the village, and the canal and the River Oise ran across marshy ground on the village's eastern edge. Here the mist had been thickest, and here, hours after it had lifted further to the west, it had still not entirely dispersed. As late as one o'clock a breathless runner from the 7th Royal West Kents brought a final message from Colonel Crosthwaite, who was fighting the Germans off at his battalion headquarters, not very far in front of Ly-Fontaine. It read, 'Holding out 12.30 p.m. Boches all around within 50 yards except rear. Can only see 40 yards, so it is difficult to kill the blighters. Signed J. D. Crosthwaite.'

After that no more was heard of the Royal West Kents. It was less than forty-eight hours since they had taken over from the 10th Essex in the line, and, reading the message at his own battalion headquarters before sending it on to Brigade, Major Tween of the Essex was acutely aware that, had the chips fallen differently, he might have been sending a similar message himself. Late in the morning, when the mist began to thin, the Essex had anxiously observed the firing at Crosthwaite's headquarters just half a mile away. They had also spotted small parties of the enemy creeping forward between them and the fort on the rising ground behind the village of Vendeuil.

The fort at Vendeuil had been built in the seventeenth century by the military architect Vauban to guard the road to St Quentin and the river crossing beyond. It was a classic lozenge-shape, and in front of it its outer ditches had been incorporated into a redoubt which formed part of the defensive scheme of the village. The fort itself was protected by a deep dry moat, high ramparts, and a stout stone gateway approached by a causeway and a drawbridge. As a defensive position in itself it was almost invincible. Situated on a slope behind the village, it was well sited to give covering fire to the two areas of defence in the village beyond, occupied by A and B Companies of the 7th Buffs, and also to the areas held by C and D Companies to the south of the track that ran from Vendeuil to Remigny. With a grandstand view from behind the ready-made parapets of its stout ramparts, it was an ideal observation post from which vital information could be passed to Colonel Ransome at Battalion Headquarters in Clarence Keep.

The so-called 'keep' was nothing more than a small chalk quarry half a mile along the track, and, while it provided a certain amount of shelter for the HQ staff, they could see little of what was happening in the low-lying outpost zone. But it was a long time now since there had been any news either of the fort itself or the outpost zone beyond it. After four hours' back-breaking labour, crawling across gas-soaked ground, hardly pausing to shelter from frequent tornadoes of shelling, the Battalion signallers managed to repair the telephone lines, which were cut in so many places that they gave up counting at forty. But Captain Fine, in the fort, had only time to give the briefest of reports before the line was lost again, this time for good. After that the only news of the outpost line was brought unexpectedly by A Company's cook.

Like most of A Company, this man had been rounded up by the Germans,

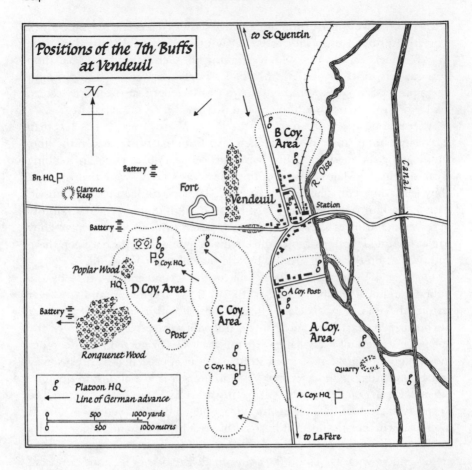

but, being in charge of the Company's stores, he had the wit to bribe his captors to let him go. He bribed them with bacon. Suspecting a plot, they had first insisted by signs that the cook should eat some himself. Raw bacon was not entirely to his taste, but, since three Germans were holding him at bayonet-point, he obligingly carved off a slice and chewed it with every appearance of relish. His captors consequently tucked into the raw bacon with so much gusto that the cook was able to slide away into the mist while their attention was distracted. He was delighted with his escapade and, although chastened by the fate that had befallen the rest of his comrades, he clearly felt that he at least had upheld the honour of his company by scoring one over the enemy.

A few other men of A Company had managed to slip away into Vendeuil fort, but it was hardly a refuge. The officers in Clarence Keep had a grandstand view of the Germans' attempt to storm it and had watched anxiously while the fort was viciously shelled, but all they knew for certain when the smoke cleared was that the garrison was still firing, still holding out, and still holding the enemy off. They had also seen the blink of a signal lamp from the ramparts, and the message was flashed at intervals throughout the long afternoon: 'Counter-attack urgently required.' But there was no possibility of a counter-attack, and Captain Fine himself must have known it. After a while the signals stopped.

Although in one sense they were picked men, not even the most partial observer would have looked on the soldiers defending the fort as élite troops. The age at which a man could be conscripted for military service had recently been lowered to eighteen, and raised to forty-two. Rigid medical standards had been relaxed, and recruits were no longer rejected on grounds of height, or because they had bad teeth. The standard of robustness had dropped, and in some cases the hardships of war service had affected even the fittest. Many had bad feet, and two of the platoons in Vendeuil fort were made up of men who were indifferent marchers and had been weeded out and sent to the Royal Engineers to serve as unskilled labourers. During the previous weeks they had been usefully, if not always congenially, employed in digging trenches, humping duckboards, toting bales of wire and excavating dugouts at the behest of the Royal Engineers, and it was something of a shock to find that they now seemed to be a bulwark in the path of the Germans. A company of REs plus a platoon of the Buffs made up the rest of Captain Fine's command. In terms of military prowess they could fairly be described as mediocre, but they could shoot, they were sticking it, and, although the Germans were all around, they were doing their best to stop them. Their best was pretty good. If the enemy attempted the slightest move, rifles blazed from every corner of the ramparts, machine-gun bullets streamed from loopholes, and the two Stokes mortar guns firing at short range deterred even the boldest from coming closer. The fort was more than a stumbling block to the Germans. It was a hornets' nest. But hornets can fly away, whereas Captain Fine was uncomfortably aware that he and his men more closely resembled rats caught in a trap.

A mile or so to the north, where fourteen German divisions had been pitched against the three British divisions holding the line that looped around St Quentin, the gunners of Lieutenant Herbert Asquith's battery on the southern edge of Holnon Wood had been firing a defensive barrage since before dawn.[1] From their position they had been shooting on fixed targets, and Asquith did not doubt that they had done some damage because, as one

1. The three divisions holding the line round St Quentin were the 36th, 30th and the 61st.

of the battery's forward observation officers, he knew that they had pinpointed their targets and registered their guns to an inch. But their forward observation post on the hill outside St Quentin had vanished, like the hill itself, in a whirlwind of explosions.

For several weeks Asquith had climbed almost daily to the post on the eastern slope of the hill. From this sturdy concrete emplacement the officers observing for the artillery could look directly into the sizeable town of St Quentin, half a mile away. It was a haunting sight. The great bulk of the cathedral loomed over empty streets. Not a wisp of smoke rose from innumerable chimneys. When the wind rose, a shredded curtain might flap from a windowless house, but, despite the rumble and roar of the war and the occasional rattle of fire somewhere along the line, an eerie silence seemed to brood over the deserted city in a way that was almost uncanny. But after nightfall the infantry guarding the redoubt on the hill could hear the trundle of wheels in the streets, the muffled tramp of booted feet, the rattle of loaded wagons or, when the British guns had been active during the day, the sound of men shovelling rubble.

It had been so quiet that artillery officers had begun to regard duty at the observation post as a mere morning stroll followed by a day's sport. It had amused them to select their targets on aesthetic grounds, and one particularly ugly modern villa which offended their artistic sensibilities had come in for a good deal of punishment in the course of registering the guns. They were gratified to observe that it had been more or less demolished by the third shot. The roof disappeared in an avalanche of shattered tiles, the walls bulged and crumbled, and a large object slid across a teetering floor and see-sawed to a precarious halt, half in and half out of the top storey. Raising his binoculars, Asquith saw that it was the frame of a four-poster bed. More and more it seemed to him that St Quentin was a city of the dead, both ghostly and sinister, for in the run-up to the battle not a gun on the German side had replied. But now that the Germans had unleashed all the might of their artillery the vantage point on the edge of No Man's Land in front of St Quentin was getting the full force of the bombardment. Before the war the hill had been a favourite spot for picnics and Sunday outings. There was a pleasant inn on its lower slopes and a fine view from the top. The people of St Quentin called it '*la montagne de la ville*', but to the British Army it was 'Manchester Hill', for it was the Manchesters who had captured it in the spring of 1917 in the last skirmish of the German retirement to the Hindenburg Line.

It was quite a coincidence that a battalion of Manchesters was again in possession of Manchester Hill when the German assault came, and in Colonel Elstob's view it was a happy one, for both he and his men regarded it as a point of honour to defend it. Manchester Hill was a good defensive position.

It had an all-round field of fire, it was well entrenched, and well-wired machine-gun posts were set up at intervals around its forward slopes. On the reverse slope a small quarry had been fortified, and machine-guns and Stokes mortars had been strategically sited to defend it. There were shelters and dugouts for the cooks and signallers, and another for Battalion Head-quarters, and for many hours since the attack had been launched the Man-chesters had been standing fast.

The 2nd Battalion, which had first captured Manchester Hill, was the old 96th Regiment of Foot. It had first come into existence in 1760, and had been part of the Manchester Regiment since 1881. The regimental battle honours ranged from Egypt in 1801 to Ladysmith in 1900, via the Peninsular Wars, the Crimea and the Afghan War, with many other half-remembered engagements on the way. Since 1914 a new generation of Manchesters had added another honour to the Regiment's escutcheon, for the 2nd Battalion had arrived in France in time to distinguish itself at Mons.

The soldiers of the 16th Battalion who now held Manchester Hill were infants by comparison, for their own battalion had come into being only in August 1914, a full ten days after their seniors had landed in France. But they were infants no longer, and, although they had been at the front for less than two and a half years, they had given a good account of themselves. They had captured Montauban on the first day of the Battle of the Somme, and had also served with distinction at Ypres the following year. More to the point, they had been recruited in Manchester – the first of eight battalions raised by the city's lord mayor – and, unlike other service battalions, whose recruits were drawn from surrounding districts, they considered themselves to be Manchesters in the truest sense. As such, these sons of the city had no intention of losing Manchester Hill, and no one was more heartily determined to hold on to it than their Commanding Officer, temporary Lieutenant-Colonel Wilfrith Elstob. The Colonel had not been born within the city boundaries, but his home in the village of Chelford was just a stone's throw to the south, he was a graduate of Manchester University, and it was in Manchester that he had joined up on the first day of the war. He had enlisted as a private, and, although he was no more a soldier than any other man in his unit, the Colonel's military career was some weeks longer than that of the Battalion itself.

Elstob had not served long as a private soldier. In the first hectic days of the war, when men of all types and from every level of society had flocked to join the Army, the number of would-be soldiers soon outnumbered the peacetime establishment, and rapidly burgeoned into a force whose enthusiasm far outstripped its capabilities. The number of officers who could be pulled out of retirement was far from sufficient to organize it into anything like a fighting force, and the ranks had been scoured for men who could be trained to officer the raw battalions of Kitchener's Army. Elstob was an obvious candidate. He was a man of culture and education and, above all, a man of intelligence.

Wilfrith Elstob's life and background could hardly have been less likely to fit him for the role. His father was a country vicar, and like many sons of the clergy Elstob spent his schooldays at Christ's Hospital, dressed like a sixteenth-century clerk in holy orders, in the knee-breeches, long blue coat and yellow stockings which had been the uniform of the school since its foundation. He had flourished as an athlete, and, although he was no swot, he had a flair for languages that took him on to Manchester University and a more than respectable degree. He intended to be a schoolmaster, took a diploma in education, and followed it by two years' study in France, first at the Lycée in Beauvais and then at the Sorbonne. By 1914 he was employed as a schoolmaster at Merchiston Castle in Edinburgh, where two years spent teaching French to inky schoolboys of varying aptitude had not quenched his enthusiasm for France and its language. Elstob was a scholar, a born schoolmaster, and he loved his job.

Until the war had rudely interrupted his summer holiday in the quiet vicarage at Chelford, Elstob had never envisaged a military career. Now, three years after being commissioned as a humble second lieutenant, it was hard to envisage any other. He had won the Military Cross, he had been awarded the Distinguished Service Order, he had been through the mill with his battalion, and now, as its Commanding Officer – albeit a 'temporary' Lieutenant-Colonel – he was in command of the 16th Manchesters at the most critical moment of the Battalion's existence. It was up to him to conduct the defence of Manchester Hill, and he was perfectly confident that his men would not let him down.

Two nights earlier, when the Battalion had taken over the position, Elstob had made the situation plain to his officers as they mulled over a plan of the defences. Jabbing his finger on the quarry redoubt to which, in the last resort, they might be pushed back, he had said, 'Here we fight – and here we die!' The language was a shade colourful, the sentiment a little on the dramatic side, but, right down to the rag-tag of cooks and orderlies at the tail-end of the Battalion, there was not a man who did not agree with it. By noon on 21 March they were doing exactly what he had predicted.

The line from the observation post to Asquith's battery had long ago been ruptured, but a forward observation officer managed to get back to the battery position south of Holnon Wood. He hardly needed to report that the situation was desperate, since to the right and left of Manchester Hill they could already hear machine-gun fire drawing closer and the sound of savage fighting near the villages of Savy and Salency. When the battery was ordered to retire to the battle zone, no one was surprised. Asquith's section stayed on to cover the retirement. The guns were screened by an outcrop of trees on the edge of the wood, and when all the remaining shells had been fired the horses were brought forward and the guns were limbered up and pulled back to the new position near Etreillers.

Now, if the battery was to be of any use in stopping the advance of the enemy, if its fire were not to be haphazard, a new vantage point would have to be found and, for lack of any other means of communication, messages would have to be semaphored across the open ground and possibly in view of the enemy. Asquith volunteered to go forward with one signaller to direct the battery's fire.

*Lieutenant Herbert Asquith, C 149 Bty., Royal Field Artillery*

In front of Holnon Wood the ground slopes gradually upward to the Round Hill, then there is a slight dip in the land, and beyond it are the lower slopes of Manchester Hill. A dead corporal lay on the slope, and halfway up the hill a platoon of our infantry was retiring in open order towards the battle zone.

When I reached the crest, I saw that our outpost redoubt at the Brown Quarry, that held out so gallantly for more than seven hours against the full tide of the attack, was now cut off on the north and west by the German infantry. A large number of grey misty figures, easily recognizable as Germans by the shape of their helmets, stood halted on the skyline of Manchester Hill, and two platoons had detached themselves from the mass and were advancing towards us down the western slope. They were about 500 yards in front of us, advancing in close order, grey steely lines, with low-flying German aeroplanes passing above them.

There was heavy machine-gun fire, and bullets whizzed past us probably aimed at our flag as we sat signalling the target from the edge of a shell-hole. Some British shrapnel burst above the German troops in glinting spirals of smoke, and to avoid it they turned slightly to their left, advancing near the line of the St Quentin railway.

The German artillery were pouring their fire on the battle zone behind, and there was a continuous background of thunder which seemed to extend for many miles on either side of us.

We were now in a new No Man's Land between the two armies. After repeating our signal several times, we went down to another gun position at the foot of the hill and warned the officer of the line of advance. This gun opened rapid fire on the enemy, and while it was doing so a German aeroplane swooped down out of the mist and fired at us with a machine-gun from a height of about 200 feet. The crew

drove it off with a Lewis-gun, and I went to the battle-zone O P to
report the German advance to the major.

On Manchester Hill itself, although the battle had outflanked it, the last
remnants of the Manchesters were still holding on to the quarry. The village
of Savy had not yet fallen, but the Germans had advanced well along the
road and had infiltrated the trench that linked it to the redoubt. 'Here we
fight,' Colonel Elstob had said – 'and here we die.' And he had meant it.
Elstob was as good a shot as any man in the Battalion. He took his turn
firing from the parapet, he carried ammunition, he directed the defence.
Now there was not much left to direct and all that remained was his own
Battalion Headquarters staff, a few orderlies and signallers, and a handful of
D Company pushed back into the quarry redoubt. Many of them were
wounded, including the Colonel himself, but, although it was plain to see that
the situation was hopeless, Elstob had no intention of giving in. The enemy
were on the edge of the quarry itself, and had even entered it, fighting hand to
hand, but they could not pass the barricade of sandbags that now blocked the
trench. There were only a few to defend it, but a supply of Mills bombs was
piled within easy reach and cooks and clerks and first-aid men who had seldom
lobbed anything more lethal than a cricket ball hurled them with such enthusiasm that, again and again, the Germans withdrew to count their losses and
recover their shaken strength before launching another attack.

Each time they lunged forward, Colonel Elstob was waiting on the
barricade, urging on his bombers, hardly troubling to take cover as he fired,
taking careful aim, making every bullet count. He was firing his revolver,
for a rifle was a slow and unwieldy weapon in the circumstances, and the
Germans too were hampered by the narrow limits of the trench. Time and
again they called on the Manchesters to surrender. '*Ergeben Sie sich!*' As a
linguist, Elstob must have understood, but he did not deign to reply in
German. The men heard him call out 'Never!' just a moment before he was
struck. The bullet that killed him drilled a neat hole in the centre of his
forehead.

When their Colonel fell, the heart went out of the men, and very soon
the Germans swarmed across the barricade to take possession of Manchester
Hill.[1]

★

1. Lieutenant-Colonel Elstob's body was never recovered, and he is commemorated on the memorial to the missing of 1918 at Pozières on the Somme. He was
posthumously awarded the Victoria Cross. The citation read: 'For most conspicuous
bravery, devotion to duty and self-sacrifice during operations at Manchester Redoubt,
near St. Quentin, on the 21st March 1918.

A thousand yards away, on the northern edge of the Holnon plateau the few remaining men of the second-line battalion of the 4th Ox & Bucks who were holding out at Battalion Headquarters at Enghien redoubt had been almost surrounded since three o'clock. It was only a matter of time before the enemy closed in, but even at this late hour they believed they could fight their way out. Still, they were unwilling to retire without orders, and they should have been able to obtain them, for their deep-buried telephone line to Brigade Headquarters was still functioning. The trouble was that there was no one at Brigade HQ who had the authority to give the order that would release them. Many hours ago, to his astonishment, the Brigade-Major, Harold Howitt, had found himself to all intents and purposes in command of the 184th Brigade and, for a General Staff Officer, grade 3, even one who was acting as Brigade-Major, it had been a disconcerting discovery. When the bombardment began in the early hours of the morning he had been sharing a dugout with the Brigadier. It was a comfortable dugout, for Brigadier-General White was an officer of the old school, who insisted on maintaining mess standards even in the trenches.

The mess basket that accompanied Brigade Headquarters to its forward battle position contained an ample supply of linen tablecloths and napkins, silver cutlery and glassware, and, even if the cooking facilities were basic and the dishes owed more to the efforts of Messrs Crosse and Blackwell than to those of the mess cooks, they were served on china plates. Even after the most modest of repasts the Brigadier-General insisted that the King's health should be drunk in port or, if supplies failed, in whisky. White was a stickler for etiquette, and did not regard the proximity of the enemy as any reason

---

'During the preliminary bombardment he encouraged his men in the posts in the redoubt by frequent visits, and when repeated attacks developed controlled the defence at the points threatened, giving personal support with revolver, rifle and bombs. Single-handed he repulsed one bombing assault, driving back the enemy and inflicting severe casualties. Later, when ammunition was required, he made several journeys under severe fire in order to replenish the supply. Throughout the day Lieutenant-Colonel Elstob, although twice wounded, showed the most fearless disregard of his own safety, and by his encouragement and noble example inspired his command to the fullest degree.

'The Manchester Redoubt was surrounded in the first wave of the enemy attack, but by means of the buried cable Lieutenant-Colonel Elstob was able to assure his Brigade Commander that "The Manchester Regiment will defend Manchester Hill to the last." Sometime after this post was overcome by vastly superior forces, and this very gallant officer was killed in the final assault, having maintained to the end the duty which he had impressed on his men – namely, "Here we fight and here we die." He set throughout the highest example of valour, determination, endurance and fine soldierly bearing.'

for failing to observe this indispensable formality. If need be, he would have obliged his officers to drink the loyal toast in water.

In the cubbyhole he shared with his Brigade-Major the sleeping arrangements were adequate, if not luxurious, but the strength of the dugout was not. It was a deepish dugout, but, since it was not in the forefront of the battle zone, it had been only sketchily reinforced and was not nearly strong enough to withstand the pounding of heavy-calibre shells. The ground shook and rumbled and shivered alarmingly. They could feel it trembling even through the soles of their boots, and it was not many minutes before Howitt saw the ominous sign of loosened chalk trickling from the roof and realized that it was about to fall in. He shouted a warning, pushed the General up the ladder, and scrambled hastily after him. As Howitt cleared the last rung, the ladder slid from beneath his feet and vanished in a shower of chalk and brick as the dugout collapsed and buried all their possessions from shaving gear to steel helmets.

It was bad luck about the steel helmets, for the whole place was alive with missiles, and almost at once a flying shell splinter furrowed the General's scalp and knocked him to the ground. Howitt was appalled. He was hugely relieved to find that the General was still alive, but he was bleeding profusely, he was half unconscious, and he was clearly *hors de combat*. Howitt hastily patched up the General's wound with his own field dressing, summoned two orderlies to take him down the line, and, with quaking trepidation, realized that it was up to him to co-ordinate the three battalions of the Brigade in the greatest battle of the war.

The one saving grace was that the telephone lines to the signallers' dugout had held, and time and time again during the course of the long day Major Howitt blessed the engineers who had laid the communications and buried them deep. He kept in close touch with the Ox & Bucks at Enghien redoubt and anxiously followed their fortunes, issuing whatever orders and encouragement he could, but at half past four a message came through which stumped him.

*Brigade-Major Harold Howitt, 184th Bde., 61st Division*

The last message I received was 'We are surrounded now, Sir, what are we to do?' It was an agonizing position, so I rang the Divisional Commander and, as the whole front had collapsed, I was told to give them permission to cut their way out if they could. It was five o'clock before I was able to get back to them, and after that I heard no more. I believe that many of them did.[1] The position from then onwards was

---

1. The Official History of the War states that none of the Ox & Bucks managed to escape. The few survivors were captured.

chaos and, as brigade control was largely gone, I went along to Lawson of the 5th Gloucesters, who was my senior colonel on the right, to get his instructions. He asked me to go along to *his* right and make touch with the brigade there. So I set off.

The Germans were advancing fast by then, now that Enghien redoubt had gone. I met a group of disorganized men whom I got into position *just* as some Germans tried to get through. We drove them off, and when they had retired I continued down a sunken road to try to contact the brigade on the right. I saw another group of men and, knowing that the situation was critical by now, I ran towards them to ask for their help – hoping, of course, to repeat the last performance. The light was going by now, but when I was very close I saw by the shape of their tin hats that they were Germans! They fired at me and they missed, but they were at such close range that the blast from their rifles knocked me over. The next moment I was on the ground with Germans all around me, pointing their bayonets at my middle. I was a prisoner – and I couldn't do a thing about it!

They stripped me of everything I had of any value and marched me away. The first stop was at their company headquarters, which had been established in one of *our* gun emplacements, and they sat me down on a pile of shells. I couldn't help admiring the young officers I saw at the desk. There they were, just arrived, a mile or two behind our old lines and with no accurate maps of them, and yet they were working out their plans by candlelight in a most efficient manner. They kept asking me questions, pointing down the road and saying '*Kamerad?*' – obviously intending that I should tell them where my friends were.

After a time they handed me over to two soldiers armed with revolvers and I was sent outside. I could see the next assault being prepared, mules carrying machine-guns and mortars, and all in full array.

But it was late in the day and, although the front of the 61st Division was fluid, the redoubts in the forward zone had fought stubbornly and had fought for so long that the German sweep forward had been seriously dislocated. It was true that the situation on the left of the 61st Division was shaky, but they had thrown back a defensive flank from south of Maissemy to Vermand. The encroachments into the battle zone were haphazard, and across the whole of the corps front it was largely intact. In places the Germans were even having the worst of it. Few of the guns had been overrun, and the bulk of the forward guns – now back in prepared positions – were still firing vigorously as evening approached, and out in front the infantry were giving as good as they got. Some even managed to counter-attack.

*Leutnant Hermann Wedekind, 11th Coy. Commander, 79th Infantry Rgt., 20th [German] Division*

Suddenly, there was heavy firing from machine-guns, and infantry came towards us from somewhere in front. Our artillery was laying down its shells far beyond and must have missed these hidden enemy nests. We threw ourselves to the ground. Everyone seemed paralysed, but soon we overcame the surprise. I screamed to my men, 'You must defend yourselves and shoot back, otherwise the English will pop you off like rabbits. Set sights, 600 metres!' I shook a comrade lying next to me and yelled, 'Shoot, man! You have to shoot!' But he made no effort. He was dead! Not far from me a machine-gun began to fire. I knelt up in order to better observe the direct hits on the ground, and within minutes my left shoulder was struck by a terrific blow. I had been hit by a bullet, and blood began to spurt from my sleeve. A man jumped up, ripped my coat open, and tried to bandage my shoulder with the strap of a bread-bag.

I managed to drag myself back to the nearest trench, which was now full of reserve troops. There I met the Regimental Commander, who wished me a fast and speedy recovery. Soon I had the good fortune to get emergency bandaging from a field doctor, and got a ride to the rear in a truck which had brought up trench-bridging materials.

Leutnant Wedekind was in considerable pain, and the jolting progress of the cart did not help to soothe him. But at least he was out of it with a 'good wound' – the *Heimschuss* which, like the British soldiers' 'Blighty', would guarantee a trip home to the Fatherland and a welcome period of convalescent leave. Even the loss of his equipment did not much concern him. Shortly before he was wounded he had polished off the last of the good red wine in his spare water-bottle, and it was some consolation to know that it had not gone to waste.

General Gough had moved his army headquarters to an advanced position at Nesle, roughly fifteen miles in a direct line from the nearest point of the front, although Gough suspected that the 'front' was now a good deal closer. All morning he had fought the impulse to go forward to his divisions and brigades to judge their situations for himself, but long years of discipline and experience had taught him to curb his inclinations. His job was to stay put, to keep his distance, and to take the overall view of his forty-mile front as reports came in. But the reports had been few and far between. The eleven divisions under his command were divided into four corps, and the news that filtered through from the hard-hit battalions in the confusion of the fighting line took a long time to travel back from battalions to brigades, from brigades to divisions and on to Corps Headquarters. By the time it was passed on from Corps HQ to the commander of the army, it inevitably described circumstances which had existed two hours earlier.

But Gough contained himself. He was a sensible man. Early that morning, when he had been wakened by the bombardment and received the unwelcome news that it was falling all along his front, he had issued a few orders and, knowing that for the present there was no more to be done, had then gone back to bed and slept soundly for another hour. Years of soldiering in India and campaigning in the Boer War had taught him the value of proper rest and proper food. If he neglected them, no man, from a private soldier to the commander of an army, could do his job efficiently — and so, at the end of an anxious morning, despite his reluctance to be parted from his telephone, the General and his staff officers had sat down to lunch. It was not a happy meal. Messengers came and went incessantly, the conversation was subdued, and General Humbert, whom Gough had courteously invited to join them, did not add to the conviviality of the occasion. General Humbert was embarrassed.

When he had arrived from French Headquarters a short while earlier, he had been greeted with open arms. Gough had personally rung French HQ to report the position on his front, and, remembering Pétain's promise to support him in case of need, he reasonably supposed that the French troops under Humbert's command were already moving to his assistance. The French general reluctantly disabused him. General Pétain, justifiably fearful for his own front, had put no troops at the disposal of the British. Gesturing towards the pennant that hung on the bonnet of his staff car, Humbert said despondently, 'All I have is my fanion.' It came as a severe shock. It meant that, for the moment at least, the Fifth Army was on its own. Two divisions in GHQ Reserve had already been ordered to proceed to the front, but they were a long way away and it was a moot point where the 'front' would be by the time they got there. Indeed, it was not at all clear where the front was now, or even if it was still intact.

Now that the fog had lifted, the Royal Flying Corps had taken to the air, and the first reports came in while the staff were at lunch. An officer who had hastily excused himself came back and whispered in Gough's ear. Masses of Germans had been seen moving forward, and for miles behind their line every road was teeming with troops. They were all making for the Fifth Army front, and they were coming in such numbers that there was no longer the slightest doubt that they meant to overwhelm it.

# Chapter 9

General Gough had already ordered his car and, shortly after General Humbert took his departure, he set off to visit his four Corps Headquarters. It would entail a round trip of more than sixty miles on narrow country roads which had never been meant for fast travel, and he would be away from his telephone for at least three hours, but it was a risk that he felt obliged to take. Before leaving, he took the precaution of telephoning each of his four Corps Commanders in turn to ascertain the present situation.

It was almost 3.30 before he breezed into III Corps Headquarters at Ugny-le-Gay, deliberately showing a cheerful front to General Butler and his staff. It was Butler's first engagement as a Corps Commander, and his line on the extreme right of the Fifth Army was seriously threatened. The enemy had penetrated across the River Oise on his 58th Division front. The Buffs at Vendeuil had actually seen a contingent of German soldiers marching north on the St Quentin road, passing between their outposts half-hidden in the mist. But, although much of the outpost line had now been lost, the 18th Division was still fighting on in its battle zone. The trouble was on their left, where the flank of the 14th Division had given way.

Gough did not allow himself to show dismay. He merely confirmed the order he had given earlier: that III Corps was to pull back, as previously arranged, to the line of the Crozat canal a little way behind. But he impressed on General Butler that it must be no haphazard retirement, and that the troops should keep in touch with the troops to right and to left. The afternoon was wearing on, and in two hours the light would start to fail and the fighting would surely abate; until then he was confident that III Corps would not give way. The 3rd Cavalry Division had already been ordered to move south to support them, and General Humbert had promised to do everything in his power to persuade General Pétain to keep his promise to send French troops to their assistance. Gough was sure that Pétain would do so. He left his Corps Commander feeling a good deal less anxious and a great deal more cheerful than he felt himself.

It was just fifteen miles from Ugny to XVIII Corps outside Ham, where General Maxse had set up his HQ near the canal. His battle zone was still unbreached, although he had taken heavy casualties in the outpost line and the flanks of the battalions on his right and on his left were 'in the air'. He was, nevertheless, absolutely certain that his troops could hold on – and they *were* holding on, even in the outpost zone at Manchester redoubt, at Enghien redoubt, at Holnon Wood and on Holnon plateau, where they had thrown back a flank to protect the battle zone from being entered from the north. But his force was seriously weakened. It was self-evident that Maxse would be forced to pull back his flanks to keep in touch with the troops on either side, but Gough made no bones about the fact that the longer Maxse could keep the Germans occupied on his front while the other corps retired, the better it would be. He was glad to be able to tell him that the 20th Division was on its way to help him.

At XIX Corps Headquarters, at Le Catelet, near Péronne, General Watts's situation was more serious. In principle his position between the valleys of the River Omignon and the River Cologne should have been more favourable, for it was billowing country of shallow valleys and low ridges well placed for defence. The distance between the two rivers was barely five and a half miles, and General Watts had two divisions to defend it. He also had a cavalry division in reserve. But the undulating ground from which, even in bad visibility, the Tommies might have repulsed a massed frontal attack was perfectly suited to an assault based on the Germans' new tactic of speedy infiltration, and the mist clinging to the shallow depressions behind the British positions on the ridges had masked the fast-moving parties of enemy soldiers as they filtered through. The news that they had entered Templeux-le-Guérard from the north reached General Watts shortly after noon. It came as an unwelcome surprise, for this village was well inside the battle zone and the British line was a full mile ahead of it, on higher ground on the edge of Hargicourt village.

Between the two villages, the long, low valley where the River Cologne ran its leisurely course was pitted and scarred by a number of shallow quarries, many of them long and straggling where veins of chalk had been gouged haphazardly from the soil. The British Army, and in particular the Royal Engineers, had every reason to bless the local quarrymen who had unknowingly constructed such a splendid line of defence in the years before the war, for the use of an army which was not then in existence, in a war which had not yet begun. It had been a simple matter to link up the indentations and to convert this rough ground with its ready-made parapets and dugouts into a powerful redoubt, and indeed the main line of the battle zone had been sited round Hargicourt for this very reason. No one had conceived that the enemy would simply walk round it.[1]

When General Gough arrived at XIX Corps Headquarters the Corps Commander was obliged to inform him that his outpost line had gone, that his battle zone had been penetrated on his left flank, and also that, with the loss of Maissemy, his right flank too had been turned. So far as he could ascertain, his troops were fighting back, and they were fighting hard, but it was as clear to General Gough as it was to Watts himself that two weak divisions and some dismounted cavalry could not hold the Germans back indefinitely. Both men fully understood the seriousness of the position, and Gough did not feel obliged to adopt the same breezily cheerful attitude with which he had encouraged General Butler. He laid his cards on the table. He had earmarked the 50th Division to assist XIX Corps in case of need, but it was still at Guillaucourt, roughly twenty-five miles distant on the road to Amiens, and with the best will in the world it could not possibly reach the battlefront until morning. Neither man expressed the thought that, after a sleepless night culminating in a ten-mile march from the railhead, the men would hardly be at the peak of their performance when they did arrive. Still, the essence of the confused reports that reached Watts's headquarters from the battlefield was that the centre of his front was holding, and Gough was able to cheer him with the reassuring news that XVIII Corps had formed a line south of Maissemy to cover his open right flank. He urged him to hold on to his existing front as long as possible, and to bend back his shaky left to join hands with VII Corps to the north.

General Gough did not have to impress on his Corps Commander the importance of 'keeping in touch'. Even if the whole Fifth Army was obliged to fall back (and already he privately feared that it must), all would not be lost so long as the line remained intact as it retired. Now that the mist had dissipated, the advantage of well-sited positions had reverted to the defenders and, from the information he had – sparse though it was – General Watts was persuaded that his troops could keep the enemy at bay, at least until the arrival of the 50th Division.

As the crow flies, only four and a half miles separated Le Catelet from General Congreve's VII Corps Headquarters at Templeux-la-Fosse, but the

---

1. The troops in the quarries comprised two companies plus the headquarters staff of the 2/7th Lancashire Fusiliers, and two companies of pioneers of the 5th Border Regiment. Although they were attacked from both sides as well as from the rear, they held out until five o'clock in the afternoon, when they were forced to surrender. While the fighting was going on for Templeux-le-Guérard, a runner had been sent ordering them to retire, but he had not managed to reach them. Only a few men succeeded in breaking out when they were surrounded.

roads that meandered across country were little more than lanes, and Gough's car was forced to travel almost twice as far, along the main road through Péronne. When he eventually hurried into Congreve's office he was rewarded with better news. It would not be true to say that the General was in high spirits, but he was reasonably satisfied with his position. He was also vastly relieved, because, as he confessed to the Army Commander, only a few hours ago he had feared that his line had given way on the 16th (Irish) Division front. But the Irishmen had fought so doggedly and counter-attacked so brilliantly that assault after assault had been thrown back. It was true that his extreme right had been broken near the Cologne valley, where the flank of his neighbour General Watts had given way, but he had three divisions in the line and the 39th Division had been close by in reserve. Already, on his own initiative, he had ordered it up to fill the gap and to link up with the remnants of Watts's XIX Corps on its right. Congreve was quietly confident that he could hold on, and Gough knew his old friend well enough to believe it. 'Well done, Walter,' he said. There was no need to say more. Time was pressing. It was now more than two hours since he had left General Butler's headquarters at the southern limit of his army, and matters might have altered radically since then. A fresh batch of reports would be waiting at Army Headquarters. He half dreaded the news they might contain, but he took comfort in the fact that here, on the extreme left flank of the Fifth Army, VII Corps was standing fast.

The 9th (Scottish) Division stood at the important juncture of the front where the left of the Fifth Army met the right of the Third, which continued the line to the north, and it was a position that was both vulnerable and dangerous. The boundary between the armies lay just north of Gouzeaucourt, and the outpost line east of that village dipped across the fields in front of the German-occupied villages of Gonnelieu and Villers-Guislain. The Scots had been in and out of this sector since February, and one sergeant whose task it was to allocate sentries to posts in the forward line never tired of a well-worn jibe addressed to the man on the extreme left. 'There you are. Now if General Gough gives the order "The Fifth Army will right wheel", *you'll* be marking time for the rest of your life.' The unfortunate Jock, realizing that he was the last man on the Fifth Army front, did not always appreciate this pleasantry.

It was an axiom of military doctrine that the junction of two armies was the weakest point of a defensive line, and a wily enemy would attack it if he could. This particular junction was more vulnerable than most, because it adjoined the Flesquières salient, which had been thrust deep into enemy territory in the Battle of Cambrai. Three divisions of the Third Army straggled round its rim, and, since it was the only ground which

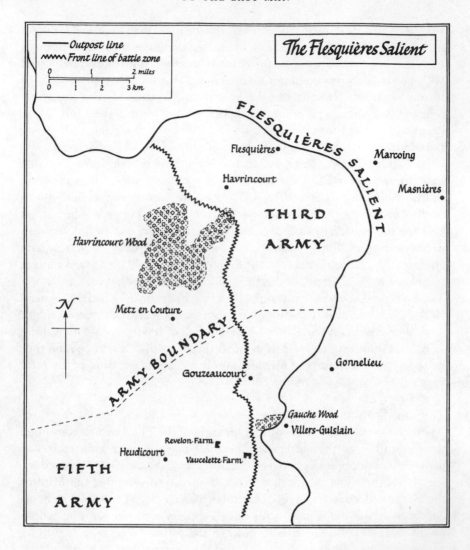

the Germans had not later won back, it was almost a point of honour to
retain it.

It was not the enemy's intention to mount a full-scale assault on the
Flesquières salient, although the men who were holding it might have been
forgiven for supposing otherwise. The bombardment had fallen on them
just as heavily as it had on their right and their left, they had been soaked
with mustard gas, and throughout the day their thinning ranks had thrown
back a succession of violent attacks which had given every appearance of
being the real thing. But they were not. They were a feint. It was the

Germans' intention to exhaust the British troops, to incapacitate them by means of gas and high explosive, and to pin the Tommies down until their own troops south and north of the salient had pushed westward. Then, converging on Havrincourt, they would pinch the salient out. But south of Gouzeaucourt, where the 9th (Scottish) Division stood at the hinge of the salient, the attack was intended to succeed, to punch a hole in the British defences, to swarm through it – and to keep on going.

At Gouzeaucourt on the extreme left of the 9th (Scottish) Division a company of the Highland Brigade was standing-to under the noses of the enemy in a line of scattered posts in front of Gonnelieu barely 500 yards distant on the slope ahead. A nervous sentry, acutely conscious that only a few hundred yards, a single sandbagged parapet and a narrow strip of barbed wire lay between him and the Kaiser's Army, did not much relish being at the razor's edge if the Kaiser were to launch an assault. But the Germans did not assault at Gouzeaucourt itself, and it was doubtful if they had ever intended to. More than once during the course of the morning, parties of enemy soldiers were seen approaching across the fields from Gonnelieu, but their progress was half-hearted, and the British guns had responded so speedily and fired so accurately that the Germans had soon turned tail. The posts remained intact.

The full ferocity of the attack fell on their neighbours, a stone's throw away on their right, where the outpost line ran down the hill along the forward edge of Gauche Wood. It was manned by B Company of the 1st South African Infantry, and Captain Garnet Green was in command.[1]

In May 1916 the South Africans had been sent to replace the 28th Brigade in the 9th (Scottish) Division. Most of them were not displeased, and some of them were positively delighted, for, although it was officially the 4th South African Infantry, one of the regiments which made up the Brigade was known more familiarly as 'the South African Scottish'. They wore kilts of Atholl tartan, had a full-blown pipe band, and were referred to affectionately by the other battalions of the Brigade as 'Our Jocks'. Their presence had mollified their new comrades, and somewhat reconciled them to the loss of the battalions of native Scots. Any lingering resentment had long ago been dispelled, for the South Africans had proved themselves to be 'bonnie fechters', and the homely vernacular compliment, never lightly bestowed, was no mean tribute to their prowess in the arts of war. In the

1. In March 1918 the 9th (Scottish) Division comprised: 26 Brigade (8th Black Watch, 7th Seaforth Highlanders, 5th Cameron Highlanders); 27 Brigade (11th Royal Scots, 12th Royal Scots, 6th King's Own Scottish Borderers) and South African Brigade (1st South African Infantry, 2nd South African Infantry, 4th South African Infantry, which was the South African Scottish).

eyes of the Division, no matter what their individual territorial allegiances might be (and they ranged from Natal via the Transvaal to the Cape), all the South Africans were accepted as honorary Scots, and some of the Lowlanders even assumed that the few Afrikaans-speaking soldiers in the South African Brigade were speaking Gaelic.

Like the Australians, every man in the South African contingent was a volunteer, and their sharpness of eye and their skill with a rifle – perfected in pursuit of small game on the farms and veldts of their native land – were legendary. Nor had they arrived as raw recruits, for the South African Brigade had come to the 9th Division straight from Egypt, and there, fighting in difficult desert terrain as part of a mixed force, they had put the Turks to flight at Agagia and occupied Barrani and Sollum. Some, like Captain Garnet Green, had fought in South-West Africa in the first year of the war.

Green had served as a hard-riding, sharp-shooting trooper of the 1st Royal Natal Carbineers, and he could out-ride and out-shoot any man in a brigade in which these skills were ten a penny. He liked to be where the action was, and when the South-West African campaign ended with the surrender of the Germans in July 1915 he had transferred to the South African force then preparing to leave for the war in Europe. One year later, and almost to the day, as a newly commissioned second lieutenant, Green led his men into Delville Wood in the Battle of the Somme. He was one of only two officers and 140 men who came out again.[1] If any in the 9th Division had regarded the South Africans as cuckoos in the nest, they had changed their minds after Delville Wood.[2] Now Green and his Springboks were to face the German onslaught at yet another wood. There were all too few of them to defend it.

The line ran round its southern perimeter, facing the German line in front of Villers-Guislain. It was not much of a line, for there were only two posts just inside the wood, with another redoubt on the open ground near the south-western corner. The Springboks had two trench mortars and two

1. Garnet Green was awarded the Military Cross. A year later, at Passchendaele, he added a bar to this decoration and was promoted to the rank of captain.

2. The South African National Memorial has in recent years been placed at Delville Wood. It is the right and proper place for it, but it is only fair to say that the gallantry and suffering of the entire 9th Division at Delville Wood deserves acknowledgement, although it is natural that the performance of the small but valiant South African force has tended to overshadow that of their comrades. By comparison with the mass of the Allied forces, there were so few South Africans on the Western Front and their losses were so disproportionately heavy that Delville Wood grew to be the symbol of the South African sacrifice, and the battle – then as now – has been adopted as their own, in much the same way, and largely for the same reason, as the Australians have 'adopted' Gallipoli.

machine-guns positioned to cover both arms of a part-sunken Y-shaped track that ran up the hill from Villers-Guislain, just a five-minute walk away for the woodcutters and occasional courting couples who had once used it. Paul Maze had sketched the position the day before from a vantage point south of the wood near Vaucelette Farm.

Although he was a Frenchman born and bred, Paul Maze had been part of the British Army since the first contingent of the Expeditionary Force had landed in his home town of Le Havre in August 1914. The French military authorities had declared him unfit for military service, but, armed with nothing more than a letter of introduction from the British consul at Le Havre, a gift for languages and a determination somehow to get into the war, he had sought out the colonel of the Royal Scots Greys and, in impeccable English, offered his services to the Regiment. It was all quite irregular, but the times were chaotic and the colonel, newly arrived, was struggling to arrange a thousand essential matters through official interpreters whose command of English was far inferior to that of Maze. So, with the encouragement of the colonel's second-in-command, on whose plate most of the problems had landed, and the help of a friendly sergeant-major, who managed to produce various items of khaki kit which gave him some semblance of military appearance, Maze was co-opted into the regiment and set off for the war.

He had stuck with the Scots Greys through the retreat from Mons to the Marne, covering possibly twice the distance of any other man in the Regiment, sometimes on horseback, frequently by bicycle, carrying messages, liaising with scattered bodies of French troops, occasionally becoming hopelessly lost, and on one occasion narrowly escaping being shot as a spy. His services during the retreat had been invaluable. They soon became indispensable. Shortly after the Battle of the Marne, now respectably attired as a soldier of the French Army, he was officially attached to the staff of General Gough. Gough was then Commander of the First Corps, and when he was later appointed to the command of the Fifth Army Maze had remained on his staff.

In a sense, Maze was Gough's window on the war, for Maze was an artist, and his meticulous drawings of the terrain, sketched in detail on the ground, were often of infinitely more use to the General than the flattened images photographed from aircraft a thousand feet above it. Furthermore, Maze could travel where the Army Commander could not, and he spent more time in the forefront of the line than at Fifth Army Headquarters. The officers of the official French liaison staff barely concealed their irritation at the presence of this upstart who so clearly enjoyed the confidence of the Army Commander, but Gough did not give a hoot. In his view Maze was worth a dozen mere interpreters, and he valued him not just for his artistic skill but for his artist's eye. Maze was an acute observer, and the reports he brought back of what he had seen and heard, the information he gleaned on his travels, were of considerable importance. Maze had a roving commission, and Gough personally saw to it that he had the entrée to every corps and divisional headquarters on his front and in his army.

Travelling fast on a powerful motorcycle, Maze could negotiate congested roads and reach the front even at the height of battle. No one questioned his right to go where he liked, and his laissez-passer bore not only the official stamp of every corps and divisional headquarters in the Fifth Army, but the signatures of its highest-ranking officers. Although officially he held the honorary rank of sergeant, not the least of this paragon's attributes were his charm and ease of manner, which made him just as welcome in a mess presided over by a brigadier as it did in a front-line post in the charge of a corporal. The General was equally interested in Maze's impression of both, particularly on the matter of morale.

Sometimes, as he sketched the tortured landscape of his native France, Paul Maze's impressions were more personal and more painful. Looking across the ruins of St Quentin, remembering the pastels of Maurice de Latour which had hung in the museum, he was saddened to think that they too might be lying among the wreckage and the debris of the town. He had felt much the same sadness on the slopes of Chapel Hill on the eve of the German push. In the battle zone across the ravaged farmland, he could see the skeletal roofs of ruined Gouzeaucourt and the trench that straggled down to protect the flank of the 9th Division. Off to his right all was quiet at Gauche Wood. It was late in the afternoon and, being careful not to expose himself to the eyes of the enemy, Maze made his way down to the post they still called Vaucelette Farm. Any resemblance to a farm had vanished long ago, but he found the battalion headquarters of the Northumberland Fusiliers in a deep dugout nearby and stopped there to beg a cup of tea. He found almost a party-like atmosphere, for there was a wind-up gramophone and a selection of popular records, the officers were youthful, and their unspoken attitude seemed to be that, since there was nothing to do but wait, they might as well be cheerful while they could. It might have been a sixth-form beanfeast. No one mentioned the coming attack.

Maze produced his sketchpad and, by the light of a hurricane lamp, made lightning sketches of the young officers round the table. The Colonel was an older man, and Maze could sense the anxiety beneath his carefree manner. A little later, when dusk fell and it was safe for Maze to retrace his steps to the place where he had left his motorcycle, the Colonel went up the long stairway to the dugout entrance, shining his torch to light the way. Outside it was eerily quiet, with a hint of the mist that would shortly begin to gather. Across the valley to the north Gauche Wood was a barely discernible smudge on the hillside, but, although the land was sinking into the dark, Maze could see it clearly in his mind's eye, for he had sketched every cleft and gully. Now that they were alone, Colonel Howlett spoke of the attack. It might be tonight, he thought, or might be tomorrow, but whenever it came they would be ready. He seemed to have something else on his mind and, as Maze shook hands and wished him luck, he said hesitantly, as if by an afterthought, 'You know that sketch you did of me just now in the dugout? I wonder if you would send it to my sister?' Turning his back on the line to mask his flashlight, he scribbled the address on a piece of paper. As he tucked it carefully into his top pocket, Maze wondered if Howlett had had some kind of premonition.[1]

When the assault was launched on the 9th Division front, the full force of the attack fell on Gauche Wood. The storm troops swarmed towards the hill, and a heavy smokescreen mingling with the mist as they approached hid them from even the most vigilant of lookouts. They came with rifles slung and stick bombs at the ready; they came for once in silence; and they seemed to come from everywhere, flinging themselves en masse at the eastern fringe of Gauche Wood, plunging along its southern edge towards Garnet Green's redoubt.

Machine-guns firing blindly into the mist traversed the front by instinct and by guesswork, but the enemy soldiers were upon them, and even behind them, almost before they knew it. Filtering along the very dips and gullies Paul Maze had so assiduously plotted in his sketches, they had slipped between the outposts to take them from the rear. Two of the posts were overwhelmed straight away. Leaving the moppers-up to deal with the remnants, flinging bombs, and fighting hand to hand, the German soldiers began to carve a path through the wood. Second Lieutenant Meller Beviss had barely half his platoon left, but they fought like furies, and yard by yard they battled their way through the wood to the open ground behind. And when the Germans halted among the battered trees to gather their scattered force, they began to dig, and they dug like men possessed. It was only a brief respite, but it was long enough to establish a feeble line only fifty yards from the edge of the wood. Glancing to his right, Beviss could see that Green's redoubt had gone and that Green and the survivors of his command were fighting their way back to join them.

By the time they got there the enemy was preparing to assault, and there were fewer than fifty men with rifles plus a single Lewis-gun to meet

1. Lieutenant-Colonel Reginald Howlett, DSO, MC and Bar, did survive the war and continued to serve as a Regular Army officer until his retirement as a brigadier in 1939.

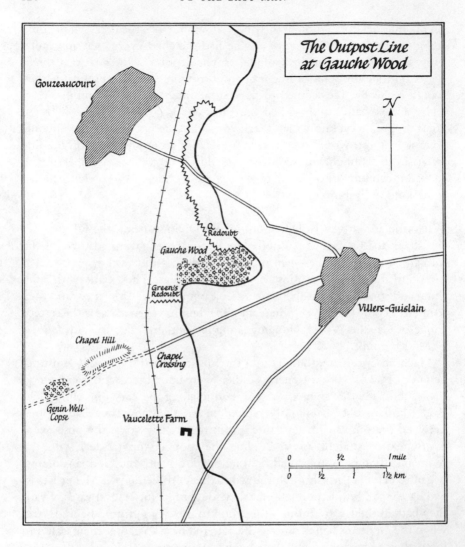

them when they came charging from the wood. The Germans charged in
full-throated cry and they flung themselves forward in long lines, three deep.
And they charged with infinite courage, without the support of artillery or
machine-guns. The distance was so small, the outcome seemed so sure. But
they were at point-blank range, and now that the smoke had dispersed and
the fog was lifting, now that, at long last, there was a visible target, the
dazzling marksmanship of the South Africans came into its own. It stopped
the Germans in their tracks. The assault ground to a halt, and, when the
lines wavered and the enemy soldiers tried to dig in on the edge of the

wood, the bullets spitting from the Springbok rifles caused such mayhem that they soon retired into the wood for shelter. It was eleven o'clock in the morning, and the fight for Gauche Wood had gone on for more than two hours. For half an hour longer the Springboks kept the Germans at bay and then, to their exquisite relief, the guns, which had been firing on the SOS line in No Man's Land on the far side of Gauche Wood, shortened range and began to pound the wood itself. Some desperate runner had got through with the message that Gauche Wood had been lost – and he had made it not a moment too soon.

At 9th Division Headquarters disturbing messages had been coming in all morning, and General Tudor was in a quandary. No attack had yet developed on the front held by the Highland Brigade at Gouzeaucourt and, thanks to the stand of the South Africans in the outpost line, the front line of his battle zone was safe. The flank, however, was not. News of the 21st Division on his right was confused and contradictory, but by midday it seemed certain that the strongpoint at Vaucelette Farm had gone. The trenches behind it were still holding out, but a visual report from a divisional observer suggested that the 21st Division had withdrawn its troops from Chapel Hill. That was a serious matter. It was also a matter of some annoyance to the Divisional Commander. This area had previously been within the sector of the 9th Division, but ten days ago, when his troops had returned to the line after a much-needed rest, General Tudor found to his consternation that these vital positions had passed out of his control and been reallocated to the neighbouring division. His Brigade Commanders were equally dismayed, for Chapel Hill, lying immediately south of their battle zone, was the bastion on which they had depended to protect the Division's right flank.

It was not much of a bastion, and not much of a hill – it was a long, low knoll, a mere streak on the landscape south of Revelon Farm. But now that it had been lost General Tudor hardly needed to inform his Brigadiers that steps must immediately be taken to recapture it. The 1st South African Regiment holding the battle zone was to swing round to face south and to stand fast along the divisional boundary. The Jocks of the South African Scottish would advance to retake Chapel Hill, while the 'details' who had been left behind near Heudicourt, and the Jocks of the Lowland Brigade in reserve, were ordered forward to the third line of the battle zone to support them.

The Lowland Brigade, clustered round the village of Heudicourt, had been on the point of moving forward to relieve the South Africans in the front line, and all that could be found for A Company of the 11th Royal Scots by way of billets were some tattered camouflaged tents among the ruins. Until the bombardment started, and despite the cold, the damp and the discomfort, Alex Jamieson had considered that he was in luck. Their tents were near the gun-line, and in a dugout in the ruins close by he had had the good fortune to find an artillery canteen whose existence was known only to the gunners. What was more, Alex had money in his pocket, the canteen had just received a small supply of chocolate, and although, strictly speaking, the canteen had been set up for the benefit of the gun-crews, the corporal in charge magnanimously allowed him to buy some, if only a single bar. To a sweet-toothed boy of eighteen it was manna from heaven, and Alex set off to find a quiet corner where he could enjoy his booty. As he was about to pocket his change, it struck him that he had been given too much.

*42821 Private Alex Jamieson, MM, 11th Bn., The Royal Scots (Lothian Regt.), 9th (Scottish) Division*

I went back into the canteen and said to the fellow at the counter, 'You've given me too much change.' He looked at me as if I should have been in the Salvation Army instead of the British Army! He said, 'My God, Jock, you're an honest man!' And he gave me *another* bar of chocolate and wouldn't take the money for it, so I was well pleased, because he was only allowing one bar per man, so it had paid me to be honest. If I'd kept the extra money (it was only a few centimes) I wouldn't have been so well off, because I got *two* bars for the price of one. But it didn't enter my head to keep it. It's not that I was a goody-goody or anything like that: I just knew that it wasn't the right way of doing things.

It took more than a few months in the Army and four weeks at the front to bend the principles of a Glasgow Boy Scout.

The canteen had long ago shut up shop, and its stock had almost certainly been blown out of existence by the bombardment that had reduced the ruins of Heudicourt to rubble. When the shells began to fall, Jamieson's company was led into a small valley to shelter in the lee of an embankment. As the day wore on and the situation worsened, they moved forward into the Heudicourt valley.

*Private Alex Jamieson, MM*

We were right out on the open, and we were told to lie down on some slightly raised ground and to make some sort of protection by digging in with our entrenching tools. Well, an entrenching tool is a completely useless piece of equipment unless it was meant to protect the base of your spine when it was hanging from your belt, but it only added to the weight we had to carry when we were on the move. The small pile of earth I managed to throw up was absolutely laughable!

While we were there some men of the Lincolns of the 21st Division started coming back through us – not in great numbers, just in ones or twos, because the 21st had had a very bad time in the front line and they were getting out of it as quickly as they could, but they were stopped by our officers and told to join us. They weren't reluctant, they were quite happy to stay, but it was just that they hadn't known what to do. So we lay there for a bit, and after a while we had to move forward across a sunken road and some distance ahead there was another ridge, and we hadn't been there long when we saw the Germans coming over it. They were absolutely pouring over it, just like a crowd coming out of a football match. They were packed together coming over this ridge, and we were ordered to open fire. They must have been near enough half a mile away. I know I had my sights at the highest they would go, they were so far away. But these bullets must have been landing in amongst them even at that distance, and they just melted away! It was the first time I'd fired a rifle in anger, so to speak.

We started advancing towards that ridge and we had to cross a sunken road, and as we ran forward to occupy a rise a German machine-gun opened up and Bill Relph, who was just on my right, was hit and he fell down. Naturally I stopped to help him, but the corporal bawled at me to leave him alone and carry on. Well, it's instinct to help a pal, isn't it? But I just had to carry on. Poor old Relph wasn't more than two or three feet away from me, but I had to leave him there. When we got up on to the ridge the corporal dropped down beside me and he told me that Relph had gone west.

They were clinging to the fringe of Chapel Hill, but even with the help of part of the 2nd South African Infantry, which had swivelled round to stand along the flank between them and Gauche Wood, they could get no further. It was the South African Scottish who managed it. They were only a company strong, but there was no stopping them. They swept through the line and on to the knoll, chased the Germans from the crest, and dashed on to clear them from the captured trenches on the further slope. And there they stayed, stretching hands to join up with the ragged line on their right. By seven o'clock, to the vast relief of General Tudor, and despite the perilous gap in the line beyond it, the flank of the 9th Division had been made safe.

Later, when darkness fell, and the last of the reserves moved forward, the weary boys of Jamieson's battalion were moved back for the night to rest in whatever shelter they could find in the redoubt at Revelon Farm. Towards midnight, when enemy patrols crept cautiously out of Gauche Wood there was no one to oppose them. The Springboks had fought to the last, and the bodies of the dead lay slowly stiffening where they had fallen. Garnet Green was there. Second Lieutenant Meller Beviss and a mere handful of survivors had managed to crawl back.[1]

But the battle zone had not been breached, the Germans had been kept at bay, and at the end of the long day's struggle only the outpost line at Gauche Wood had passed into the hands of the enemy. The 9th Division had fought hard to hold their ground, and the weary remnants knew that they had done well.

1.  Beviss escaped only to be killed three days later at Marrières Wood. His body was not recovered, nor was Garnet Green's. Both are commemorated on the South African panels (96 and 97) of the Memorial to the Missing in Pozières Cemetery on the Somme.

# Chapter 10

Any fresh news from the Fifth Army front merely confirmed the overall view as Gough had surmised it in his hasty visits to the Corps Commanders and, since he still expected assistance from the French Army on his right, for the moment he was not particularly downcast. But, shortly after his return to his headquarters at Nesle, information arrived from the adjacent sector which put his own situation in a different light. The enemy had simultaneously attacked the Third Army.

It was more than twelve hours since the opening of the massive bombardment, and it had thundered across many miles, from Barisis in the south, where the British joined hands with the French, to the Arras sector to the north of it, and on across Artois to Armentières in Flanders. Altogether it was a distance of 103 miles – more than four-fifths of the entire British line. It was a powerful demonstration which was intended to keep the British guessing and, if possible, to keep them from sending reserve troops to assist in repelling the main German assault.

The reserves at the disposal of the British Army as a whole were paltry. There were only eight divisions in General Reserve to cover the whole length of the front, together with a very few local reserves to assist the individual armies. In the two months before the German assault many thousands of labourers had been employed in constructing railways which would enable the reserves to be speedily transported to any threatened front (although General Gough would have gladly employed them in strengthening the weak defences of his own front): not knowing the precise intentions of the Germans, seen from the rarefied heights of GHQ this had seemed to be the only possible course of action. But, as night fell on 21 March, the Germans' intentions were still obscure.

No attack had so far developed on the sectors of the First and Second Armies. The main force of the attack appeared to have been directed at Gough's Fifth Army (the least able to withstand it), but the simultaneous blow which had fallen on the Third Army front caused equal anxiety, and not least the situation on the Flesquières salient at the hinge of both. It was true that all the enemy's attacks had been repelled, but the casualties in the salient had been heavy. Across its entire depth it had been soaked with mustard gas, large numbers of men had died or been evacuated, and in some places even those who were still in the line were sick, vomiting, weakened by the deadly effects of the gas.

The decision to hold the Flesquières salient had been made in the belief that it would constitute a useful 'false front' from which withdrawal would not only be easy, but also considerably shorten the line. The perimeter of the snout of land that thrust into enemy territory covered twenty-one straggling miles and was thinly garrisoned, but it measured little more than seven miles across the straight base. Although it was not yet clear that the enemy's thrusts had amounted only to raids in force, and it would be premature to consider withdrawal from this hard-won territory, by the end of the day his tactics could be fairly deduced. By advancing on either side of it, it seemed that the Germans intended to make the salient untenable, to close in by a pincer movement and to pinch it out. The plan had not entirely succeeded. The Fifth Army's 9th Division on the southern hinge of the salient had stood fast, but north of it, where General Otto von Below's Seventeenth Army hit hard across seven miles in the centre of the Third Army front, the Germans had broken through.

They broke through far and fast, with little warning. For many troops even in the battle zone the first indication of the enemy assault was the sight of enemy soldiers bearing down on them out of the mist. The front line had been so taken by surprise and so speedily overwhelmed that there had been no time for any warning, any signal or any runner to reach them. On the 51st Division front the line was ruptured in the centre along a misty valley that ran through the front line to Louverval on the long straight road that ran from Cambrai to Bapaume through the centre of the front. Just south of the road, near the village of Beaumetz, Second Lieutenant Dick Gammell was in charge of the 153rd Brigade Signals centre. He was extremely proud of it, for he had set it up himself.

*Second Lieutenant Dick Gammell, 1/7th Bn., The Black Watch (Royal Highlanders), 51st Division*

I had to try and be sure that I could maintain communication from Brigade Headquarters, with battalions, the front line, the support line and the reserve line, and I established a headquarters dugout called Q404, which was really a little telephone exchange. We made our exchanges by the use of a bullet and cartridge case. You have a jack and a plug, and the jack is the thing with a hole in it and the plug is the thing you put into the hole. Well, the jack was the cartridge, and the plug was a 303 rifle bullet.

I had a devil of a time trying to establish this report centre. A signalling officer had five methods of trying to maintain communication with his battalions. The simplest was a landline – what was known as a D2 cable – and that was easy to lay along the bottom of a trench. Then you had an instrument, like a telephone. There was a very handy little trench telephone called a D3, about the size of a big ·box of chocolates, and that had a buzzer and also a microphone. But we weren't supposed to use it, because the Boche could pick it up. Then we had a thing called a Fullerphone, and we were allowed to use that a bit, because the Boche was not supposed to be able to pick it up. And then there was lamp signalling and just flag-wagging. But of course the most reliable of all was the runner – the human chap. I had about twenty runners, recruited from the battalions, and actually I had a couple of VCs, who were quite fearless – McDonald was a Gordon; I think McBeath was a Black Watch. I remember McDonald particularly. If I sent him on a message from A to B, he just cocked his tin hat on one side and walked out. He didn't seem to care a damn if there were bullets.

So I'm in my dugout at about five o'clock in the morning, and I wake up and I hear Major Adam, our Brigade-Major, talking to Division with the morning report: 'Yes, everything quiet.' The next thing I hear is a lot of shells falling in the sunken road, and before very long I hear Major Adam saying, 'Gas! Gas! Pass the whisky.' This was *his* antidote to gas. So we dropped the gas-curtain down the entrances to the dugouts, which were stairways, because we were twenty feet or more below ground.

My servant, Thomson, eventually found his way down into the dugout, and he said, 'I'm very sorry, Sir, I canna reach your britches, because there's too much gas about.' I said to Thomson, 'Well, I think I could fight a battle just as well in my slacks as I can in my breeches!' I never saw my breeches again!

It was really very unpleasant, because we didn't know what was happening to the south of us. Between us and the road there was a bit of a valley, and it was a misty morning and we couldn't see, and the line broke, just as it so happened, under this bit of a valley. The Boche had got through our front line and had come down this little valley in the mist unseen, and he very nearly got us from the side.

Gammell's report centre had been some two and a half miles behind the outpost front and a mile and a quarter from the forward edge of the battle zone. Now, like Brigade Headquarters near Beaumetz, the fighting was only a very short distance ahead and there were ominous signs that it was drawing closer still. By half past eleven the Germans had a firm foothold in the ruins of Doignies, not much more than a mile from Brigade Headquarters, and the position was becoming critical.

The guns of C293 Battery were covering Doignies – or at least some of them were, for their two forward guns had been lost and the crews of the others, firing from the grassy slopes between Doignies and Beaumetz, were well within range of the enemy's machine-guns. Already there had been casualties, the gunners of the abandoned weapons were fighting with the infantry in the village, and, in the absence of the Battery's commander, Lieutenant Mackie, who was in temporary charge, was having a hard time.

Major Ronald Ward had been in England for a month, attending a senior officers' gunnery course. As the weeks went by, returning from the range at the end of the day to the mess, where the talk was electric with anticipation of the coming battle, he was not the only officer on the course who chafed to get back to his command. He had been thankful to pack up, thankful to board the boat for Boulogne, and, at the end of a snail-like train journey that took twelve wearisome hours, he was more than content to bed down at the Battery wagon line at Favreuil in a far less salubrious billet than his quarters at Salisbury Plain. It was almost midnight on 20 March, and when the crash of the mighty bombardment roused him four hours later he had no doubt that it was the opening salvo of the battle. He heard himself speaking aloud his first conscious thought: 'Thank God I haven't missed it!'

For the two years he had commanded C Battery, and for every waking hour Major Ward had devoted every ounce of his energy to it. He had trained its gunners and drivers to such a level of skill and efficiency that, in his belief, it was superior to any other in France, and he was intensely proud of it. To have been away from C Battery at this particular moment would have been a bitter blow.

In a straight line drawn across the map, the battery's wagon line at Favreuil was a good six miles from the headquarters of Ward's Artillery Brigade at Beaumetz, and since it was not directly behind the guns of 293 Brigade, the distance was even longer by road. It had always been an inconvenient situation. Now, in the confusion of conflicting reports from the fighting line, it had become downright awkward. As the front line ran, Favreuil was only half as far from the twin villages of Vaulx and Vraucourt and, in the clamour of confusion as the hours went by and the enemy progressed, it seemed to Ward, on tenterhooks at the wagon line, that it was there to his immediate left that the battle was raging. Although his first instinct had been to ride hell for leather to his guns, he had reluctantly decided that he ought to remain at Favreuil.

*Major Ronald Ward, C 293 Bty., Royal Field Artillery*

It seemed to me that the battle was chiefly on our left front, since from that direction the roar was intense, while on the right front, where the 293rd Brigade was in action, things seemed fairly quiet. (In actual fact the enemy did not assault the 51st Division at dawn, except on its left, and my officers afterwards told me that they received no SOS from the part of the Divisional front the battery was covering.) Early in the morning a cyclist messenger came down the road from Vaulx–Vraucourt and he told me that the enemy was already in the village. As a matter of fact Vaulx was not taken by the Boche until the following day, but the news was disturbing – especially as it appeared to agree with the noise of the battle. So it seemed to me that the Brigade wagon line, with its many vehicles and its rations and forage, might soon be cut off from the Brigade itself. If the Boche had broken through to the wagon line – an event which seemed to be imminent! – then the rapid moving of all the horses, the vehicles and the stores of the four batteries, not to mention the Brigade ammunition column, first to the right and then forward to withdraw the guns, would have been no easy operation. It would have taxed all the energies of the few officers who would have been available to carry it out. So I sent a message to Colonel Main at our Brigade Headquarters to say that I was fully prepared, if necessary, to move the wagon lines to a position directly behind the gun positions, and we set about preparing to do this. But soon after noon a message reached me from Colonel Main telling me to go up to C Battery – and I was glad to get it!

I mounted at once on my horse, Prince, taking my trumpeter, Cleater, on his pony as horse-holder, and we set off over open country towards Frémicourt. The main Bapaume–Cambrai road passes through this village, and 51st Division's headquarters were there, so it was being heavily shelled, so we passed between it and Beugny and went on eastwards. I noticed that the fire was chiefly on crossroads and other points which could easily be avoided by two mounted men. During the ride I took note of possible routes for the guns, for the roads through the villages were obviously marked down by the enemy and were so damaged by heavy shells that it would be folly to try to lead a battery through them. The village of Lebucquière was being very heavily 'bumped', but we passed south of it to Vélu, a small village with a chateau standing in a large wood, and the shelling made this a particularly unpleasant place to pass through.

About 200 yards to the left front of the village three roads meet at a level crossing, and this point was an enemy target. I halted and

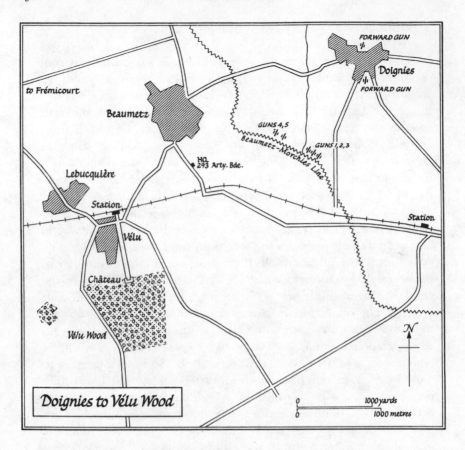

*Doignies to Vélu Wood*

watched this place. After a few minutes it was clear that the Boche was firing salvoes at the crossroads about every three minutes. I told Cleater my plan, which was to stop at the entrance to the village, wait there until a group of shells had fallen, then gallop along the street for 500 yards, swing round a corner to the right, and gallop on into the open fields beyond. We waited for the next fall of shells. Immediately they had fallen I said, 'Now then, Cleater, gallop!' And away we went.

Well, we covered the 500 yards, swung round the corner to the right – and the next instance Prince was up to his girth in coils of telephone wires which the shelling had brought down on to the road. Now Prince was a horse who would shy at anything. Once in England he climbed a steep embankment to avoid a baby in a perambulator! But he was really full of wisdom, and he showed it this time. Cleater dismounted and carefully lifted each one of Prince's legs and cleared it from the wire and, although this took several minutes, Prince stood quite still all the time, even when the next salvo of shells dropped very close to us and the splinters flew right by us. As soon as he was clear we galloped on again, extremely thankful, because it was a nasty corner and it was, to say the least, an exciting ride!

Although the open land beyond was far back from the original front, it was honeycombed with reserve-line trenches. Cleater turned back, leading the Major's horse, and Ward crossed the last difficult mile on foot. His battery had not let him down. The guns had kept firing until the breeches had jammed; only one of them was still in action, but the gunners were fighting on, firing Lewis-guns and rifles with the infantry. They were firing from trenches some way behind the guns, there was nothing in front of them, and the guns themselves, now completely exposed, might at any moment be overrun by the enemy.

*Major Ronald Ward*

Presently the only remaining gun, which had been shooting at the Boche infantry advancing west from Louverval, began to fire with open sights at a Boche battery of three guns advancing along the high ground and winding their way down a hillside. We got a few shells into them, but our men were tired, and the firing from our one gun, its breech now so stiff that it could hardly be opened, was not fast enough to stop them from getting quickly down the slope and into a little valley less than a mile away. A few minutes later a salvo of three shells burst amongst us, and two more salvoes. We were lucky to get off with only one casualty.

It was now 5 p.m. We had only four shells left and it was clear that the battery could do no more, so I ordered the retirement. I knew that no teams could possibly arrive to pull the guns out within several hours, so my object was to get the men away at once and, if possible, to get teams up as soon as it was dark to withdraw the guns – although it seemed very improbable that we could manage this before the enemy captured them. So the sights and breech-blocks were removed, as well as any important equipment we could carry – telephones etc.

Behind the battery position the ground rose for nearly a mile, and all this was now open to the enemy's view and to machine-gun fire. It meant two treks across exposed grass slopes, with a dip about halfway. I sent the others on ahead over these open spaces, two at a time, and told them to run their fastest. Three were wounded by machine-gun fire, and we had to leave behind one of them who was very seriously wounded. I left one man to take care of him, but I doubted if he would last more than an hour. Of course I obeyed the old seafaring rule that the Captain is the last to leave, and when my turn came at last I got a good move on. Once over the hill our difficulties were ended, and I was decidedly glad to reach cover intact!

A short distance north of the abandoned gun positions the Scots of the 51st Division had been gradually thrust back to the rear line of the battle zone. So had the 6th Division north of them, and part of the 34th Division on its left. At the end of the day they were still holding on. Of necessity the headquarters of 153rd Brigade had been obliged to move back, but, although the Germans were now dangerously close, the work of the signals centre continued, and in the dugout in the sunken road Dick Gammell was carrying on as best he could. The wires had long ago been cut, but relays of runners battled bravely on to carry the messages that were so vital to appraising the situation and to the all-important need to 'keep in touch'. As the hours went on and the fighting came closer, as man after man disappeared into the maelstrom and did not return, there were fewer and fewer runners available for the job.

### Second Lieutenant Dick Gammell

We didn't give during the day of the 21st. In fact reserves were coming through our sunken road and going on to the front line – and very unpleasant it was, because there were a lot of bullets flying about. We were so close to the fighting now that there wasn't much shelling round about us (they'd be afraid of shelling their own troops), but there were a *lot* of bullets. It was very unpleasant indeed!

Everything had broken down, and I was completely without communication except by runner. Well, we had to get a message to the brigade on the right. It was little Smithie who was due to take it, and I said, 'Look, it's pretty tough but you've got to get through.' I admired his courage enormously, because he came back to me and said, 'I canna get through, Sir.' So I said, 'Well, Smith, you've *got* to get through. You go down to Nine Elms and skirt round there, but get through!' And he *got* through, and he got back. I was terribly pleased. I got him a Military Medal for the job. He got back with a message from my Brigadier, Beckwith. It simply said, 'HOLD ON'.

South of Essigny, where the Germans had penetrated deep into the British battle zone on the flank of the 18th Division, the remnants of C83 Battery were still working their last remaining gun. Later, Walter Lugg would look back on it as a day of hair-raising adventures. For the time being there was no time to think of anything but the moment, and Captain Heybittel had decided that it was high time to get out. They had been firing now for more than twelve hours, and for almost eight of them they had been face to face with the approaching Germans, beating them off, falling back bit by bit as one by one the guns had been lost, resorting to rifles to protect the final position and the one remaining weapon. They had kept it firing until the last glimmer of daylight. They had accomplished miracles – but it was pointless to continue. It was too dark to detect a target, and too dark to see the Germans closing in on them in the gloom. Heybittel's immediate concern was to save what was left of his detachment and to get his men away before they were entirely surrounded.

*Gunner Walter Lugg, MM, C 83 Bty., Royal Field Artillery*

At one time we used to think Captain Heybittel was a bit stand-offish, but in that battle we saw his true worth. He was one in a million, he really was. His leadership that day! He got the DSO, and he definitely deserved it.

The Captain gave the order and we all knew that we didn't have much time, so we started to disable the gun. It was absolutely burning hot – and what a job we had to get that breech-block out! Of course, more haste less speed! But we managed it and dumped it in a sandbag, which I was given the job of carrying – not for the first time that day! We decided we would give the Germans one more surprise, so we took out the pins that held the wheels on, so that when the Germans drove them away the blooming wheels would fall off. Ha ha! We did that with malice aforethought, and we did it off our own bat.

While we were there, someone spotted a movement just on our right and shouted out, 'Who's there?' No answer. So we realized that they were Germans. Charlie Stone was lying there covering us, and he got up and went out – he'd got his rifle – and he walked right out towards the place. He said in a kindly voice, 'Come on, Fritz. Come on, Fritz.' Next thing, they fired a shot and Charlie Stone fired back, and then somebody else fired. The Jerries started running away, but Charlie ran after them, right out into No Man's Land. I was right by him, but I couldn't go with him because I had the breech-block in a sandbag on my back, so obviously *I* couldn't go. But he went. 'Come on, Fritz,' he said – just like that! These Germans were actually in the *rear* of us, and Charlie went right after them – *chasing* after them. He chased one for about a hundred yards before he caught him. Of course some other fellows had followed by then. They captured two prisoners,

and Charlie even brought in their old machine-gun on the way back.
He got the Victoria Cross for that, and if ever a man earned it it was
Charlie Stone. He was a coal miner in civil life, and a great friend of
mine.

We started making our way back, prisoners and all. It took us a long
time in the dark, and then when we got back to our wagon lines they
were completely deserted. All our horses had gone, the wagons had
gone, and of course we'd lost all our guns. They'd all been captured
– but we'd made sure that they wouldn't be much use to the Jerries.[1]

The gunners were too exhausted to feel much emotion other than profound relief tempered by a mild satisfaction that, at the end of it all, the
Germans had not entirely had things all their own way.

Far to the north, on the Third Army front, the gunners of C295 Battery
had also indulged in a last defiant gesture before their battery was overrun
by the enemy. They too had fought until the last possible moment, and,
having disabled their guns and seen the gunners safely on their way, the
officers were the last to leave the Battery dugout a little way behind the guns
– and a long way behind the old front line through which the Germans had
advanced. It was a comfortable dugout, for it was constructed within the
sandbagged ruins of a cottage. In peacetime it had been a modest peasant
dwelling, but it was commodious enough to provide a room for an office
where the business of the Battery could be carried out, and another which
served as a kitchen, as well as a room for use as a mess and sleeping quarters
combined. It even had an open fireplace and a few shabby armchairs on
which the officers had been able to make themselves comfortable in quiet
times. On the table stood a large wind-up gramophone.

The officers quitted these splendid premises reluctantly and in a hurry,
leaving even precious pipes and tobacco pouches on the mantelpiece. But
there was no time to lose, for already the Germans were almost on top of
them. The Battery commander, Captain Parrish, had been the last to leave,
and the papers he had burned were still smouldering in the grate when he
dashed back again, struck by a rebellious thought. If they must go, he
reasoned, they could at least leave the incoming residents an appropriate
welcome. It was the matter of a moment to select the gramophone record

---

1. Walter Lugg himself was awarded the Military Medal. The citation for Charlie
Stone's Victoria Cross read, 'After working hard at his gun for six hours under heavy
gas and shell fire, he went to the rear section with an order which he delivered. At
dusk he helped to capture a machine-gun and four prisoners – a gallant act, which
undoubtedly saved the detachment serving the gun.'

he had in mind, for it was a favourite of one of his subalterns, who had played it endlessly. Parrish placed it on the turntable, gave the handle a few hasty turns, and placed the needle on the record. The tinny strains followed him as he dashed off again, slamming the door behind him.

> There's a task that England is out to perform
> With Russia and France to assist,
> And some help now and then from the brave Belgian men,
> And it's this: to defeat the Mail'd Fist.
> It's a terrible task and we had to combine,
> But together we'll wind up the Watch on the Rhine.

It was the voice of Harry Tate, and by the time the well-known soprano of Violet Loraine joined in the chorus the Commander was out of earshot. But he knew the words by heart.

> When we've wound up the Watch on the Rhine,
> How we'll sing 'Auld Lang Syne'!
> You and I – 'Hoorah!' we'll cry,
> Everything will be Potsdam fine.
> When we've wound up the Watch on the Rhine,
> Then they won't have the option of fine,
> Since to jail they'll be lugged,
> All the Herrs will be jugged,
> When we've wound up the Watch on the Rhine.

There had not been time to wind up the gramophone fully, and the record had wailed to a halt a long time before the Germans did arrive. They got there rather later than Captain Parrish had expected: they had been halted by their own guns firing short, and when they eventually arrived they were in no mood to appreciate what they found. A heavy shell had landed among Leutnant Ernst Junger's detachment and killed four men. The others had turned and run. It was some considerable time before he had been able to gather them together and move forward. Silence had fallen all across the front, and it was quite dark by the time they reached the gun-pits. There was nothing more to be done. The officers began to call the roll and to collect their scattered men, and the soldiers themselves, exhausted by the effort of the day, blundered round in search of shelter for the night. But Junger searched further afield and stumbled on the battery headquarters. He entered cautiously, shining his flashlight around the darkened room. It was Fusilier Haller who found and lit the lamp, and Haller who curiously wound up the gramophone on the table. It whined

into life in the middle of the record and, gaining momentum, blared out
through the brass horn.

> *When we've wound up the Watch on the Rhine,*
> *How we'll sing 'Auld Lang Syne'!*
> *You and I — 'Hoorah!' we'll cry,*
> *Everything will be Potsdam fine.*
> *When we've wound up the Watch on the Rhine,*
> *The half-a-Crown Prince must resign,*
> *For instead of the loot, he'll be getting the boot,*
> *When we've wound up the Watch on the Rhine.*

Junger was an educated man with more than a working knowledge of
English, and the message came across loud and clear. After their ordeal of
the last hour his nerves were already jangling. He was livid with rage. Captain
Parrish would have been delighted at the result. The gramophone was too
heavy to lift, but, shoving it with all his might, Junger sent it careering across
the table. The needle screeched across the bakelite. As the machine teetered
on the edge, one more shove sent it crashing to the floor, and there, after a
final protesting wheeze, it lay silent.[1]

Hans Schetter was tired and dirty, but he was well content. Now that they
were at rest, looking back across their lumbering progress to the start of the
long tumultuous day, it seemed to him that the frustrating hours of waiting
for the early mist to clear had been the most exhausting part of it. It was all
that he could clearly remember, for the last few hours had passed in a blur
of noise and danger and excitement. Only fleeting impressions remained in
his mind, and the episodes that stood out most clearly were trivial ones. He
remembered kicking an English football along the road to Epéhy, and
unescorted groups of captured British soldiers who put their hands up as his
squad approached them – as if, he thought mockingly, 'they had been fed
the English propaganda about the German barbarians!' He remembered the
scattered bodies of British and German dead, and the sight of the wounded
still lying among them. And he remembered the horror of the moment
when a comrade had picked up a pair of good British boots and found the
bloody stumps of the wearer's feet still inside. That had shaken them all. But
war was war (as he had reminded himself), and the squad had soon recovered

---

1. By a happy coincidence, Leutnant Ernst Junger's sequel to Captain Parrish's
story appeared in his book *The Storm of Steel* (English translation, Chatto & Windus,
1929). Junger served with the 73rd Hanoverian Fusilier Regiment, 111th [German]
Infantry Division.

in the elation of their triumphant progress in the wake of their advancing troops.

The evidence of their success was all around them, and by and by, as the sun and the march grew hotter, they felt safe enough to take off their heavy helmets and carry them under their arms. At the next halt, while Leutnant Mack scouted ahead for a new observation point, Schetter, sheltering fortuitously in a British dugout, helped himself to six tins of British bully beef. He put them into his helmet and humped them for the rest of the day. The extra weight did not add to the pleasure of the march, and he rather regretted it when the observers stopped for the night at another British dugout and found what, at first glance, seemed to be enough food for the whole German Army let alone their own small team. It had clearly been inhabited by senior British officers, because it was a long way back from their original line. These splendid quarters had been requisitioned for the German boys by their lieutenant.

*Musketier Hans Schetter, 3rd Coy., 231st Reserve Infantry Regt., 50th [German] Reserve Division*

It is a large English dugout with above-ground living quarters built with sandbags. The enemy obviously left this place in a great hurry. Tables in the kitchen are still covered with meat, cauliflower and other vegetables. The dugouts are full of provisions, and we help ourselves to cigarettes, chocolate, corned beef, condensed milk, sugar, biscuits, marmalade and other good things to eat.

More prisoners are coming back in bunches now. They are Irish soldiers, for they have a shamrock patch fastened to their upper sleeves.[1] Our lieutenant talks with a wounded enemy officer who has been hit in the eye and arm by a shell fragment. We are astounded that he has the guts to talk to us. The lieutenant tells him that we are on our way to the English Channel. But he replies with pride, 'There are trenches over trenches all along the way!'

But they had advanced a good five miles, and ahead their infantry was still pressing forward to gain what ground they could in the little daylight that remained. For the time being their own work was over. Although it had been a cloudless, springlike day of unremitting sunshine, the smoke of battle and the clouds of dust thrown up by countless shellbursts had mingled into a haze, and for more than an hour now observation had been impossible. The British gunfire had abated, and the roar of their own German guns, still

1. They were men of the 16th (Irish) Division.

searching far ahead, was reassuring. They could see nothing of the actual fighting, but between the whistling of flying shells and the thud of distant explosions they could clearly hear the rattle of musketry and the intermittent stammer of machine-guns.

The telescope had been packed away for the night, the observers had already picnicked eagerly on British rations, and they were looking forward to another good meal before turning in. To cap their satisfaction, an orderly arrived with a sack of British Army socks, and the German soldiers lost no time in exchanging them for their own. The air inside the dugout was not made sweeter by a dozen men removing their boots to tear what now amounted to little more than shreds of matted fibre from their sticky, aching feet. Wriggling his toes with pleasure at the delightful sensation of soft Australian wool, Schetter lit a postprandial cigarette and went outside to savour the excellent English tobacco. It was past six o'clock, the light was going fast, and behind the haze of battle the sun was setting blood-red in the west. Some field guns had been moved forward into a nearby field. They were silhouetted against the evening sky, and they were preparing to open fire.

# Part 3

# The Endless Road

*The endless road moves to a darkening sky,*
*A road where withered trees and shadows sigh*
*Across the years, where memories lie*
*With friends long-dead in Picardy . . .*

LIEUTENANT J. R. T. ALDOUS
210 Field Coy., Royal Engineers,
31st Division (1914–1918)

## Chapter 11

In the German territory beyond the Fifth Army front, the British soldiers captured during the day's fighting had been rounded up and several thousands of them were herded into St Quentin. Before the battle began, the Germans had wired off certain fields to serve as makeshift prisoner-of-war camps until the captured Tommies could be shifted to the rear, but for the moment no one but the sentries had time to bother about the prisoners. They had arrived in such numbers that there was no time to search each man individually, so, although they had lost their kit and most of their possessions, some still had a bite or two of food in their pockets and a pipe or a few cigarettes to smoke. It was a crumb of comfort – and the only crumb of any description they were likely to receive for some time to come. In the circumstances it was impossible to feed such numbers, still less provide them with any shelter.

The Tommies had been dressed in battle order when they were captured, so there was not a greatcoat nor a blanket among them, and they stretched out, shivering and despondent, on the bare ground. It grew cold after the sun set, and would grow colder still as the night wore on, but it was thirty-six hours since most of them had slept and, despite chill, hunger and acute discomfort, some men did manage to drop off through sheer exhaustion.

But the cages were full, and prisoners were still streaming in. Although the flow slowed to a trickle after dark, hundreds were still crowding the streets of St Quentin, and their unfortunate German escorts had no idea where to put them. They were very much in the way. The town was full of second-line troops weighed down with battle equipment, ready to move forward to pursue the advance. There was no need now for silence or discretion, and the night rang with voices, shouting orders, occasionally cursing, as line after line of supply vehicles tried to carve a path through the press of waiting troops. In the main square where some battalions were congregated there was room enough for them all, but the passage of wheeled transport was hampered by the residue of rubble, only hastily swept aside.

In streets near the square, British prisoners had been pushed close to the battered walls to let the vehicles pass, and it seemed to their astonished eyes that the Germans had requisitioned anything on wheels to get supplies forward. Lorries were few and far between. There were horse-drawn farm wagons, carts pulled by mules or donkeys, ancient cabs and carriages, even milk floats drawn by bewildered dogs – and there were countless hold-ups when horse-drawn ambulances stuck fast while attempting to cross the tide of traffic, and brought it to a dead stop. Horses whinnied, donkeys brayed, drivers cursed, and dismayed officers, trying to restore order, bellowed torrents of malediction. But, for all the delays and despite the apparent chaos, the supplies, like the troops, were inexorably moving forward, and it seemed to the dejected prisoners, dazed by the overwhelming assaults of the day, that the German Army was unstoppable.

They were not alone in this assumption. Some thirty miles away, on board his Imperial train, the Kaiser was exultant. This was a battle he had been reluctant to undertake, but the evidence of his own eyes had converted him to his own cause. He had watched his troops advancing far and fast, and what he had seen had convinced him that the battle they called 'the Kaiser's Battle' was a glorious success. He was happy now that it had been fought in his name. He had no doubt that his Army would continue bowling forward, that the British would be smashed, the French would be scuppered, and the Allies would soon be ready to make peace on German terms. In the elation of the moment he lost no time in telegraphing the jubilant news to Germany. 'Victory is complete,' he crowed.

Ludendorff's impressions of the day were not so sanguine as those formed by the Kaiser, and the communiqué he issued took a less triumphant line.

> From south-east of Arras to La Fère we attacked the British positions. After a heavy bombardment of artillery and trench mortars our infantry assaulted on a wide front and everywhere captured the enemy's first lines.

Ludendorff was of the opinion that the Kaiser's shouts of 'Hurrah!' and 'Victory!' had been decidedly premature. The reports that reached him during the evening clearly showed that, while in certain places the British outpost positions had been overrun, the British were holding out and fighting hard. Only at four points had their front been substantially penetrated. Ludendorff's intention to break through the British defences on a wide front and to surge on to capture the artillery positions behind them had not been achieved. Although many field guns had been captured, the British artillery had inflicted huge casualties and frequently brought the assault to a standstill. Even in the sectors where it had succeeded, some isolated strongpoints were still holding out and tying down far too many of Ludendorff's storm troops, who were obliged to stay behind to deal with them. It had not been a clean sweep.

In Ludendorff's initial plan, once the breakthrough had been achieved, he had intended to shift his heavy artillery northward, to support a second hammer-blow that would crush the British while they were still reeling from the first. Weighing up the reports that were still coming in from the field, he did not yet feel justified in doing so. The heavy artillery must remain where it was, to assist the troops to renew the attack next day, and the question of launching a fresh onslaught would have to wait until they succeeded.

The matter of reinforcements also placed Ludendorff in a quandary. He had plenty of them – at least in the short term – and they were even now awaiting orders. Should he send them to the north, where the German troops who had not quite broken through could certainly do with their help, or should he send them to the south, where the front of the British 14th Division had given way and where the 18th Division on its right would consequently be in difficulties?

In later years, with all the clarity of retrospective vision, some analysts of the battle concluded that Ludendorff's decision on this momentous night was so ill-judged that it cost the Germans the battle and even affected the outcome of the war. But, in the immediacy of the moment, weighing up the situation from a confusion of reports, Ludendorff was swayed by one overriding consideration. He knew very well that the right of the British front adjoined the front held by the French Army, and that, given the circumstances, it was now all too likely that reserve troops of the French Army would soon come to the assistance of their British allies. He therefore decided to throw the bulk of his reserves behind General von Hutier's force south of St Quentin, and having come to this decision he gave the order that would set them on the march.

The Crown Prince and the Kaiser passed the evening in a euphoria of self-congratulation. 'Little Willie', as the Kaiser's son was derisively nicknamed by the British, was no strategist and certainly no tactician, but he was in titular command of the German Eighteenth Army and he had shared his father's elation at what he believed to be a triumphant achievement. If General Ludendorff had expressed his reservations, they carried no weight with the Crown Prince. Early in the evening he issued his personal orders in a communiqué to his troops:

> The Eighteenth Army will continue attacking – even during the night. North of the Somme it is important to cross the road Tertry–Beauvois–Le Hamel as soon as possible. The task of the Army, to facilitate the advance of the Second Army by attack in the flank and rear of the enemy still in front of that Army, remains good in its widest sense.

If the order to continue attacking during the night reached the weary German fighting troops, they ignored it – and they ignored it because there was no possibility of obeying. They had been on the alert or on the move for thirty-six hours, few of them had slept, they had been fighting all day, and they had strained themselves to the limit. They had done their utmost for the Kaiser, and for the moment they had nothing left to give.

Just outside Essigny-le-Grand, where the 7th Battalion, the Rifle Brigade, had been overrun by the Germans that morning, the 2nd Battery of the 5th [German] Artillery Regiment had pulled into position, and within half an hour the men were slumped asleep round their guns. They had fired all through the bombardment, and later in the day they had trailed slowly forward to this new site in captured territory. Leutnant Herbert Sulzbach lay there with his men. Next morning they would be on the go again, but for the present they were dead to the world. Not far away Reinhold Spengler, wrapped in his waterproof sheet, was also slumbering in the open. In the small hours of the morning, frost settled on the ground, but even the bitter cold did not arouse them.

Hermann Wedekind was safely tucked up in bed. He was luckier than many of his German comrades, for he was well behind the line in a field hospital at Bohain, but he passed a painful and uncomfortable night. Early in the evening, while a doctor was removing the bullet from his wounded arm and making good the damage, Wedekind vomited spectacularly under the anaesthetic. He brought up what appeared to be a large quantity of blood – a clear sign to the flustered surgical team that he also had internal injuries. Although they could find nothing which might account for a haemorrhage, nursing orderlies were instructed to keep a close eye on the patient during the night, and Wedekind was frequently disturbed by their solicitous attentions. He had no idea why, nor was he in any condition to explain, or even to realize, that the cause of the 'haemorrhage' was the quantity of red wine he had consumed during the battle.

It was past eight o'clock in the evening of 21 March before General Gough was able to sit down to a hasty meal. On the whole he was satisfied with the results of the day and with the praiseworthy performance of his army. With the concurrence of the Commander-in-Chief, withdrawal to the reserve line in the event of a powerful assault had been envisaged long ago, and the plans had been carefully worked out. In the early part of the evening Gough confirmed his provisional orders, and repeated the instructions he had given verbally to his Corps Commanders that afternoon. Above all there must be an orderly retirement, and the moving line must be gradually adjusted to present an unbroken front to the enemy. The key was 'keeping in touch' and, as Gough reiterated to his staff, the importance of this could not be overstated. Corps Headquarters would move back to selected localities already equipped with the vital telephone lines and communications which would enable them to direct the efforts of their troops. Divisions would swing back in conjunction with those on their flanks. At all costs '*touch must be maintained*', so that, in theory, even a single platoon would know the whereabouts of its neighbour.

General Gough was too much of a soldier to think that it would be easy – but he believed that it could be done. Obviously it was not yet possible to ascertain how many men had been killed or wounded, captured or cut off, but the number was clearly many thousands. What remained of his force was critically weak, his front would be fragile, but judicious retirement would buy time until reinforcements arrived to strengthen it. Until they did, he believed, without undue optimism, that the Fifth Army could hang on. But Gough needed support and reinforcements – and he needed them fast!

Immediately after dinner, when he reported to GHQ by telephone, he found to his consternation that his view was not shared by the General Staff. Nor, it seemed, were his misgivings. In the course of a heated conversation with Field-Marshal Haig's Chief of Staff, it became clear that no reinforcements would be immediately forthcoming. General Lawrence's response to Gough's request that reserves should be promptly sent to assist him was, it seemed to Gough, a distinctly patronizing attempt to reassure and encourage him.

*General Sir Hubert Gough, GCMG, KCB, KCVO, Fifth Army Commander*

I told him of the number of divisions which the Germans had brought into action against us and the masses still in the rear. I then went on to express very considerable anxiety for the next and following days. The Germans would certainly continue to push their attack on the next day, Friday, and it would undoubtedly continue with unabashed fury for many days. Could our tired and attenuated line maintain the struggle without support? That was the question, and it was a grave one. Lawrence did not seem to grasp the seriousness of the situation. He thought that 'the Germans would not come on again the next day'. 'After the severe losses they had suffered,' he thought that they 'would be busy clearing the battlefield, collecting their wounded and resting their tired troops.' I disagreed emphatically, but I failed to make much impression. It has always been my opinion that G.H.Q. did not fully grasp the magnitude of the assault on the Fifth Army or the desperate odds it had to contend with . . .[1]

1. General Gough's words are quoted from his book *The Fifth Army* (Hodder & Stoughton, 1931).

Since General Lawrence was Sir Douglas Haig's Chief of Staff, it could be presumed that his attitude reflected Haig's own. Gough was both worried and baffled. He sent for Paul Maze, who had just returned, exhausted from the exertions of the day, and handed him a message with instructions to deliver it to French Army Headquarters away to the south. Maze had 'gathered from General Gough that the French reserves were not coming up as he had hoped, and that beyond the two divisions of reserves which he had at the start, no others were forthcoming'.

Puttering southward on his motorbike, Maze felt limp with weariness and dazed by lack of sleep, but it needed no exercise of wit or imagination to guess that the sealed envelope in his pocket contained an urgent request for help.

It was close to midnight when a priority signal from GHQ arrived at Fifth Army Headquarters. It was signed by the Commander-in-Chief himself. In view of the strength of the attacking force and the determination of the foe, Sir Douglas Haig considered that the performance of the British troops was 'highly creditable'. He sent his personal congratulations 'and his thanks for their efforts – and he instructed that this appreciative message should be 'communicated to all ranks'.

It was kindly meant and intended as encouragement, but it did not encourage General Gough. With much of his scattered force in a state of disarray or engaging in a difficult withdrawal, how, when and even where Haig's message could be communicated 'to all ranks' was not, for the moment, apparent.

All along the front – ragged in many places where the enemy had penetrated – battalions had been split, companies had fallen back piecemeal, and stragglers were adrift in the night. There were small groups, often a mere handful of men, who had been cut off or left behind when the order to retire had come too late or not at all. But there was safety, of a kind, in numbers. It was far worse for solitary wanderers with only a hazy idea of the whereabouts of their comrades, trusting to luck and fearful of stumbling into the Germans while they searched for their own lines. Harold Howitt was particularly anxious to avoid them, for he had had quite enough of their company for one evening and he was only too thankful to have given his captors the slip.

Sitting despondently on his shell-dump between two watchful guards, he had felt both angry and ashamed, cursing the ill luck that had thrown him into hands of the enemy, and speculating miserably on the indignity of a bleak future as a prisoner of war.

Gold and silver star-rockets soaring above their front gave the signal for the Germans to continue their advance, and it was obvious that the presence of their reluctant prisoner was an embarrassment. They had no idea what to do with him. As it was impossible to send him back, there was no alternative but to take him with them. Howitt had not the smallest objection to being marched towards the British lines. Urged on by his guards, he trailed along at the end of the column, shoulders hunched in a semblance of meek compliance, but inwardly preparing to leap at the first opportunity of escape. Dusk was closing in when luck, assisted by some obliging British gunner, gave him his chance.

*Brigade-Major Harold Howitt, 184th Bde., 61st Division*

Looking ahead I saw a dip in the road full of mist and smoke, and, as luck would have it, when we were at the bottom, one of our shells dropped unpleasantly close and, looking over my shoulder, I noticed that both my guards had ducked into a shell-hole behind. I had no plan in my mind, but I instinctively leapt at the first man to get up, seized him by the revolver wrist and the throat, and started shaking him. By this time the other man was up and, as I didn't have another hand, all I could do was to throw one man against the other and roll them both into the ditch at the side of the road. For a moment I wondered what to do next; however, I recovered my wits and ran for it.

They were soon up and emptying their revolvers at me, but they missed and I kept running. I decided that I would make across country to where I could see a burning ammunition dump on the roadside at Beauvois. I think I was right to do this, though the dump was an unpleasant neighbour as I ran beside it, and I must have showed up against it, because several pot-shots were also taken at me. But somehow or other, after *hours* of dodging about, I got through safely to Beauvois. It was quite empty except for some dead casualties, because we had been driven out of it by gas-shells earlier in the day. It was *not* nice to go through it, but I had to, so I did, and managed to get on to the Ham road beyond.

Beauvois was well behind the rear line of the battle zone, and the Ham road on the other side of the village was not a healthy place. For all Howitt knew, a detachment of German soldiers might come marching along at any moment; but he had to risk it. It was now pitch dark, and since he had no idea of the whereabouts of the enemy – or of the British for that matter! – it would be even more dangerous to strike across country. The road led south-west, and he followed it cautiously, hoping for the best. He bitterly regretted the loss of his revolver, now the property of the Germans who had captured and disarmed him. It had cost Howitt the tidy sum of three guineas, but in his present situation he would have paid ten times as much for the reassurance of its trusty grip. He had never felt more exposed.

In normal circumstances, even on quiet nights, there were always star-shells shooting above the lines, which provided a pointer to their general direction. But tonight they were few and far between. Nor were there many 'lines' as the Army normally understood the term. Here and there a burning cottage threw a lurid glare across a nearby field, but the fires were haphazard, and the light they cast was of no assistance to a fugitive whose sole desire at present was to escape the notice of a sharp-eyed enemy.

As he walked on, listening hard, he picked up the sound of footsteps on the pavé. Guessing that a patrol was coming towards him, he dived into a field on the left-hand side of the road. He started to crawl slowly forward, hoping to pass unseen, but when he reached the edge of the field he almost ran into a manned post. To make matters worse, it proved to be one of several posts strung out along a ditch. Slowly, and with infinite caution, Howitt retraced his painful progress on hands and knees, and when he was at a safe distance he slipped across the road and tried the same manoeuvre in the field on the other side. And with the same result!

Howitt was desperate now. Lying close to the ground between two of the posts, he decided to make a run for it, to dash between them, and pray that the men who held them would not be extra vigilant or that the disturbance might be mistaken for the scurry of a nocturnal animal. He was tensing his muscles to spring when he heard a sharp expletive. It was a single familiar Anglo-Saxon syllable, uttered in a tone of deep disgust, but it was music to Howitt's ears for it could only have come from the lips of a British Tommy. He could have wept with relief.

*Brigade-Major Harold Howitt*

I knew then that I had got through the German patrols and had bumped up against our own rearguard line.

My next problem was how to give myself up. I began to call to them in English, and gradually showed myself, with my arms up. A Jock of the Gordons came at me with fixed bayonet, and luckily stopped with it very close to my abdomen. I told him I was an escaped prisoner, which he did *not* believe, so I asked him to take me to one of his officers. Thus I was marched through our lines! Within the hour orders came to retire beyond the Somme and blow up the bridge at Ham. So I had a narrow escape in many ways.[1]

Major Ward was also out in the night, but he knew exactly where he was going. He was making for the front, where he had been forced to leave his guns, and if it were at all possible he was going to do his damnedest to get them back. He was well aware that the venture might be as pointless as it was dangerous: the Germans had been so close and advancing so rapidly that it was more likely than not that the guns had been captured hours ago. All in all, Ward did not feel particularly hopeful.

*Major Ronald Ward, C 293., Royal Field Artillery*

Lieutenant Ogilvie had moved up all the limbers and firing wagons during the afternoon and set up an advanced wagon line, so I got together five teams and gun limbers, with five gunners, Ogilvie and myself. (I would gladly have had a few more men, but none were available and there was no other officer.) At 11 p.m. we started forwards. We pushed on to Vélu, avoiding roads as far as possible, for they were now impassable for wheeled traffic in many places, and got to the village and on to the one road Cleater and I had galloped along. Now all was quiet.

Beyond Vélu the road was difficult, for there were many new trenches and a good deal of barbed wire. But a more serious and unexpected difficulty was the mist, which now settled down again, very thick and white, so that one could only see two or three yards. For a mile and a half I had great trouble in maintaining direction

---

1. Days later, when at last there was time to write letters, Howitt regaled his friends and family with the tale of his adventures. There was an unexpected outcome: 'I received a letter some time afterwards telling me that in a newspaper serial entitled "Mr. Standfast" there was a description of an incident somewhat similar to the one I had written about. I couldn't understand this, but later, when I was on leave at home, I happened to mention it to my Brigadier when I went to visit him in hospital. He roared with laughter and confessed that a friend of his – John Buchan no less! – had called on him and said that he was hard up for copy for his next instalment and he was hoping that Bobby, just back from the big attack, might have a story for him. The Brigadier explained that he hadn't, because he had been wounded early on, *but* that he would show him a letter he had received that morning from his Brigade-Major (me!) who had had an exciting experience. So that's how it came about. And after the war Buchan asked me to take tea with him at the House of Commons, so that he could meet "Lefroy" – which was the name he gave "my" character.'

through it, whilst finding a way in and out of trenchlines. We moved very slowly forward, the teams keeping well closed up, passed through a gap in the main trench, and arrived at the battery position. There stood the three guns just as we had left them, faintly seen in the hazy light that pierced the mist from the low-lying moon, looking very lonely and forgotten.

*Now* was the most anxious time. The trench 200 yards in rear of the guns was manned with scattered infantry. This was good, but it showed that this trench had definitely become our front line, so the guns were now in No Man's Land. I knew that the enemy was close by and doubtless all ready to prevent us from saving the guns. (I did *not* know until later that during the evening the 19th Division had made a counter-attack towards Doignies. It failed, but it had no doubt checked the enemy's advance for the moment.)

From now on all instructions were in whispers. In silence I led three teams forward to the three right guns. The drivers did their work beautifully, and in almost complete quiet we limbered them up and then moved them back about fifty yards. Then Ogilvie and I took teams to the other two guns, 400 yards away from the main position over the hill to the left. Any moment I expected a burst of machine-gun fire or shelling, but during the hour we were on the position everything remained wrapped in complete silence, which was made even more intense by the deadening effect of the heavy mist. No gunfire. No rifle fire. It was as peaceful as a night on Salisbury Plain – a strange contrast to the noise of the day just past.

Removing the other two guns was a much more difficult job. They had been in that position for two months, and the effect of the enemy shelling and their own firing had caused the heavy roofs of the pits to sink, so that there was not enough overhead clearance to run the guns out from the back. After a lot of hard work and some digging we were still no nearer clearing them, when fortunately I found an officer and about thirty men in the trench behind and they came to help. With all this manpower we hauled the guns out of the front of the pits on to level ground in a few minutes.

The intensity of the silence about us made our movements sound terribly noisy, and I have never in my life been so anxious as I was then. I expected to see the enemy appear through the mist at any moment. But the worst work was completed, and I led these two guns back to the other three.

We were all delighted with our success!

A little over a mile away, Dick Gammell and his signallers were also getting out, taking advantage of the stillness, the darkness and the mist to make their way back with the weary infantry and to carry on, if they could, in a new position. Apart from a couple of signal lamps, there was no hope of salvaging any of the equipment, so painstakingly constructed, and Gammell was loath to leave it for the benefit of the enemy, or even to leave the dugout intact for his convenience.

They smashed up what they could and climbed up the steep stairway for the last time. Gammell was the last man out. When he reached the top of the steps he emptied the contents of a can of petrol down the stairway and set it alight. It ignited with a satisfactory bang. The walls of the stairway and the rooms below were lined with boards of timber and, although it was twenty feet below ground and far from damp-proof, there was just a chance that the dugout would burn. Then he turned away, thankful to have escaped the rigours of the day with a whole skin and with nothing worse to complain of than scorched eyebrows.

All along the road weary men were plodding westward through the mist, some in a semblance of platoon formation, others in twos and threes. After a while Gammell noticed that his own party had been augmented by a number of waifs and strays who were happy to place themselves under the orders of an officer in the innocent belief that he would lead them home. He marvelled at their confidence, for he himself had no idea where 'home' was to be found. But he kept them together and, by and by, when they came to a small quarry by the roadside, he led them into it, and as the dawn approached he set about organizing some kind of defence. It was all he could do.

Although it had been pushed back on part of its front, the Third Army seemed to be in a more secure situation than the Fifth. But the position on the Flesquières salient where the two armies met gave some cause for concern. The force defending it was seriously diminished by casualties and, although no ground had been given, the troops could hardly be expected to withstand a fresh assault. They could easily be cut off if the Germans continued to advance on their left – as they showed every intention of doing. It seemed only sensible to withdraw them – not, initially, as far back as the battle zone at Havrincourt, but to an intermediate line which would shorten their front and enable them to keep in touch with the neighbouring 51st Division to the north. General Sir Julian Byng, in command of the Third Army, had also been in touch with GHQ, and the Commander-in-Chief had agreed that this was the sensible course. The intermediate line was ready-made, for it was nothing less than the strongly fortified Hindenburg Line, which, less than four months previously, had been so gloriously captured by the British Army.

The news of the withdrawal from the front line of the Flesquières salient on the northern hinge of the Fifth Army caused General Sir Hubert Gough to reappraise his position, for there was no alternative but to order the withdrawal of his own 9th (Scottish) Division to conform to the new line. The warning order was issued during the night, and when it filtered down to the men in the line they were far from pleased. They had given little ground. They had saved their flank, fought hard, and stuck it out. They had suffered much, but they knew that they had done well, and it was hard to come to terms with a retiral that would leave the field to the enemy. But orders were orders.

The private sentiments of General Gough were similar. Despite the precarious position of the 21st Division on its right flank, he had hoped to swing back on the hinge of the 9th Division line, to readjust the front of his army, and to hold on until reserve troops arrived to strengthen his weak, attenuated force. He had not envisaged a wholesale retreat, and he did not do so now. He intended to fight a battle in retreat, and that was a very different matter.

Although Gough had good reason to suppose otherwise, the Commander-in-Chief was not so insensitive to the difficulties of the Fifth Army as Gough himself believed. Haig had already ordered the 8th Division to go to Gough's support, and after Gough's telephoned report that evening he had decided to dispatch the 2nd Division too. But, since it was now behind the Flanders front, it would be a little while before it reached the Fifth Army.

Field-Marshal Haig was obliged to take a broad view of the situation, and he was not convinced that the day's events showed beyond doubt the main thrust of the German assault. He had always believed that this was more likely to fall on the fronts of the Third and First Armies, or even astride the Franco-Belgian frontier, where the Second Army held twenty-three miles running from the left flank of the First Army to a point north of Ypres. These three armies were the guardians of the Channel ports on which the fortunes – even the fate – of the British Army depended, for through them stretched the lifelines across the English Channel which linked the Army to its home base and kept it active in the field. Every transport carrying drafts of reinforcements, every shipload of food for its men, forage for its horses and ammunition for its guns, every plank of timber and every small necessity, from stone for repairing roads down to the last nail and horseshoe, reached the Army through the bottlenecks of Calais, Dunkirk, Boulogne or Le Havre. Le Havre was inconveniently situated a long way to the south, and Calais so close that it could be shelled by the enemy's long-range guns, but the ports constituted the only lines of communication. By comparison, the French Army was abundantly endowed, with a sprawling network of roads and railways running from the French front through the deep hinterland of unoccupied France to the coast of the Mediterranean.

The ground behind the British front was narrow – the fronts of the Third and First Armies were roughly fifty miles from the coast, and on the left flank of the Second Army less than thirty miles lay between Ypres and Dunkirk. If the enemy succeeded in breaking through this lightweight front with a crushingly superior force and managed to leap forward, a hop, a step and a jump would take him to the coast, the British Army would be pushed into the sea, and the war, so far as Great Britain was concerned, would be lost. It was this danger, and this consideration more than any other, which had influenced Sir Douglas Haig in planning the disposition of his denuded force to meet the German assault – and the force at his disposal was far far weaker than he desired.

The reorganization of divisions in January had brought their component battalions if not to full strength then at least to something approaching it, but, with one battalion fewer in each brigade, each division had been diminished by a quarter of the peacetime force. Reserves were few, even though it was an axiom of military strategy that assaults on weak forces could be repelled only if fresh troops could be thrown in to reinforce, and to counter-attack to recapture lost ground. The question which had perplexed Haig and his Staff was, Where would the assault be launched? And how should they dispose their fragile force to meet it? The Germans' show of preparation across many miles had strengthened Haig's conviction that the enemy strike would be aimed directly at the Channel ports.

To the British General Staff, trying to deduce the German plans, the distribution of a slender force to best advantage across 126 miles had been the subject of deep discussion and much perplexity. In the final allocation the vulnerable armies closest to the coast had come off best.

On the left of the line the Second Army, with Dunkirk at its back, had twelve divisions to dispose along its twenty-three-mile front. South of it, the First Army, holding thirty-three miles between Armentières and Gavrelle, slightly north of Arras, had fourteen, which included two divisions supplied by the Portuguese. General Byng's Third Army continued the line with another fourteen divisions across his twenty-eight-mile front. The Fifth Army, with the longest front of all and which was known to be the weakest, was allotted only twelve divisions to defend it. It was forty-two miles long.

The First Army had two divisions in local reserve, and the Second Army had three. The Third and Fifth Armies had four apiece, and this in General Gough's case was less generous than it seemed, for three of them were cavalry divisions, whose strength in manpower was only that of an infantry brigade. When these arrangements had been made there remained only eight unallocated divisions in General Reserve. The best that could be done was to place two behind each army, ready to move at a few hours' notice to any part of the front where they were needed.

Even with luck and the recently improved communications, even by using every available train, every bus and every lorry, the movement of a whole division of 9,000 men, with its horses, wagons and stores, with its guns and ammunition, could not be speedily accomplished. But, remembering the slogging progress of previous campaigns, Haig had banked on the belief that, even in a successful offensive, any German advance would be slow, giving his troops time to withdraw so gradually that there would be days or even weeks of grace in which reserves could be sent to assist them.

It is only fair to say that his opposite number, General Ludendorff, had taken a very similar view. But he, at least, had ample resources with which to exploit the situation, while the British commander could not easily draw on the few resources at his command in order to contain it. It would be the height of folly for Haig to strip his other fronts of their all too meagre reserves when it might conceivably be part of the enemy plan to trick him into doing so. Who could say that the attack on the southern sector of his front was not a feint, and that soon another, even stronger, blow would not be struck elsewhere?

Haig was very conscious of the weakness of the long Fifth Army front, but he had not intended to present its commander with an impossible task. For one thing, since the Fifth Army was much further from the coast, the extent of the territory behind him would give Gough room to manoeuvre if the worst should come to the worst. In the event of an assault on the Fifth Army, the General Staff had counted on two things: that the obstacles of the River Oise, with its marshlands and tributaries, and the proximity of the dense forest of St Gobain would compensate for the sketchy defences at the southern extremity of the front, and that General Pétain would honour his agreement to send French troops to Gough's assistance.

Pétain had every intention of doing so – albeit with the same qualms and doubts as Sir Douglas Haig. He too had the security of a front to consider – the long, bitterly contested French front that ran from the right of the Fifth Army to the mountains of the Vosges. With the prize of Paris always in the Germans' sights, as he believed, might not the main thrust of the enemy onslaught be directed at the French? One division was already preparing to set off to assist the British, but could he afford to part with more reserves which might soon be badly needed elsewhere? During the day, despite General Gough's urgent entreaties, Pétain had hesitated and pondered. But honour was at stake, the danger was on his flank, and General Humbert's reserve divisions were close at hand. At nightfall he finally issued the order that would release them. Like the British reserves, they could not be moved in an instant, but the wheels had been set in motion and they would soon be on their way.

All evening the wires behind the British front in Flanders had hummed with urgent signals from G H Q. By midnight, the colonels of most reserve battalions had received the curt preliminary order: 'Prepare to move.' It was the first indication that a great battle had begun in the south, and that soon they would be in it.

# Chapter 12

At the Army School in the village of Caix, almost thirty miles from the battle line, Tom Witherow and his friends had listened all day to the distant sound of the guns. News was scanty but rumour was rife, and in the evening no one was surprised when the course was abruptly abandoned and the officers were ordered to pack up and prepare to return to their battalions at the front. With a fair idea of what was in store, Witherow donned his old shabby uniform and carefully folded his dapper new tunic into his valise. He never wore it again.

Very early in the morning of the second day of battle, they set off for the station, passing farmworkers on their way to the fields, where swathes of green shoots predicted a bountiful harvest and the war seemed very far away. It was more than an hour's tramp, and a chilly one, but to fit young men it was invigorating, and Witherow was enjoying it. After a while they came to a barn where a military band had mustered for early practice. They were playing 'The Last Rose of Summer', and the melody followed them through the still morning air as they marched on.

Although the murky dawn had broken a long while earlier, Major Ward was still out and about. He had been on his feet for more than twenty-four hours, but he would not allow himself to give in. The teams had rescued all their guns, but as they were dragging them away one sank into a shell-hole and Ward could not bring himself to abandon it. Having escorted the first four along the first mile of the road to safety, he returned to his old battery position, where the gun still lay, drunkenly askew, where he had left it. The gun team, however, was no longer there, and without hefty manpower Ward could do nothing. But he was not entirely despondent. The Battery had done well. They had retrieved four of their guns, and, cheered by the thought that he still had an active unit, Ward rode back in reasonably good spirits, satisfied with the night's work. This pleasant sensation lasted until he reached Vélu and was met by the sight of his four guns parked, abandoned and forlorn, beside a wall.

*Major Ronald Ward, C 293 Bty., Royal Field Artillery*

To this day I don't know what happened, but somehow my orders had been misunderstood and the NCOs had thought that the guns were to be left there ready for detachments to come up from the wagon lines. It was a bitter disappointment. Once again the guns seemed as good as lost, for by now it was obvious that another great attack was developing. Shelling was becoming more intense, and I could hear rifle fire too. I hurried back towards the advanced wagon lines near Frémicourt, two and a half miles away, and collected four teams and limbers and two gunners. No one else was available!

The Germans were now firing on the village of Lebucquière only half a mile away, but we reached the guns safely and limbered up. The route between Lebucquière and Vélu was under heavy shell-fire, and the road was very much damaged. The only certain way of getting out of the village was to go down a road not more than four yards wide, with the wall of the chateau on the left and a bank over five feet high on the right. Fortunately, a hundred yards down the road, there was a depression in the bank where the height was only about four feet. Over this part of the bank the guns must go. There was no other way.

I explained carefully to the drivers what they had to do and then sent the best team at it, telling the others to follow in turn. I knew very well that, if any horse jibbed, failure would inevitably follow. A leg over a trace, the wheel-round made too late, or the turn up the bank made too sharply, and the gun would stick there and possibly overturn. Shells were falling in the wood and on the level crossing. The first team started off at a trot, then broke into a canter and then to a gallop. Down the narrow road they went, and as they reached the place where the bank was lowest the lead driver held back his hand-horse for an instant, swung his ride-horse hard round to the right, and up the bank they sprang with the centre horses following them. The traces had been left just slack enough to allow the wheel-driver to keep the gun and limber well against the wall on his left, and at exactly the right moment he made a fair turn, the limber and gun took the bank squarely, and the gun bounced up the bank and into the field of grass beyond. The other three eighteen-pounders followed in perfect style. It was a great moment – and I *was* happy! So I got back to the advanced wagon lines with all four guns. Things could have been worse.

Things could have been a good deal worse. It was true that in one or two places the enemy had a foothold in the battle zone, but along most of its length the Third Army had given little ground and most of its battle zone and even parts of the outpost zone further north were still intact. On the Fifth Army front, where the enemy had struck hardest, the situation was worse, but by no means did it seem to be catastrophic. In places where the enemy had scythed deep into the line, the troops on either side of the breach had swivelled on some steady point and swung round to form defensive flanks, while the men who faced the brunt of the attack counter-attacked where they could or, in the last resort, fell back fighting for the vital time that would enable supporting troops to form a line behind them. Men clung to forward positions in sharp, uncomfortable salients or were pushed back into deep re-entrants which stretched their original frontage to twice its previous length. Frequently, in places where a diminished force of survivors extended to join hands with their neighbours in front or behind, there were fewer men to defend far more ground than they had held at the start of the battle. But they were 'in touch'. Nowhere had the retirement been a rout. The line had yielded. It had been bent – but it had not been broken.

Long before daylight the remnants of the 14th and 18th Divisions were safely across the Crozat canal and the bridges were blown up behind them.

There had hardly been time to count the cost or estimate their losses, but when the 10th Essex assembled in Frières Wood, behind the canal, Major Tween was not surprised to learn that, diminished though it was, the Battalion was the strongest remaining unit of the 53rd Brigade. The Buffs and the Berkshires had been almost decimated. While the weary Essex and the remnants of the Buffs and Berkshires snatched what sleep they could, the 54th Brigade and some dismounted cavalry, with a hotchpotch of pioneers, spread out in a thin line to stand sentinel along the canal.

The Germans had already begun to filter forward. They started off at dawn in the early mist. By sunrise, when the mist began to lift, Reinhold Spengler's company had reached Montescourt – although not without difficulty. A handful of British soldiers were still clinging to positions in the one-time outpost zone. They were isolated, and far from help or rescue, but they continued to harass the enemy for the rest of the day.

*Leutnant Reinhold Spengler, 2nd Coy., 1st Bavarian Infantry Regt., 1st Bavarian Division*

Again and again we encountered English machine-gun nests, but the field battery accompanying us gave the battalion considerable support. Its guns often fired at the enemy from only 200 or 300 metres away.

In Montescourt the enemy had been totally surprised by our attack.

The place was a perfect picture of headlong flight. Even the wounded in an English field hospital had been left behind. With great pleasure we discovered an enormous food depot nearby. Unimaginable treasures were found inside, but we could only pick up a few things to carry along – bacon, ham, corned beef, chocolate, cigarettes and real tobacco. (Our own smokes were terrible!) We did not have much time to be choosy, because the progress of the march was more important.

Towards noon, when we neared Jussy, a terrible enemy machine-gun fire met us. The English had thrown infantry and artillery reserves into the village. Jussy lies along the Crozat canal, and some 500 metres behind the town runs a railroad embankment. The canal and embankment were very convenient for the defence of the village. Repeated attacks were stopped short of Jussy with heavy losses. The artillery battery with us could help little, because the English machine-gun crews behind the embankment constantly changed position.

All day the remnants of the British divisions, augmented by an entrenching battalion, by pioneers and by amorphous groups of survivors, continued to beat the Germans off and hold the line of the canal.

The River Somme, rising in the high ground east of St Quentin, runs south-west before looping north to Péronne, and it described a wide arc round the critical sector held by the British Army, until it turned sharply west of Péronne to carve a meandering course through Amiens to the sea. The river was important to the economy of northern France. In the places where it was narrowest and least navigable, canals had been constructed in Napoleonic times to allow barges to ply along the Somme and to link it to the River Oise, a mile or so to the east.

North of St Quentin the River Omignon ran south-west to join the Somme. The previous day, as the line was thrust back and the Germans filtered along the valley of the Omignon, the left flank of the 61st Division was dangerously exposed along the depth of its battle zone and even behind it across the Holnon plateau. The danger was that the enemy might filter round it and capture Holnon Wood from the rear. A thin defensive line flung back south of the valley was hard-pressed to hold it. By mid morning on 22 March the enemy were pushing hard against the northern edge of Holnon Wood. They were also attacking its long frontage from the east. Holnon village had been captured, Manchester Hill had gone, and just behind it the enemy had a foothold in the village of Savy. The 61st Division had retired, but only a short distance, and the line had been reformed round the perimeter of Holnon Wood and behind the village of Etreillers to the south of it. They had good artillery support, there was no shortage of machine-guns, and during the morning the Germans made little progress. But it was not for want of trying. Their casualties were immense, a second division had already been sent in as reinforcements, and that morning Walter Bloem's reserve battalion was ordered forward.

After their day of anxious waiting, it came as a huge relief, and his men were only slightly subdued by their march through the old No Man's Land past the scattered bodies of comrades cut down in the first assault the day before. Passing through ruined villages, they tramped in open order up the slopes of a hill above Holnon Wood to the left of the captured village and halted to wait in a sheltered position just below its brow while Bloem sent his orderly officer to make contact with the battalion in front. Almost two hours passed.

Machine-gun bullets were spurting and spluttering over the crest, but from time to time Bloem crawled to the summit to see what he could of the fight in front. But it was hard to make sense of the confusion.

Eventually, as the tumult ahead began to ease, a report was thrust into his hands. It had been scribbled in haste by the young officer, and the wording of his note was quite unmilitary: 'Infantry which can storm like this are unconquerable. Without a doubt Holnon Wood is ours.' Bloem could hear for himself the hurrahs of the triumphant troops, and shortly afterwards he was ordered to move his own men forward towards the south-east corner of the wood.

*Hauptmann Walter Bloem, 12th (Brandenburg) Bn., [German] Grenadier Regt.*

I deploy the Battalion and we pass obliquely over the crest quite unopposed. Before us is a wide plain; on the right the captured wood, full of mystery. Not a shot. We march quietly on. Suddenly infantry and machine-gun fire opens from the left! Some Tommies have ensconced themselves as snipers in a group of trees. I order my leading company to take up a position and open fire. Good Lord! The Grenadiers of 1918 do not shoot like those of 1914, especially at long ranges – practically all they know about is fighting in trenches. The scoundrels in the treetops continue to loose off merrily, and the advance of the whole division is held up by that score of men. My companies have had to dig in. I send back word for a *Minenwerfer* section to be brought up. We wait half an hour. We smoke and curse.

At last the *Minenwerfer* arrives, and hardly has the first bomb burst in the treetops when the impudent snipers jump to the ground. I order the Battalion to advance, then out of the group of trees a single Tommy approaches. Is he fed up with the war? We wave to him to come into our shell-hole. He grins and makes a face. He actually picks up a clod of earth and throws it at us! One of my runners, very annoyed, raises his rifle to shoot him, but he runs off. I take the centre of Holnon Wood as direction – we enter it without hindrance.

It was a relief to be on the move and in action at last. It seemed an eternity since the reserves had set off on their slow crawl forward and an age since the leading wave of the assault had punched through the British line the morning before. Although there was no formal announcement, the news of the breakthrough spread like wildfire through the ranks of the reserve battalions. Excited and exhilarated, the German soldiers braced themselves for battle and the orders that would send them forward to share in the victory. But they kicked their heels for many weary hours before the orders came. They came a good deal later than their army commander had intended, for the progress of his troops had been slower than General Ludendorff had meant. Given their strength, which far exceeded the strength of their British opponents, they should have advanced miles, with the back-up troops following on their heels within hours of the first assault. According to the original plan, the reserve battalions now penetrating Holnon Wood were almost a day late.

Notwithstanding Bloem's officer's rapturous praise of the invincible German soldiery, their conquest of the wood had not been quite such a glorious feat of arms as the ecstatic report had suggested. The 61st Division had put up an obdurate defence, and, when the Germans finally succeeded in pressing into the wood, the bulk of the British force had voluntarily retired. It was a deliberate and disciplined retirement. Only the rearguard was left to oppose the Germans' passage through the wood, and they had opposed them bitterly every yard of the way – lying in ambush in dense undergrowth, firing Lewis-guns from makeshift positions behind uprooted trees, fighting hand to hand in clearings, denying the progress of the enemy along rough forest tracks, and, at the last, fighting to exhaust the enemy and to gain time for their comrades to take up the position where they were to stand fast behind the battle zone. The position was clearly drawn on the Army map. It was shown as 'the Green Line', the last line of defence.

Running through the western outskirts of the village of Attilly on the far side of the forest, the Green Line curved north across open ground a few hundred yards beyond Holnon Wood and south in the other direction to skirt behind the village of Etreillers. It was not much of a line. The trenches were sketchy and shallow, in places they were only a few inches deep, and, even if much more time had been available, even if the situation had been less critical, the fighting soldiers were not equipped with enough spades and pickaxes to improve them. On other parts of the XVIII Corps front some men were still fighting on the forward edge of the battle zone, but they could hardly be left there when neighbouring battalions had retired. General Sir Ivor Maxse saw no alternative but to order the whole Corps front to retire to the Green Line. The order was issued shortly after midday, but even then Maxse was having second thoughts, and a short while later he issued another order. His better judgement told him that the Green Line was no place to stand and fight, and if his men remained there, weakened as they were, his line would soon be broken and overwhelmed. It seemed to him that there was nothing for it but to swing back in a south-westerly direction and to take up a line on the banks of the River Somme. Here they would stand, and here they would fight – and here, surely, the reserves that must now be on their way would reach him. The loop of the Somme did not run parallel to the original line, and the front would be a long one for his depleted force to hold. But it could not be helped.

The 2nd Royal Scots Fusiliers were disposed round Etreillers in the sector of the 30th Division south of Holnon Wood. When the battle began Etreillers had been well behind the forward line of the battle zone, and Second Lieutenant Pat Hakewill-Smith was with his platoon in a small redoubt in a field north-east of the village. This was their battle-station, and the previous morning they had moved through the bombardment to reach it. Directly ahead, and between them and the enemy, the Bedfords were defending the village of Savy. The Royal Scots Fusiliers had had a comparatively peaceful day on 21 March. Occasionally Hakewill-Smith's platoon had helped out with long-range fire from their solitary machine-gun, and, although Etreillers behind them was being gradually reduced to ruins, his platoon in the field ahead were only slightly troubled by shelling. They had watched repeated attacks on the Bedfords, and applauded their own artillery when they repulsed them. They had cheered on the battalion on their right as they counter-attacked, and cheered louder still when they returned with a haul of prisoners. With rations and water for forty-eight hours, and plenty of ammunition, Pat felt reasonably secure.

Night fell, the mist gathered, and they could no longer see what was happening in front. From time to time there were scattered bursts of firing or a salvo of explosions nearby. None of them slept, and the night seemed very long. The morning brought no comfort. Sheltering from a fearsome bombardment, they guessed, correctly, that the enemy was making a final bid for Savy. Not far to their left they could see the fierce fight for Holnon Wood, and on their right it was clear that the village of Roupy was now in the hands of the enemy. It was equally clear that, apart from a thin and scattered line beyond them, they were now in the front line. The hours dragged on.

*Second Lieutenant E. ('Pat') Hakewill-Smith, 2nd Bn., Royal Scots Fusiliers, 30th Division*

I collected some odd men coming back, and this brought the strength of the platoon up to about sixty. I was lucky enough to get hold of a stray Vickers machine-gun and its team, and I also got another Lewis-gun off one of our aeroplanes, which was forced to land near my trench. This meant that I now had three machine-guns and about sixty rifles and, but for the fact that my trench was unwired, I should have felt very confident. But our position by then was like this:

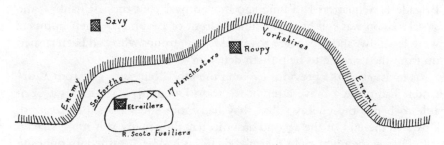

Shortly after four o'clock in the afternoon the enemy began to push on again. There were simply swarms of them – line after line, coming about five paces apart. I counted thirty lines and then got tired of counting, there were so many of them. Just at this time we got a very nasty enfilade machine-gun fire from our left, which I didn't like a bit, but luckily we spotted the gun, fired at it like billy-o, and managed to make it shift. The Boche came slowly plodding along, simply thousands of them! I waited until they were 600 yards away and then opened up with machine-guns and rapid rifle fire. There were so many of them that we couldn't miss! We simply *mowed* them down, and they weren't making much ground. But suddenly we saw *more* Boche behind us, coming through Etreillers and working round our rear. I turned a Lewis-gun on them and this held them up, but only for about two minutes, and then I saw the Boche on our right flank pushing on, so the situation was like this:

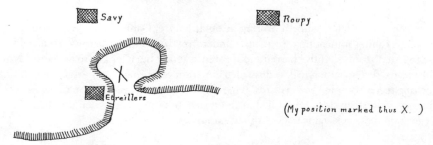

(My position marked thus X. )

I hadn't liked the situation in the least for the previous fifteen minutes. None of our field guns had been firing, and I heard no rifle fire either from the rest of my battalion or from the battalion on my right, and I knew that if they had still been in position they would have been fighting hard. But my orders were to hold on to the last.

In the sunken road at Beaumetz, the former Brigade Signals dugout was only superficially damaged, although Dick Gammell had done his best to destroy it. But even by the evening of 22 March no curious enemy soldiers had set foot in it. The Germans had got no further than Doignies. The two Brigade Headquarters had long ago moved back, but the left flank of the 51st Division was still holding a line in front of Beaumetz. Their numbers were few now, and they were thankful for the troops who had been rushed up from the rear line to help them defend it.[1]

As long ago as the previous evening the 8th Gloucesters and 10th Worcesters had made a brave attempt to storm Doignies. They had not been able to budge the enemy – but they had more effect than they realized. Towards the end of the second arduous day the enemy was more shaken still. During the night eight German divisions had been rushed up opposite the IV Corps front. They were far from fresh. They had been fighting all day and had had little sleep, but, although they had suffered many casualties and their numbers were far fewer than twenty-four hours previously, they still greatly outnumbered the remnants of the stricken British force in the line they were intended to break. It was held by only eight weak brigades, and the Germans had every reason to suppose that their task would be a walkover.

At dawn on the second morning of the battle, the German heavy artillery began to pound the British lines and the first of many infantry assaults was launched. Again and again the Gloucesters and the Highlanders in the trenchline east of the old sunken road beat them off. Between Morchies and Vaulx–Vraucourt, north-west of Beaumetz, and therefore actually behind it, the supply of ammunition had almost run out, and as the front wavered

1. Nine years later, while motoring through France, Gammell made a detour to Beaumetz and, rummaging through the undergrowth, found the stairway to his old dugout. It was only slightly charred and apparently intact, but it looked so dangerously dilapidated that his father-in-law dissuaded him from venturing into it – to Gammell's lifelong regret. Not long afterwards, when the road was resurfaced, the many deep dugouts in its steep sides were filled in and sealed, but in winter, when the roadside vegetation dies back, faint traces of their entrances can still be seen.

and the Germans filtered through the widening cracks a six-mile gap was gradually opening in the line between Beaumetz and Mory. If it were not filled, the arrow-straight road from Cambrai would be wide open and there would be nothing to stop the Germans walking straight through to Bapaume. The tanks were ordered up from Haplincourt to plug the gap and stop them. It was the last and only chance.

The 2nd Battalion Tank Corps was more than five miles behind the tenuous line, and when their section commander hurried along shortly after lunch the subalterns of Robert Watson Kerr's section were lounging in shirtsleeves near their tanks, enjoying a postprandial snooze in the afternoon sun.

*Lieutenant R. Watson Kerr, MC, 2nd Bn., Tank Corps*

He shouted, 'Look slippy! You're going into action at once!' That made us jump, and in a moment or two we had got our tunics and Sam Browne belts on, pocketed our loaded Colts, and crossed the road to our tanks. 'Here!' I shouted to the reconnaissance officer when I had got my tank under way – 'where's the front line?' 'There isn't one,' he replied. 'Well, where's the Boche, then?' He pointed over the sunny fields ahead. 'Just walk right on and you'll find them soon enough!'

We set off walking beside our tanks, with our crews inside them, but after we had covered some distance across country there was a slight tension in the air. Guns were firing somewhere near. Then suddenly, to our right, about a hundred yards or so away, we caught sight of a battery of British field guns firing in the open.

We stopped. So did the battery. Then to our amazement we heard the artillerymen shout, 'The tanks! The tanks!' and they followed this up with enthusiastic cheers, led by the officer waving his cap above his head. We waved back – a little embarrassed – thinking that the gunners must have been feeling pretty desperate to cheer us like that.

Pipsqueaks were now dropping unpleasantly around and beyond us, and so we separated to our own tanks. It was safer there, and any minute now we might come on the infantry who were supposed to support us. But that was where we made a mistake! There were no infantry ahead of us. We were on our own, and the battery of artillery had apparently been the front line. No wonder they had cheered![1]

---

1. The 9th Welch, who were garrisoning Beugny astride the crucial Cambrai–Bapaume road, had been intended to go forward with the tanks, but in view of the precarious situation it was decided to keep them where they were to defend the village in the event of the Germans breaking through.

Apart from some scattered clusters of infantry, the tanks were on their own. The roar of the powerful motor, the crashing of gears, the rattle of vibrating ammunition racks as the tank lurched along its ponderous course made it quite impossible to hear anything but the loudest of explosions outside its armoured walls. It was also difficult to see, for a narrow steel flap gave only a limited view of the ground ahead, and it was some time before Watson Kerr realized with some trepidation that the rest of their section had disappeared.

*Lieutenant R. Watson Kerr, MC*

There was a knoll ahead, with hillier ground on the left, and I decided to leave the valley and take to the slopes. The tank began to mount it gently. Then suddenly I saw what looked like a whole German Army, in full marching order, with banners flying and the harnesses of horses sparkling in the sun. They were coming towards us over the crest of a grassy slope several hundred yards away, battalions of them against the distant skyline, a swarming mass marching towards us in open country in full marching order, in brilliant sunlight, and with nobody apparently to stop them but ourselves. And *what* a target! My driver and I couldn't believe our eyes at first!

After the first shock of surprise we quickly got our guns going, and in the concentrated fire the huge host ahead melted back over the horizon.

It seemed fantastic, incredible. And it was all over in a moment. There was only the bare hill ahead now.

The tank crew were dumbfounded. It seemed to them in the elation of the moment that they had single-handedly driven off the cream of the Kaiser's Army. They whooped and cheered, grinning with delight. They could hardly believe it. But just as Watson Kerr was about to close the flap he saw with dismay that, in their blind plunge forward, they had blundered into a maze of trenches swarming with enemy infantry and machine-gunners. The enemy soldiers were even more disconcerted by the sight of the tank. They began to run, scrambling towards the shelter of a wood on the slope above. The tank thundered after them in pursuit.

With the aid of fascines – those weighty bundles of tight-packed faggots which could be automatically dropped to form a bridge – a Mark V tank could travel across trenches as it lumbered straight ahead, but manoeuvring the bulk of its twenty-seven tons among such a labyrinth of earthworks was a very different matter. It was perilous going. Peering through the flap, holding his position with considerable difficulty, thrown from side to side as the tank jolted and juddered across the uneven ground, Watson Kerr could see nothing but a crazy jumble of crumbling earth, scrambling legs, gaping holes. Inside, as the engine strained to haul the monster up steep slopes, the noise, the fumes, the heat mounted. Above the roar of the tank's engine and the grind of its revolving tracks, streams of machine-gun bullets rattled against its outer walls. They bounced off the heavy casing as harmlessly as hailstones, but, as the metal lining flaked beneath the impact, flurries of red-hot splinters showered down on the crew. They cursed and dodged them as the tank roared on, hoping with every buck and plunge that their luck would hold, gambling on the chance that they would not bog down, dreading the next shuddering jolt that might herald disaster. Watson Kerr soon decided that it was high time to make for home.

*Lieutenant R. Watson Kerr, MC*

I shouted to the driver, and we turned carefully so that our nose faced the steep side of a trench. The tank began to mount, slowly, slowly, its tracks biting into the loose soil and its tail dipping dangerously low. Slowly the earth in front crunched away, the tank's engine roaring itself out. Then something terrible happened. Suddenly the engine stopped, and there was silence. A grim, hellish emptiness after all that bedlam!

I think all our hearts stopped with that engine. Then I scrambled back from my seat. 'Come on!' I shouted. 'Get her going again.' Our voices sounded hideously loud!

We got the starting handle, fixed it, and, crouching down, prepared to turn it. 'Now!' I said, and we swung it round – and the miracle happened. The engine spluttered into life, and in a moment or two we were out of the treacherous ground, careering down the valley, knowing that we had done all that one tank could.

We eventually got back to camp in the twilight, and my crew of six and myself, feeling very exhausted, went in search of food.

Despite their first, delirious impression, Watson Kerr and his crew had not quite defeated the entire German Army. They had not been on their own, though of the twenty-five tanks which went into action only nine returned. But they had panicked the leading companies of the German 24th Reserve Division and, as the panic spread to the companies behind, the whole division retired in a disorderly rabble, and it was some considerable time before it was reorganized. By then it was far too late to try again to advance that night.

Between them, the tanks and the gunners had closed the gap in the Third

Army front. Had there been enough infantry to follow through, they might have closed the line and stood their ground. As it was, they had gained precious time – long enough to form a new and stronger line behind, and long enough for the guns to be moved back to support it. The heavy guns of the German artillery inadvertently assisted by firing short and shelling their own troops, and when they scattered in confusion for shelter more than 200 enemy soldiers ran into the eager arms of 153rd Brigade, who delightedly took them prisoner. The situation was still critical, but it was a heartening episode in a long, grim day.

On the Fifth Army front, Pat Hakewill-Smith and his men were still 'holding on to the last' in their isolated position in front of Etreillers, and by five o'clock he had no doubt that 'the last' had already come and gone. He was right. The order to withdraw had never reached him, and it was a long time since the rest of the Battalion had begun to make their way back.

Now the enemy was closing in. It was clear that they would very soon be encircled and, without so much as a strand of wire to protect their position, there was no chance of holding back a force which outnumbered them many times. Reluctantly Pat Hakewill-Smith alerted his small force and prepared to withdraw. He gave the order calmly, but he was very much afraid that he might have left it too late.

*Second Lieutenant E. ('Pat') Hakewill-Smith*

The Boche had nearly joined up around us. We couldn't withdraw to our rear, so we slipped off to our right rear. Naturally, as we left the trench, we came under rifle fire and machine-gun fire, and they also got a couple of guns on to us and sprayed us with high shrapnel, but by a miracle we got across the open only dropping about a dozen men, who most unfortunately had to be left.

After covering 200 yards of open ground, we got under cover of a hedge round an orchard, but it was only just out of view and we still got it fairly hot. Fortunately I knew the ground, and we worked our way into a shallow railway cutting where we were fairly safe. The enemy didn't follow us up, and five minutes later we were out of sight and out of trouble. I only had about thirty men left by this time, and two of my machine-guns had been put out of action. About a quarter of a mile further on we came into the rear zone and ran into a battalion of the Rifle Brigade, to whom I attached myself. They told me that the order to evacuate had been given at three o'clock and everyone else had gone by 3.30, whereas we did not leave until 6 p.m.

We went on down the railway line and cut across country when

we were out of sight. We were now in some trenches on a small incline
in a shallow valley on the right of a village called Vaux. Here we got
a generous dose of eight- and ten-inch shells, and then, just as it was
getting dark, the enemy attacked in force. As our wire was uncut and
we had a good field of fire this was easily stopped, but shortly after we
had beaten off this attack a hostile aeroplane flew over us very low
down. As it was now dark we couldn't see it, but when it was directly
over us it dropped a phosphorus bomb that burst in the air with a great
shower of 'golden rain'. Although it was very pretty to look at, we
did *not* like it and, sure enough, about two minutes later we came in
for fairly accurate shelling from the *rear*! We knew then that the enemy
was past us on both flanks, so at 9 p.m. on the second day the situation
was like this:

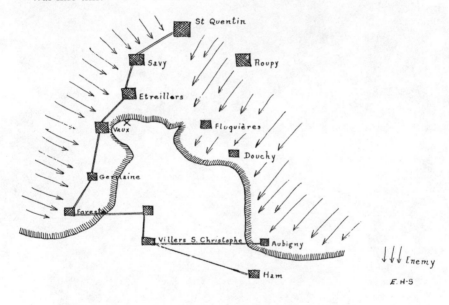

Plodding on, keeping just a step or two ahead of the Germans, they skirted
the village of Foreste, which was already in enemy hands, and, keeping to
lanes and cart tracks, struck out across country. It was hard going in the
dark, but they knew very well that the Germans were at their heels.

By evening on 22 March, Reinhold Spengler's regiment was still stuck at Jussy
on the northern bank of the Crozat canal. The Germans had tried repeatedly
to get across, and Spengler's regiment had been in the thick of the fighting. At
dusk they braced themselves for one final effort. The attack failed.

★

The men cut off at Vendeuil fort had given up all hope of a rescue. It was a long time since the last encouraging message had been flashed from the fort at Liez, they had fired their last bullet, and Captain Fine knew that the time had come to surrender. He intended to do so in military style. The men had already trickled down from the ramparts, and, when they had piled their useless rifles and formed up, they swung open the heavy gates and marched out. The Captain took his place at the head of the bedraggled column, carrying a white rag nailed to a stick – but he carried it like a banner. The Germans held their fire and rounded them up in an almost comradely manner. Then they marched them up the road to St Quentin. It was a long way for hungry, exhausted men, but they marched with backs straight and heads held high in a final gesture of defiance. They were disappointed, bone-weary and thoroughly fed up, but they had given the enemy a run for his money.

# Chapter 13

The thousands of soldiers lying out on the battlefield spent a comfortless night. The clear starlight had long ago disappeared behind the gathering mist, and the dark gave way reluctantly to the murk of another thick, grey dawn. For many of them, manning the guns, trekking through the night, or standing on the alert for a move by the enemy, there had been no chance of rest, and those who had managed to snatch an hour or so of fitful sleep woke stiff and numb to the booming of guns, the chill of damp garments clinging to weary flesh, and the prospect of a third punishing day.

The second company of the 3rd Bavarian Regiment had passed the night in a gravel pit close to the canal bank north of Jussy. By chance or design, this was a target for British guns, but most of the shells had exploded in the centre of the pit and, although the men had been forced to stick like burrs to its steep perimeter slopes, there had been no casualties. This was a considerable relief to Hauptmann Eugen von Schobert. After the losses of the past two days, and the last costly attempt to cross the canal, his company was already short of men, and in an hour's time, when they renewed the assault, it would be in the leading wave. Early in the morning his men clambered from the gravel pit and made a meagre breakfast of iron rations. There were a few looted titbits to supplement rye bread and the cold sausage of uncertain provenance, but there was nothing to wash down the dry, unappetizing fare – not even the familiar brew of lukewarm ersatz coffee – and it had not been possible to replenish water-bottles, drained in the heat of yesterday's fighting.

Von Schobert gathered his company round him and spoke to them soldier to soldier, and man to man. They were dishevelled and hollow-eyed, they had fought hard for seventy-two hours, they had performed magnificently, and the Captain congratulated them on a fine achievement. But the battle was not yet over. One more effort was needed. There were painful gaps in the ranks and they were all conscious of the loss of dear comrades, but the enemy had also had heavy casualties and the line defending the canal was feeble. One more push and it would surely give way. Von Schobert's speech was inspiring. His men could not cheer him, for they were within earshot of the enemy and had been warned to be quiet, but he had roused their fighting spirit and, as he led them towards the canal, they marched with the purposeful tread of men who had the scent of victory in their nostrils.

Twenty-four hours ago, when the last of the British troops were safely across the canal, the bridges had been blown up. But some were only partially destroyed, and the previous evening, before his company retired after its last abortive attack, von Schobert had trained his binoculars on the bridge at Jussy. Its girders were twisted and drunkenly askew, its centre had collapsed into the canal, but there were no impassable gaps, and von Schobert had judged that, given time and a modicum of luck, it would be just possible for his men to pass over the debris. Now he blessed the fog that might muffle the sound of their passage and hide their movements from the British soldiers on the other side. One by one, clumsily, ghostlike in the mist, the men worked their way across.

They crossed painfully slowly in groups of four or five, lurching awkwardly across the sagging girders, hanging from precarious handholds, swinging unbalanced by the weight of rifles and equipment, scrabbling in search of a half-submerged foothold, straining to reach the hand of a comrade stretched over a dangerous gap. Von Schobert was one of the first to cross, and he waited on tenterhooks on the far bank, aware that a single footfall might be enough to alert the enemy. The scrape of booted feet, the chink of equipment, the occasional splash, a stifled curse, an involuntary exclamation – every tiny sound jarred on his ears like the blare of a thousand klaxons. Georg Maier and his light-machine-gun sections had the worst of it. 'Light' it may have been, but the dragging weight of forty-three pounds slung on the back, the unwieldy boxes of ammunition, passed from hand to hand along a chain of limpet-like men, made for slow and tortuous progress. It was a miracle that they made it.

*Gefreiter Georg Maier, 3rd Machine-Gun Coy., 1st Bavarian Division*

As soon as we crossed over the canal bridge the enemy was alerted and opened fire. Thanks to the fog, he was not able to hit us hard, and our infantry quickly stormed the position where the firing came from and we followed with our machine-guns. The town was soon on fire. It looked grotesque through the dense fog, and we became confused by all the noise of shell-fire, rifle and machine-gun fire, and the cries of the wounded. Because of the fog we couldn't see much of the enemy – or even of our own forces – but we stormed on through the streets among the burning houses. All at once we came under fire from English Lewis-guns. In the fog they could not see us clearly, and the bullets fell rattling on the street. This caused quite a panic! We pointed our own guns in the direction of the shooting and, by good luck, we found the aim. They soon stopped firing and fled.

In spite of the fog, our infantry stormed on towards a railway embankment, driving the English in front of us. They stopped and fired at us from the top, but they were soon driven off and took cover on the other side of the embankment. We got there about the same time with forty or fifty men and four machine-guns, while behind us the rest of our boys were still fighting the English we had overrun in the streets of Jussy.

We were lying on one side of the embankment, the English on the other. What to do? We had no hand-grenades, and neither did they. Soon we had lost three men out of four shot through the head by snipers – but the worst was still to come.

Our own artillery began firing on the embankment. They were unaware that some fifty men and our four machine-guns already were there. One shell dropped between the tracks on top of the embankment and killed a few of our infantrymen. Another man from one of the machine-guns had his left arm torn away. Suddenly, to our horror, we got fire from machine-gun teams in the rear. The thick fog of the morning had helped us to take Jussy, but now we were unable to call off the artillery fire. We shot rocket flares into the air, but they could not be seen. Because of this we sent runners back twice, but they were killed on the way. As soon as the fog disappeared we would be seen by the English, and then what? To make yet more trouble, our ammunition was dwindling down to almost nothing, and we had to search dead and wounded men for any they had. Our machine-gun officer, Leutnant Hirschberger, went from gun to gun telling the men to save ammunition.

One man near me was shot through the lung and slowly died from internal bleeding. I can remember how he gradually lost his colour and his voice, sinking slowly into delirium, begging us to deliver his last message to his loved ones if we should ever again see our homeland. It was terrible seeing a young comrade slowly bleeding to death with no help around, surrounded only by the enemy. Well, if we did not soon get help from the rear, we would be dead, too – or, at best, taken prisoner.

*Leutnant Reinhold Spengler, 2nd Coy., 1st Bavarian Infantry Regt., 1st Bavarian Division*

The next hour was pure hell. Only two sets of tracks separated us from the English, and our artillery was still dropping shells on the embankment. Lying there, it occurred to me that I had had nothing to drink for the past twenty-four hours. Thirst gnawed at me – all my comrades were the same. Suddenly, one of our infantrymen threw himself down beside me. It was Hans Weissenbrucker, a friend of mine from Munich, who had been with me since we joined the regiment on the Somme in 1916. He said, 'Here, Reinhold, drink!' He gave me his water-bottle – and that water tasted wonderful. How Weissenbrucker came upon it remains a mystery to this day!

Finally our brave artillery liaison officer managed to get through to tell of our predicament, and the firing from our own guns stopped.

*Gefreiter Georg Maier*

About 9 a.m. an officer finally reached our reserves and told them of our situation. By 10.30 the sun broke through the fog, and immediately reserves from our regiment and the 24th Bavarian Regiment advanced, taking all the English prisoners who we had overrun in the town earlier. As soon as the English saw help approaching, they quickly left the other side of the embankment. When we saw the enemy retreating, we put our machine-guns on the top of the embankment and fired at them streaming across a large field between Flavy-le-Martel and Faillouel.

Myself and a friend were the first to go over to the other side of the embankment and begin looking for souvenirs. There were many dead Englishmen. We found hundreds of cigarettes in the dead soldiers' knapsacks, along with chocolate, fine biscuits and lots of good things *we* didn't know any more. I didn't smoke, but I took all the cigarettes I found and gave them to my comrades. I also found a picture in the knapsack of one of the Englishmen lying dead at the embankment. It was a girl, and after the war I had it in mind to make enquiries in England, but I could no longer read the address on the back. I still wonder where she lived and where the dead soldier had come from.

When we were finally relieved we looked over the English prisoners, especially the ones who had harassed us so much from the rear. I guess they were glad to still be alive. The war was over for them – but not for us! I met two schoolmates from my home town among the troops who were advancing, and we shook hands and chatted of home before they had to go ahead. After it was all over we rallied our men from the 3rd Battalion and went back into Jussy. There we found an English provision depot and a barrel of porter beer, which we opened with one shot of the pistol – and, boy!, at this moment it tasted heavenly! We rested a few hours, and our commander came along to congratulate us and thank us.[1] At 4 p.m. we followed our advancing troops as reserves.

The Green Line on the canal had gone. It had been the line of last resort, but there had simply not been enough men to hold it. To the right and left of Jussy, other German troops had managed to cross the canal across improvised bridges under cover of the fog and, now that the Bavarians had captured Jussy, they spread out to smash other pockets of resistance and inch by inch sweep away the defence. By mid-afternoon the British line between Tergnier and St Simon had been pushed back nearly two miles along most of its length.

Everyone was on the move: the German Army pushing forward, swelled by large contingents of fresh troops; the British Army fighting hard as it fell back; the French moving rapidly into the Fifth Army sector to support it; and Fifth Army HQ hurriedly quitting Nesle to take up new quarters at Villers-Bretonneux, twenty miles to the north-west.

Paul Maze had spent the night at Nesle – the last he was destined to spend in a bed for days to come. He had risen early, but Nesle was already teeming with townspeople rushing about, calling from door to door, from window to window, desperate for news. At General Gough's headquarters, clerks and orderlies running hither and thither were loading mountains of papers, signalling equipment and personal effects, in preparation for the move. The lorries were drawn up in the yard, and large numbers of panicking civilians were clamouring at the gates, urgently pleading that they and their household possessions might also be loaded up and carried westward to safety. It was a sad sight, for nothing could be done to help them. *'English soldat no bon!'* shrieked one woman, shaking her fist at a departing lorry. Her meaning, in the pidgin French which was the lingua franca between the Army and French civilians, was easily understood. It was dispiriting to say the least.

Maze caught up with the commander of the Fifth Army artillery. Oblivious to the chaos, General Uniacke was calmly making his way to breakfast. He had dressed, washed and shaved, and he looked as spick and span as if he were walking to the mess at Woolwich or Aldershot. He was decidedly pleased with himself. The Fifth Army, to be sure, had lost many guns, but Uniacke was equal to the challenge. Without a by-your-leave from General Headquarters, he had taken it upon himself to requisition more than enough guns to replace them from GHQ's own reserve gun parks, and they were

1. Shortly afterwards, Hauptmann von Schobert himself received the congratulations of the Regimental Commander and was awarded the Bavarian Order of Max-Joseph for his feat in leading the battalion across the canal.

even now on their way to make good the losses. Questions might well be asked, but, the General implied, he would be perfectly willing to deal with them when the time came. Meanwhile he was happily confident that his guns would go a long way towards turning the tide.

Maze found General Gough grave, but resolute. He had no choice but to move back to a position from which he could survey the shifting fortunes of his army and exercise overall control. Nesle was already far too close to the fighting line, a scant mile and a quarter across the plateau above the River Somme, and it would clearly be the enemy's next objective. But at all costs the Somme line must hold. The earliest dispatches, the news that the Crozat canal had been breached, had made dismal reading, but Gough was not a man to be dismayed. The 8th Division was even now detraining, and the vanguard would very soon arrive to defend the Somme. Better still, some French troops were already on the spot, and others were moving into position to help his hard-pressed force now over the canal on the southern edge of his front. Gough issued his orders quietly. Maze was to go in search of the French, to make contact with French Headquarters, and to report back. Above all he was to keep in touch with the French, and with XVIII Corps, and to impress on both how vitally necessary it was that they should keep in close touch with each other. Come what may, there must be no occasion for the enemy to swarm through a gap. 'Whatever you do,' he told Maze, 'impress on the troops with whom you are in contact that on no account are they to retire without warning units on either flank. The line must bend and give, but the enemy must not be allowed to break through.'

Tom Witherow was also in Nesle. The train which had been destined for Ham had never got there, for Ham had been already under bombardment and was on the point of being evacuated. He had spent the night at Nesle rather less comfortably than Paul Maze, for after reporting at Army Headquarters the only billet he and his companions could find was in an outhouse.

*Second Lieutenant Tom Witherow, 2nd Bn., The Royal Irish Rifles, 36th (Ulster) Division*

We were awakened early in the morning, as there was a general state of alarm. It was some time before we could succeed in getting definite orders. We were to report at 36th Division Headquarters, which were at a place called Fréniches. This place was pointed out to us on the map, and we had to get there as best we could. By this time there was great chaos in Nesle, and everybody who could do so was clearing out. The difficulty with us was our kit. We packed it up, and I left mine in charge of Robinson with instructions to try and get it back

to Roye, which was the next town on the main road and the place to
which Corps Headquarters was moving. This of course was easier said
than done, as the valise with all my belongings must have weighed
eighty pounds. Still, Robinson was a cute fellow and I knew I could
safely leave it with him. He got hold of an old handcart, put the valise
on it, and joined the throng on the Roye road. Before he got far out
of Nesle, cavalrymen appeared over the ridge and everyone thought
they were the enemy, so a great stampede occurred which resulted in
my kit being left on the roadside, where it no doubt eventually fell
into the hands of the enemy! The cavalry in question were I believe
French.

When we set off, every road was now a sad sight with a long,
unending stream of French peasants trying to escape. Whole families
with their farm carts packed with the most valuable of their possessions
mingled with military. What a scene of confusion it was! And the
sadness and tragedy of the whole thing, and the look of hopelessness
on the faces of these poor homeless people, made an indelible impression
on my mind. I can never forget the sights I saw that day.

With very great difficulty we made our way to our divisional
headquarters. The guns were sounding nearer and nearer, and we knew
the enemy could not be far off. We were lucky enough to get a lift
on some passing motor lorries, and in spite of the crowded conditions
of the roads we arrived at long last at our destination. We duly reported
our arrival, but were merely told to wait outside. After a long time
Marshall and I were at last given definite orders to proceed to the
fighting. General Hesse of the 109th Brigade had come to HQ and,
as he had evidently asked for officers, we were ordered to accompany
him back in his car to the front. There was no clearly marked front
line – only a series of posts. It was simply the line reached by the
advancing enemy when darkness put a stop to the fighting.

Eventually we reached the farmhouse which was the HQ of the
Brigade, where we found a number of very dirty, unshaven officers
discussing the situation. Colonel Peacock of the 9th Royal Inniskillings
was there, and we were ordered to be attached to his regiment. There
was a discussion about an attack which was to be carried out in the
morning and which both Marshall and I were to take part in.

Witherow's brigade HQ was in the village of Villeselve, south of Ham,
south of the Somme canal and south of the main road that ran for seven
miles from Ham to Flavy-le-Martel and on across the fields beyond Jussy
where Maier and Spengler had watched the British streaming back and their
own German reserves advancing to pursue them. But the advance had not

been plain sailing. The wooded country beyond gave ample cover, and the British rearguards had opposed them all the way. But the British were few, and the Germans were many. Slowly but inexorably they pressed on, taking heavy casualties, but filtering always forward into the wood and inching steadily onwards.

Earlier that morning, the 10th Essex had marched thankfully down the forest track from Frières, meeting cheerful parties of French infantry and exchanging jovial shouts of greeting as they passed. The sight of the French was comforting. At last, at long last, the Tommies believed, they were going to be relieved. This had also been the hope of General Gough, but events had moved too quickly for the plan to be methodically carried out, and the French were plunged into the fighting almost from the moment of their arrival. Already part of their first two divisions had been rushed up to assist the beleaguered 58th Division in the fight at Tergnier on the right extremity of the British line. Bill Ballard met them in the early hours of the morning as his wagon lumbered along congested roads to reach the gun battery.

*945278 Driver Bill Ballard, Royal Field Artillery, 58th Division*

Our guns were at Tergnier. That was a big railway depot, but it had been blasted by the Germans. The houses were all blown to bits and the cellars were open, so we were using these ruined cottages as flash cover. We always did that, because eighteen-pounders had a more or less low trajectory. We had our wagon lines and our billets in Chauny, which was a bit south of Tergnier, and it was really cushy there. We had beds and everything in our farmhouse. Wonderful it was after coming down from Passchendaele! Our front lines were somewhere near La Fère, almost running through it, and there was the Gobain Forest, where our infantry were. My brother was in the 6th London Regiment. I found out where he was and went to see him, and I found him in the front line in the Gobain Forest. The 6th and 7th Londons were on the extreme right of the Division, where the British line ended and the French line began.

When we got down from Passchendaele and took over that part of the line, we thought what a hell of a lovely time the French had had in these good billets, though the defences were nothing to write home about. We were just on the outskirts of Chauny in a big farm, and one of our chaps said, 'There's a big dump in the town – food and all sorts of stuff.' So we stacked our wagon with all this wine and sugar, cocoa and tins of milk – the lot. Yes, it was all there! You had to live by your wits to a great extent really. It was a war, and you'd got to live! But someone saw our chaps rolling these barrels of wine along the road to the wagon, and there was an awful row. The British military police made a raid on our billet, but we'd been tipped off, so we buried all this stuff down a well so that we could get it again. It turned out that it was the French mayor's civilian dump. Of course the MPs didn't find the stuff, but we were all stopped three francs from our pay, and the officers were stopped five francs – because the officers had some of the stuff as well, you can bet your life! We didn't mind too much, because we had plenty! When I met my brother I gave him a box of lump sugar, and he was delighted. It was a nice life while it lasted. But of course it soon went when we were attacked.

I was at the wagon lines when the barrage started early in the morning. It absolutely shook the ground! The shells were coming one after the other from heavy great guns, but you don't know what's going on and naturally I was worried about my brother!

The next night we were going up to Tergnier. *I* didn't know what for. As a driver, you don't know what the orders are, and all *we* knew was that we were going up to our battery. On the way up some voices called out to us, 'Where the hell are you chaps going to? This is the front line.' This was our infantry, and they were lining the road! Well, we got to the battery, and our gunners got drag ropes and put them round the guns and pulled them out of the cellars and brought them all down the road to where we were. They said they could hear the Germans talking, they were so close. The gun-line had become the front line!

When we got about two miles back down the road, there were stacks of lorries coming up – French lorries – and all the French troops were coming out of their lorries and going across the country with fixed bayonets, in open order. We thought, 'What the hell's all this?' We'd got another few miles to go, and here are the French coming up as if the Germans had broken right through. We were going along at walking pace, and a French soldier came up to me. I was on my horse, and he said, 'Hello, Tommy.' He was just an ordinary *poilu*, but he spoke perfect English. I said, 'You speak good English.' He said, 'Yes, well I was a waiter at the Savoy Hotel in London.' I always remember he said to me, 'I shall never come out of this alive.' Some men had a premonition. But of course he had to carry on with his regiment.

The French soldiers attacked at dawn – gallantly, but fruitlessly. They were no match for the rushing tide of the powerful German force. Bayonets could not prevail against a hurricane of bullets from machine-guns, and the

French had only as much ammunition as each man could carry. There was no more to be had, but they held out until they had fired their last bullet. When the survivors were forced back, the impetus of their retirement carried the exhausted British soldiers with it.

When Paul Maze made contact with the French, this was not yet clear. Thanks to his trusty motorcycle, Maze had made good time, squeezing past the many hold-ups on the encumbered country roads. Reaching a French regimental headquarters, and having placed himself at the disposal of the colonel, he set off to see for himself what he could make of the situation.

*Paul Maze*

I overtook some companies of French dismounted cavalry who were labouring with their loads across the open in order to keep off the road. They were the tail-end of a regiment hurried up to Bois Hélot. They said something about looking for their ammunition transport, which had not followed up.

I climbed on to a wooded knoll, from where I had a survey of about 300 yards of partial visibility and could watch the progress of limbers and carts on a road below. Shells were leapfrogging over my head and bursting on the roads behind me. The continuously increasing thundering on the whole line from north to south sounded most ominous. The fog had thinned a little, which permitted me to see vague groups of men ahead, and gradually a further patch of country rose to view beyond. Immediately the tac-tac of machine-guns was heard on the right, which brought to their feet a number of men I hadn't seen before, who started running – obviously for shelter. The fog then completely lifted, and the volume of machine-gun fire increased. Aeroplanes swooped down on our troops and dropped flares that brought an immediate response from their artillery. I certainly apprehended the worst, but, unexpectedly, to my forward left Bois Hélot sprang to life with debouching lines of French infantry advancing to counter-attack under cover of a machine-gun barrage. This seemed to divert the enemy's fire from the British, who were now springing to their feet and quickly retiring.

Bois Hélot was barely two miles west of the hamlet of Rouez, where the 10th Essex had breakfasted and were happily relaxing after more than forty-eight stressful hours of violent exertion. Rouez was hardly even a hamlet. It consisted of a solitary chateau and a large farm whose barns and outbuildings straggled round the elbow of a narrow unpaved road flanked by a finger of copse thrust out from the wood. Tiny though it was, there was ample room for the whole of the 53rd Brigade, which at full strength would have required three fair-sized villages to accommodate its men. When they were paraded for roll-call, the bedraggled remnants were a miserable sight. The colonel of the Royal Berks was disconcerted to discover that his command now consisted of his own headquarters company and a handful of men from his trench-mortar battery, a few machine-gunners, and a few dozen survivors of the Royal West Kents. Tucked into a sheltered position in the shadow of the wood, Rouez had so far escaped the worst of the shelling. There were green buds on the trees, a carpet of daffodils and clumps of purple crocuses in the chateau grounds, and even an ornamental lake, where some battle-stained Tommies were able to swill off the worst of the skin-crawling grime.

Very soon the noise of rifle and machine-gun fire, which had sounded reasonably distant up to mid-morning, began to crackle much louder and much closer, and a French liaison officer galloped up shouting that the Germans were in the wood just a few hundred yards away on the road to Frières. Hastily mustering the skeleton companies, the Essex filed through the spur of woodland between them and the road which, only a few hours ago, they had marched happily down to Rouez. There was barely time to form a line across the grass along the roadside before the Germans were upon them.

*Captain R. Chell, DSO, MC, 10th Bn., The Essex Regt., 18th Division*

On they came out of the wood, rank after rank, but, working their bolts like the Old Contemptibles, the Essex rifles scorched through them like jets of fire. New lines sprang up, and were mown down again until one almost sickened of the slaughter. There were at least three battalions of the enemy, and again and again the waves were crippled and sent back. The Essex paid a heavy price too. There was a gamekeeper's cottage right on the edge of the wood, and the Huns had a machine-gun at every window, and D Company took the full force of this deadly fire. Then, just after midday, the enemy broke through to a vantage point on our right. All the rifles were in the line, holding the Germans back in the wood, so Major Tween decided there was nothing for it but to attack with Battalion HQ – just a handful of pioneers, signallers, runners, even sanitary men. He led the attack himself, running in front shouting the men on. Alas, Tween himself was mortally wounded and died a little later – but they hoofed the Germans out and took the position.

We were fighting shoulder to shoulder with the *poilus*, and *they* were unfortunately short of ammunition, because their supplies hadn't caught up with them, but French armoured cars dashed up and down simply pouring out bullets, and the Germans got no further. It may seem to have been a small and unimportant attack in relation to the whole battle, but every moment at that vital junction point with the French, every moment gained by us or by the 58th Division was of incalculable importance in preventing the wedge which Ludendorff was pressing with all his might from biting into the gap on our left.

But, nevertheless, the Germans were advancing on both flanks. By nightfall they were well behind us, and only a narrow exit corridor remained. Another two hours and we should have been surrounded. As it was, it was a miracle that any of the Battalion got out at all. But we left many, many behind.

It was an anxious day in London. The news of the big attack had come as no surprise, least of all at the War Office, where Sir Henry Wilson, as Chief of the Imperial General Staff, had already given instructions for men on leave to be immediately recalled. He went personally to Victoria Station to see the Staff train pull out and to speak to officers on their way back to France, pausing also to have an encouraging word with groups of Tommies, who were clearly less than delighted by the abrupt summons to return to the front. Wilson then drove to Downing Street to see Lloyd George, and stayed there for the next five hours. It was a fine day in London – warm enough for the two men to sit for part of the time in the garden as they chewed over events in France.

News from the front arrived via a tortuous chain of communication, dispatched in the heat of battle via runner to brigade headquarters, by dispatch-rider to corps commander, and on by telephone or signal to an Army HQ. When all of these headquarters were simultaneously on the move, information was necessarily sketchy and long out of date by the time it reached the headquarters of the Commander-in-Chief, to be assessed and relayed across the Channel to the War Office. In London, although it was clearly understood that the situation in France was serious, the full gravity of the position had not yet been realized. Wilson was still inclined to look far ahead, and he urged the Prime Minister to take a long-term view. He urged him, in particular, to take immediate steps to conscript men up to the age of fifty and, furthermore, to extend conscription to Ireland. The CIGS was convinced that nothing less than a mass levy of every available man would, in the long run, win the war.

When the War Cabinet met at four o'clock Wilson went in with all guns firing, expounding his views with the force of a bombardment, stressing the necessity to recruit more and still more men and 'the importance of taking a long, broad view of the future'. His sole supporter was Winston Churchill.

But, although the Cabinet was not yet able to grasp the full significance of events in France, they were alive to the short-term danger, and the arrival of a King's Messenger with an urgent dispatch from the Commander-in-Chief did not reassure them. They learned, with some dismay, that the Fifth Army was in the process of falling back towards the Somme, and that the Third Army, although it had given less ground, was being forced to conform to the retirement of the Fifth. This news swung the balance. Fifty thousand boys under nineteen years of age were now encamped in Britain, fully – or almost fully – trained. It was reluctantly but unanimously decided to waive the lower age-limit for service overseas and to send them forthwith to the front.

Sir Douglas Haig had also made use of the King's Messenger to send a personal package to his wife. Although a King's Messenger travelled daily to London from GHQ, it was not the usual custom of the Commander-in-Chief to make use of him for personal purposes, but the circumstances were exceptional. Less than a week previously Lady Haig had given birth to a son. Food was scarcer in England than in France, and Haig's chef had made a quantity of rich beef tea from the plentiful supply of meat available to the Army. Reduced to a small quantity of solidified jelly, which could be diluted to build up the strength of the new mother, it was contained in a small, stout package which took up very little space in the dispatch bag. It was accompanied by a hasty, affectionate note from the Commander-in-Chief to his wife, and a War Office messenger delivered both items to Haig's house on Kingston Hill, where Lady Haig was nursing his newborn son.

Haig himself was concerned with weightier matters than the well-being of his family. The situation of the Fifth Army was much more to the point, and, having acquiesced in Gough's decision to withdraw to the line of the River Somme, the Commander-in-Chief was appalled to discover that Gough's force was now on the other side. Gough was barely installed in his new headquarters at Villers-Bretonneux when Sir Douglas Haig arrived in person and made no attempt to conceal his surprise at this development. He fully understood Gough's difficulties, but he was also acutely aware of the peril of the situation and the woeful consequences that would inevitably ensue if the gaps widened, if the French could not fill them, if the retirement of the Fifth Army should leave the Third Army 'in the air'. Taking a broad and objective view of the situation, with no knowledge of the valiant individual efforts that had held up an overwhelming force, he confessed, 'I cannot make out why the Fifth Army has gone so far back without making some kind of stand.' It would be a long time before it was accepted that the Fifth Army had been strained to the limit – and beyond.

On returning to his own headquarters, the first act of the Commander-in-Chief was to issue an uncompromising order:

The Fifth Army must hold the Somme at all costs. There must be no withdrawal from this line. It is of the greatest importance that the Fifth Army should effect a junction with the French on their right without delay. Third and Fifth Armies must keep in closest touch in order to secure their junction and must mutually assist each other in maintaining Péronne as a pivot.

Between leaving General Gough early in the afternoon and issuing that order at half past five, Haig received a visit from General Pétain. Pétain had fulfilled his obligation under his agreement with the British Commander-in-Chief. He was no less anxious than Haig that the French and British armies should keep in touch, and was willing to commit a far greater force than he had originally promised. But as for the twenty divisions Haig now demanded, *that* was impossible. If he denuded his own force in order to support the position of the British Army he might well be sacrificing the cause of France itself. In his belief that the Germans would very soon attempt to break through in Champagne, even march on Paris, Pétain had a powerful ally – and it was Germany herself.

That morning the German secret weapon had been unveiled. A mammoth gun had opened fire and begun bombarding distant Paris, seventy-five miles from a secret position deep in the forest of St Gobain.

20. The sunken road south of the village of Beaumetz where Second Lieutenant Dick Gammell's Brigade signals HQ was burrowed into the high bank beyond the tall tree. The HQ of Major Ronald Ward's 293 Artillery Brigade was close by, and when modern hedging machines have peeled back the undergrowth the traces of the entrances to these and many other dugouts are still discernible.

21. *Above*: Major Ronald Ward of C293 Battery, who rescued his guns from beneath the noses of the Germans advancing at Doignies.

22. *Right*: Major Ronald Ward, C293 Battery, caricatured by an artist comrade.

23. Looking towards Doignies from the sunken road at Beaumetz across the fields where the guns of C293 Battery were disposed – and later rescued by Major Ward.

24. The forward gun of C293 Battery was situated in this field on the edge of Doignies. Cows now graze in the rough pasture, still pock-marked with traces of the fighting.

25. The redoubts that formed the front line of the British battle zone round Hargicourt village are still evident on the chalky soil.

26. The entrenchments in the old quarries at Templeux-le-Guérard, where two companies of the 7th Lancashire Fusiliers and two of the Border Regiment held out until they were surrounded.

27. *Above*: The temptation of abandoned British supply dumps to the badly fed German soldiers significantly slowed the progress of their advance. 'Unimaginable treasures were found inside, but we could only pick up a few things to carry along – bacon, ham, corned beef, chocolate, cigarettes and real tobacco. (Our own smokes were terrible!)' Leutnant Reinhold Spengler. (Photo: Imperial War Museum).

28. *Left*: Brigade-Major Harold Howitt, MC, leaving Buckingham Palace with his wife, Dorothy, after receiving his Military Cross from the King.

29. *Above*: The village of Lechelle, where Battalion Headquarters, 23rd Londons, was overrun.

30. *Left*: Battalion HQ at Lechelle was in the farm at the top of the road. 'I was belting up that road as hard as I could. I hadn't gone more than thirty, forty yards before four Germans stepped out in front of me, all with their rifles trained on my stomach, and that was the end of my fighting!' Captain George Brett, MC.

31. Lieutenant L. Chamberlen, MC, 2nd Rifle Brigade, who was wounded at Pargny on the River Somme. '... we could see the Hun coming down the hill on *their* side while we ran down the hill on ours. We went like hell!'

32. Leutnant Fritz Nagel, whose anti-aircraft gun-crew K Flak 82 was roped in to help the German infantry attacking from Albert on 27 March 1918 (Photo: Richard A. Baumgartner).

33. To prevent injury from flying glass during air raids and bombardments, windows throughout Paris were reinforced by a network of gummed-paper strips in designs which were often elaborate in smart premises like these.

34. The operation of the long-range 'Paris Gun', which bombarded the French capital from a distance of seventy-five miles.

35. Private Horace Haynes, 2/6th Royal Warwicks, (*left*) with another of the young soldiers who were rushed to the front. 'When we went on parade, instead of saying "13 Platoon, Attention!", our platoon officer said "56 Draft, Attention!"'

36. *Right*: Capitaine Désiré Wavrin, 62nd [*French*] Division. 'I honestly believed that my last hour had come when the enemy brought up their awful *Flammenwerfers* and hosed us with liquid fire. The flames were less than a metre from my face. I wondered if I was going to be grilled like a piece of pork!'

Brave "Soixante-quinze", orateur pathétique
Qui jamais d'éloquence à court ne demeura,
Coffre fort et point asthmatique,
Des bords de la Marne au Jura,
C'est de toi surtout qu'on dira :
« Il a la gueule sympathique ! »

37. *Left*: The fast-firing French gun the 'Soixante-quinze', the most famous artillery-piece of the French Army, was prized for its performance.

## Chapter 14

When the first shell fell on Paris, people assumed that a bomb had been dropped from the air. Air raids were not unusual, and since the end of January, when the bombing had increased, Paris had taken on an unfamiliar appearance. The statuary in the Place de la Concorde had disappeared beneath strange sandbagged structures surmounted by jaunty slanting 'roofs' which gave them an odd resemblance to giant hats. Stockades of sandbags protected the sculpted panels of the Arc de Triomphe, the base of the column in the Place Vendôme, the mighty monument in the Place de la République, and a thousand statues and ornamental fountains in the city's parks and squares. To prevent injury by flying glass, windows throughout the city were reinforced by a network of gummed-paper strips, some in remarkable patterns which presumably gratified the taste of the residents but were not always appreciated by others. One householder caused particular annoyance to his neighbours by using paper of a lurid shade of blue, adorned with pink paper rosettes at the intersections of the strips. Smart shops employed professionals to apply the protective paper to plate-glass frontages and produced intricate designs that were both striking and artistic. Some incorporated the name of the firm, or advertising slogans, or even the ringing patriotic maxim '*On les aura!*', with its implication that, despite the temerity of the enemy in raining bombs on Paris, sooner or later the French would wipe the floor with the Germans.

On the whole, Paris endured the raids philosophically. Restaurants and theatres stayed open, and if a show ended while a raid was still in progress the cast would improvise an entertainment to keep the audience under cover until it was over. The bombs were not powerful and the damage was not extensive, although one bomb caused a sensation. It exploded in front of a taxicab, which promptly drove into the crater, fitting it as neatly as if it had been tailor-made to accommodate it. Next morning it attracted crowds of sightseers, and the driver, who turned up to inspect the damage, was the hero of the hour. He was quite unhurt, and, affecting a nonchalant air, was happy to repeat his story many times to a succession of eager listeners who plied him with cigarettes and even cigars.

Strictly speaking he should not have been driving during a raid, for the regulations laid down that all private and public transport must come to a halt. This caused maximum inconvenience to people who happened to be travelling on the Métro when their train stopped between stations and they were forced to continue on foot through the tunnels. Fortunately, most air raids occurred after dark, when the traffic was lighter than in daytime, and the sound of an explosion at seven o'clock on a fine spring morning was something new. The weather was clear in Paris, but there was no sign of an aeroplane in the cloudless sky, no sound of anti-aircraft guns, no familiar tattoo of warning drums in the streets. But there had undoubtedly been an explosion. Twenty minutes later, almost to the second, there was another. When the detonations continued at regular intervals, people retired to cellars and shelters. Shops and businesses stayed shut, traffic stopped running, Paris ground to a halt, and the morning passed in a buzz of rumour, counter-rumour and wild speculation.

Towards lunchtime, when the puzzled and hungry shelterers emerged in search of food, the explosions had stopped. The afternoon newspapers carried the astounding news that Paris had been shelled by a colossal gun which experts estimated was fired from a distance of at least seventy-five miles. Since no one could predict when it might fire again, or where the shells would fall when it did, the Government urged every citizen to 'take precautions'. The precise nature of the precautions they could take in the circumstances was not explained, but this was enough to send most people hurrying back to shelter.[1]

Later in the afternoon the Prime Minister, Georges Clemenceau, paid a morale-boosting visit to children sheltering in the basement of their school. They rewarded him with a spirited rendering of 'La Marseillaise'. The experiences of a long life had endowed Clemenceau with a certain imperturbability of character. It was not for nothing that he was called 'The Tiger', nor was it the first time he had heard German shells fall on Paris. He was already a man of thirty when the siege cannons of the Prussians were bombarding the city in 1871. But the singing of the children doubtless did a good deal to cheer him at a profoundly anxious time.

★

1. The 'Paris Gun', as it was properly known (although later confused with the gun known as 'Big Bertha'), was a combination of a 15-inch gun and an 8.2-inch gun, with two extensions to the barrel, each some forty feet long. To support its enormous weight, it was fixed to an overhead gantry with a pulley mechanism. The maximum range of the Paris Gun was roughly eighty miles, and to propel a shell of 280 pounds across such a distance it required a charge of almost twice as much explosive. There were three such weapons, in scattered emplacements near Laon in the forest of St Gobain. One burst its breech after firing two shots on 25 March; the third came into action on the 29th.

For the Kaiser, the news that the gargantuan gun had successfully begun bombarding the French capital set the seal on an excellent day. He was on board the palatial Imperial train on his way back from Ludendorff's advanced headquarters, travelling just a little more slowly than in peacetime, beneath the tinkling chandeliers in the white and gold magnificence of his private drawing-room. He was still elated by the success of the offensive, and he could hardly restrain himself from spreading the good news. As the train with its shining coachwork of blue and ivory pulled in from Avesnes, the waiting stationmaster was astounded when the Kaiser himself bounded from the train, shouting like a schoolboy, 'The battle is won! The English have been utterly defeated!'

By the Kaiser's personal orders, flags were flying throughout Germany and schoolchildren were given a whole day's holiday to celebrate the victory. But the German people – shabby, hungry and beset by weariness – craved less for victory than for peace to put an end to the killing and privation. Conditions were worse than ever. Prices were sky-high; rations – meagre though they were – were not regularly honoured, although the same goods were available for sale to the highest bidder on the black market; and the first spring vegetables (officially price-controlled) were openly selling at astronomical prices. A cabbage could cost half a week's wages. Although eggs should have been more plentiful with the coming of spring, they could be bought only in twos and threes and with a doctor's prescription. Public transport in towns was reduced to a few overcrowded buses and trams, slow and ramshackle. In Berlin, elephants from the zoo were pulling coal carts, although the 'coal' available to civilians was only a meagre ration of briquettes formed from compressed coal dust. There was no fuel for hot water and no soap to wash with, no tobacco for the consolation of a smoke, no sewing cotton to mend the holes in shabby garments, no medicines, no drugs. Growing numbers of industrial workers were going on strike, and there were violent disturbances in the working-class districts of Berlin and, elsewhere, rumblings of discontent that could not be quieted for long by waving flags and shouts of victory unless they were a certain guarantee of peace and better times. All that was certain in the aftermath of an offensive was the long, long lists of casualties, bringing heartbreak to the families of men who had died in the Kaiser's Battle to secure the Kaiser's victory.

One casualty of the battle was the stepson of General Ludendorff, whose plane was shot down on the second day of the battle. The news of his death had reached Ludendorff the same evening, but, although the General's grief was genuine, his personal feelings had to be set aside. He was first and foremost a soldier, moulded in the dutiful tradition of military service, and his first duty was to concentrate on the job in hand. Notwithstanding the Kaiser's roseate view, the situation was not developing entirely along the lines that Ludendorff had desired or planned.

The German Eighteenth Army, attacking with the greatest weight of numbers against the weakest sector of the British front, had attained un-expected success. But it had never been intended to pursue the battle beyond the Crozat canal. The original aim had been to divide British from French and, by holding-attacks against the French flank, to engage reserves which otherwise would be sent to assist the British. But now the temptation to exploit the new situation was considerable, although it had not been central to Ludendorff's strategy to seek a full-scale battle on the extreme right of the British line, where there was no strategic advantage to be won.

If the objective of 'pushing the English into the sea' was to be fulfilled, it was in the centre and north of the British line, closest to the Channel ports, that the push would have to succeed, and it was the Second and Seventeenth German Armies in this sector which had been meant to thrust home the momentum of the offensive. But in that all-important sector the British defences were remarkably obstinate. The centre of the Third Army line had been driven in, but north of the breach at Louverval and Beaumetz the line had merely swayed back to conform with troops retiring to the south, while north of the Scarpe, on the Arras front, neither the extreme left wing of Byng's Third Army nor the right wing of the First had budged an inch. If Ludendorff's grand strategy was to succeed, the First and Third Armies must be conclusively defeated.

Although the progress of his troops had been neither so swift nor so overwhelming as Ludendorff would have wished, the preliminary reports on which his decisions would be based had been encouraging, and those he received from his Seventeenth Army were particularly optimistic. They were also exaggerated and misleading. General von Below claimed, among other 'successes', that Monchy-le-Preux on the Arras front had been captured after a stiff fight. But the British had voluntarily evacuated the village, and the Germans had moved in without firing a shot. It was true that von Below's army had pushed well into the battle zone north of the Flesquières salient, but he was not the only German general to fall into the trap of believing that because an army had retired it was beaten. Nor was he the first. In the dog days of August 1914, as he followed the tiny British Expeditionary Force on its long retreat from Mons, General von Kluck had been under a similar misapprehension. Now, after four long years of conflict and stalemate, that same heady sense of exhilaration was sweeping through the German armies, and, dependent as he was on the judgement of his subordinates in the field, Ludendorff himself was not immune to its influence. General von Below was so certain of the accuracy of his own evaluation that he issued an uncompromising order to the right wing of his army: 'Follow the retreating enemy and prepare for the breakthrough.'

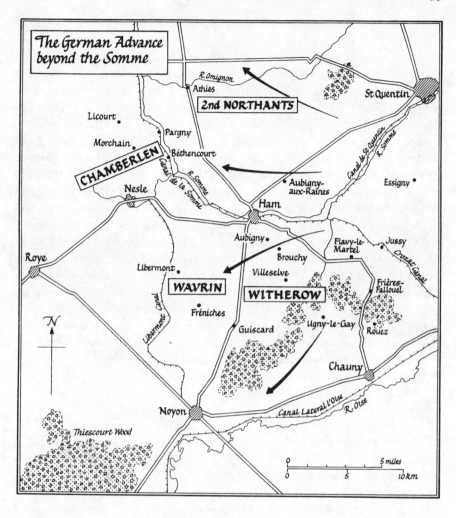

The German Advance beyond the Somme

Ludendorff also was thinking ahead, and in the light of the impression he had formed he revised his strategy. General von Hutier's Eighteenth Army was to exploit its success by pressing on to the south-west far beyond its original objective. On his right, where the Somme flowed east to west, the German Second Army would advance on a wide front on both sides of the river, while the Seventeenth and Sixth Armies attacking further north would drive the British into the sea. Outlining his new plans at a meeting with the Chiefs of Staff of the two army groups which were to carry them out, he added, 'We shall continue attacking at new places in order to bring the whole British front to ruin.' General von Kuhl, who attended that meeting, was astonished by the scope of this remarkable change of strategy.[1]

In order to facilitate the new plan and press home the victory as speedily as possible, Ludendorff sent three more divisions to swell von Hutier's Eighteenth Army, and three more from his own Army Reserve were ordered to move into position and stand ready to assist in extending the offensive to the north.

Speed was of the first importance, but, among the glowing reports from the battlefront and from the air above roads that were clogged with refugees, transport and retreating troops, some disturbing messages had reached the ear of the German commander. There were rumours of whole companies leaving the line of march to forage in abandoned British supply dumps, and of delays due to gorging and even drunkenness, which slowed up the progress of an entire regiment. The age-old instinct for looting, the temptation of almost unheard-of luxuries, in many instances overcame the German soldiers' inbred sense of discipline. Indeed, although some officers were complaining that they could not easily control their men, the officers themselves were not impervious to temptation. On 23 March, Leutnant Rudolf Binding recorded in his diary, 'Our cars now run on the best English rubber tyres, we smoke none but English cigarettes, and plaster our boots with lovely English boot polish – all unheard-of things which belong to a fairyland of long ago.' He might have added that large numbers of German soldiers were also marching in 'English' boots, wearing 'English' shirts and socks, and washing – when they had a chance to wash at all – with 'English' soap. Even the horses were starting to fill out on lavish feeds of corn and oats, by courtesy of the British Army – a welcome improvement on their accustomed diet of grain eked out with a quantity of crumbled leaves, collected by the ton the previous autumn by German schoolchildren.

In the turmoil of the retreat, the abandoned dumps and canteens were a blessing to British soldiers too. The Army continued to do its best to get rations to the men, but its efforts were haphazard to say the least, particularly where the gap between the Fifth Army and the Third was slowly widening. By 23 March the situation was becoming critical. On the southern edge of

1. Von Kuhl wrote nine years later: 'Such a dispersal of the Armies in three directions was thinkable only when, as Ludendorff said, a great victory had been achieved – that is, when the enemy had been beaten on the whole front . . . The situation was considerably different . . . thus there was a complete change of plan. Hitherto the main feature had been the attack of the Second and Seventeenth Armies against the British. To the Eighteenth Army fell only the protection of attack from the French. Now the French and British were to be separated and both attacked simultaneously. This meant shifting the attack a good way to the left.'

the Flesquières salient the 9th (Scottish) Division had retired to the Green
Line on the further edge of the battle zone at Nurlu, and they were not
impressed with what they found there.

*42821 Private Alex Jamieson, MM, 11th Bn., The Royal Scots (Lothian
Regt.), 9th (Scottish) Division*

The Green Line was supposed to be really something outstanding in
the way of a defensive line, but it was never completed, and when we
came back into it we thought the trenches must have been intended
to trap tanks, they were so wide! They were twice the width of a
normal trench – about twelve feet wide – and they had no fire-steps.
That was the first moment that I was frightened, really frightened,
because the orders came along, 'This position must be held at all costs
until the last man.' Well, you've got to be in that situation to understand
what it means. I was only nineteen, I'd only been in France a little
over a month, and I thought I was going to be killed. I had a sinking
feeling in my tummy. Everybody was thinking, 'How on earth can
we hold this position? It's impossible!' That was on the night of the
22nd. Of course, what happened was that, when daylight came on
the morning of the 23rd, we had been outflanked and we were out in
the blue. The order came to retire once again, which I must say was
a great relief to me.

Very near this Green Line was a big Expeditionary Force canteen,
which had been well behind the lines, of course, and as we hadn't had
much to eat for several days we were told to lift what we could and
find our own breakfast. This canteen had taken a direct hit, but in we
went. It was a marquee, or had been, and everything was all over the
place. All I could get hold of was some cigarettes – good cigarettes –
and some biscuits.

After we grabbed what we could and were going to continue retiring,
a South African officer who had been seconded to us said, 'The Africans
haven't got through yet. We must cover their retreat.' This was wrong,
as it happened, but he ordered us to go forward to this ridge, and I
remember seeing a few Germans running into a farmyard just a bit
ahead and everybody opened fire. I remember at least one of them
fell. Then we got the order to come back again. But having been out
in the blue, so to speak, our own people saw us coming, thought we
were Germans, and opened up on us as we were coming back.
Everybody was trigger-happy, because there were troops all over the
place, and if they saw anybody moving they were inclined to just let
go. You knew so little of what was going on except within a few yards.

But we all had the idea that it was all a deliberate trap and we were to go back a certain distance, form a bag, and entice the Germans into it. I don't know whether this was officially put out or whether it was the troops' own idea, but we thought we were leading the Germans into a trap and that would be that. If it hadn't been for everyone thinking that, it could have been a rout, I think. Of course we, as private soldiers, had no idea that the German offensive was covering such a wide front.

*Captain Geoffrey Lawrence, 1st South African Bn., 9th (Scottish) Division*

Early on the morning of the 23rd Major Ormiston came up and gave the officers our orders. He said, 'You are now the rearguard to the whole of this front, and you are to hold this line. You will fight to the last man and the last round. There will be no surrender and no retreat. All forward troops of ours retiring will be stopped on this line, if necessary with your revolvers, and you will shoot any man who refuses to stand.'

When he left, we set about improving our defences and waited for the enemy. It's difficult to describe the feeling that came over me then: that this was to be our final sacrifice. No heroics, but almost a feeling of uplift. Here we stand and here we die. Shortly after midday we could see troops of our adjoining division streaming back on our extreme right. There were bursting shells falling everywhere, dumps of ammunition going up, and burning supplies giving off great clouds of black smoke. I saw a driverless horse harnessed between the shafts of a mess cart rushing at full speed back towards us and being followed by exploding shells from the enemy gunners. He swayed between the shell-holes and somehow got back without upsetting the cart.

The enemy was following closely behind and was soon close to our line hoping to break through. We stopped many men of several divisions with our revolvers in our hands, but we never needed to use them. I stopped a young corporal of the Northumberland Fusiliers in charge of a Lewis-gun team, who said at once that he was quite prepared to make a stand and only too pleased to be given definite orders. Between us we sited his gun to fire in enfilade across our front, and just then a terrific racket broke out on our right with heavy enemy shelling and machine-gun and rifle fire from our troops. I suggested to Captain Hallack that we go down to the trench to see what was happening. As we were making our way along, the Jerries, who had by this time reached our wire in front of us, fired a grenade. It exploded in the trench, and Captain Hallack was severely wounded in the back.

Stretcher-bearers came forward, and I ordered them to take Captain Hallack and get back to Moislains as best as they could.

I went on, and found our men were holding on well. The enemy was halted, and his infantry was clustering behind a series of square-shaped manure heaps left by the French peasant farmers. Our line formed a long inverted arc, and I could see that, although the Germans were well protected by the manure dumps here on the right, they were vulnerable to fire from our position on the left, so I got back as fast as I could and told the Lewis team to follow me.

We climbed out of our low trench and crept up to some Nissen huts divided by a sandbag wall. Peeping over, I could see that I had a clear view of about ten of the enemy behind their manure heap less than fifty yards away. I said, 'Give me the gun,' and I let loose with a half-drum into the bunch of Jerries. There seemed to be only one survivor, who staggered away into the mist. Then I raised my fire to the groups sheltering further down. I was horrified to see the flashing flight of my bullets in a curving trajectory. It seemed that earlier on the Lewis-gunners had loaded their drums with one tracer round of ammunition to every five ordinary rounds, for anti-aircraft fire, and of course this gave our position away to the enemy artillery and they immediately started firing at us with bursts of shrapnel and high-explosive shells. We moved fast!

We got back to our trench, but things were getting very critical, with the enemy actually in our wire close by, and I could see in the distance that the division to our right was moving back, which would leave us all but surrounded. Major Ormiston appeared and ordered me to get all my men away in sections to our reserve line at Moislains and to stay with the final section myself, to give covering fire. They went off in relays, while the rest of us gave rapid fire at anything we could see, to hide our *very real* weakness. Then I got the last section of ten men, told them to follow me closely in single file, and we hopped out of the trench with the Hun now actually in our wire, firing wildly.

I put on a sharp pace and led off at right angles to our trench. The enemy by this time had got his field guns on a rise and started firing point-blank over open sights at us. One shell flew just over our heads and burst in front of us. The blast of it actually lifted our helmets. The next two ploughed a furrow at the side, barely a few feet away. As soon as they had our range I took a sharp left incline to put off their aim, and when I thought they had made their new correction I switched quickly to a right incline. And I was right! Their next shells burst *exactly* where I had been. I kept going like this until our little squad reached a fold in the ground out of sight of the gunners and we were soon clear of artillery and rifle fire.

We passed an enormous shell-hole (a small house could have fitted into it!), and in it was a group of our wounded. One little fellow pleaded and begged not to be left. I could only say that I was sure Jerry would attend to them. It was terrible having to leave them to their fate! He kept pleading, 'Don't leave us, sir.' That rang in my ears for a long time.

It was now, as 23 March drew to a close, that the fateful decision to hold on to the hard-won Flesquières salient began to exact a high price. To the south of it the Scots on the extreme left of the Fifth Army were retiring in good order, and fighting as they went, intending, as instructed, to keep in touch and join hands with the men of the Third Army who held the salient on their left. But, as the long day wore on, it became disturbingly clear that their left flank was in the air and that the vital liaison had been lost. To the north of the Flesquières salient the line had been driven in at the centre of the British front, and the enemy had pushed well ahead. It was only now that the men of the 47th and 63rd Divisions, holding the Flesquières salient, were ordered to withdraw, keeping in touch as they went with the troops to their right and their left. As the furthest forward, they had the most ground to cover, and their numbers were weak. They had endured a terrible night of bombardment as the enemy closed in, pressing closer and closer to the ever-narrowing exit, and they had not begun to move until well into the morning.

As the 47th Division retired, it became plain that a gap was opening between them and the 9th Division, and that the Germans were making an all-out effort to drive a wedge between the Third Army and the Fifth. It was vital to protect their vulnerable right flank, for this was the southern boundary of the entire Third Army.

The 9th Division was retiring to Manancourt, uncovering the right-hand battalion of the 47th Division, which was consequently within range of enemy machine-guns. It was suffering badly, and two companies of the Royal Welch Fusiliers were sent post-haste to reinforce the exposed flank of the battalion. This was a blow to Captain George Brett, in temporary command of the 23rd Londons, for their removal left a gap between his own battalion and the 21st Londons, 300 yards away along the Metz switchline, and before they could extend to fill it the enemy attacked. The Metz switchline was badly sited, the scantily wired trenches were barely three feet deep, and in the few hours that had elapsed since they moved into them there had been no opportunity to improve them – and no need, for, although the 142nd Brigade was rearguard to the Division, it would be off

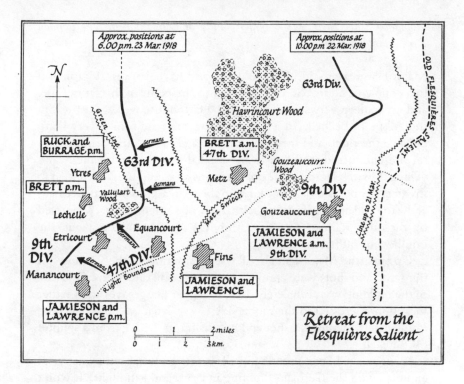

Retreat from the Flesquières Salient

and away by early afternoon. Now, in the first light of morning, when the Germans struck in massed ranks and in wave after heavy wave, it was forced to defend a position which was all but indefensible.

The 23rd Londons were holding the high ground near the cemetery east of Metz, and it was clear that the enemy meant to have it. Brett and his men were equally determined that he should not. By noon they had beaten off two strong attacks; by two o'clock they had repulsed a third; and twice, as the enemy fell back to regroup, they had counter-attacked and put his rearguard to flight.

When the time came for the Brigade to retire, the Germans had lost heart. Brett was able to collect his men in his own time, and march them off unmolested. This one battalion had held up the Germans' advance for almost six hours, and they were very weary as they set out on the three-mile trek across country to Lechelle. It was five o'clock before Brett reached Battalion Headquarters, fervently hoping that the enemy would stay his hand until next morning.

*Captain George Brett, MC, 23rd (County of London) Bn., The London*
*Regt., 47th Division*

Major Hargreaves said, 'You go down and have first rest. I'll call you
in a couple of hours.' So I went down in the cellar of this farmhouse,
and I fell asleep very soundly. Now the farmhouse we were in was in
the village of Lechelle, at a corner where the road took a very sharp
bend to the right, and the cellar faced straight on to the bend, with a
second entrance directly on to the road. I woke up with the Major
yelling down, 'George come up! Germans all round us!' I tried to grab
my steel helmet and then, looking up the staircase, I saw two Germans
at the top and one had his arm back, throwing something in. I scrambled
up the other staircase into the farmhouse and, just as I got out, the
bomb went off behind me.

Upstairs, the Major had got all the men lining all the windows in
our farm, and shots were coming in at us from all directions. One side
of the building was completely dark, so Major Hargreaves and I rather
incautiously crossed to the moon side to see what we could see, and
immediately there was a shot and he was hit in the leg from a splinter
off the wall.

By now we'd been shooting in all directions for about a quarter of
an hour, with the Germans shooting in at us, and I thought, 'It won't
be long before the Germans rush us and we shan't be able to stop
them, so the best thing we can do is to get out and report back that
the Germans are through.' The Major agreed. I said, 'Can you run?'
He said, 'Yes, I'm all right, I can manage. You carry on.' So I told the
men what we were going to do. I said, 'We're all going out through
this door here, so follow me, and, when we get to the road, turn left
and run like blazes until you get to the first British post and get the
warning through.'

I went out first, with my pistol in my hand, but just as I got to the
corner of the road two Germans with rifles and bayonets came round
it. I shot them both on the run, and then I turned to my left with the
men − and at the very same moment four rifle shots came smacking
across at us from the ditch on the other side of the road, and I was hit
through the arm. As I was falling I can remember I felt something
running along my chest and I thought, 'I've read about that in books
− that red-hot, searing pain in the lungs.' I remember my pistol falling
out of my right hand and clattering across the road, and thinking that
I must get away before they had time to reload. So I was up on my
feet and belting up that road as hard as I could. I hadn't gone more
than thirty, forty yards before four Germans stepped out in front of

me, all with their rifles trained on my stomach, and that was the end of my fighting!

One of these men tried to shoot me, and I found that the trouble was I hadn't put my hands up – so I indicated that I *couldn't* put my hands up. I showed them the blood pouring down my hand, and I showed them my empty pistol holster, and that was that. I was hit not only in the arm but in the hand, in my chest and on my left shoulder, so I had been hit by certainly three out of those four bullets. I began to feel rather faint as a result, and I thought the more faint I could make myself look the better. So I sat down on the wall and held my head in my hands and looked as tragic as I could, and I had a really great groan. And then the NCO in charge of this party indicated to me to get up, and he sent me off with one of the men. He took my arm and led me down the village, and round the corner were simply massed German troops, lined up in fours waiting to get through. I was led further down the road, which was completely filled with German troops, until we found one German soldier standing as a sentry over a wounded British soldier, and I was handed over to this sentry as a second chap for him to look after. Here I waited for I don't know how long. Germans came up and up and up, shuffling forward and then stopping, then another lot marching forward then stopping, and so on. They were obviously held up somewhere or another.

From the lane outside Lechelle it was hard to tell what was happening, but even in the dark the larger village of Ytres was perfectly visible from a mile away. Ytres was on fire, the country glowed in the light of the flames, and a cannonade of explosions cracking interminably from the heart of the blaze sounded across the fields like the crack of doom.

The village was on the line of retirement of the 63rd Division, and one of the unfortunate battalions caught up in the mêlée at Ytres was the Artists' Rifles. All the way back from the Flesquières salient, young Charles Ruck's greatest difficulty was a torn trouser leg. He had ripped it clambering through barbed wire the night before and, although he had fixed it as best he could with two safety pins from his standard-issue field dressing, this was not sufficient to keep the ragged fabric from flapping irritatingly against his leg. They had been on the move for twenty-four hours.

*30473 Rifleman Charles Ruck, 1/28th (County of London) Bn. (The Artists' Rifles), The London Regt., 63rd Division*

We went back from one set of old enemy positions to another, and then into rearguard actions which never came to a showdown, followed by short advances covered by the Lewis-gun, and long retirement marches. That night, however, we were held up at Ytres by confusion at a blazing ammunition dump, which the Boche exploited. They got through and cut off half of our battalion, but such was the confusion that most of our lads got away again. At one moment our section was given the doubtful honour of holding the road pending a further retirement. My chief worry during the interminable wait was whether the darned gun would go off when I pressed the trigger. A Lewis-gun needs regular cleaning, which it had *not* received any more than we had. Fortunately we were ordered out before it could be put to the test. By that time we could hear the Germans spreading themselves, as if to attack.

Miraculously, we got clear of the dump and were digging in again to the tap-tap-tap-tap of their machine-guns, which, as usual, had secured commanding positions. It was clear that we were in a weak defensive position and that we would have to retire again. Before we left, we had time to see to some of our seriously wounded who had been left behind in the confusion of the night. We had no means of getting them out. All we could do was to give them some words of comfort, and hope the Boche would do the decent thing by them.

Ruck had at least got clear of Ytres before the enemy closed in. Private McLelland-Burrage was not so fortunate. Lying in a prepared line of trenches in front of Ytres, he and his companions had been encouraged by the sound of the thunderous explosions behind, happily assuming that British guns were firing to support them.

*Private A. McLelland-Burrage, 28th (County of London) Bn. (The Artists' Rifles), 63rd Division*

I should have been rather hot and bothered if I'd known the truth. The station was on fire; and also the sidings, on which there were many truckloads of shells, and what we actually heard was these shells exploding. Still no direct attack came, but even the least intelligent of us knew that we were holding on much too long to an untenable position. Our gallant colonel, having already lost communication with Brigade, had received no orders to retire, and it was not until midnight that he did so on his own initiative. Then, of course, it was too late. We came to a sudden halt in the streets of Ytres. We were already surrounded. We heard the '*Hoy! Hoy! Hoy!*' of Germans shouting quite close to us, but that was all. A very brave lance-corporal named Talland-Brown, who could speak German, volunteered to get through the enemy line to Barastre to let Brigade know where we were and ask for instructions. He was challenged by a German sentry, and he replied in good colloquial German something to the effect of 'Shut your bloody mouth! Do you want to get us all shot?' So the sentry said, 'Pass, friend.'

While we waited, I was starving for a smoke. I knew Ytres and I remembered two large Expeditionary Force canteens in marquees close to the station, so I left the fragments of the platoon and went off on the scrounge. It was pitch-dark inside the marquees, and I felt my way about, putting my hands into broken crates. I found bags of cigarettes but nothing to eat – except Epsom salts, of which, at that time, I was not in particular need.

Suddenly the world seemed to come to an end with the first of the two worst explosions I have ever heard. I was flung down between two piles of crates, and a storm of bricks came crashing through the top of the marquee. I picked myself up and was hardly on my legs when the second explosion came, and down I went again. I hurried back to my platoon – or rather the spot where I had left it. I had seen a few ghastly sights, but nothing to equal that. It was the only time I ever saw a gutter literally running with blood, lit up by the red flames of the burning dump and station. Only one man out of the platoon was left alive, and he was lying on his back crying, and another fellow was hanging on to a severed artery in his thigh above a gaping wound. I had nothing with me to make a tourniquet, and our clumsy attempts to hold the artery seemed useless. We could do nothing but watch him bleed to death. He died crying for his mother.

When Talland-Brown had got safely back with orders, we were led out of Ytres and told to dig ourselves in with our entrenching tools. (This should have been done before. Indeed, I don't know why we weren't taken straight on to Barastre.) Suddenly it seemed to me that the fellows walking about began to move hastily in one direction. I poked my head up to have a look, and an officer saw me and waved to me. 'Come on,' he cried, 'we're all going!' And go we did. It was the last time I did a non-stop run for two miles.

So far we had been fed with absurd rumours. 'Our troops had advanced in the north and were halfway through Belgium. Down in the south the French had advanced about twenty miles. The Germans were being led into a very pretty little trap.' But tonight most of us realized the appalling truth that we were a defeated army in headlong retreat.

But the troops were gradually regrouping. One brigadier reported back that he now had under his command 900 men of eleven different units.

*Second Lieutenant Dick Gammell, 1/7th Bn., The Black Watch (Royal Highlanders) 51st Division*

There were stragglers all over the place and we collected them all together, and when we assembled things really were chaotic. There was quite high ground in front of us, and the Jocks were simply streaming back. Wilson and I decided to become infantry officers, as it were, and try to steady things. So far as I was concerned, signals didn't matter any more! So we went forward and collected some Jocks and formed a sort of line. They were all from different units, so we were in complete disorder.

It was the bush telegraph that saved the whole thing, and it was quite extraordinary. They'd managed to get the field kitchens up just behind us, and the rumour went round, and before we knew where we were the men began to congregate. They say that if a man's hungry he'll find out where the food is, and that's quite true, because *that* is really how the Division assembled – what was left of it!

Along the length of the stricken front, every man had been thrust in to help to hold the line – the bootmakers, the shoeing smiths, the orderly-room clerks, the signallers, the entrenching battalions, the sappers, the tailors, the cooks, the storemen, the armourers, the drivers, grooms and servants: any man of the rag, tag and bobtail of ancillary troops who was fit and capable of holding a rifle.

As the hours dragged by, the exhausted men who were falling back or clinging to desperate positions waited with mounting anxiety for some sign of the reserves who were surely on their way to reinforce or, better still, to relieve them.

But it was not so simple.

The situation had been foreseen, and the staffs of the reserve divisions had been working for weeks on the detailed arrangements which would enable these divisions to move at short notice and as rapidly as possible to another part of the front. Even after the reorganization of battalions, and although most were still understrength, a division comprised more than 7,000 infantry, but transporting so many – together with some thirty tons of food for the men, and sixty tons of ammunition for their rifles – was almost the least of the difficulty. There were three companies of Royal Engineers, with their wagons and tool carts and equipment, and eight batteries of artillery, each gun requiring six wagons to transport its personnel, its stores and its ammunition. There was a divisional signals company, with all its radio equipment, its carts and miles of cable. There were two companies of machine-gunners, with their weapons and ammunition, and three field ambulance units, with stretchers, medical equipment and supplies. There was the divisional transport, and the transport sections of three brigades, with the men and wagons and horses which would keep a division mobile in the field, and the divisional ammunition column, which, like each transport unit, needed the space of an entire railway train to transport it. A whole division required twenty-four long trains of heavy rolling-stock to transfer it from one sector of the front to another.

Nor could the loading of the trains be haphazard. In routine moves in quieter times, supplies could be sent ahead, a depot established, dumps and transport lines set up, and billets prepared in an area where the division could concentrate and shake down before moving its component battalions in rotation to the front. But in circumstances of urgency, when battalions must be sent off piecemeal, prepared to go into the line or even into action right away, the method of loading the trains was of vital importance, for it was imperative that each complement of men should have sufficient resources immediately available for sustenance, supply, communications and back-up.

On the Belgian front the staff officers and quartermasters of the 8th Division had laboured long hours drawing up detailed lists and issuing a spate of contingency orders on the disposition of space and allocation of priorities right down to the placing of the divisional laundry in the last of the twenty-four trains. But even with the most meticulous forward planning, and the Herculean labour of hundreds of men, the move could not be quickly accomplished. The trains could only be brought up one at a time to three entraining points, at Hopoutre, Godvaersvelde and St Omer. The loading of horses, transport, supplies and men was a lengthy business, and the trains could only set out at three-hourly intervals on the slow, trundling journeys across the overstrained railway system that would bring them to the battle in the south.

The first train left at six o'clock in the morning of 22 March. The situation was fluid and, as the vanguard of the 8th Division rumbled southward, it was changing by the hour. That same evening, a billeting party of the 2nd Northants which had gone on ahead made their way forward to find billets for their battalion in Athies. Long before they had finished their task the village came under attack. Fighting their way out of it, they escaped by the skin of their teeth and struggled back for new orders. Athies was two and a half miles east of the River Somme. In the early hours of the following morning, when billets were finally found for the battalion, they were in the village of Licourt, two miles west of the river. It was a long way back from the area on which the 8th Division had been instructed to take up a support line. But that was already in enemy hands. One by one, as the battalions detrained on 23 March, they were rushed to fill a four-mile gap on the eastern bank of the river. Their job was 'at all costs' to prevent the Germans crossing it.

*Lieutenant L. Chamberlen, MC, 2nd Bn., The Rifle Brigade, 8th Division*

We detrained at Rosières and were rushed by lorry due west to Morchain, where we dumped our kit with the quartermaster, and from there we just ran. We were told to get to the river at Pargny before the Hun, and the Hun weren't firing much at us, but you could see them coming over the downs on the other side of the canal. We were within a mile of them, and we were on higher ground, with the village of Pargny and the Somme river and canal between us, and we could see the Hun coming down the hill on *their* side while we ran down the hill on ours. We went like hell! I got my company eventually into position. There was a sunken road running down the hill into Pargny, and I was on the high ground above the sunken road with A Company. (A Company and C Company were in reserve a few hundred yards behind the village, with B and D in the front line.) A Hun aeroplane came swooping along the sunken road, then suddenly, a quarter of an hour later, two bloody machine-guns began firing straight at us from a ruined cottage in the village at the end of the lane, and we knew then that they must have been infiltrated. I said, 'Come on, you blokes. Bring that Lewis-gun and get some blokes on the other side. We've got to get rid of that bloody machine-gunner.'

I ran in front of them down the road to the village, and we were very fortunate, because there was a big log from a tree which had fallen down and we managed to get behind that just as the machine-gun got on to us and began firing at us like hell. Of course *we* were firing *back* like hell! The last thing I remember for a bit is feeling something like a very, very sharp blow from a hammer just below my throat. It knocked me out, knocked me to the ground, and when I came round I was lying in the mud, and I couldn't move. I was paralysed from the waist down, so I just lay there, dazed. I remember thinking that it was really quite nice to have a rest! I didn't feel anything. My little corporal, Smith, crept out and took me by the legs and pulled me back to the sunken road, and the stretcher-bearers came down. Luckily, by then the Hun had taken fright and stopped firing and sloped off.

But it was only a temporary respite. By the time Lieutenant Chamberlen had been carried back to Morchain and found, to his relief, that he could move his limbs again, the Germans were tightening their grip on Pargny. During the night, while he jolted painfully towards Villers-Bretonneux on

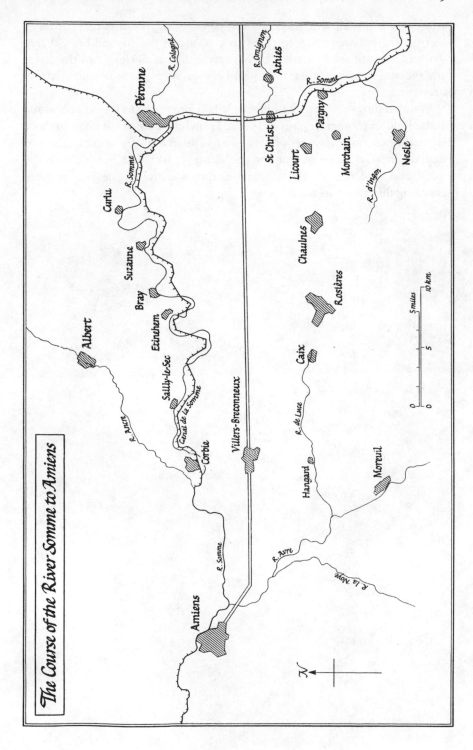

The Course of the River Somme to Amiens

a lorry packed with wounded soldiers, all along the Somme line parties of Germans were attempting to filter forward across the myriad bridges that spanned the streams and rivulets that spread like tentacles from the river, and picking their way along the ancient causeways over the marshes that lay between.

Four centuries earlier, when Henry V had attempted to cross the Somme at the head of another English army, the French had dug deep holes in those same earthen causeways to obstruct him. But there was nothing now to impede the Germans, except for the clammy mist that hung above the marshland, and the widely scattered outposts of the fragile British force guarding the river and canal beyond.

## Chapter 15

It was Palm Sunday, the first day of Holy Week, and in Germany, in France and in Great Britain, where the calendar of the ecclesiastical year unfolded regardless of international conflicts, Christian churches held the usual services, singing traditional hymns and blessing and distributing sprigs of foliage in token of the palm leaves that were strewn in the streets of Jerusalem. In British churches the hosannas of the familiar joyful hymns rang hollow. There was little cause for rejoicing. In letters an inch high the headlines of Sunday newspapers thundered the ominous tidings: BRITISH FORCED TO WITHDRAW 15 MILES. It was the worst news of the war, and in every church throughout the land special prayers were fervently offered to implore the assistance of that same Divine Providence to whom, in similar services on this Palme Sonntag, German priests and pastors were offering equally fervent thanks for news of victory.

All across Great Britain young soldiers were being warned for the front. At their training camp in Northumberland, Horace Haynes and his friend Curly Courtland had expected the official order almost as soon as they heard of the German breakthrough. It had amused the two boys to start the rumour that they were on forty-eight hours' notice to leave for France and that no one was allowed to leave the camp, and this news had been relayed back to them so often during the course of the day that they themselves had begun to believe it. On Saturday morning, to their amazement, the 'rumour' became reality.

*2565 Private Horace Haynes, 2/6th Bn., The Royal Warwickshire Regt., 61st Division*

When we went on parade, instead of saying '13 Platoon, attention!', our platoon officer said, '56 Draft, attention!' We went down to the quartermaster's stores and we got handed out a gas mask, field dressing and steel helmet. We were told not to leave camp, but we did, some of us, and we went down to Blyth to the picture palace. But then during the picture they flashed up on the screen, 'All men of the Royal Warwicks return to camp immediately.'

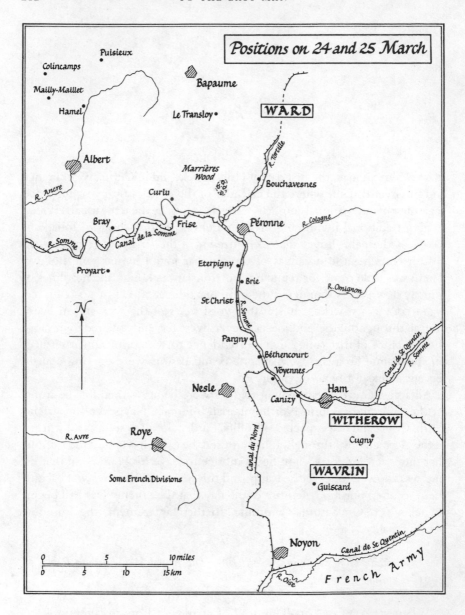

Positions on 24 and 25 March

Sunday morning we was lined up about eight o'clock, in full kit, and marched down to the station. We was all excited. We were singing, 'How can I bear to leave you? A parting kiss I'll give you . . .' We were singing that on the station. Then the train came in, and away we went – eight of us to a compartment and the doors locked. It stopped at Newcastle and it stopped at York, and all the way along we picked up different drafts. There was two trains, one following the other, and we arrived at Folkestone at 2.30 the next morning. We got a pot of tea and a biscuit and a lump of bully beef, and then we marched to Dover, got on the boat for France. There were three boatloads of us, all young chaps (we was all eighteen), and we had a destroyer each side of us and an aeroplane over the top, and the pilot waved goodbye to us as we got to France – waggled his wings and waved to say goodbye.

On Wimbledon Common, where Derick Haywood was training, the boys of Platoon 16a were disconsolate, for everyone seemed to be going except themselves.

*537288 Private Derick Haywood, 15th (County of London) Bn. (Prince of Wales's Own Civil Service Rifles), London Regt., 47th Division (diary entry)*

*24th March, Palm Sunday*: Large drafts off to France and, since then, three officers and NCOs were taken off parade and warned for France immediately, including Lieutenants Holder, Bonner, Lloyd-Jones, Sergeants Haig, Steven and Corporal Mitchell of our platoon. Pateman spoke on behalf of our platoon and volunteered us for France, but they said we have to finish training first. Later in the day a second large draft left for France. I was guarding kits in a hut while the boys went out for the last time, and Walker, another eighteen-year-old pal who was on the draft, came in for a chat. He tried to look cheerful, but I could see he wondered what was in store for them out there as the news is so alarming. He is a decent lad. Until now nobody has been sent out until he is nineteen, but things are so grave that we are to go as soon as training can be rushed through. I wonder what will happen to these boys. We're nearly all eighteen, or nineteen at most. Later, Ball, Wordley, Walker and I, with Clayton, Sissy Fellows, Gordon Ivey, Gough, Sloane and others, had a final bust-up with them in the canteen. Afterwards we went to Wimbledon Station to see them off and came back nearly in tears. Some came into our hut to say goodbye, and others called out as they passed down the lines at 10.30 p.m. on their way to the station. I wish we could have gone out with that fine crowd. They're mostly boys from jobs in the city, or just left school. They went off singing 'Goodbyee' and other songs. I shall always remember this night.

Sentimental songs did not have much currency in France among the seasoned soldiers, particularly among the French, who had long ago had sentiment knocked out of them. As they travelled towards the British front, any singing that enlivened the long, weary journeys by train and lorry was desultory and in quite a different vein. Their taste leaned towards the scatological and anti-German, particularly among the regiments from the north of France, whose home country had been invaded by the same enemy twice in forty years, and whose families, in many cases, were cut off behind the lines in German-occupied territory, at the mercy of the hated 'Boche'. Anti-German jokes were popular in northern France, and the crudest of them had their genesis in the trail of ordure which, according to local folklore, had marked the progress of the Germans' march into France in the Franco-Prussian war. This had given rise to the belief that the Germans suffered from abnormal intestinal activity due to their animal appetites and the sauerkraut which supposedly was the principal element of their diet. It was the theme of much crude humour and many sonorous, flatulent songs, which were popular in the lower type of café-concerts and were enthusiastically taken up by the troops. Even schoolchildren delighted in the hoary old riddle 'When three Germans dine together, why can you never see more than two of them?' Answer: 'Because one of them is always in the lavatory.'

On their way to Noyon, where the British 58th Division was falling back, the songsters of the 144th French Regiment had whiled away the journey with songs from an extensive repertoire of parodies composed by their own Sergent Ricard and set to popular tunes. Their favourite was 'The Song of the Monkey', which was particularly insulting to their German opponents and, under present circumstances, seemed to fit the bill. It ran to many verses in which a monkey bemoans the fact that, if man is descended from the ape, the Kaiser must logically be a member of the monkey's genetic family. But there was consolation in the last verse: 'Oh Monkey! Dry your tears and do not reproach Darwin. He said that man was descended from you – he said nothing about the Boche!'[1] And that, so far as the *poilus* were concerned, put the Kaiser in his place.

1.                          *O Singe!*
                           *Calme ton émoi*
                           *À Darwin ne fais nul reproche*
                           *L'homme, a-t-il dit descend de toi*
                           *Il n'a jamais parlé du Boche.*

Four French divisions had already arrived, and others were on their way. Late on Saturday night, on the eve of Palm Sunday, the 62nd Division had reached its destination at Guiscard and, in silence, the 307th Regiment began the long march to the line. Although they could hardly be said to be full of the legendary French *élan* and were not exactly raring for a fight, their spirit was philosophical and Capitaine Désiré Wavrin, marching at the head of No. 6 Company, was confident of his men. In the six months since he had been given command of the Company, with the specific task of restoring its morale, he had seen a remarkable change in their demeanour.

The Regiment had been under a cloud since the previous year, when indiscipline had spread like wildfire through the ranks of the French Army. It had begun on the notorious Chemin des Dames, where successive regiments had fought long and bitterly for possession of the heights above the Aisne. They had been gained and lost many times, and the cost in lives and suffering had been incalculable. On 16 April 1917 the battle had come to a head in the great offensive planned by General Nivelle, which was intended to smash the German lines and win the war. After the removal of Joffre in the aftermath of the terrible battle at Verdun, Nivelle was the new broom which would sweep clean and sweep the armies to victory. Visiting the French Sixth Army on the eve of the battle, he had declared, 'The hour has come. Courage! . . . Have confidence.' The troops had believed him. But despite Nivelle's plans and preparations, despite the enormous weight of artillery which was to pave the way, the attack of 16 April 1917 had been pure and simple disaster. The German defences were stronger on the Chemin des Dames than on any other part of the long front. The French bombardments made little impression, and when the troops went forward with all the courage and obstinacy that any general could have desired, they were assaulting positions that were virtually impregnable. The gains were minimal. The casualties were huge – 120,000 in a matter of hours. Courage and confidence alike were engulfed in a welter of blood, and the indomitable spirit which for so long had been the capital of the French Army languished and died. After the Calvary of Verdun, the Chemin des Dames had been too much.

Nivelle was determined to continue his campaign, but he had broken his army. The troops held the line, but they refused to attack again. By May the insurrection had spread like a malign epidemic through half the Army, and the 62nd Division, which had already been decimated at Verdun, was easily infected. It was understandable that its troops were sullen and demoralized, and Désiré Wavrin, who had begun the war as a simple soldier and had been commissioned from the ranks, understood as well as anyone. As a schoolmaster in civil life, he understood the importance of discipline and justice, and he believed his men had every reason to feel dispirited and aggrieved. He had taken command of the company at the beginning of October, when the regiment was holding the line in the village of Moÿ near Vendeuil, and found morale at a low ebb. Several of the officers had been replaced, or demoted; others had left for the Salonica front at their own request.

*Capitaine Désiré Wavrin, 22nd Coy., 6th Bn., 307th Regt., 62nd [French] Division*

The first thing I did was to have a meeting of the officers and NCOs at my command post, to get to know them and to establish friendly relations. The first night I did nothing, but about eleven o'clock in the evening on the second night I went round the trenches with my faithful orderly, Quéfille. All the sentries and the corporals were at their posts, keeping a conscientious lookout, but the officers and sergeants were nowhere to be seen. I found them in their dugouts, asleep with their equipment and their boots off. I didn't say too much, but all the same I let everybody understand that henceforth they had to be a great deal more alert, and on the following nights when I went round the trenches (which I was careful to do *not* at a fixed time: sometimes before, sometimes after midnight, and often during a relief) I made sure that everyone was present at his post.

At the same time I had made it my business to find out the feelings of the troops, and for one thing I found a lot of men grumbling about the food. So, the first time we went out to rest I went unannounced to the cookhouse. There on the table I saw the meat, divided into two portions. One of them was only a *very* little smaller than the other but it was of *much* better quality, and when I asked the orderly corporal about it he replied, 'Oh, that's for the NCOs.' I asked him why only fifteen NCOs were entitled to almost as much meat as the rest of the company put together. Well, it's true that in the tradition of the Army the NCOs should come off a *little* better than the men, but, under present circumstances, that was hardly the point! So I instructed him, 'In future, whether we're in the line or out of it, every day I want you to bring me an account of all the rations you've drawn and how you propose to distribute them. Every day I shall detail a platoon leader to come and collect a share for his platoon and, without fail, I shall want to know what it is.'

I soon realized that the captain who was my predecessor hadn't bothered about the men – nor had he ever gone round the trenches during the night to see how things were. Naturally the NCOs hadn't bothered either. I had a couple of officers, Lieutenant Rigout, who was a pork butcher at Limoges, and Sous-Lieutenant Dehone, who was a brewer from Douai, and I promoted them immediately. They were good chaps. They soon took charge of things, and soon we were good comrades. Naturally, at the start, if the men were more satisfied some of the NCOs were *not*, but little by little they came to understand that I was not a rotter and that when we were in the line I myself never jibbed at doing my own bit and that I spent a good part of the night going round the trenches and talking to them – always in a friendly manner. So things began to go quite well in the company. I had my reward a few months later, when we were inspected by the Divisional General when we were out of the line and he halted our battalion and in front of everybody he said, 'I congratulate the 22nd Company. By its good appearance and by its good performance, it has wiped out its past record. It is no longer in disgrace.' How happy and proud the men were! And so was I! From that moment on my company did whatever was asked of them without a murmur. I can honestly say that it became the best company of the regiment – in fact we had the honour of having the *Croix de Guerre* added to our flag.

Of course, it wasn't entirely due to me. We had a new Battalion Commander: it was Commandant St Julien, and he was a real gentleman. What a man! He was always in a good humour – I never saw him when he wasn't smiling. He came round the trenches to visit us, day and night, it didn't matter to him! If the weather was fine he used to say, 'What lovely sunny weather!' And even if it was raining he used to say, 'What lovely rainy weather!' One day he came into our extremely muddy trench and catching sight of me he called out, 'Well, at least it's very clean where you are!' I said, 'Do you think so?' 'I certainly do,' he replied, all smiles. 'In the trench where I've just come from I was up to my haunches in mud. Here it only comes up to my calves!' He was a great man!

We made several attacks in that sector, and threw back a number of German attacks. Certainly we had casualties, but we inflicted more casualties on the Germans! When the English relieved us in January we marched all the way on foot towards Paris and went into rest near Enghien-les-Bains. We were only twenty minutes from Paris – and what a temptation *that* was for the men. The Commandant turned a blind eye, so quite a number of our chaps were able to go into Paris every day to enjoy a bit of life. That was *some* rest period. In fact it was a little *too* good to be true, considering what was in store for us!

We left on 17 March for the Chemin des Dames – and unfortunately the Commandant left us then. We were expecting a German attack there, but we had hardly arrived and done a bit of reconnaissance, and our artillery had barely moved into position, when new orders arrived. The Germans had attacked the Fifth English Army in the very position we'd left not long before, and the English were falling back, so, before we had properly settled in, our 62nd Division had to rush away again to form a first line of reserve behind our allies. Or so we were told! We set off in lorries, and during the night of 23 March we arrived at Libermont, north-west of Guiscard.

They rested for an hour or two, and early in the morning of Palm Sunday they moved up to the north-west corner of Hospital Wood. A mile or so away and almost directly ahead of them, Lieutenants Witherow and Marshall had passed an anxious night near the village of Villeselve.

*Second Lieutenant Tom Witherow, 2nd Bn., The Royal Irish Rifles, 36th (Ulster) Division*

About 800 yards in front of us the sunken road led into a village called Brouchy, and beyond that was another village called Aubigny, which we were to capture from the enemy. The whole attack turned on the point, Was Brouchy occupied or not? If it was, then attack would probably end in a costly failure, for, with machine-guns in its houses, the enemy could break up any attack long before we could reach Aubigny. If it had been our own men that were going into the attack matters would have been different, but a gather-up of 200 men, including pioneers, butchers and other Army Service Corps men, was all we had. It was not a pleasant prospect, and we did not look forward to it. But, as dawn approached and the bombardment began, word arrived that the enemy was attacking on our *left*, down the Ham–Noyon road, that he had broken through and the attack was to be abandoned. We were not sorry.

About a mile away was the town of Ham, where the enemy were now installed. We could see them all over the country, because there were no trenches, and on our left we could see our men lying in the open fields with very little protection. To the right my own battalion the 2nd Royal Irish Rifles – or what was left of them! – were occupying a position, and the French troops were beginning to come up and were scattered about behind our very thin line. We saw the cavalry going out to reconnoitre in the direction of Brouchy, and no sooner had they approached the village than a tremendous fire opened out from the houses and they immediately turned and galloped to the shelter of our lines. So much for the story that the enemy was not in occupation of the village!

About a thousand yards away a large body of men who looked like the enemy advanced into a ploughed field in extended formation and started to dig themselves in. I directed machine-gun and rifle fire on them, but I was very doubtful about the situation and almost as soon as the fire started I ordered it to stop, just in case the men might be our French allies. It was so difficult to decide who was who, even at a very short distance. Unfortunately they turned out to be the enemy, and we had allowed them to dig in just in front of us! About 1,500 yards away I could see a number of German staff officers standing under a tree reading a map and directing operations.

I was the senior among six officers, including a machine-gun officer, and consequently I had to make many decisions that day in the course of the fighting, moving continually along the long line – a most dangerous operation, because the road was not sunken. The fire was exceptionally accurate, and every time I went along the line the enemy opened fire and I had to dodge as best I could. It was very difficult to evacuate the wounded, because there was no cover whatever. The enemy began to shell our position heavily, and to make matters worse his aeroplanes swooped down to within a few feet of our line, firing all the time. We mounted a counter-attack with the assistance of the French, led by Colonel Peacock, but it ended in nothing, and things were now becoming very serious. I knew it was only a matter of time before we would be forced to retire. My ammunition was beginning to run short, and I sent urgent messages to Brigade Headquarters in Villeselve for a fresh supply.

Two wounded men came into our line from the right. They belonged to my own battalion, the 2nd Royal Irish Rifles, and they said that the remains of the Battalion were surrounded and would shortly be captured. No ammunition had arrived, and we were running very short indeed now. The machine-gun officer had been continually urging me to retire, until I actually had to threaten him. At last, when I saw that the enemy had broken in our right rear and we were nearly surrounded, I *had* to give the order to retire.

There was only a narrow strip of ground running towards the village which was not occupied by the enemy machine-gunners. I gave orders to the nervy machine-gun officer that he should go back to a hedge and cover our retirement from that position. He was delighted to be off, but that was the last I saw of him! He left us in the lurch at the critical moment, and it will always be a miracle to me how *any* of us survived that retreat. Bullets were falling round us like hail, there was not a piece of cover, and we were too tired to run.

*Capitaine Désiré Wavrin*

When we took up our position we were *supposedly* in support of the English – or at least so we had been told, and that was what we believed. My company was holding the northern corner of Hospital Wood, but hardly had we moved into place than the rear lines of the English started falling back, and instead of reinforcing our allies we found ourselves in contact with the enemy. I could clearly see that the Germans were massing in great numbers in a ravine some 300 metres from the wood, and so could my men. They got very excited, and demanded to know why I didn't send word for an artillery bombardment. Alas! I had no means of doing that! No one had given us the SOS code for artillery assistance. A trooper of the cavalry came up on liaison duties, and I gave him a message to tell the battalion commander what was happening and asking him as a matter of urgency to let me know the code. A quarter of an hour later, the trooper returned and handed me a paper. It read, 'I do not have the signal code. In any event it would be useless, because we have no artillery. It is not expected to arrive for another twenty-four hours at the earliest and there are only a few British guns in the sector. I shall ask them to send over some shells.' Quite soon five or six shells did fall, but they didn't in the slightest prevent the Boche from massing in greater and greater numbers.

They made a reconnaissance attack, which left quite a number of them dead on the field, but, thanks to good cover, they began to filter into the wood. There were far too few of us to man it completely, and they burst on top of a section of the 24th Company on my right. Their lieutenant was killed, and their fine captain (who was well known to be a coward!) was at Battalion Headquarters instead of being with his unit. So I sent a message to Headquarters, and shortly afterwards I received an incredible reply. It was signed by this famous captain. He made no mention of the death of his lieutenant, which I had reported, but informed me that what I thought were Boche breaking into the wood were actually *Americans* who were coming to reinforce us! I ask you!

I demanded that they should send up a patrol of 'Americans'. They didn't dare refuse, but the patrol, when it arrived, consisted of men of the 22nd and 24th Companies of our own troops. I sent it off under the guidance of one of my sergeants. Ten minutes later they returned with a German prisoner, having stumbled across a lookout post, killed one of the sentries, and captured the other. The Boche prisoner said to me, '*Nein Kaput! Nein Kaput!*' He was begging me for his life, but there was no danger of my killing him – I was much too happy to have got him alive. I sent him down to the Commander with this message: 'Here is one of Capitaine G.'s Americans!' That put me in bad odour with both of them!

If the French had only the haziest idea of what was happening, they were not alone, for the Fifth Army was fighting in small fragmented groups of weary men – 'gather-ups', as Lieutenant Witherow had put it – of half a dozen or more different units, who could judge what was happening only on their own particular line – if lines they could be called. In front of Libermont, where the Germans were rapidly encroaching from the direction of Ham, a dangerous gap was appearing, and only the French troops – newly arrived, ill-equipped, short of ammunition, and lacking information – stretched out a tenuous arm across the enemy's path. They were there, as they thought, to reinforce their allies, but many British troops – weak and worn and wearied by three days' strenuous fighting – believed sincerely and with infinite thankfulness that the French troops had come, at long last, to relieve them. Yesterday they had been bone-weary. Today they were soul-weary. It was hardly surprising that communication was scant and that, consequently, co-ordination between the armies was poor. The British Command had done its best. III Corps had already been transferred to the command of General Fayolle, in the belief that unity of command in this dangerous southern sector would stem the tide and restore the situation. But in the confusion of the fighting, as von Hutier thrust forward his reserves, neither General Fayolle at Montdidier nor General Gough at Villers-Bretonneux knew with certainty what was happening hour by hour.

In the sky above the battlefield, aeroplanes buzzed and swooped and observers tried to make sense of what was happening on the ground. Second Lieutenant Robert Best was flying above the village of Villeselve, where only three days before he and his observer, Lieutenant White, had spent the night on a British airfield. Now the airfield was no more, and on the ground, a thousand feet below, Lieutenant Witherow was preparing to retire with his men. Best and White could plainly see long lines of Germans advancing in perfect formation on either side of Ham, and, having carefully noted the position, they flew off westward to pass on this information.

*Second Lieutenant Robert Best, 53 Squadron, Royal Flying Corps*

I must explain that the messages were put in bags, and these were wrapped up in long streamers so as to make them easy to see when we dropped them from the air. Unfortunately Whitey threw the message bags overboard without rolling up the streamers, and they got caught up with some of the tail wires, so there was nothing for it but to land at Villers-Bretonneux. As soon as we examined the machine

we saw that this one wire had been shot through. While it was being
repaired, Whitey and I went off for lunch, where we had one or two
glasses of wine. Thus fortified, we thought we ought to deliver the
message bags ourselves at Fifth Army HQ, and so off we went.

Immediately we were overwhelmed by red tabs. (The music-hall song
'I'm on the Staff' kept running through my head!) We were told that we
should report our story to General Gough in person, and we were shown
into his office. After some heavy saluting, I explained to the General that
while we were in the air I had seen the German troops advancing
perfectly clearly, and marked their forward line on my map. He heard
me courteously and patiently, but this did not prevent him from smacking
me cheerfully on the back and telling me that I was mistaken. It seems
we had counter-attacked in the morning and I had probably mistaken
the blue of the French uniform for the field grey of the Germans. But
the General was soon to find out who had been mistaken.

Unless his duties took him away from GHQ, it was Sir Douglas Haig's
invariable habit to attend morning service at the Church of Scotland hut at
Montreuil, but on this of all Sundays, in the midst of the greatest crisis of
the war, his chaplain hardly expected to see him. The Reverend Mr Duncan
was waiting outside the modest barrack on the ramparts which served as a
soldiers' restroom on weekdays and, by the addition of a makeshift altar
covered with khaki cloth, was transformed into a place of worship on Sundays.
A few minutes before 9.30, punctually as always, the Commander-in-Chief
appeared. Duncan was astonished and, hardly knowing what to say, remarked
as they shook hands that he 'hoped things were not too bad'. Haig looked
him straight in the eye. 'You will remember,' he said, 'what you once read
to us from 2nd Chronicles: "Be not afraid nor dismayed by reason of this
great multitude, for the battle is not yours, but God's." ' And, leaving
Duncan suitably impressed, he walked unhurriedly into the hut and sat down
in his accustomed place. Haig was a man of steadfast faith, and was glad of
a period of calm reflection and spiritual sustenance to assist him through the
rigours and responsibilities of this most critical day.

He paid close attention to the sermon, later noting in his diary that the
theme indicated 'Why we can and should rely on the Gospel of Christ to
guide us in the present and future', and describing it as 'excellent'. At the
end of the service he again surprised his chaplain, by inviting him to lunch
at his personal quarters in the chateau of Beaurepaire. It was a small party.
Apart from the Chaplain and the Commander-in-Chief, only his Chief of
Intelligence, General Cox, and an ADC were present. Haig, unsurprisingly,
was preoccupied and, although General Cox conveyed to Mr Duncan some
fascinating technical details about the Paris Gun, conversation was otherwise

desultory and there were frequent interruptions which obliged the ADC to leave the room. It was a modest lunch, for Haig preferred simple food – a little soup, a plain grilled sole or a cutlet followed invariably by a milk pudding were sufficient to satisfy his appetite, if not that of his guests.

As soon as lunch was finished Haig excused himself and went off with General Cox to consider reports which, after a quiet morning, were beginning to arrive in quick succession. The news was not good, and even a telephone conversation with General Byng, in command of the Third Army, brought only a little comfort. His left was holding fast, but the right wing of the Third Army beyond the dangerous gap between it and the Fifth was being pushed back rapidly as the Germans advanced.

From his observation post, a mile beyond his battery, Major Ward had seen them coming with his own eyes. Until that moment he had every reason to be satisfied, for, since the guns of A and B Batteries had been overrun the previous day, his was the only battery of the Brigade which still had guns in action. As well as the four he had rescued at Beaumetz and retrieved for a second time when they were left behind in Vélu, two more guns had fortuitously arrived from ordnance. C Battery was once more at full strength and was now in position on the outskirts of the village of Villers au Flos. But Ward had selected an observation post well ahead of it – perhaps too far ahead – on the high ground between Bancourt and Haplincourt, and, although it gave a remarkable view of the country as far as Vélu, it required an inordinate length of fragile telephone wire to connect Ward to the Battery. This single vulnerable link was the only means by which he could direct the fire of his guns, but the risk, he concluded, was worth it, for the panoramic view from the OP on the high ground would give early and ample warning of a frontal attack.

Shortly after midday, when the morning mist had cleared and when Haig's guests were sitting down to lunch some twenty-five miles to the west, Major Ward went forward with two signallers to the observation post.

*Major Ronald Ward, C 293 Bty., Royal Field Artillery*

When we got there we were pretty heavily shelled for about three-quarters of an hour, so, leaving the signallers to repair the telephone wire, which had become cut by this shelling, I walked on for another three-quarters of a mile to the left front, where I saw some of our infantry digging a trench on a little hill. They proved to be a company of a pioneer battalion, troops which were not usually employed in the front line. I always wore the bronze letters HAC on my shoulders in addition to the regimental buttons, since of course I was originally commissioned into the Honourable Artillery Company, and I remember being considerably bucked when the captain in charge said, 'It's all right if the HAC are here.'

But it was not all right. As he and I stood looking down over the gentle grass slopes that lay between us and Vélu Wood, he suddenly touched my arm and pointed eastward. And indeed it was a surprising sight. A few moments before all had seemed comparatively peaceful – and no place more so than Vélu Wood. On the west this presents a straight side 900 yards long, bounded by a hedge. A moment before this had been only a hedge; now it had suddenly become a continuous grey line of infantry advancing, with about three paces' interval between files, and, as the first line cleared the wood, others followed them. It was very impressive, for the ranks extended for more than half a mile – and what a target! They were 3,500 yards away from me. The range from the guns was a bit long, it is true, but high explosive would have had a wonderful effect from six guns at 'gunfire'.

At the moment, obviously, I could do nothing, for I was a long way from my telephone, and so I hurried back at top speed towards the OP. But alas! there were no signallers to be seen anywhere, and so no telephone! They had worked back almost to the Battery repairing the wire, and had not yet returned to the OP. It was tragic enough to miss such a target, and more tragic still not to be able to support the pioneer company. One British eighteen-pounder battery was firing at the line of Boche infantry from somewhere far away on my right, but it could not stop the attack alone, and neither could two of our tanks, which I saw advancing from that side. I trust the company commander of the pioneers realized all this promptly, for while we two were talking together I had noticed that there was no one at all visible on our right, and in that direction the country was quite open for a mile and a half, so, as our left was certainly in retreat, he was entirely 'in the air'. It was useless to stay where I was and so I hurried on, but I had to cover a total distance of two miles to reach the Battery, and it was a very long and depressing journey.

When I got there, I learned that I had been given up as missing, and certainly it was not an unreasonable view to take, for there had been a lot of shelling and I had been out of touch for a long time. During my absence the Battery had not been too comfortable, for in the morning they had been shelled from the direction of Barastre – that is, from the east – and several horses had been hit. Then at midday eight enemy aeroplanes had come over low down, and one driver and a few more horses had been wounded.

The colonel arrived just as I reached the guns and gave me the order to retire at once, and so at 4 p.m., having called in Morris and his signallers, we 'front limbered up' and moved off just at the very moment when the position again came under shell-fire, no doubt as a result of the aeroplane reconnaissance. To move out of the position, it was necessary to do so from the left flank, the teams coming up from the left rear and then in front of the guns. I kept the Battery firing throughout this operation, each gun stopping only for an instant whenever any team crossed its line of fire, and Cease Fire was not ordered to the left-flank gun until the last limber was in position beside it ready to front limber up. All the other guns had by then been withdrawn. Thus fire was maintained until the last possible moment, which was very much to the credit of all the men and horses concerned.

It was a very good thing that we moved when we did, for we heard the next day that by that time the enemy had already taken Villers au Flos; and, worse still, by the afternoon they were well across the Bapaume–Péronne road near Le Transloy, so, at the time we pulled out from our position, the German infantry was less than three miles away on our right *rear*.

Sir Douglas Haig received this unwelcome news when he rose from lunch, and he reluctantly acquiesced to General Byng's desire to pull back the right wing of his Third Army as far as Longueval. The main body of troops, with the 9th (Scottish) Division on its right, had already begun to move, and the enemy had pushed forward to the Bouchavesnes Ridge, where the old road ran along the crest from Péronne towards Bapaume. It overlooked the rank and cratered tundra where, in November 1916, the Somme campaign had fizzled out in the waterlogged slough in the valley. It had taken the Allied armies five months of punishing effort to get that far. Now, after the long leap forward to the Hindenburg Line, they were back where the Battle of the Somme had ended. Soon, moving back across the hard-fought ground, past the barely discernible traces of woods and villages that had consumed the flower of Kitchener's Army, they would be back where it had begun.

Only the South African Brigade, in front of Bouchavesnes, had not received the order to retire. The runners who were carrying it were caught and presumably killed by the German barrage, and the situation had altered drastically since the previous evening when General Dawson had received instructions from 9th Division's commander in person. The South Africans were to move to the high ground behind Marrières Wood, to extend a thin line as far as Priez farm, and to protect the right rear of the Division. 'And there,' added General Tudor, 'you must hold on at all costs.'

The Springboks had carried out his order to the letter. But the cost was higher than anyone had imagined. It was nothing less than the annihilation of the South African Brigade.

# Chapter 16

Even when they straggled into position the previous night, the South Africans were a brigade in name only. Their prodigious stand at Gauche Wood and Chapel Hill, and their casualties during the retirement of the 9th Division, had reduced the entire Brigade to a skeleton force of some 500 men – barely the strength of a single weak battalion. In normal circumstances, on completion of a move, the divisional rearguard should have moved into support, but the circumstances were so far from normal that every man of the Division was needed to form a line – and a line, moreover, which was more than five miles long. When the Germans attacked on the morning of 24 March it was inevitable that gaps should appear between the brigades. Inevitable too that the enemy should press forward between them.

The position of the South African Brigade was not an enviable one. The left flank of its fragile line was soon 'in the air'. On the right, although at first the Springboks had been in tenuous contact with the 21st Division, it was soon apparent that the enemy had encroached, that the right flank was also open to the wide, and that the enemy was attacking from three directions: the south, the east and, disturbingly, also the south-west, almost at their backs. They had very little to fight back with, and the ground was difficult to defend. There was one stretch of decent trench, a few others which were little more than token scrapings, plus a considerable scattering of shell-holes. The men each had 200 rounds of ammunition, and there were a number of Lewis-guns with a reasonable supply, but the four Vickers machine-guns had only four belts of ammunition apiece. During the night, General Dawson sent three of them back and told the teams to link up with the transport, if they could find it. The last remaining gun and the weary men who manned it would have to do the job with all the ammunition there was. And it was little enough.

In the three days since Gauche Wood, hardly a man of the surviving Springboks had slept for more than an hour at a stretch, but they were as stubborn as the enemy was persistent. They held out for far longer than even the most sanguine would have thought possible – husbanding their meagre supply of ammunition, making every shot tell and, by the same unerring marksmanship that had baulked the Germans at Gauche Wood three days earlier, repeatedly holding off a force ten times their number. Even when the enemy crept forward under a smokescreen, even when field guns were manhandled forward, the Lewis-guns dispatched their crews before they could come into action. But defeat was only a matter of time, and by two o'clock in the afternoon the South Africans were surrounded. By four o'clock only a hundred exhausted men remained. Now trench mortars were bombarding at close quarters, their ranks were thinning fast, and their ammunition was almost exhausted. Half an hour later, when the last shot had been fired, the few who remained were engulfed in a sea of enemy soldiers and made prisoner. As they were marched back behind the German line, their captors helped to carry the wounded and treated their prisoners with a respect which was close to admiration. Brigadier-General Dawson was at the head of the ragged band which was all that was left of his brigade. Leutnant Rudolf Binding met them as they went.

### Leutnant Rudolf Binding

Out from the lines of our advancing infantry, which I was following, appeared an English general, accompanied by a single officer. He was an extraordinary sight. About thirty-five years old, excellently – one can almost say wonderfully – dressed and equipped, he looked as if he had just stepped out of a Turkish bath in Jermyn Street. Brushed and shaved, with his short khaki overcoat on his arm, in breeches of the best cut and magnificent high laced boots such as only the English bootmakers make to order, he came to meet me easily and without the slightest embarrassment. The sight of all this English cloth and leather made me more conscious than ever of the shortcomings of my own outfit, and I felt an inward temptation to call out to him, 'Kindly undress at once', for a desire for an English general's equipment, with tunic, breeches and boots, had arisen in me, shameless and patent.

By way of being polite, I said with intention, 'You have given us a lot of trouble; you stuck it for a long time.' To which he replied, 'Trouble! Why, we have been running for four days and four nights!' It appeared that when he could no longer get his brigade to stand he had taken charge of a machine-gun himself, to set an example to his retreating men. All his officers except the one with him had been killed or wounded, and his brigade hopelessly cut up. I asked for his name, to remind me of our meeting, and he gave it. He was General Dawson, South African Brigade.

It was almost dark as they marched through Bouchavesnes and up the hill beyond, but it was light enough to distinguish the mass of St Pierre-Vaast

Wood on the left and the ground that swept down to the village of Moislains in the valley. It was also light enough to see troops and guns and transport in a continuous double line that stretched far to the east, jamming the road for miles. General Dawson had the satisfaction of knowing that for more than seven hours his tiny force had dislocated the immediate plans of the German Army and kept it from moving forward.

In the confusion of the previous evening, as the South African Brigade moved back to Marrières Wood, Lieutenant Geoffrey Lawrence had been caught up with the stragglers, too late to catch up and rejoin his unit, and much to his annoyance he was ordered to join up with the 'details' at the makeshift transport line at Bray. Here, to his pleasure and profound relief, he found his brother Reg. Both boys had been in the thick of fighting for three ferocious days, and it had seemed to each of them almost too much to expect that the other had survived. In the wake of the day's debacle it seemed doubly miraculous that they had, and they embraced as if they had not met for years.

When the wounded had been accounted for and sent off, of the entire South African Brigade there were barely 300 survivors, mostly non-combatants. Later, when it became clear that no one else would be coming back from Marrières Wood, they were split into groups of a hundred men, each representing a regiment, and with the rest of the 9th Division they set off on the next stage of the retirement through Combles. At least they were retiring as a body, but it was a body which could be better described as the ghost of the South African Brigade.

Not all their comrades were so fortunate. The three brigades of the Division had been so split up that there were crowds of stragglers. Harry Atherton and his friend Higgins of the 28th Field Ambulance were cold and wet and uncomfortable, for they had not properly dried out in the three days since they had been rushed to the line at the start of the battle. It was unfortunate that the Field Ambulance boys had been taking the opportunity of a brief rest in an abandoned farmhouse to do their laundry, and had hung their clothing out overnight to dry. But it had not dried, there had been a keen frost, their garments were still frozen stiff when their unfortunate owners were obliged to put them on, and three days of warm sunshine and unremitting exertion had not sufficiently penetrated the layers to thoroughly dry them out before another night of fog and frost struck chill into their bones.

*Private Harry Atherton, 28th Field Ambulance, Royal Army Medical Corps, 9th (Scottish) Division*

We could tell by the sound of the gunfire that the Germans were getting very near, and we didn't have long to wait, for in the distance we could see a line of our infantry coming towards us. They turned round and lay flat on the ground, fired a few quick rounds, got up, crossed the road, and shouted to us, 'Come on, mate!' Then another line came in sight and did the same – a few quick rounds before crossing the road. They were fighting a rearguard action. We couldn't see anything else in the distance, but now we seemed to be alone between two armies, and Higgie and I decided it was time to go, so we followed the infantry, but keeping well to the right of them so that we wouldn't be in their line of fire. We were lost, and we didn't know where our new headquarters were, so we kept on walking. It was moorland, with not a building in sight. The area was around Combles, and it was suddenly so quiet that one couldn't think there was a war, yet it was so near. Two soldiers of the Signals who had a post there asked us what was happening. We told them to get moving, because Jerry wasn't far away.

We'd been going on for a while when we saw someone coming towards us. We could see he was an airman, and he asked us what was happening. We had dropped on an airfield, and it was my brother George! We were very glad to meet each other so far from home. It's a small world! He didn't know me in my tin hat. We had a few minutes with him, and before we parted I told him I would tell mother, who would be very pleased. He asked us if we had any cigarettes, so we gave him a packet before we said our goodbyes and we were on our way again.

In the distance there was a crowd of soldiers, and when we got nearer there was a notice chalked up: 'Stragglers Post'. The Regimental Traffic Officer told us the way, and also that we had another six miles to walk! Before we started we were given some tea and bread and jam, and it tasted good – we were ready for it! It was almost dark when we finally arrived, and we had to report on what we had been doing and to explain our absence. They simply said, 'Very interesting. Dismiss!' Some of the boys had found a few bottles of wine in a house that had been evacuated, but the CO confiscated them. They ought to have kept it dark!

In the course of that same evening, 24 March, an unexpected visitor arrived at GHQ in the person of Lord Milner, en route from London to Paris to confer with Monsieur Clemenceau. In view of the seriousness of the situation in France – more serious even than the War Cabinet yet realized – Lloyd George had sent this trusted senior member of the War Cabinet to confer with the French Prime Minister. Lord Milner had been travelling all day, but he broke his journey at Montreuil to pay a courtesy call on the British Commander-in-Chief. But Sir Douglas Haig had already left for Bernaville, where General Byng had now set up Third Army Headquarters and where, for convenience, Haig was also to meet his own Chief of Staff, General Lawrence, whom he had sent to visit General Gough earlier in the day.

Lawrence had found Gough in good heart. General Fayolle had been with him, for now that the Fifth Army was technically under the command of the French the two men were working closely together and they had arranged for a joint counter-attack to take place the following morning. They had outlined the details, which Lawrence now passed on to the Commander-in-Chief, and it was reasonable to believe that this would re-establish at least part of the line along the Somme. The right wing of Byng's Third Army was falling back, but, where the situation appeared to be most precarious, newly arrived divisions had been ordered piecemeal into battle to plug gaps which might appear as the troops retired. Byng could only reiterate the orders he had issued on the instructions of the Commander-in-Chief, in the confident hope that they would be carried out.

Even so, there was cause for anxiety – so much so that, before leaving his headquarters at Montreuil, Haig had telegraphed urgently to London to request that Sir Henry Wilson, as Chief of the Imperial General Staff, should come to France. His message read, 'Situation is serious. Morval Ridge lost so Third and Fifth Armies are separated. Junction with the French can only be re-established by vigorous offensive action of French while I do all I can from the north in conjunction with them. I meet Pétain tonight.' He was unaware that Lord Milner was already speeding to Paris.

At this juncture Haig badly needed backing, and he needed it particularly in his relations with the French. A staff car was standing by, and immediately after dinner Haig was to set off to drive to Dury, south of Amiens, to confer with General Pétain, who was driving north from Compiègne to meet him at eleven o'clock that night. Before Haig left Third Army Headquarters he impressed on General Byng that 'at all costs' he must maintain the left wing of his army where it met the First in the north, and stand fast in front of Arras. They would not be alone, he assured him. General Plumer had agreed to thin his line in the Belgian sector, and, by taking some divisions from the First and Second Armies, it was the intention of the Commander-in-Chief to concentrate a reserve line behind Arras. Meanwhile, he added, it was of the most vital importance that the Third Army should cling to its ground.

Apart from necessary adjustments to maintain contact with the retirements on its right, the Third Army was indeed clinging to its ground, but further south, where its right wing was swinging back in a wide arc, things were not going quite in accordance with the orders which had been issued by Third Army HQ. Although the retirement had been carefully plotted on the map so that the line would remain intact, replicating those theoretical movements on the ground while being harried by an unco-operative enemy was another matter. In the tumult of attack and counter-attack, of piecemeal withdrawal and haphazard infiltrations by the foe – and, above all, in the unremitting shell-fire – the signals services had virtually collapsed. Even when orders reached a divisional headquarters, despite valiant individual efforts they seldom got through to the brigadiers whose task it was to orchestrate the movement of the troops. Telephone lines were smashed; runners could not cover the long distances from divisional headquarters; and, in the absence of conventional communications, mounted staff officers sent off to search frantically for brigades in the 'line' did not always succeed in finding them. When they did, more often than not the position in the so-called line had altered so drastically that the orders were no longer relevant. Divisions were retiring less in accordance with instructions from Army Headquarters than by improvised arrangements between individual brigadiers as circumstances demanded. They were not running, but they were fighting as they went, and it was hard to know what was happening. No matter how brigades and battalions tried to 'keep in touch', it was no wonder that gaps appeared. As darkness fell, they grew wider.

Even in daylight, moving across the old Somme battlefields had been difficult. There were few landmarks. A few haphazard heaps of rubble or a trace of brickdust among the old shell-holes was all that remained to show the location of a village pulverized in the fighting of 1916, and here and there a skeletal cluster of jagged stumps marked the site of a wood. A maze of old trenches littered the wasteland. They were deep and treacherous, festooned with barricades of rusting barbed wire – formidable obstacles in the path of troops trying to take up a line or to make their way across country. But the enemy, endeavouring to thrust forward, was encountering the same difficulties. Here and there, fighting patrols of fifty or a hundred, pushing blindly into strange terrain, were actually moving parallel to some British battalion as it withdrew, unbeknown to either. The going was slow. Although the roads had been patched up, they were frequently blocked by a line of transport wagons or guns moving back to new positions.

*Sergeant A. Dunbar, A 236 Bty., Royal Field Artillery, 47th Division*

After we had fired all our ammunition we were ordered further back and into another field for the night and to replenish our ammunition. A couple of dozen wagons of live shell had been ordered from the divisional ammunition column, and our CO had also asked for a dozen empty wagons to recover the piles of empty cartridge cases that we had left on our last gun position in our hurry to get away. The empty wagons duly arrived, and I was detailed to act as guide back to the old position. I was *not* amused. At the time we got our guns away we thought that at least a whole battalion of German infantry were in the next field, and it seemed madness to try to recover those cases. However, orders is orders, so we started back.

I was tired out and half-asleep most of the time. Also it was dark, and we were on unfamiliar ground. More important, we did not know where the Germans were or how far they had advanced since we left the gun position. I really didn't know just where I was, and it was strangely quiet. The only sound was the rattle of our horses' harness and the clatter of their hooves. I didn't like it one bit. I was leading a column of twelve wagons, thirty-six drivers and seventy-two horses, to say nothing of a DAC officer (and his horse), and I was leading them straight into the arms of the Germans for all I knew. It was a shattering thought!

After about an hour, and more by luck than by my judgement, we found the position. The cases were still there, scattered about the field, and we got them loaded into the empty wagons as quickly and as quietly as possible. All the time I was sure that we were being watched by hundreds of German eyes the other side of the hedge! There were a few cases left over when our wagons were full, but I advised the officer in charge that we should get away as quickly as we could and not push our luck. He led the column this time, and I brought up the rear. All the time my eyes and ears were working overtime. I could almost *feel* Germans all round us. But our luck still held, and the further we went the better I felt. I rode up and down the column once or twice to see that all was OK. This was standard practice, but on the last occasion I counted the wagons. There were only eleven! I checked again. Still eleven! I rode up to the officer in front and reported. 'You must have left one on the position,' he said. 'You'd better go back and find it.' My heart sank, but it was an order and I had no option. I turned back alone, and this time I was quite certain that I would end up a prisoner of war or, worse, dead in a ditch at the side of the road.

We had come back a few miles, and my horse didn't like leaving the others. Come to that, neither did I! After a time we came to a fork in the road, and, although I was quite sure the left fork was the one we should take, my horse badly wanted to take the other. I had my way, however, and off we went again. Half a mile further we turned a bend, and fifty yards away there was a group of men in the road.

Without thinking, I rode up to within a few yards and saw that there were six or seven men sprawling and sitting on the road and one held out what appeared to be a mug to me. Suddenly I realized they were in field-grey uniforms and not khaki! I whipped my horse round and shot back at the gallop. I dropped the reins on his neck and he got the message. For the next hour he went on and on without hesitation. Turnings, crossroads, forks in the road made no difference – he knew the way all right. We finally caught up with the column and I reported to the officer that I had found no trace of the missing wagon. 'Oh, that's all right, sergeant,' he said, 'I remember now – we only had eleven wagons to start with.'

The men I saw were undoubtedly a German patrol. Probably they had raided a British canteen somewhere and were all too drunk to recognize me or to fire. Thanks to my horse, I got away with it that time, but for hours I was in a cold sweat!

More than twelve miles to the south, where von Hutier's Eighteenth German Army was on the heels of the 58th British Division and the French who had come up to assist, the 1st Bavarian Infantry Regiment had reached Guivry and had rested there all day. The terrain was easier going than on the old battlefield of the Somme, but they had now been marching and fighting with little sleep for three days and nights, and they were thankful for the respite. They had also had little food since their feed at Montescourt three days earlier, but in Guivry they once again struck lucky.

*Leutnant Reinhold Spengler, 2nd Coy., 1st Bavarian Infantry Regt., 1st Bavarian Division*

Shortly after arriving, we found a French provision depot. It was not as assorted as the English one we left in Montescourt, but to us it was a hungry man's paradise. The depot was stocked with all kinds of meat, sausages, mountains of white bread, real coffee, cocoa, canned milk, tea, cheese, chocolate and candied fruits. We stayed here the rest of the day, and had plenty of time to feel like guests of the French.

One man of my light-machine-gun platoon delighted us with a juicy roast. He loved to cook, and an hour after settling down in Guivry he served a delicious baked chicken. That night we had pork roast and bread dumplings – a feast so well loved in Bavaria. All of this proved too much for my stomach, which was not used to such delicacies (not by my own choice). Soon I was sick, and the next morning I looked like a living corpse, barely able to stand on my legs. During

the next several days I took my place in the baggage wagon that
followed the company.

Sated for once with good food and the pleasant sensation of full stomachs,
the Bavarian boys gave little thought for tomorrow as they settled down for
the night. Things were going well. A little way to the south the sky glowed
and flickered above the burning town of Noyon. Behind them their guns
were still firing, and ahead, where the dull thud of other explosions sounded
along the Oise, engineers were blowing up the bridges that crossed the
river.

Noyon was on the road to French Headquarters in the town of Compiègne
– and Compiègne was almost halfway along the main road to Paris. The
Staff at GQG[1] in Compiègne were used to hearing the drone of German
bombers following the line of the River Oise as they flew towards Paris.
They had learned to ignore them, and even to disregard the din of anti-aircraft
guns in the forest firing salvoes at the raiders overhead. But now Compiègne
was the target, and for the last three nights a series of violent air raids had
driven the Headquarters' Staff to shelter in the deep catacombs beneath the
palace where they were based. Emergency telephone lines had been installed,
and tables and chairs had been carried down from the galleries above, but,
although the subterranean passages ran so deep that the sound of neither the
bombs nor the guns could be heard, working under these conditions was
not easy, and in the present critical circumstances GQG was working round
the clock. The catacombs were as cold and clammy as the grave, the
emergency lighting was far from adequate, and a constant invasion of soldiers
and even civilians seeking shelter during raids made it almost impossible to
concentrate. General Pétain had already decamped with his most senior
officers to a villa on the edge of the forest.

On the third night the raids began earlier and were more violent than
ever. Parts of the town were already badly damaged, most civilians had now
been evacuated, and, as the gravity of the military situation increased, the
Staff at GQG fully expected to be ordered to move. The fall of Noyon was
to be the signal for their departure. It had always been anticipated that, in
the event of an emergency, GQG would go back to Chantilly, where
suitable premises had already been prepared, but now the plans were changed.
During the afternoon of Palm Sunday, Colonel Valentin, who had been at
Chantilly since the previous day, making final arrangements, was ordered
to proceed to Provins. The enemy had advanced too far, and Chantilly was
far too close to the line for safety. Provins was well to the south, near the
forest of Fontainebleau to the east of Paris. Although Pétain himself proposed

1. GQG – *Grand Quartier Général* – was the equivalent of British GHQ.

to remain at Compiègne with his advanced headquarters, the news of GQG's departure did not reassure Sir Douglas Haig when he learned of it at Dury late that evening. Provins was a long way from the area where the threat was greatest and where the crisis was deepening all the time.

The order to pack up came as no surprise to the French Staff at Compiègne, but they had hardly expected to receive it at 10.30 in the evening in the middle of an air raid and to be told that baggage must be ready for removal by six o'clock in the morning. In seven sleepless hours the Staff, their clerks and orderlies, and the officers' servants, hastily summoned from billets in the town, were now obliged to accomplish a task they would have been hard-pressed to complete in seven days.

There were mountains of paper to be packed and removed to safety, for every department had its own irreplaceable archives. These ranged from the plans for the reorganization of divisions to the transport schemes of the Railway Department, which would not only be of inestimable value to the enemy if they were to fall into his hands but would paralyse the Army if they were lost or destroyed by fire or shelling. It was clear that it was going to be a long night.

For almost a year French Army Headquarters had been installed in the sprawling palace which dominated the town of Compiègne and the forest beyond. GQG was the last of a long line of occupants, for the chateau had originally been built in the time of the Merovingian kings who ruled Gaul after the fall of the Roman Empire, and had been enlarged and rebuilt a thousand years later by Louis XV. He liked it best of all his residences, and his favourite hunting ground was the lush forest outside its walls. A balustraded terrace overlooked the sandy avenue – then the King's private thoroughfare – where he had once ridden out to meet the carriage that brought the Austrian princess Marie Antoinette to her unhappy destiny as the bride of his grandson, the Dauphin. Here too, at Compiègne, the Emperor Napoleon had held court (and married another Austrian princess), and the chateau had been refurbished in his own distinctive style. Napoleon's marble statue still brooded in the salon where, a century before, in the throes of another war, he had laid vainglorious plans to invade and conquer England.

In 1914, in the first hectic days of the present war, before the battles that threw them back and the start of the long stalemate, German uhlans had briefly occupied the chateau of Compiègne as they swept through France on the heels of the Allies. Now that the stalemate was broken, in the flurry of preparation for departure through the long hours of the night, it seemed perfectly possible that the Germans would soon be back.

Travelling to Dury to meet the British Commander-in-Chief, General Pétain was not in the happiest frame of mind. He struck Sir Douglas Haig as being 'very much upset, almost unbalanced, and most anxious'. It was hardly surprising. The rapid advance of von Hutier's army southwards and the deliberate bombardment of Paris by the German long-distance gun weighed heavily on Pétain's mind and was drawing him to the inexorable conclusion that the threat to the French capital outweighed all other considerations. He was convinced that the Germans' attack in the British sector was intended to push the British Army aside before launching a major thrust against the French in the Champagne, there to break the line, sweep on to Paris and, in effect, conquer France as they had done in another war half a century before. The falling back of the southern wing of the British Army adjacent to his own did nothing, in his view, to inspire confidence. Nor did it incline him to accede to Haig's desire that he, Pétain, should extend his forces northwards to keep in touch with Haig's own force, and to make a stand at Amiens. Pétain had already fulfilled his initial obligation by sending such troops as he could spare. How could he further denude his own army of men who might be badly needed to thwart another German blow which would strike at the heart of France? He strongly suspected that it was part of the machiavellian German plan that he should do so.

In Sir Douglas Haig's view, Amiens, at the hub of the vital rail communications in the north, was the Germans' main objective. The prising apart of the French and British armies would enable them to capture it. Moreover, if the British Army were driven back to the coast, and consequently out of the war, the Germans doubtless hoped that the French themselves would collapse.

The midnight meeting was not a happy one. Both commanders were tired, and, despite Haig's competent command of French and the presence of bilingual liaison officers during their discussion, misunderstandings arose – or so it was subsequently said.

Each man, the other later claimed, had gained a false impression of the intentions of his opposite number. It was probably true that, when challenged to speak plainly, General Pétain admitted that, in the course of unforeseen events, he might ultimately be forced to retire southward on Paris. It was probably equally true that Sir Douglas Haig hinted at the possibility of being forced to retire northward to the Channel ports. In retrospect, neither commander's recollection of the meeting entirely matched the recollection of the other. Nevertheless, Pétain had revealed his thinking in an order to the French Army, and he handed a copy to Haig. After an assessment of the military situation, it went on:

INTENTIONS OF THE GENERAL COMMANDER-IN-CHIEF
Before everything to keep the French Armies together as one solid whole; in particular, not to allow the Grande Armée de Reserve to be

cut off from the rest of our forces. Secondly, if it is possible, to maintain liaison with the British forces.

The words 'if it is possible' reinforced the suspicion of the British Commander-in-Chief that the French were not to be relied on. Although the French Commander reiterated his wish to assist Haig to the limit of his ability, he made no secret of the fact that his orders from the French Government were 'to cover Paris at all costs'. But Haig himself, despite his declared conviction that only the combined force of the British and French armies could meet the crisis and repulse the German assault on Amiens, had conveyed the impression that his own position was ambivalent, if not directly to General Pétain then certainly by his instructions to the Third Army.

General Byng had undoubtedly received that impression, and early the previous day he had informed his corps commanders that it was not yet certain whether retirement would be made towards the west to keep in line with the French, or north-west to cover the Channel ports. On the Commander-in-Chief's instruction, he had also made arrangements for the construction of a new line to which the Third Army could fall back, running north from Dernancourt south of Albert, to link up with the Arras defences. As soon as sufficient men could be found, work would begin on a further system of trenches which would extend from west of Doullens to cover the ports of Boulogne, Calais and Dunkirk. If the worst came to the worst, it was there that the British Army would make its last stand.

To find sufficient labour, they would have to scour the bottom of the barrel, and every man who could be spared from the lines of communication was detailed for this task – the Royal Engineers, the personnel of camouflage parks and factories, the staffs and officers of the Army schools of instruction, the men who had operated the forward light railways, whose task of carrying supplies to the old front line was redundant now that it was no more. Drivers and transport troops were co-opted, along with men employed at salvage dumps and base camps, and every man who could be spared from any branch of the unwieldy administrative machine that supported the Army in the field and who was not capable in the last resort of fighting in the line.[1]

It was thought to be a necessary precaution.

General Pétain's journey on the main road to his headquarters took him through Montdidier and the area where the troops of his reserve army were assembling to form a line. Nearing Compiègne, his vehicle was forced to slow down to a crawl. Despite much blowing of the horn and the voluble

---

1. During the next few weeks, 5,000 miles of new trenches were prepared and 23,500 tons of barbed-wire entanglements were erected on 15 million wood or steel pickets.

imprecations of his driver, the big staff car had great difficulty in squeezing past the cavalcade of lorries streaming across the river and inching up the narrow streets towards the chateau, where the preparations for departure were in full swing. Capitaine Jean Pierrefeu was hurrying through one half-emptied gallery, where the marble eye of Napoleon seemed to glare with cold displeasure at the feverish scene below. The great man had chosen to be immortalized, larger than life, in the robes of a Roman emperor, and Pierrefeu was now struck by the thought that he looked uncannily like a commander abandoned by his troops.

It was three o'clock in the morning by the time Sir Douglas Haig reached his quarters near Montreuil. Until tomorrow, there was little he could do. General Byng had his orders, and the Commander-in-Chief was hopeful that the Third Army north of Péronne was even now forming a flank along the straggling westward course of the River Somme. But south of Péronne, where the Fifth Army had already passed into French command, it was now up to Pétain to save the situation.

But ultimately it would not be up to Pétain. It would be up to General Foch.

# Part 4

# The Bottom of the Barrel

*The tide ran in, that day, so deep*
*The sun was drowned; yet friendship flows*
*Deeper, from springs which childhood knows,*
*Mirrored in ageing memory.*

LIEUTENANT J. R. T. ALDOUS
210 Field Coy., Royal Engineers
31st Division (1914–1918)

## Chapter 17

No one could say with certainty who first proposed that General Foch should be invited to co-ordinate the command of the Allied armies. Doubtless the seed was planted and the idea slowly grew in the course of various meetings between the interested parties on Monday 25 March. But it was blindingly obvious to all concerned that something would have to be done, and when he reached Montreuil at 11.30 that morning Sir Henry Wilson made no bones about it. Nor did he hesitate to say 'I told you so' at his meeting with Sir Douglas Haig.

*Extract from the diary of General Sir Henry Wilson*

I could not resist reminding him that it was he [Haig] . . . who killed my plan of a General Reserve, nor could I resist reminding him of what I had both told and written to him on the 6th March – that without a General Reserve he would be living on the charity of Pétain.

These observations could not have delighted Haig; nor were they necessarily true. The French were already contributing a greater number of troops than had been mooted by the Supreme War Council earlier in the year. The difficulty was, in Haig's view, that it was not great enough and that, given the state of mind displayed by General Pétain, it was unlikely to increase soon enough to affect the Allies' fortunes in the battle. The British Commander-in-Chief was genuinely perturbed by Pétain's apparent change of outlook and, consequently, by the change in the strategy he seemed likely to adopt.

But Pétain's stance had not changed overnight, although there was little doubt that the realistic view he had previously held had swung to a mood of downright pessimism. Pétain was no fire-eater. With regard to military matters his mind was cold and calculating, and, in the aftermath of the costly Franco-British campaign on the Somme, and in the wake of the failed Nivelle offensive of the previous year and the disenchantment which had brought about his own appointment as Commander-in-Chief, his view had crystallized. By eschewing the old tenets which had held a sacred place in

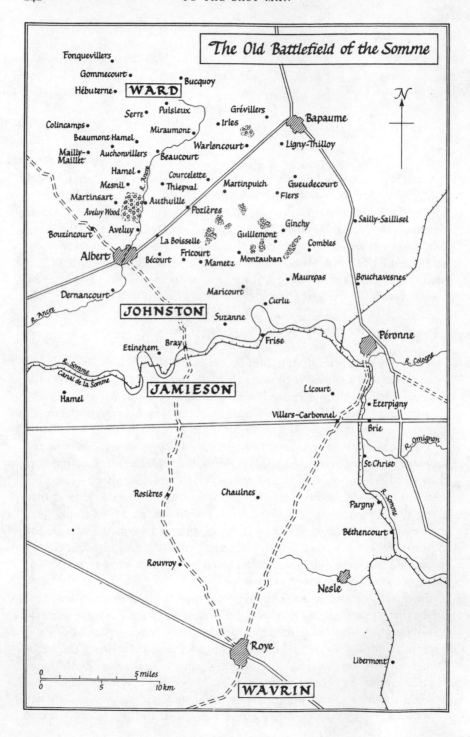

The Old Battlefield of the Somme

the French military mind and imagination since time immemorial, by careful preparation and the overwhelming support of artillery, Pétain had restored the situation at Verdun in 1916. With cold, objective assessment he had analysed the fatal weaknesses which ran deep within the hierarchy of the French Army. Single-handedly he had imposed the reforms which restored discipline after its near-collapse and had set about the task of restructuring and retraining which would enable the Army to take the offensive when the time eventually came. Until then – and until the Americans were in a position to add the weight that would tip the scales – Pétain's policy was to stand on the defensive. This had been his policy in May 1917, when he was given the post of Commander-in-Chief and the task of picking up the pieces in the wake of the mutiny, and neither the result of Haig's Passchendaele offensive, which he had reluctantly supported, nor the outcome of the Battle of Cambrai at the fag-end of the year had given him cause to change his mind.

He was not alone in his approach. For more than a decade before the war there had been a new school of thought in the upper echelons of the French Army Command, and Pétain had been one of a handful of high-ranking officers at the École de Guerre who were reassessing the value of the nineteenth-century death-or-glory tactics which still dominated the Army and were beloved by France. But in the present war they had cost the country dear. In its first six weeks the casualties had amounted to almost half a million, and the dead alone outnumbered the whole of the original British Expeditionary Force. Now, four years later, with casualties compounded, with a weakened conscript Army whose morale had been badly shaken, reeling under the weight of an overwhelming assault which he doubted that the Allies could defeat, Pétain's instinct was to draw in his horns, to retrench, to defend the French capital, and to save his army to fight another battle another day.

But the French Government ministers, who less than a year ago had hailed Pétain as a saviour, were less in sympathy. General Foch was now Chief of the French General Staff, military representative at Versailles and technical adviser to the French Government. He had the ear of the politicians, and the vigour of his offensive spirit – that untranslatable *élan*, that rebellious, revolutionary spirit of brotherhood and patriotic fervour which had toppled thrones and sent troops wild-eyed into battle – was seductive. At this crisis of the war the political masters found Danton's stirring cry of '*L'audace, l'audace, et encore l'audace!*' more attractive by far than the sober pronouncements of Pétain. Foch was the Danton of his day, and to Georges Clemenceau, who had become Prime Minister in November, he was a man after his own heart. His forceful temperament was in fiery contrast to that of Pétain – stoic, cold, impassive. The ringing words of his famous message to General

Joffre in 1914 were already legendary and would ring on through the annals of military history: 'Hard pressed on my right. My centre is yielding. Impossible to manoeuvre. Situation excellent. I am attacking.'

Foch's star had waned after the Battle of the Somme, but it had risen again by the sheer power of his magnetic personality, and under the present circumstances his influence was great. He was on good terms with General Sir Henry Wilson and the two men, each Chief of his respective General Staff, had kept in close touch. On Saturday evening, as the Germans had advanced and the crisis had deepened, Foch had telephoned Wilson in London. No record was made of their conversation, but now, according to Wilson's own account of his interview with Sir Douglas Haig at Montreuil, after discussing the necessity for united action, Wilson proposed that Foch should be invited to co-ordinate the action of both Haig and Pétain. 'In the end,' he added, 'Douglas Haig agreed.'

Haig was not a man who either quickly or impulsively adopted new ideas and, although he was a courteous listener, he was not readily inclined to attribute new ideas to others. He suggested, in an entry in his diary, that a similar thought had occurred to him. It hardly mattered. In the light of the impasse with Pétain, Haig was not slow to realize that such a move might well be in his interest. The seed took root – and it was nurtured by the news from the front of the Fifth Army that the Franco-British counter-attack on which General Gough had placed so much reliance had not come off.

Haig was disappointed, Gough was perturbed, but, at XVIII Corps Head-quarters, General Maxse was fuming. Beyond the western bank of the Somme, now in the hands of the Germans, there was a gap of nearly a mile between his XVIII Corps and the XIX Corps north of it, commanded by General Watts. It was tenuously covered by the battered remnants of the 24th Division, in reserve three miles in the rear. Immediately to the south, a weak and badly mauled brigade of the 61st Division had been extended to cover no less than one and a half miles of front. It was a precarious position. Although Péronne itself was now in German hands, in front of the town and south of it Watts was clinging firmly to six miles of the Somme round the wide curve that sent the river looping to the west immediately south of the gap which separated him from the Third Army on his left flank. On the right, where his line had been pushed back at Béthencourt and Pargny in front of Nesle, another gap now lay between his force and the line held by Maxse's XVIII Corps and the French troops who extended it. Unless the situation could be immediately retrieved it was plain to see that the Germans would easily brush aside the handful of men strung out behind the gap, and the French and British armies would be irrevocably separated. The situation was more than critical: it was potentially catastrophic. Only the French could save the day, and from the early hours of Palm Sunday the French 22nd Division had been arriving at Nesle.

The plan was that the French would attack from south to north towards the river on Maxse's side of the gap, while parts of the British 8th and 24th Divisions would simultaneously attack from west to east. Thus, between them, they would close the gap and retain the line of the Somme. The plan had been devised by General Gough in conjunction with his Corps Commanders, Watts and Maxse, and with General Robillot in command of the French, and it had been agreed with General Fayolle. Zero hour was fixed for the morning of 25 March, and during the night the 24th Division was moved forward. After their exertions and losses during the past few days the men could not accurately be described as fresh, but they had had a little rest, for they had been in reserve since Saturday and, although they had been digging trenches for most of Sunday, they had at least had a chance to sleep and a respite from the fighting. General Maxse had no small difficulty in collecting sufficient troops for his part in the assault, because the men in the actual line were all he had, and the line must still be held and manned when the assaulting force advanced. With no supporting troops, no reserves of infantry at his disposal, he had to do the best he could with what he had – one battalion of pioneers (22nd Durham Light Infantry) and one field company of Royal Engineers, newly arrived that morning. They moved into the line to replace the two brigades, or more precisely to replace the remnants of the two brigades, which were to make the assault.

It had been arranged for 8 a.m. and, since the French troops as yet had no artillery, the guns of XVIII Corps were to back up their attack. But, at the request of the French commander, zero hour was postponed until eleven o'clock, because his troops were not yet ready in position. But the Germans were. They attacked ferociously, and they attacked all along the line. By eleven o'clock, when Maxse still had hopes that the combined effort might halt the enemy – or at least enable the divided force to keep in touch if it must fall back – General Robillot's force had already begun to retire. It was retiring in a south-westerly direction, it was carrying XVIII Corps artillery with it, and the space between the armies was swinging wide.[1]

No assistance had come from the French, and it was unfortunate that the front-line troops of the 24th Division did not know it. When the first enemy parties appeared, they progressed for some distance before so much as a single shot was fired to stop them: in the misty light of early morning the Tommies assumed that the grey-clad figures half-seen in the distance were

---

1. When General Maxse later tackled General Robillot to ask why the joint attack had been aborted, Robillot looked at him with astonishment. 'But it was no more than a plan!' he replied ('*Mais ce n'était qu'un projet*').

French troops who had managed to get a head start. When they realized their mistake they fought back – and fought hard all morning, holding the enemy in check and causing so many casualties that again and again the Germans hesitated and stopped. It was not until after one o'clock that the line was forced to retire and the Somme line was irrevocably lost.

In front of Libermont, where Désiré Wavrin and his comrades were holding Hospital Wood, the battle had started at 6.30 in the morning.

*Capitaine Désiré Wavrin, 22nd Coy., 6th Bn., 307th Regt., 62nd [French] Division*

It was such a violent attack right across our front that it was impossible to withstand it. During the night the enemy had infiltrated all through the wood and my company was cut in two. I managed to get out of the wood with a group of men and, splitting up and shooting all the time, we managed to reach the edge of Libermont, which the 4th Battalion was defending. Here the resistance hardened up, although the shells were simply pouring down on us, causing terrible losses.

When it was coming on for four o'clock in the afternoon, long columns of enemy soldiers poured out from Esmery-Hallon and massed in front of Libermont for an assault. I counted sixteen waves of them at least. Very soon it became impossible to hold out any longer, and we had to fall back a long way to the other side of the canal. It was at that moment, after ten hours' fighting, that I began to feel completely washed out. I had managed to send back the remains of my company, and only Quéfille was still with me. The whole ground and the shallow trenches were thick with dead bodies, and the Boche were only about fifty metres away. I felt limp as a rag. I said to Quéfille, 'I give up! I can't go on any longer. Let them capture us and be done with it.' He shouted back, 'What are you saying! Let them capture us? What if they do us in instead! We have to clear off!' He was some man! He grabbed me by the sleeve, and I let him pull me along, crawling across the rough grass and under bushes, and we ended up out of breath on the bank of the canal.

We managed to go across it on a little bridge, although we were being swept with bullets. There were some scraped-out trenches on the other side, and to get our breath back Quéfille jumped into one and I jumped into another. Three machine-gunners got there at the same time, and at that very moment a volley of shots came over and killed every single one of them. I think my guardian angel must have been there, because I wasn't touched, but I didn't hang around. The bridge must have been mined, and just then it went up. My only thought was to get out of there as soon as possible. But then something absolutely farcical happened with dire results: the buttons of my braces burst, and my trousers tumbled down to my ankles so that I was hobbled like a goat! I could neither stand up nor walk forward, so I had to crawl like a worm for about a hundred metres before I was able to throw myself into a ditch at the side of a road. When I'd fixed my trousers as best I could, I started off again – still of course with the faithful Quéfille. Somehow or other we managed to get back to the regiment – or what was left of it.

We went back to Ognolles, l'Abbaye-aux-Bois. Then we crossed Champien Wood, carrying our colonel, who was wounded there, and took up position on the outcrops of rock at Amy. The Regiment regrouped somewhere towards Crapeaumésnil, and there we defended first the east side of the Bois des Loges, then the west. It was there that I was reunited with the other part of my company – or with the rump of it, as you might say. At last the Regiment reached the village of Roye-sur-Matz, where there was a firm line which allowed us to reorganize under the protection of the artillery, which had at last arrived. So, fighting all the way, outnumbered ten to one, we had pulled back fifteen kilometres. We had kept the enemy from getting through with nothing but our rifles and machine-guns, but it was terribly sad to have to retreat!

Matters were not much better on the front of the Third Army. The men were tired, and, if they were not wholly dispirited and still philosophically trusting to luck and the wisdom of Higher Command to get them out of trouble, it was disconcerting to be giving up ground which had cost so much soul-destroying effort to attain. Delville Wood, Guillemont, High Wood, Bazentin, Mametz – the very names rang like a knell as they plodded back, cold and hungry and weary. Even the men of the divisions which had arrived only in time to fill the gaps and stiffen the line as it fell back fighting were exhausted by two days and nights of continuous exertion, and the business of preparing to depart had been so frenetic that they had been tired before they started.

Major Harrison Johnston of the 15th Cheshires found it difficult to believe that the officers had been hosting a fancy-dress party when the summons reached them near Ypres on the night of 21 March. The party was not the most glittering of social occasions. The room was bravely, if sparsely, decorated with greenery, but the 'fancy dress' owed less to the art of the costumier than to the ingenuity of the guests – turbans contrived from khaki scarves; beards and moustaches daubed on with charcoal; eyepatches manufactured from scraps of tarpaulin. There were a few 'ghosts' draped in tablecloths borrowed from the officers' mess, and some unlikely representations of the Kaiser, liberally adorned with cardboard medals and helmets painted silver with camouflage paint. The evening was enlivened by a contingent of nurses from local casualty clearing stations, who made congenial dancing partners (although they wisely had not adopted fancy dress), and mess servants, encouraged by a liberal supply of beer or tots of port and whisky, took turns to wind the gramophone and keep the music going. The signal from Divisional Headquarters put an end to the festivities and, looking back on that happy evening only five nights ago, it seemed to Johnston, now trudging along the road from Maricourt, that it had all been an illusion.

It was his third night without sleep. The Battalion had marched eight miles to the railhead near Ypres, and a wearisome journey – twelve hours of jolting and stopping and starting – had brought them to Méricourt l'Abbé, on the Somme, at four o'clock in the morning. They had then started right away to march the seventeen miles to the front, sustained by the promise that breakfast would be waiting when they got there. They had hardly swallowed it before men of the 21st and 9th Divisions had come streaming back with the news that the Germans were on their heels, and the Cheshires were plunged into the fight.

They were far from fresh, but they were a good deal fresher than the divisions they went to support. But they did more than support them. Together the Cheshires and the 15th Sherwood Foresters counter-attacked and regained the Cléry Ridge, south of Marrières Wood. They advanced more than a mile, and there they held on, drove the enemy back, and held up the advance all day. And when the enemy attacked in a mass which far outnumbered them, when the gap between the Cheshires and the Sherwoods widened and they were almost surrounded, they fought their way out, carrying their wounded, and fell back to Battalion Headquarters in a sunken road just west of Hem Wood. And there they stayed until finally they were ordered to withdraw.

*Major Harrison Johnston, 15th (Service) Bn., The Cheshire Regt., 35th Division*

I left the sunken road feeling pretty done in. I found a boy of nineteen lying in a ditch at the roadside and a man trying to persuade him to get up. He was shot through the mouth, which had swollen terribly. The poor kid had been shouting all day, and I'd spoken to him many times. Now I tried to get him up, but he didn't want to come and had chucked up the sponge. I told him he must make an effort or fall into Boche hands. I told him how brave he'd been all day, and that he must stick it and come. At last we got him up, and practically carried him for half a mile to the next position we were to take up. Here one of our cookers was waiting with hot tea. The General met me and told me to line the road from the junction to the river – a frontage of about 1,000 yards. Ye gods, I had about 150 men then! However, I met some South African stragglers and put them in position – they didn't want to be roped in, but I snaffled all I saw, no matter what regiment.

As I got back to the top of the road, the General blew me out by the roots, because late arrivals were having tea near the cooker instead of lining the road. Of course the poor lads were famished, but the General was right, as the Germans followed us up quickly. We got patrols out in front, and mounted our Lewis-guns in good positions and so on. Night had fallen now, and there was a strong hoar frost. I had no overcoat and felt the cold, but I had to walk up and down my line to keep the lads awake. If I sat down I slept too. Doran brought me the CO's coat and I put it on. The poor old sportsman was missing, and I felt it looked a horrible thing to wear his coat, but I was starved and I was glad of it.[1] We lost fourteen officers and over 300 men in that day's work, and we could see there was more coming, but everybody was splendid.

In the morning, 25 March, we were shelled heavily from dawn. At first we thought we were getting a few shorts from our own heavies, but it became evident very soon that the shells were Boche and that he was getting the range of our position accurately. Casualties increased, and it soon became evident that we could not stay. Our W Company, who had missed the previous day's fighting, had come up to reinforce us during the night. I therefore sent Milne with his whole company to take up a position on a high ridge and cover the retirement of the rest of the troops.

The retirement was orderly and our men were easily rallied outside the village of Maricourt. I am very sorry to say that these remarks do not apply to all units, and I was roped in to assist some staff officers in stopping the rot and making men return and reinforce our new position. Revolvers had to be produced, and it was extremely difficult to hold the mob.

The new position was a strong one, with a splendid field of fire. The enemy followed up quickly, and it was strange to see him moving up and occupying the position we had left. I saw some Boche approaching a hut I'd had my breakfast in. Here I had left the CO's coat with

1. Lieutenant-Colonel H. P. G. Cochran, DSO, in command of the 15th Cheshires, did not reappear, and much later Harrison Johnston learned that he had been killed that day, 24 March 1918. Major Johnston took over command of the Battalion.

my flashlight in the pocket. We got a few Boche during the day, but they did not make a definite attack on our new position. At about 9 p.m. that night a Boche patrol of two officers and sixteen men met one of our patrols who were just going out. Our patrol was only half their strength, but our fellows killed nine and captured two of the other fellows. About 10 p.m. we were relieved by the 17th Lancashire Fusiliers and we proceeded towards billets at Suzanne, where hot food was provided in huts.

As we came along that road I saw in the darkness many things that did not exist. I saw distinctly heaps of women and children, also umpteen animals, lying dead by the roadside, and as I came along with Binks, who had come up that morning early to act as adjutant, I had to ask him at last if he could see some of the horrible things. He said, 'No.' I stuck it for a while longer, then I saw a large building with a big green flag hanging in front of it and a large red cross on the flag. I said, 'This looks like a possible billet.' He took my arm and said there was nothing bigger than a grassy bank in sight. It seems strange that such things can happen – but take it from me they can.

After my hot drink and food I was quite all right again and very thankful. I feared I was going barmy!

The guns too were retiring, and with no little difficulty along the congested roads. Notwithstanding his hair-raising adventures in the forefront of the German assault, it was only the previous evening that Major Ward had appreciated the full gravity of the situation.

*Major Ronald Ward, C 293 Bty., Royal Field Artillery*

We got to Ligny-Thilloy and it was just like all the other villages: it was a pile of rubbish. Just outside the village and to the north of it are three crossroads on the top of a little hill, and here there was a sight that made one think a bit. A battery of six-inch howitzers was in action firing briskly, but the grim fact was that the two sections were in action almost trail to trail. In other words, two howitzers were firing due north, and the other two were firing in almost exactly the opposite direction, namely south-south-west. The peculiar disposition of these four howitzers made it rather painfully obvious that the situation was serious. We passed them and moved on a few hundred yards more to the north, and there came into action beside the road. In half an hour the howitzers had limbered up and left the position.

They had retired to the west of Grévillers, and now Major Ward was in a more optimistic frame of mind. For one thing, that morning he had at last had some food. It was only hot tea and bread and jam, but it was the first food he had eaten since breakfast on the first day of the battle, and it did him good. Soon afterwards his spirits rose even further.

*Major Ronald Ward*

At 10 a.m. on the 25th we got fresh orders and were pleased to find that they were of the cheerful kind, for we were to advance a mile to a position north-east of Irles. There the Battery came into action on open grass slopes. It was the sort of position that I liked – out in open country and on good soil where shelter trenches could be dug for the protection of the detachments, and of course the guns and their flashes were concealed from the direct view of the enemy by rising ground in front. From this position we did some good shooting at enemy infantry advancing against Loupart Wood, for Grévillers was taken by noon.

Soon after midday it became clear again that things were not going well, and, looking across the village on our left, we could see our infantry retiring from Achiet-le-Grand, one and a half miles away. The lines ran in the bottom of the valley, about 600 yards behind the guns, and I was presently startled by unexpected explosions from that direction. These proved to be due not to the enemy but to our own Engineers, who were blowing up sections of the railway track to prevent the Boche from using them. It was a further sign of the seriousness of things. A little later one of these men walked up to the Battery. He was a large American sapper, who had enlisted in the British Army. He carried *outside* him a rifle with the bayonet fixed and some cartridges, and *inside* him a large quantity of whisky plus a burning zeal to discover the enemy. I think it must have been the duty of burning the canteen the night before which had so fired his courage, for he asked me more than once just exactly where the Boche might be found, explaining that he was finding demolitions too dull. I gave him precise details, and, having shaken me warmly by the hand, he set off in the direction I indicated, though rather slowly. I saw him no more, but I fancy that discretion took control over valour before he had gone very far.

An hour later we were ordered to move back towards Puisieux-au-Mont. I remember that march of one and a half miles well, for it was terribly slow, the roads crowded with ammunition carts and with infantrymen, whom we gradually overtook. Infantrymen retiring after five days of such fighting were a sad spectacle. They were wandering along the road, wearily, in little groups, men of one regiment mixed up with those of another, and the confusion of battalions was particularly noticeable, because some were Highlanders in kilts and some were from English units. There was no sort of panic, and each man still carried his rifle and his kit, but they were dead beat, and utterly fed up. As I passed in and out amongst these exhausted men, toiling along the rough track, I felt ashamed to be riding a horse. I don't think I saw an officer anywhere, except at one place where a young staff officer was rather excitedly trying to form a line. It was a useless task, for, though the men stopped at once and faced about, he could not give them any detailed orders about occupying positions, and as there was no enemy in sight they felt his efforts were futile. Presently, as more tired troops drifted up, they wandered on again towards the west. (It has to be said that there were by now very few infantry officers left, and that some units in actual contact with the enemy were quite out of touch with their own infantry brigade headquarters.)

At last we came into action near some deserted huts just to the east of the ruins of Puisieux-au-Mont. Having arranged the lines of fire towards Irles and arranged a telephone line between the OP and the battery, I gave the order 'Stand Easy.' A few moments later, looking at the Battery through my glasses from the OP, I could not see a man anywhere, except the signallers. They had all got into shell-holes in little groups of three and four, covered themselves over with blankets from the wagons, and were fast asleep. The men were by now utterly worn out. The gunners slept whenever there was a 'Stand Easy', and at night the drivers went to sleep in their saddles as soon as their teams got off rough ground and were travelling smoothly along anything resembling a road. I don't think the men felt that they were in any way beaten, for the moment any call was made upon them – as, for example, when rapid and accurate fire was necessary – they became as alert as any battery commander could possibly wish. While they rested, I stood where I was, with my sergeant-major and two signallers, feeling rather like a father watching over his family. Soon the last of the retiring infantry had passed us by, and C Battery was once more alone.

A few miles to the south, where the open flank of the Third Army now rested on the River Somme, the position was even more hazardous. The Third Army's front had swung back, pivoting on its left, and, although its line in the north had hardly moved and the divisions on its left flank were only a little way behind their original positions, the right of V Corps had retired as much as seventeen miles from the tip of the Flesquières salient to the old battlefield of the Somme. The 9th (Scottish) Division was at the end of the line, and beyond it the enemy was advancing through the gap which divided it from the Fifth Army.[1]

After their battering on Palm Sunday and the loss of the South African Brigade there was not a man in the fragmented ranks of the survivors who did not thank his lucky stars that the 35th Division had come in the nick of time to relieve them. Isolated at St Pierre-Vaast Wood, with both flanks open and the Germans closing in from either side, Alex Jamieson's brigade had got away by the skin of its teeth. At Bray, when the roll of the 11th Royal Scots was called for the first time since the battle began, only thirty men of A Company were there to answer their names. 'Blood Company' Captain Will Darling had called it, and the name now seemed chillingly apt. The Division was a sorry sight. As they slogged along the road to Bray they passed the Divisional Commander watching from the roadside. He made no attempt to disguise the fact that he was in tears.

Now they were resting at Etinehem, a once idyllic village on the River Somme, much favoured by fishermen, who had spent long, leisurely hours on peacetime summer Sundays seated among the reeds and verdant willows casting their lines into the plentiful waters of the river. When the Division first arrived a few men had waded in to splash off the worst of the battle grime, but most had sought the shelter of barns and cottages, stretched out their weary limbs, and, before long, every man of the Brigade was fast asleep. Even the growl and thunder of gunfire growing ominously closer did not rouse them. They were utterly worn out.

*42821 Private Alex Jamieson, MM, 11th Bn., The Royal Scots (Lothian Regt.), 9th (Scottish) Division*

Even when we managed to get away the day before our troubles weren't over, because we were shelled all the way back. In fact it seemed that we'd become a target for the German artillery! We moved up quite a stiff incline to some old British trenches of 1916, and my exhaustion had got to such a stage that I didn't even attempt to drop to the ground, even when the shells were bursting quite close. But someone nearby did, and then he started kicking and yelling, so in spite of the state I was in myself I managed to drag him into a trench. He was only shell-shocked, but it was having such a bad effect on everyone that a sergeant ordered me to take him to a field dressing

---

1. Although the 9th (Scottish) Division had been the last on the left of the Fifth Army, and properly belonged to it, the line of its retirement, as the situation developed, had made it expedient to place it under the orders of the adjacent corps of the Third Army.

station we could see across the valley. By the time we got there it had moved on, so there was nothing for it but to follow. I was supporting this chap, and carrying his rifle as well as my own, because he was so shocked and his legs were just like jelly, but gradually I was getting to the stage of being as bad as he was, or even weaker. We found a medical aid post on the Combles road, and they wouldn't take him in, but I asked the doctor to give me a note that I had reported, so that I wouldn't be charged as a deserter.

Eventually we reached a casualty clearing station at Maricourt (this was the place where we had detrained a month or so earlier), and they took my casualty over and directed me to a compound for regimental stragglers. When I got there I was given some hot food, but as soon as I got the plate in my hand and sat down to eat it I promptly fell asleep. I was as hungry as could be, but I don't remember if I ever ate that food at all. A few hours later I went off again – with another chit from the stragglers post, of course – and I joined up with what was left of the battalion at Bray. Then we moved back to Etinehem, and all the way along the road we were bombed and machine-gunned from a very low altitude by four aeroplanes with British markings. We couldn't understand it. We wondered if they were planes that had been captured and were being flown by Germans. That was the optimistic view, but some of the lads thought *not*![1]

The same aeroplanes had the temerity to fire vigorously at Brigadier-General Croft. It was the final indignity, and he was beside himself with rage.

General Gough spent the afternoon visiting the headquarters of his three Corps Commanders. He was deeply disappointed by the failure of the Franco-British counter-attack on which he had pinned such hopes. Although his Fifth Army had now passed from the jurisdiction of British GHQ and was under French command, as yet he had received no orders from General Fayolle. Nevertheless the situation as General Gough perceived it was now clear, and drastic action was called for. If the Germans were to be stopped, they must be confronted by an unbroken line; and, since it was plain that the men now stretched to the limit on a vulnerable line could not indefinitely stem the enemy's march on Amiens, a strong line of defence must be formed well to the rear. Amiens was the key which, one way or the other, would

1. In 1984, when visiting France in the author's company, Alex Jamieson was able to recognize the very barn in which he had rested in Etinehem sixty-six years before.

38. The elaborate sculptured façade of Mailly-Maillet church was protected from shell-fire by wattle screens. It was used by the New Zealanders as a dressing station. 'I'm lying there ... looking at a wall of bricks forty or fifty feet high ... Of all the bloody places to put a wounded man! One smack from a shell and tons of them would be down on us' Private George McKay, NZ Rifle Brigade.

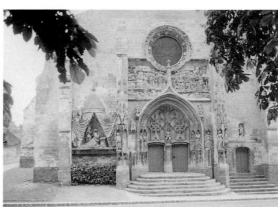

39. A modern view of Mailly-Maillet church. Although the village was in ruins by the end of 1918, the fine façade of the church escaped destruction.

40 and 41. *Above*: Private George McKay safe in hospital after being wounded in March 1918 and (*right*) at home in New Zealand more than seventy-five years later.

42. New Zealand soldiers posing for an official photograph in a respite from the battle.

"MON, IT'S DANGEROUS TO
BE ALIVE HERE !!"

"C'est rudement dangereux d'être vivant ici !"

43. Probably the humour of the postcards
soldiers sent home was not always
appreciated by their anxious families.

TO THE CHILDREN OF FRANCE
GOOD-LUCK AND VICTORY

A NOS ENFANTS DE FRANCE
BONHEUR & VICTOIRE

44. French women, evacuated far from their
homes, supported themselves by manufacturing
silk postcards and creating the kind of patriotic
dolls reproduced on this postcard.

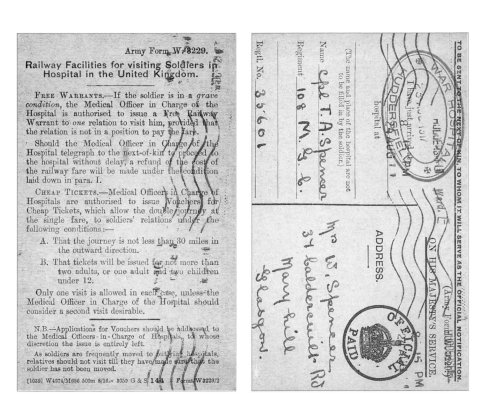

**Army Form. W. 3229.**

**Railway Facilities for visiting Soldiers in Hospital in the United Kingdom.**

FREE WARRANTS.—If the soldier is in a *grave condition*, the Medical Officer in Charge of the Hospital is authorised to issue a Free Railway Warrant to *one* relation to visit him, provided that the relation is not in a position to pay the fare.

Should the Medical Officer in Charge of the Hospital telegraph to the next-of-kin to proceed to the hospital without delay, a refund of the cost of the railway fare will be made under the condition laid down in para. I.

CHEAP TICKETS.—Medical Officers in Charge of Hospitals are authorised to issue Vouchers for Cheap Tickets, which allow the double journey at the single fare, to soldiers' relations under the following conditions:—

A. That the journey is not less than 30 miles in the outward direction.

B. That tickets will be issued for not more than two adults, or one adult and two children under 12.

Only one visit is allowed in each case, unless the Medical Officer in Charge of the Hospital should consider a second visit desirable.

N.B.—Applications for Vouchers should be addressed to the Medical Officers-in-Charge of Hospitals, to whose discretion the issue is entirely left.

As soldiers are frequently moved to outlying hospitals, relatives should not visit till they have made sure that the soldier has not been moved.

[1039] W4974/M686. 500m 8/16. iv 3059 G & S 144 Forms/W3229/2

45 and 46. Such postcards were sent to wounded soldiers' relatives, who could be given free or cheap railway passes to visit the injured. There were also free travel facilities if a badly wounded soldier was in hospital in France.

47. Lieutenant Jim Aldous, MC, (*right*), with Captain West, MC, at rest after the touch-and-go fight at Adinfer Wood.

48. *Above*: The chateau of Grivesnes, sketched on 13 April, two weeks after the epic fight to defend it.

49. *Left*: The chateau of Grivesnes, restored after the war, but now derelict and abandoned.

50. In the aftermath of the fight on 31 March, dead German soldiers lie in the chateau park at Grivesnes, beneath a notice which ironically reads, 'It is expressly forbidden for troops to enter this property.'

51. *Left*: A *poilu* of the 350th Régiment d'Infanterie sketched two weeks after the first German assault, on guard at a barricaded window in the chateau of Grivesnes.

52. *Above*: Lieutenant-Colonel Lagarde with survivors of the 350th Régiment d'Infanterie who defended Grivesnes.

53. Plaques on the wall outside the chateau commemorate both French and German regiments which fought here between March and August 1918, when Grivesnes was in the forefront of the line.

54. British veterans welcomed by Monsieur Claude Dubois, mayor of Grivesnes, in July 1996.

55. Lance-Bombardier Robert Ford. 'I wanted to be a signaller in the Royal Engineers, but they wouldn't have me because I wore glasses. So I joined the Royal Artillery. They didn't care. You said you were nineteen and that was good enough for them.'

56. Major Harrison Johnston, in command of the 15th Cheshires. 'The general met me and told me to line the road from the junction to the river – a frontage of about 1,000 yards. Ye gods, I had about 150 men then!'

57. Although many guns were lost in the early stages of the retreat the gunners continued to give sterling service very close behind the allied lines. Again and again guns like these 18-pounders thwarted the enemy's attempts to storm forward.

58. Private Stanley Sutcliffe, 51st Battalion, AIF, who helped to thwart Ludendorff's final bid for Amiens. 'It seemed a strange thing that we should be fighting on the very same hill on which a year before we used to practise attacks in making ready for Bullecourt.'

59. *Below*: Seventy-five years after he was taken prisoner, Private Walter Hare was welcomed by the owners of the farm close to where he was captured. '... the Germans got a machine-gun into a farmhouse on the left and they were shooting down the road at us. It was murder!'

60. The letter written by Brigade-Major Harold Howitt to his wife during a respite from the Battle of Amiens.

turn the fortunes of the opposing armies, so the Amiens Defence Line must be manned. Such a line was already in existence fifteen miles in front of Amiens, where seven and a half miles of trenches had been constructed by the French in the first year of the war. Some were in a poor state of repair, and some had vanished altogether when the front moved eastward and French farmers returned to cultivate the land, but it was still a perceptible line of defence, and Gough was profoundly thankful that some precautionary fate had made him veto an earlier proposal that the remaining trenches should be filled in. His difficulty was to find a body of men to reorganize the line and help defend it. He turned to his chief engineer, Major-General Grant, and put him in command. Somehow Grant was able to collect 3,000 men, mostly engineers, including 200 Americans, and Gough himself diverted a brigade of new arrivals to join them in the task.[1]

It was the best, the only thing, that could be done. By late evening on 25 March the arrangements had been put in hand. At first light next morning, work would begin on the Amiens Defence Line, and with this comforting knowledge Gough was able to breathe a little more easily. His customary optimism had not deserted him, but now that he had scraped the bottom of the barrel he was well aware that, as a formation, the Fifth Army was fighting literally to the last man.[2]

Even in the light of reports from the Third Army front which were undeniably confused and sketchy, Sir Douglas Haig had not revised the orders which he had issued the previous evening, when visiting Sir Julian Byng. Instead, early in the afternoon of 25 March he sent a signal to General Byng confirming them. He was playing for time. Despite his misgivings after the night meeting at Dury, Haig had not given up hope that Pétain would be forced by French Government pressure to send him help, and his aim now was to hold on until more French troops could reach him. Accompanied by Sir Henry Wilson, Sir Douglas Haig set off at three o'clock to drive once more to Dury, where Wilson had arranged to rendezvous with General Foch and Prime Minister Clemenceau. But only Foch's Chief of Staff was there to meet them. This was General Weygand, who made his chief's apologies and explained that his absence was due to another, more pressing, engagement. The President of France, Raymond Poincaré, had taken a hand, and was travelling personally to meet Pétain at Compiègne, where General Foch's presence was also required, as well as that of Monsieur Loucheur,

1. The 150th Brigade of the 50th Division.
2. Three days later, when Major-General G. S. Carey arrived back from leave and was given command of this composite body, it became known as 'Carey's Force' and, ever since, Carey has been erroneously given credit for forming it.

the French Minister of Munitions, and Lord Milner, who would represent the British Government.

It was now too late for Haig to reach Compiègne in time for these proceedings, and his own discussion with General Weygand at Dury was brief. Haig handed Weygand a note to pass on to General Foch. It repeated his request for twenty French divisions to be sent as a matter of urgency. Haig then returned to Montreuil and his duties at GHQ, but Sir Henry Wilson, anxious to know what had transpired, left immediately to travel to Versailles, to await the arrival of Lord Milner at the headquarters of the British Mission.

It was nine o'clock before Milner returned, but the news he brought was good. Pétain had now agreed to release fifteen divisions. Of more interest and importance was the fact that all those present at Compiègne, from the President downwards, had favoured the appointment of General Foch to unify command of the French and British forces. In the absence of the British Commander-in-Chief and, more important, of the authority of the British Government, Milner had felt unable to accede on their behalf, but Wilson was not deterred. Although it was now 10.30 in the evening and he had risen at five that morning, he drove straightaway to Paris to visit Foch. It was after midnight before he got back to Versailles, but he was well content. Another meeting had been arranged, this time of all the interested parties. A signal was dispatched to British GHQ to inform Haig that it would take place at Doullens at eleven o'clock that morning. The Doullens Conference, as it would later be known, was destined to be historic.

## Chapter 18

In front of the Third Army the Germans were pressing on, but Rudolf Binding still had time to scribble in his diary, 'Tomorrow we hope to be on a level with Albert where there will be villages again.' They had spent two uncomfortable nights on the Somme in the inhospitable wastes of the old battlefield, sleeping as best they could in the open air. But it was more than the cold that kept Binding awake: it was the excitement of the chase, the desire to press on, to consolidate the victory, and to be marching again through unsullied countryside where there were farms and villages, and trees turning green with the fresh tints of spring. 'Here', he wrote, 'the villages are merely names. Even the ruins are ruined. Yesterday I was looking for Bouchavesnes, which used to be quite a large place. There was nothing but a board nailed to a low post with the inscription in English: "This was Bouchavesnes." One only longs that there shall be no rest until we can feel the first breath of the Atlantic in Amiens.'

Leutnant Fritz Nagel had enjoyed a more comfortable night. He and his gun team had appropriated an abandoned British lorry, in which they had slept for the last two nights. The canvas cover slung over the lorry's iron frame was only a flimsy protection, though it kept out the worst of the cold and gave the illusion of shelter. Better by far was the storage space the lorry provided. During the many halts on the road to Albert, as the lorry trundled slowly behind the gun-carriage, the men of K Flak 82 had ample opportunity to raid abandoned supply dumps, and by the evening of 25 March the vehicle was crammed with cases of condensed milk, tea, cocoa, corned beef, sugar, bacon, tinned butter and biscuits, and with countless cartons of Woodbine cigarettes.

*Leutnant Fritz Nagel, Anti-Aircraft Gun Bty. K Flak 82*

Our mouths watered and we were most anxious for night to fall so we could stuff ourselves with these incredible goodies. It was a treasure beyond price. We were always hungry and completely sick of Army slop. That evening some of the soldiers drank the first cup of real cocoa

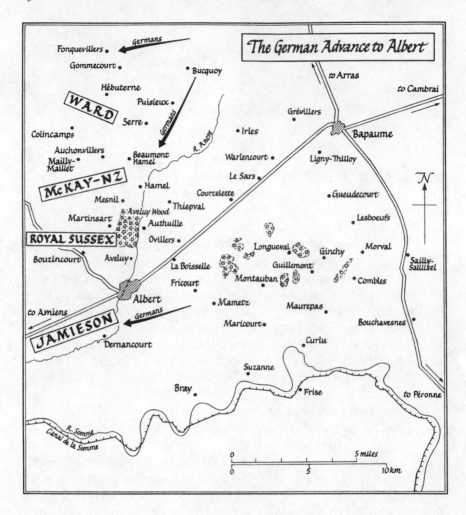

The German Advance to Albert

they had tasted in years, and loaded up on biscuits and jam, plus tea and milk.

We had hardly made a dent in our supplies when we began to worry that some staff officer might order the lorry off the road as unnecessary baggage. But, all in all, it had been a good day and we were looking forward to an elegant breakfast with coffee and bacon. My men began stirring when it was still pitch dark. They were hungry and could not wait.

The forward drive continued, though very slowly. We were still on the main highway, but soon I felt that we had to get off this road or be blown to bits. Judging from the shelling, I thought their artillery must be massed wheel to wheel, and we could not move forward while tons of steel splinters were zooming all around us. We stopped and jumped into a narrow ditch, which felt like a haven of safety.

As I looked out of the ditch, I saw that the artillery and infantry had left the highway and were scattered over the neighbouring fields to escape the shelling. The highway now seemed more or less free, so we jumped on the gun and dashed off with our precious lorry behind us. I had never driven the gun at top speed, but all I could do was put my foot down and let her go. Nobody was hit, and that astonished me, but I couldn't find a side road. After driving forward for a few minutes we caught up with a regiment of infantry marching along without being molested by artillery. Looking behind we still could see geysers of dirt shooting up as high as trees.

So far we had advanced about ten kilometres, and the town of Albert was in front of us, some five kilometres away. But our slow and very bloody progress did not look like a breakthrough to me, nor could I detect the slightest sign of a British collapse. Judging from the many dead and the never-ending stream of our wounded coming back, it was evident the enemy had no intention of quitting.

Early in the morning a motorcycle rider brought an order to abandon the lorry. It was needed for more important duties, so we had to load all our treasures on to the gun-lorry, and that was *not* easy. Our pockets were stuffed, and the rest of the biscuits and tin cans rolled around on the floor.

Unlike their German counterparts, the 11th Royal Scots had not enjoyed 'an elegant breakfast', and Alex Jamieson's platoon would have had none at all had he not been sent with a small party with orders to scrounge what they could from an abandoned canteen. It was the early hours of the morning, and during the night the remnants of the 9th Division had gone back through Albert to take up a line just behind it. It was a macabre journey. The shell-fire hardly diminished, and the night was lurid with the glare of burning canteens and depots and the thunderous conflagrations of blazing ammunition dumps, which the British were destroying as they went. Now that the British Army was nearing its supply lines there were plenty of stores. This in itself was galling, because, despite their abundance and despite the monumental efforts of transport and supply officers, it was extremely difficult to get rations to battalions on the move across country or along roads clogged with troops and refugees. There was nothing for it but to forage, and the dumps were a godsend. Nevertheless it was imperative that neither supplies nor munitions should fall into the hands of the enemy if it could possibly be avoided. In many cases it could not, but certain officers in each division were given the task of destroying such depots as they could. In the 9th Division this task had been given to Captain Will Darling, the fire-eating officer with whom Jamieson had crossed swords at Brigade Headquarters many weeks earlier and many miles away.

*42821 Private Alex Jamieson, MM, 11th Bn., The Royal Scots (Lothian Regt.), 9th (Scottish) Division*

We'd taken up a position near the railway line at Albert, and the canteen wasn't very far away. It was in a big, camouflaged marquee tent, and it was in total darkness. But there was a full moon that night, so it was light enough to see by, and the officer had given us his torch and told us to pick up what we could. There were four or maybe five of us, but I had the torch and I was first into the canteen. As I went to lift up some tins of biscuits a voice said, 'Hands up!' I got the shock of my life! At first I thought the Germans had caught up with us, and then I turned round and found myself staring straight at Will Darling. He was shining his torch into my face, so that I was nearly blinded, but I could see that he was covering me with his revolver! Well, Captain Darling was *not* a man to mess about with, so I did my best to explain that I'd been sent to get food by the officer. The others had turned up by then, but he refused to take our word for it and he sent one of the lads back for the sergeant in charge. It seemed like ages before he came, and all the time the Captain never took his eyes off me and never lowered his revolver. The other lads were keeping well back, and he had me in his sights as his target. I can't say that I was easy in my mind all this time. Looting was a serious crime in the Army, even in those circumstances.

Eventually the sergeant arrived and corroborated our story, so Captain Darling let us pick up the biscuits and go back. But we didn't have a chance to look for anything else, and that's all we had in the morning – dry biscuits. There wasn't even a drop of water to go with them, and if you haven't tried to eat a big Army dog-biscuit, with nothing to spread on them and nothing to wash them down, you've no idea how difficult it is, even for hungry men. If you had strong teeth you could just about manage it, but some of the older men and some of the fellows whose teeth were bad couldn't get on with the biscuits at all unless they soaked them first. But there was nothing to soak them with – no tea, no water, nothing. When we left the marquee Darling and his party were pouring petrol over the stores, and not long after we left the canteen went up with a *whoosh* and the blaze lit us all the way back.

The 11th and 12th Battalions of the Royal Scots, or what was left of them, had been stretched out in a line from Dernancourt to the railway line which ran westward out of Albert. The town itself was to be given up. Albert, lying in low ground behind a steep hill, would be too difficult to defend; if the Army was to make a stand, as it was hoped, it would be far more advantageous to form a line on the higher slopes behind the town and to the north of it. The town of Albert had been the pivot of the Battle of the Somme, and the proposed new line ran across ground that was depressingly familiar to the men who had fought there in the summer of 1916. North of Albert the line ran through Aveluy Wood, above the western bank of the River Ancre, across the heights at Auchonvillers in front of Beaumont Hamel, and across to the village of Hébuterne. It had been easy enough to trace it on the map. The trouble was that there were not enough troops to man it.

From the old British position of 1916 above the village of Beaumont Hamel, where the 2nd Division had flung out a defensive flank, a huge gap stretched all the way to Hébuterne. Not a single British soldier stood along the four miles of empty ground, and if it could not be plugged and the Germans continued to advance there would be nothing to stop them sweeping through it.

It was the New Zealanders who did it. They were not yet sufficiently organized to attack as a division, for they had been rushed down from Ypres. Their transport had only just arrived, their artillery was still on the way, but the infantry had been gradually moving towards the line and the 1st Battalion of the New Zealand Rifle Brigade were within shouting distance at Colincamps.

It was half past one in the morning before the New Zealanders' Divisional Headquarters was set up at Hédeauville. Although the bulk of the New Zealanders were still west of Amiens and there was a shortage of lorries to transport them, the first arrivals, moving hurriedly forward, had marched the last ten miles from Pont Noyelles in the dark. There had been many delays along the dusty roads as they marched against a stream of military transport, stragglers, and refugees streaming westward, and it was six o'clock in the morning of 26 March before the 1st New Zealand Rifles passed through Mailly-Maillet and pressed forward towards the right-hand side of the gap, adjacent to the flank of the 2nd Division that straggled up the hill from the village of Hamel. Here, it was hoped, the Kiwi riflemen would secure the right flank of the main New Zealand advance, which would fill the gap between Beaumont Hamel and Serre and, if it could not drive the Germans back, might at least halt their forward progress.

That was the plan, but it could be put into effect only when the main force eventually reached the line. Meanwhile the Rifles were entirely on their own. They had snatched a few hours' rest, dozing uncomfortably without removing their equipment and accoutrements before they were rudely awakened. But they were fresh and full of zest – so fresh that they felt little sympathy for the dull-eyed stragglers they met on the way, dead beat and numbed by days of stiff fighting. George McKay was with one of the two sections of machine-guns.

*25921 Private George McKay, B Coy., 1st Bn., NZ Rifle Brigade*

There's no use telling those fellows to turn round and fight – there's not a weapon amongst them. Not a rifle. Not a revolver. Soldiers! Can you imagine it? We go up a long series of slopes and we come to a rise of ground and here's two dead soldiers – British soldiers – and two of my men hadn't been in action before, and they pulled out and jumped down into a hollow. *'Take cover, take cover – you'll get shot here.'* I said, 'Get up and get into your place in the section and *I'll* tell you when to take cover. There isn't a Hun within a thousand yards of us. You stay in your place in the section.'

We went on past those two dead Tommies and down on to a road, and we were going to cross the road and go over to start climbing up the general slope on the opposite side of the valley – Auchonvillers Ridge – when a runner came up to me. 'Oh, Mac,' he says, 'you've got to take that section up on to that point and wait for the Germans coming across the skyline.' So I was heading that way when we came on a British officer standing on the road. I took no notice. He was stopping runaways and he had one of these revolvers, one of these buggers that bores great big holes, and he had me covered with it. 'Halt!' he said. So we halted. Everybody stopped dead. Well, I was in charge of the section carrying the gun. McArthur was No. 2 – he was carrying the spare-parts bag. Both of us carried revolvers, but you couldn't reach for a revolver when this bugger had got you in his sights and only had to press that trigger.

'Take that section across the road there,' he said. 'We want your ammunition.' 'Well,' I said, 'I'm acting under orders from my own lieutenant and I can't take orders from you.' I'm standing there, loaded with ammunition and machine-gun and everything, and I can't move because I didn't want a bloomin' great hole blown in my stomach. I said, 'If you shoot me, you won't live long afterwards. This section will kill you!' And I think that saved my life. But I could see I was on a spot – a real spot. Life was the penalty for making a mistake, so I thought I would talk him out of it. I said, 'Anyway, that crater where you've got those troops is quite unsuitable for a Lewis-gun. If you put your gun there, the Germans can climb up close and handy and bomb you out before you know where you are. You couldn't see them to shoot them, because they're down under cover, but they'll reach you with their bombs.' I told him why I had to go on to that spur and where I had to look for the Germans coming and everything. Well, he spent about ten minutes there arguing, and at last he said, 'All right, go on.' So off we went.

I got about a quarter of the distance up to this rise when I met our Lieutenant Nees coming down at the double, and he was fuming. 'Where the hell have you been, McKay?' I said I'd been hung up down on the road, that a Tommy captain had me covered and ordered me to take the gun across the road there into that crater, and I said he'd threatened to shoot me if I didn't. Nees pulled his pistol out and he said, 'I'll fix him!' I said, 'Look out he doesn't get the drop on you, or he'll make *you* dig in too!' So off he went, this Lieutenant Nees – a first-class soldier: a small man but a very active one.

I headed for this bit of a ridge, where we could see the country for a thousand yards all round us – all except one point on the left. I estimated that to the skyline would be about a thousand yards. Well, we had hardly got settled when over they came. Band out in front and all, just marching. They had taken France, in other words, and they were home and dry. So I gave them the first blast at a thousand yards. And, of course, as soon as they come under fire they scattered, broke up their formation, and took to the long grass. Well, then all I had to do was just pick out bunches of them, and that's what I was doing. I looked on that as one of the best day's sport I've ever had! Loads of ammunition and plenty of Huns. And you can see that parties of Huns at a thousand yards coming towards us was quite good shooting.

We got them slowed up a bit in the long grass, and they started using smoke bombs. A rifle grenade would fire forward, and it would burst and the smoke would just gradually pass through, and when it cleared these buggers would be a bit closer. Well, Lieutenant Nees paid us a visit at one point, and he's looking at the smoke. 'Ah,' he says, 'I can see through that with these glasses. You can see the figures coming forward. Here, take my glasses and put an observer on and fire in their direction.' So we did that from then on. We slowed them down a bit more. When there would be a curl of smoke, this fellow would say, 'Under the third curl to the right there's a bunch coming forward.' And I would shoot at them. I was shooting on the blind of course, but we slowed them down.

Well, that went on a bit, and eventually they got right down to this road and there was a trench along there, and they were all waiting to jump across and get into dead ground. Had they got across *that* road they could have come around the back and shot us in the rear, and that was my danger. I didn't think there was anybody in there to stop them. If they had got through, they would have come round and sniped us. They would have been shooting down on us. That's when my experience stood me in good stead. I'd been fired on when a road was frozen and I knew what a ricochet could do, so I let them have a ricochet deliberate. The party was going to cross there, bunched up, and I would hit the road about thirty yards on the nearside and let them have the broken-up bullets. Of course the bullets howl and shriek – a ricochet bullet can make all sorts of noises – but it slowed them down. But soon I saw the whole lot of them come up and start firing across the road, so I fired up and down and among them. *Then* I could see what they were firing at: the one and only bayonet charge that I've ever seen. A party of anything between thirty and fifty of our fellows with their bare bayonets, rifle and bayonet, charged down across the road and into them. Of course as soon as they got to the road I stopped firing on the Germans, so the New Zealanders crossed the road and into them. That put us safe! They stopped it!

They had not stopped it entirely on their own. Major Ward and the guns of C Battery had helped considerably to disperse the German troops, to stem the tide of their advance, and to gain the precious breathing space that would give the New Zealand reserves time to form a line along the critical gap.

The previous evening, before they were yet again ordered to retire, C Battery had been isolated on the extreme right corner at the end of the unbroken British front on the very edge of the ominous gap that stretched all the way to the heights above Beaumont Hamel. Unknown to Major Ward, the infantry had already retired behind them. It was past midnight before the Battery reached the new Brigade wagon lines just west of Fonque-villers, where their arrival caused something of a stir, for they had been given up for lost. They were all exhausted. Never before in his life had Ward felt so tired as he crawled into his valise beneath the officers' mess cart and thankfully closed his eyes – although the sleep he longed for did not last long.

*Major Ronald Ward, C 293 Bty., Royal Field Artillery*

At 1 a.m. Rimmer, our adjutant, wakened me. It seemed that the Colonel was lost – probably dead or a prisoner – but orders from

Division had arrived and, being the senior Major, I must issue instructions to the Brigade to move off at dawn. Dawn was not far off, and these orders were very important, for I knew better than anyone how near the enemy were, and so I made a very special effort to cope with the situation. But it was a terrible undertaking, for Rimmer was quite as tired as I was. We were crouched under the mess cart in a little circle of light from a candle, he writing while I dictated, and it took us an hour to compose about ten lines. While I was studying the map and thinking out what to say, he dropped off to sleep, and when at last I succeeded in framing a sentence I found I had to wake him up. Then, as soon as I had succeeded in rousing him and started him off writing the orders, *I* slept. He went to sleep three times and I went to sleep twice – how long for I don't know, but on the last occasion I only wakened when my fingers began to be burnt. The papers I was holding had caught fire in the candle. But the job was done at last, and I remember no more until the first light of 26 March woke me to the consciousness of another day.

At first the day promised to be a good one, for there was little firing to be heard and, better still, the orders over which Rimmer and Ward had laboured so long during the night had been cancelled and new orders had arrived from Division. They gave the welcome news that the enemy advance appeared to be slowing down. It was thought unlikely that he would attack that day, and the batteries were to advance to the high ground south of Hébuterne and select new positions behind the crest where the old front line had stood before the Battle of the Somme. They could do so at leisure, it was implied, and as soon as the guns were in position battery commanders were to see that the men got some rest and a chance to clean up. Major Ward's spirits rose. He enjoyed a proper breakfast in peace and comfort, and gloried in the unaccustomed luxury of a shave and a proper wash with no need to hurry. The two hours' sleep he had eventually managed to snatch had done wonders for his morale, and he was further cheered by the arrival of his missing colonel, who had not, after all, been killed or captured.

Ward had already given orders for the battery to advance, but Colonel Main wished him to send out two mounted patrols to find out the whereabouts of the Germans, while Ward himself was to accompany the Colonel to reconnoitre towards Colincamps, behind the crest of the hill where, a little way to the right, the first trickle of New Zealanders had arrived and George McKay was setting up his Lewis-gun. Having given the appropriate orders and set the mounted patrols on their way, Ward set off on horseback to catch up with the Colonel.

*Major Ronald Ward*

It was very pleasant trotting over open country, and across a long, straight road lined with trees, towards the high ground in front. The road we crossed was covered with transport, ammunition carts, GS wagons and led horses, all jogging along cheerfully. A sixty-pounder battery was amongst them, its teams of eight huge horses slowly pulling along those splendid heavy guns. Up the easy grass slopes we went, towards the long, level skyline, and about a hundred yards short of it we found Colonel Main and his small staff. With the colonels of three other artillery brigades, he was engaged in dividing up this stretch of ground, nearly a mile in length. It offered very suitable gun positions, for the hill continued to rise steadily from where we stood and gave ample cover from the front. It was going to take some time to get all the battery positions settled, for in addition to the colonels and staffs there were a lot of battery commanders with their own staffs awaiting orders – perhaps some fifty or sixty officers and men with their horses. It was about 7 a.m., and I was just getting my instructions from the Colonel, when suddenly a gunner subaltern came running back towards us from the crest a hundred yards in front, and as he drew near he called out, 'Do you know the Boche are just the other side of the hill?'

This really was a shock! Only a few minutes before everything had been going smoothly forward at the beginning of a perfect day, and now, in another moment, we were to see enemy infantry against the skyline in front, and then we should probably all be blotted out at once. All around we could hear people shouting orders to mount, and very swiftly all the officers and staffs were galloping down the slope, back to their own batteries. I am honestly certain that this was done more from a desire to clear the batteries back into safety than to keep a whole skin, for it was obvious to everyone that if the enemy reached that crest there was a wonderful prize before him. The wide, open valley was crammed with helpless transport of every possible kind, but, more important still, if he gained the line of the hill he would have an uninterrupted view for many miles to the north-west and he would promptly have seen our lack of reserves and realized his chance of success if his advance were pressed at once.

In describing how rapidly the party of gunners dispersed from the ridge, I have not included the 293rd Artillery Brigade (or rather what was left of it, namely, Colonel Main and his tiny staff, ourselves from C Battery, and a small party from the two howitzers of D Battery), because Colonel Main did the right thing – a very obvious thing to do, and yet completely neglected by everyone else. He called out to me to wait and then ran up to the crest. I saw him reach it, pull out his glasses for a brief look, and then come running back again. He gave his orders at once. The enemy infantry were there all right – skirmishers in front and about two battalions following – but what was all important was that they were *not* in actual fact 'just the other side of the hill'. They were still crossing the bottom of the valley, south of the village of Hébuterne, on their way to mount the gentle grassy slopes and over the crest to where we stood. I was to bring C Battery into action and to open fire into the valley.

Off I went at the gallop down the hill towards the Battery, which I could see approaching. Before me was a wild scene! All the transport was reversing and trying to clear themselves away to the rear, and one of the sixty-pounders had been upset in attempting to turn. When I reached the road, I found that it was jammed tight with transport, and I halted for a moment to see what was best to do. I had faced round to the front, and my mare was standing on the top of a bank just over four feet high above the road when someone galloped past us and brushed her nose. She threw up her head and jumped back, and her hind feet slipped over the edge. Down we went into the road, and as she fell on me she planted one forefoot on the inside of my right knee. It did not hurt much, though I was a bit shaken, but I was disgusted to see a great swelling of the knee joint appear immediately. After a little time someone gave me a pull from a whisky flask, and presently I felt well enough to stand up. Then I saw that Mackie had promptly taken charge and, seeing that the Battery could not cross the blocked road, he had wheeled the head of the column to the rear and was forming line on the right.

During this manoeuvre an ammunition wagon passed me, and I halted it. Someone helped me on to its limber, and there I rode while C Battery came into 'Action Rear'. Then I climbed down, put the nearest gun on to its line, and gave the extent of target to the section commanders, who threw their guns into the right direction. Really it was a good show, done quickly when everyone was terribly tired, and done accurately, for Colonel Main and Lieutenant Greenfield, who had joined him, observed our fire from the crest and saw that it came down where it was wanted. They were having an anxious time up there. The Colonel had found a few scattered infantrymen – about twenty – and these he had formed into a firing line and told to open up on the advancing enemy for all they were worth.

After our first very intense burst of gunfire we presently slowed down, and gradually got more settled. Greenfield was now established in front in an OP, and we had lamp signalling from him to the guns, so that fire could be accurately corrected. (To show how tired everyone was, I may mention that one of my best signallers was unable to read the Morse from flag *or* the lamp, and became quite incoherent in the attempt. He had to have several days' rest before he recovered and was able to do the signalling that was really second nature to him.)

Presently Colonel Main came back and gave us orders to retire. It was about 11.30 a.m., and by now my knee was so distended that it was almost bursting through my riding breeches. It was clear that I was useless to everyone, so I handed over command to Mackie and was helped by a gunner to climb into an infantry ammunition cart passing along the road nearby. Never before, and never since, have I felt so unhappy as I did just then. To leave my battery in such a crisis – no reserves anywhere and the enemy just over the hill in front, and also on the right and on the left. We did not know that the New Zealanders were already coming forward and that by night the line would be held. But on that morning of 26 March 1918 the Boche had been stopped on our little, but very important, bit of front – and stopped for good and all, for they never advanced any further. No doubt they thought that we were in strength and that supports would be necessary before the ridge could be assaulted successfully, and so they waited, and waited until success was out of reach. It was a great show, and I love to think that C Battery played a great part in it.

While these exciting events were taking place, not very far to the west of Albert the Doullens Conference was getting under way. Doullens was a small town with one long main street, a few narrow back roads, and a second wide street that straggled at a right angle up the hill to join the road to Albert. There were shops and restaurants and cafés, which were well patronized by British troops going to and from the back areas to the line, but Doullens was a town of small importance, typical of a thousand other market towns in northern France. Its most important building was a small but dignified town hall standing back from the main road, and this was the venue for the Allies' meeting. Almost four years of war had accustomed the civilian population to the incessant rumble of army lorries and ambulances through their streets, but the sight of a fleet of large staff cars, each with its fluttering pennant, was a novelty, and people stopped to gape as the cars inched through the cobbled streets and turned into the courtyard of Doullens Town Hall to deposit their illustrious occupants.

They had arrived in good time, for the meeting was not due to begin until eleven o'clock, and before it began Sir Douglas Haig took the opportunity to discuss the situation with the Commanders of his First and Third Armies. They talked in low voices as they walked slowly up and down the little garden at the back of the Town Hall. A short distance away, and just out of sight around the corner, the President of France was conversing earnestly with General Pétain and Prime Minister Clemenceau. Pétain was sunk in gloom, and he made no secret of his pessimism. The sound of gunfire could clearly be heard. 'The Germans will defeat the British in the open field,' he declared, 'then they will go on to beat us.' Clemenceau was shocked. 'Surely,' he murmured to Poincaré as Pétain turned away, 'surely a Commander should not speak in such terms!'

Punctually at eleven o'clock the politicians, the Generals and their Staff Officers repaired to the council chamber on the first floor of the Town Hall, and when they had exchanged punctilious courtesies the meeting began. No secretary was present, no notes were taken, no minutes were recorded. This would, in any event, have been an impossible task, for the formality of the proceedings frequently gave way to private colloquies between the British or the French, to consultations with liaison officers and interpreters, and even, while those were going on, to private conversations between individuals dispersed in conspiratorial huddles about the room. Later accounts of the meeting could be based only on hearsay and the recollections of those who were present. They were often at variance with each other, but they coincided on the most important issue – the decision to put General Foch in virtual command of the British and French armies.

Whatever his initial misgivings had been, Sir Douglas Haig was now completely in accord with this proposal. Indeed, he went further. It was originally mooted that General Foch should merely be given responsibility for co-ordinating the operations of a Franco-British force 'round Amiens'. Haig was quick to realize that this would not be enough, for unless Foch were given overall authority he would not have absolute control over the armies, and it therefore went without saying that he would have no control over Pétain. Although Pétain had now increased his offer of troops, at the behest of his own Government, Haig still feared that he might yet feel obliged to retreat on Paris, abandoning Amiens and with it the British Army. It was this consideration which prompted him to propose that Foch should be invited to co-ordinate the actions of all the Allied armies on the whole of the Western Front – for there were also the Belgians and the Americans to be considered. After some deliberation his amendment was accepted.

Haig's motives had not been entirely altruistic, for, though Pétain's view was ambivalent, he knew that Foch wholeheartedly shared his own conviction that the defence of Amiens and the closure of the breach between the French and British armies were of prime importance. As Chief of Staff and Military Adviser to the French Government, Foch's word carried weight. But the main essential was that he should be in a position to impose his will on Pétain, and Haig was perfectly prepared to subjugate his own authority to that of General Foch to make sure that he was, for it was obvious that no general who had two armies under his command would willingly abandon one of them. Haig had every confidence in Foch, and he was more than satisfied with the result of the meeting. 'I can work with a *man*,' he remarked as it broke up, 'but not with a committee.' By those who overheard it, not without amusement, this was interpreted as a slap in the face to General Wilson and the Supreme War Council which he had so enthusiastically embraced and which Haig had regarded with disdain. As for Wilson himself, if a snub had been intended it either went over his head or he chose to ignore it.

It was half past two before the decisions had been finalized and the conference drew to a close. There were telephone calls to be made, urgent messages to be sent, so Haig and his officers picnicked hurriedly from the Commander-in-Chief's luncheon box, which had travelled with them in the staff car. But, despite the lateness of the hour, the French contingent repaired to the restaurant of the Quatre Fils d'Aymon to continue their discussion over a proper lunch, albeit a hurried one. As they sat down, Clemenceau remarked to Foch, 'Well, you've finally got the job you so much wanted.' His tone verged on the sarcastic, and Foch was quick to put him right. It was hardly a case for congratulation, and, as he pointed out to the French Prime Minister, to take control of two armies in the middle of a retreat, in a battle which might easily be lost, was hardly a sinecure. He regarded it as an act of duty, and even of sacrifice, in the service of France. Although he spoke with icy courtesy, Foch said no more and applied himself to the business of eating his lunch. When it was over he left immediately to drive to Dury. It was here, four miles south of Amiens, that he intended to set up his advanced headquarters, and he wished to cast his eye over suitable premises. But he had another reason for making this detour. He wished to have a face-to-face meeting with General Gough and to give him his opinion straight from the shoulder on the performance of his Fifth Army.

Unlike the commanders of the Third and First British Armies, Gough had not been invited to the Doullens Conference. He had no idea that it had even taken place. The only information that reached him was a telephone message to say that General Foch had been appointed as overall commander and that he would call on Gough that afternoon. He had no inkling of the storm which was about to break over his head for, by the time Foch arrived at the little chateau to which Gough's headquarters had moved from Villers-Bretonneux the previous day, Foch was in a fine fury. To Gough's astonishment, he immediately launched into a tirade and bombarded him, even lambasted him, with questions without drawing breath and without giving Gough any opportunity to answer them. It seemed, however, that no answers were required, for the questions were more in the nature of accusations. Why was Gough at his headquarters and not with his troops in the fighting line? Why had the Fifth Army retired? What were Gough's orders to the Army? Why had he not fought as he, Foch, had fought in the First Battle of Ypres in 1914?

Gough was more than surprised. He was astounded – and he was also deeply offended. It was perfectly clear to him, as it would have been to Foch had he been in a more reasonable frame of mind, that the task of an army commander was not to lead battalions in the line but to orchestrate their operations on a wide extended front. The Fifth Army had retreated fighting all the way in a series of brilliant rearguard actions which had undoubtedly inflicted severe punishment on the enemy, considerably slowed his advance, and gained time for the reserves to reach the front. A retirement had long ago been envisaged, and was not only tactically necessary but entirely in accordance with the plan of the British Commander-in-Chief. In Gough's own view the Fifth Army had done well, and was still doing well, and he was proud of its performance. Foch gave him no opportunity to state his case, and in any event it would have made little impression. The new *Generalissimo* had already made up his mind that the performance of the Fifth Army had been woeful and that it was entirely to blame for the present situation.

The interview was conducted in French. While Gough's command of the language was sufficient for most normal consultations with the French, under the stress of the interview and in a state of churning emotions it almost entirely deserted him. He felt within himself that he had saved his army as he had all along intended, but the demeanour of a conscientious and efficient commander was not one which was likely to appeal to the man who had declared in the midst of a losing battle 'I am attacking', although that battle, and that situation, had been on an incomparably smaller scale.

The painful interview did not last long, and, by the time it ended, General Foch's voice had risen to a shout. 'There must be no more retreat. The line must now be held at all costs!' With these words he stalked from the room and returned to his car. He did not think it necessary to say goodbye.

General Gough was bitterly hurt, but first and foremost he was a soldier. By all the tenets of military discipline, the order he had received must be obeyed, and his first task was to pass it on to his troops. He then telephoned the British commander-in-chief to complain of Foch's behaviour. Haig was non-committal, vague, sympathetic. He smoothed Gough's ruffled feathers as best he could. It was a brief conversation.

It was years since the express train from Brussels had thundered along the line through Albert to Amiens on its journey to Paris, and it would be a long time before it did so again. From the edge of the town, where the

Royal Scots were defending the road to Amiens, the railway line ran back through the station and north along the valley where the River Ancre flowed through reedy marshland between the heights of Thiepval on the east and, on the west, the long ridge topped by the villages of Martinsart and Mesnil that stretched above the valley to Beaumont Hamel tucked into a deep cleft at its northern end. The Ancre had been a small and pleasant river, a mere tributary of the Somme as it ran towards Amiens on its course to the sea. But even in peacetime the Ancre valley had been marshy and treacherous, and, lying as it did just behind the British line in the Battle of the Somme, the passage of many troops and the devastation of constant shelling had transformed it into something close to a swamp, which the Germans would not easily be able to cross en masse. There were only a few negotiable crossings, and it was up to the troops in the newly formed line west of the valley to defend them to the best of their ability. North of the 9th (Scottish) there were two newly arrived divisions to take up the line – the 35th Division round the western edge of Albert and the 12th (Eastern) Division extending the line up the Ancre valley beyond. Early in the morning of 26 March the 7th Battalion of the Royal Sussex Regiment had been sent to garrison the southern-most end of the wood near the village of Aveluy, not far from the outskirts of Albert. It was hard to imagine a more awkward defensive position.

Less than two years earlier, before the German Army had been pushed back from the Thiepval Ridge in the Battle of the Somme, Aveluy Wood had been a boon to the British Army. In its thick depths troops could assemble concealed from the prying eyes of the vigilant enemy perched high above the valley, guns could be hidden, and supply wagons could travel unobserved towards the crossing-point at Black Horse Bridge to reach the front line beyond. Now that the enemy was trying to approach in the opposite direction it was a very different matter. Since the armies had moved east, the wood had become overgrown; the rides and clearings, the abandoned gun-pits, the old craters and shell-holes were a tangle of thick undergrowth and branches fallen from shell-riven trees. Landmarks had disappeared, and the wood now bore little relation to the map over which Colonel Impey was now poring with his company commanders. Some parts of the wood where he proposed to deploy them could not be accurately located, or when troops neared the approximate position they were found to be impenetrable. It was literally an uphill struggle. From the railway line in the valley the wood ran up the steeply sloping hill to the ridge above. There was no field of fire and, although the companies were deployed in depth behind it, the railway embankment on the edge of the wood was the only conceivable line of defence.

But in D Company's position there was one unexpected amenity. It was a magnificent armchair, richly upholstered in crimson plush, which had no doubt been 'rescued' from the ruins of the chateau at Aveluy by some enterprising Tommies long ago. In spite of mildew, damp and rusting springs, the Sussex boys were glad to slump into it for an occasional respite as they laboured to clear the undergrowth and improve their position. They were working under difficulties. There were no spades, no shovels, no pickaxes, no tools of any kind to assist them. But they worked more or less undisturbed. There was only a little mild shelling, and the snipers entertained themselves by shooting at small parties of the enemy filtering across the slopes on the other side of the valley. They could plainly see German soldiers in the village of Authuille, where they appeared to be engaged in looting a canteen, and the snipers made short work of dispersing them.

At eleven o'clock in the evening they heard an uproar not far to their left – bugles sounding, whistles blowing, and men cheering. A party of Germans, perhaps with the Dutch courage engendered by looted whisky, had managed to penetrate the valley and was marching up the Mesnil road, making no attempt to advance in silence. Here at the northern end of Aveluy Wood, held by the 63rd Royal Naval Division, the Anson Battalion had recently been relieved. Not long before they had received a generous rum ration, and when they were rushed back to meet the Germans they were just in the mood to show them what was what. It took them a very short while to throw them back.

A mile or so away along the ridge the main body of New Zealanders was filtering into the gap in the line. If the Germans attempted another advance in the morning, they would be there to meet them.

All day long the Royal Flying Corps had been buzzing busily in the sky as they tried to plot the course of the enemy's advance, duelling with German aircraft and dodging the German guns. Fritz Nagel's anti-aircraft battery had not yet been in action, but now they were drawing close to the battle line.

*Leutnant Fritz Nagel, Anti-Aircraft Gun Bty. K Flak 82*

Late in the afternoon of the 26th, another motorcycle messenger brought orders for me to appear at K Flak Headquarters, together with officers from batteries belonging to the same group. After sundown a small car picked me up. The purpose of the meeting was to allocate territories for the K Flak batteries to operate in. I received orders to remain in my sector and then to proceed to Albert by sunrise to protect our lines against interference from the air. Albert had been taken, it was said, and I probably would find our lines several kilometres outside of town.

The same car took me back, and before I went to sleep next to the

driver I remembered our cosy English lorry was no more and I would
have to sleep in the open again. When I woke up, our car had stopped
on a dark road with the lights out. The driver was lost and had no idea
where we were. Flares and gunfire were all around us, and we could
not tell where our lines should be. What astonished us was the absence
of soldiers. Nobody could be seen, and that was not normal at all. We
had to be in No Man's Land. It was dark, but we could see the trees
and some distance down the road. After anxious waiting, we heard
voices mixed with a few loud commands coming from a road nearby.
We could not tell whether they spoke German or English, so we stood
still, hoping something would happen to help us.

Fortunately, neither side wished to waste ammunition on this No
Man's Land road. However, it was certain we had to get away before
sunrise. Finally we made up our minds and decided to turn to the left,
going very slowly with lights out. After crawling along for some fifteen
minutes, the driver suddenly recognized a landmark. From then on
things went smoothly, and when I stretched out under the gun-lorry
about midnight I was too tired to worry about anything.

Reinhold Spengler's company, now marching westward, had spent the day
resting in the village of Béhancourt, north-west of Noyon, and he was
thankful for the respite, for, although he was slowly recovering from his
over-indulgent feasting, he was still not fully fit. There was an abundance
of food, and hot food was dished up, but he had no desire to eat. So far as
they could judge, the fighting line was now far ahead, but during the meal
a shell fell on the village and demolished a building where some of the men
had gone to eat. Six of them were killed when the building collapsed, and
one of them, to Spengler's distress, was his best friend, Hans Weissenbrucker.

At the end of this unhappy day company orders were issued. Although
they were not 'marching orders', even the prospect of a second day's rest
was small comfort. It was the date beneath the captain's signature which had
struck Spengler, for he realized with dismay that today, 26 March, was his
twenty-first birthday. It was a baleful thought, and a surge of homesickness
compounded his misery.

## Chapter 19

It was a fine morning on 27 March, chilly early on, but the sun rising into clear skies above the battlefield rapidly dispersed a few thin patches of ground mist and promised another warm day. There was excellent observation, and the Royal Flying Corps were again out in force, pinpointing ground targets, for, like the weary infantry, the objective of the fliers was to dislocate the enemy's advance. Some crews had been out all night, flying by moonlight to bomb railheads where reserve troops could be concentrating and villages closer to the line where men would have halted to rest. At daybreak they took off again, making for roads behind the German line to attack columns of men on the march.[1]

Lieutenant Geoffrey Lawrence was watching from a ploughed field where the composite battalion that stood proxy for the South African Brigade was in reserve to the 9th (Scottish) Division as they held a line dribbling from Dernancourt to the outskirts of Albert. He had never before seen so many aircraft in the sky at once.

The South Africans were on rising ground, and from his place in a hastily dug shallow trench Lawrence had a wide view of the battlefront. But his attention was fixed on the armada of aircraft, which filled the sky as far as the eye could see, swooping and diving to attack the enemy positions. It was a sight so fascinating that, despite the incessant shelling, he could not resist standing up to watch. Immediately overhead a squadron of RE8s directing artillery fire lumbered to and fro above the line. An RE8 was large and slow – an easy prey for an enemy fighter plane – and it was not long before three bright red triplanes came speeding in at high altitude to pounce. There was no mistaking that they were part of the 'Flying Circus' of the legendary German ace Baron von Richthofen – and there was not a man on either side of the line who did not instantly know it. In the next ten minutes, as the South Africans watched appalled, five of the lumbering British aircraft were brought down, and when a Bristol fighter-bomber approached innocently out of the blue the triplanes turned to attack it too.

1. During the day, the Royal Flying Corps dropped twenty-two tons of bombs in the Somme area alone and fired well over 300,000 rounds of ammunition.

*Captain Geoffrey Lawrence, 1st South African Bn., 9th (Scottish) Division*

He put up a tremendous fight. The observer in the rear cockpit blazed away trying to fight them off. Then we saw a little spark in their petrol tank grow bigger and bigger and we thought he was a goner. There was a mass of flames round the pilot's cockpit, but the pilot climbed out on to the left bottom wing of his biplane, controlling the machine from the side of the fuselage by reaching in to the joystick. By side-slipping steeply he kept the flames to one side, so that his observer was able to carry on firing until the plane had made three great circuits and landed on the ground. They came down quite close to us, and the pilot started running away from the burning plane, because obviously his ammunition was liable to explode at any moment. Looking back, he saw his badly wounded observer rolling over and over away from the flames, and, although he was wounded himself, he ran back and dragged his observer a short distance before the stuff exploded. They were both wounded again by their own bombs and by enemy artillery and machine-gun fire that opened up on them.

By this time several of our men had reached them and at great risk carried them to safety in our trench. Both of them were burnt, and in a bad way. We attended to their wounds, and Captain Ward and I cheered them as best we could.

I said to the pilot, 'Don't worry, you'll be in Blighty in a few days.' He said, 'That's just the trouble! I'd like to have a crack at that bugger that brought me down.' The observer was too bad to talk. Both of them smelt horribly of burnt flesh.

They had to stay with us all day, while we did the best we could for them, because we had to wait until it was dark enough for our bearers to carry them back to a dressing station. The pilot's name was Second Lieutenant A. McLeod. He was a Canadian, from Manitoba, and he got the Victoria Cross for that. He richly deserved it. It was one of the most remarkable and exciting things I ever saw in the war.[1]

It is perfectly possible that one of the five aircraft had been brought down by Fritz Nagel and his crew of the anti-aircraft gun K Flak 82. They were attacked from the air as they were driving through Albert.

---

1. Second Lieutenant McLeod was evacuated to Canada, where he died of his injuries on 6 November 1918. He is buried in Kildonan Cemetery, Winnipeg.

*Leutnant Fritz Nagel, Anti-Aircraft Gun Bty. K Flak 82*

First I saw explosions in front of us while we drove along one of the side streets. Looking up, I saw several Bristol double-deckers looking enormously big as they flew no more than thirty metres above us. We survived the next explosion, but it was awfully close. We were in a tight spot. It would only take one bomb to cause our ammunition to explode. There were four planes or more, flying fast – much too fast for aimed fire at so low a target. I blew 'Man the Gun', and the crew jumped on the truck and set shrapnel at point-blank range, maximum elevation, straight up. When we saw the wings of the Bristols coming over the rooftops we blasted away so fast I thought the whole gun might topple over. Within seconds I saw one plane hit, coming down squarely as if it would fall on top of us. We reloaded and waited. Again they came over the rooftops. Fortunately, at the very last split second, I recognized that these planes were triple-deckers, belonging to the Richthofen squadron, and I was thankful that the crew was disciplined enough not to have started firing before I gave the signal. To shoot down Richthofen, the national hero, would have been awful!

We were safe, but, although we had shot down a plane, there was no elation. We were getting mighty tired, and I was looking for a place where we could spend the rest of the day in a less hectic manner, without being accused of running away.

The air attack at ten minutes past ten in the morning had come on top of a much more harrowing experience. The K Flak crew was roused at dawn and entered Albert soon after six o'clock. Nagel believed from his instructions that Albert had been occupied and that the fighting line was now some way ahead of the town, but driving through the empty streets he looked in vain for any sign of German soldiers. There were none to be seen, except for a solitary wounded marine, propped against a wall nursing his shattered foot. As they moved tentatively towards the station and along the road to Millencourt, Nagel was hailed by an officer, who waved him across to his headquarters in a house at the side of the road.

*Leutnant Fritz Nagel*

The captain introduced himself as the commander of the 3rd Marine Light Infantry, and he pumped my hand and thanked me profusely for coming to his aid. The 3rd Battalion had attacked the day before, 26 March, without success but with terrible losses, and most of its casualties were caused by a machine-gun nest in a factory building a few hundred metres in front of our line. It was easy to see that the captain and the men at his headquarters were absolutely exhausted, but they had orders to attack again at 8 a.m., and the captain could only see failure and more bloody losses ahead as long as that machine-gun nest dominated the sector. Machine-guns had been placed in all six windows, which were heavily sandbagged, but one could easily see them through binoculars. Artillery was needed to knock them out, but they did not dare shoot when the lines were so close together. Now, quite unexpectedly, *we* had arrived on the scene.

I tried to explain our limitations. We were an anti-aircraft gun, ill-equipped for ground fighting. We did not have a protective shield like field artillery – but something had to be done before the attack started. According to the book, the best way to knock out the machine-gun nest was by indirect fire, but to do so the gun would have to be pulled back to the middle of the town and I would have to go forward to where I could see the target and direct the firing by telephone. But we had no telephone or telephone wire with us, and the skies were full of enemy fliers, so this was not the time for a leisurely turkey-shoot. I told the captain that the best way would be for us to roll forward with his attack, shooting as we went, hoping to hit the nest before it could do too much damage. We could clearly see the house we had to demolish about 350 metres away and about fifteen metres to the left of the road. Halfway was a country crossroad. We had to advance that far but not further, because the crossroad was the only place we could turn round. We would have to fire point-blank and hit the house quickly.

About fifteen minutes before zero our heavy artillery started a bombardment all along the line, but we were disappointed that none of our shells landed among the enemy directly in front of us. We could see geysers of mud and debris far ahead, where our artillery was trying to seal off the battlefield so that reinforcements could not come through. On the hour the attack started, and I could see marines coming out of houses, foxholes and trenches in great numbers. I wondered where they all came from! Shortly before the take-off I told the No. 2 gunner to be careful not to shoot before the driver and I had jumped off the front seats, trying to make a joke about what would happen if he shot our heads off, but nobody felt like laughing! We reached the crossroad very quickly, and my feet had barely touched the ground when the first shell came screaming out of the barrel. The crew reloaded, fired, reloaded, and fired again, with amazing speed. The first shell slammed right into the nest – and so did all the other shots. The house seemed to explode and started to burn, and I could see men jumping out of the windows. It had been quite easy!

My only thought now was to get out of there, but the gun was pointed in the wrong direction and had to be turned around. We were too slow to reach the safety of the first house in reverse gear, and the rifle fire was too heavy to risk returning on foot. We were in a tight spot! At that moment the driver, Rupp, shouted something which I couldn't understand, but he leapt up, cranked up the motor, jumped on, and turned the truck around while the rest of us held our breath. As he came alongside our ditch, we jumped on too. I've never understood why nobody got hurt on that wild ride back! One machine-gun burst could have killed the driver, who had to sit upright in his seat, and the roar of battle made it quite impossible for us to hear whether bullets were zooming round us or not. It was a magnificent performance. Rupp got the Iron Cross First Class for that. I'd never met such a character. Besides being a former racing driver, he was a top-notch mechanic and did all the repair work on the gun and the motor. His conversation was exclusively about racing, motors, women, and more women. When I asked him what made him jump on the truck under those very dangerous circumstances, probably saving our lives, his answer was, 'Well, the motor's in fine shape and I'm not going to let those sons-of-bitches shoot it up.' I was lucky to have him on the crew.

Later, in Albert, I talked to a marine officer who said that the attack of his division had petered out. Some ground had been taken, but unless reinforcements arrived quickly he feared that the marines would be pounded to pieces.

After the machine-gun post had been destroyed by K Flak 82, the marines had progressed only a very short distance before they were brought up short and thrown back by the Royal Scots. It was a dispiriting result for the Germans, but their guns were keeping up a punishing bombardment which gave every indication that a fresh attack might be launched at any moment. Alex Jamieson certainly thought so. He was one of the small party who had the doubtful distinction of being the last men on the 9th Division front. Their Lewis-gun had been set up to guard the left flank which straddled the railway line near the road to Amiens on the western outskirts of Albert. Now that the outpost line had gone and, thanks to Nagel's efforts, the covering machine-guns were no more, Jamieson's platoon was also the furthest forward, and the information that their flank towards the railway station was now open and 'in the air' did not increase their sense of ease. Most of the shells were falling too far back to inconvenience them seriously, but tension was high and Jamieson was not reassured by a spent bullet which struck him on the shoulder. It fell harmlessly to the ground, and must have travelled a long distance, but he had no idea which side had fired it.

*42821 Private Alex Jamieson, MM, 11th Bn., The Royal Scots (Lothian Regt.), 9th (Scottish) Division*

The officer told me to lie alongside a corporal Lewis-gunner between the two railway lines and fire on the Germans who occasionally tried to run across. We'd been lying there for hours and there was no sign of a full-scale attack, but of course the corporal kept firing bursts every time we saw something move, so I'd gone deaf from lying alongside the muzzle of the machine-gun. This exasperated my pal who was on my other side, not far away, because I couldn't hear what he was saying. (He was my lifelong pal – we'd been at school together and we enlisted together.) All this time we were being shelled, and they were throwing over mortar bombs, because we were that close, and they were trying to knock out the Lewis-gun. It wasn't a comfortable position by any means! My pal was always a pessimist, and he shouted, 'We'll never get out of this, Jimmy!' But I just had to forget about it and decide that we *would* get out.

Oddly enough, I never ever had the feeling that I was going to get killed. Mind you, I was only nineteen, and I'd never been under fire until a few days before, but I'd grown up all right! Youth was never our experience. I grew up in a week. I didn't feel despondent at all, because the word had gone round that we were drawing the Germans into a bag on a narrow front and when enough Germans were in it a pincer movement from both sides would cut them off. I don't know if the rumour came from above, but it certainly kept up our morale, even though it was completely false.

After a while the officer told me to move over a few yards to join the men lining the embankment, where there was some shelter from a hawthorn hedge. But a sniper had spotted us, and every now and then he was getting one of our people. I thought I knew roughly where this firing was coming from, so I put my head a little bit above the embankment. Thinking about it afterwards, I definitely took a risk, but it didn't occur to me at the time, so I put my head up and looked in the direction of the firing, and I saw a slight flash and, at the angle we were at, I reckoned that it came from between the sixth and seventh telegraph poles. The corporal machine-gunner was only about six feet away, so I called out to him where I thought the sniper was. Right away he opened up on this place, and he must have got him, because that was the end of the sniping. But we still got a lot of shelling.

After a while I saw a trench-mortar bomb coming over in the air – they're big things and they're slow, so you can see them coming. I was still on the embankment, but close up to the Lewis-gunner, and I knew the bomb was going to be very near me or him and there was nothing we could do about it. Well, that explosion! I just can't describe it. When the smoke cleared away I was all right, but I was sure the Lewis-gunner wouldn't be there. When I looked up, he was still lying in the same place with his Lewis-gun and there was a big crater between us, and on either side of him the two sets of rails were bent back, pointing upwards like four fingers up in the air. The corporal wasn't touched and neither was the gun. It was the most astonishing thing I've ever seen. He just brushed the muck off the gun, fired a burst to check that it was OK, and stayed in his position and went on firing. I remember thinking then that if anyone survived the war *he* would. He got the Military Medal for that.[1]

As well as attacking the 9th Division on the southern perimeter of Albert, the enemy were attempting to widen their bridgehead by pushing forward on the front of the 12th Division immediately north of it. There the remaining elements of the 35th Brigade of the 12th Division, much reduced by casualties, stood on the open ground, and beyond them, where the 36th Brigade was defending Aveluy Wood, the 7th Royal Sussex were in difficulty. They came so close to annihilation that at times it seemed doubtful if anyone would survive to tell the tale. When the troops on their right were forced back and the flank of the Sussex was left exposed, Colonel Impey realigned his companies in a rough L shape at right angles to each other, to cover the vulnerable edge of the wood as well as the side which faced the railway line and the river in the valley. But they were weakened by casualties after many hours' fighting, and strong parties of the enemy, vastly outnumbering them, managed to penetrate the wood, so that the companies were split up and isolated. At one stage even Battalion Headquarters was surrounded.

It was situated in a little quarry, not far behind the angle of the L, and, apart from the Colonel and the Adjutant, who was busily burning papers, there was only a handful of orderlies and clerks to defend it. There was also the sanitary corporal, the butt of much lewd humour, whose humble duties had not often required him to confront the enemy at close quarters. But every man could fire a rifle, and time and again the enemy's attempts to rush the post were beaten off, until at last the Germans gave up, the fighting

1. The corporal did not survive the war, and Jamieson was most distressed when he was killed later in the year.

died down, and the survivors retired, leaving many dead behind them. One wounded German soldier was taken prisoner. The sanitary corporal had been killed, so had an orderly-room clerk, and the Colonel's own orderly, Private Beale, had been killed too. Tom Beale was a sad loss to the Battalion, for he had been orderly to five successive Commanding Officers and knew more about its affairs than any man alive. Beale had joined the Battalion at the beginning of the war, when Impey himself had been a mere captain, and he would be sorely missed. But Battalion HQ had done more than save itself: it had also saved the situation on its front, and the Colonel's immediate task was to regain touch with his companies, now so reduced in numbers that they were disposed in platoons with wide gaps between them.

On the edge of the wood close to the railway, Lieutenant Rogers and eight men of C Company fought a battle of their own. When the company retired to a line further back, they were left behind to cover its withdrawal. With the help of two Lewis-guns, they held off the enemy for more than an hour, and even when a runner got through to report that the company was safely in position there was no chance at all of getting away. By the time a lull did come, one Lewis-gun had been knocked out and ammunition was running low. Rogers thankfully passed the word for discreet withdrawal, but they had only crawled back a few yards when a voice so loud that it seemed to be right in his ear shouted a peremptory order: 'Hands up!' It was useless to fight, hopeless to attempt to escape from the thirty or so Germans who loomed out of the bushes to surround the miserable Tommies crawling worm-like on the ground, and there was no arguing with the light machine-gun that covered them.

The German officer was pleased with his capture, and as they trudged back through the thick wood he chatted chummily to Rogers and even offered him a cigarette. He smiled quizzically as he held out the packet, and the reason was obvious. It was an English Gold Flake cigarette. Rogers struggled with the instinctive feeling that he ought to respond in a lofty manner with a contemptuous refusal, but his desire for a smoke was too strong to be denied. The friendly gesture was clearly intended to soften him up, for his captor began to question him minutely on the Battalion's positions. Rogers knew them very well, but he also knew Aveluy Wood, and the German officer clearly did not. Hoping to give the impression of affable co-operation, he gave the Hauptmann detailed information which he knew very well would lead the party straight to the 6th Royal West Kents, who were holding the line of the railway at the northern end of the wood; the rest he left to fate. And, although the party were shelled as they walked along the railway line, fate was on Rogers' side.

*Second Lieutenant V. E. Rogers, 7th Bn., The Royal Sussex Regt., 12th Division*

When we got to within about a hundred yards of the West Kents' position the German officer spotted the men stretched out between the rails and immediately tried to save himself by pointing his revolver at *me*, but he was shot in the stomach by one of the Royal West Kent snipers. His revolver went off as he fell and the shot just missed me!

The Royal West Kents shouted to us to stand to the side of the railway, which we speedily did, and they opened fire on the Germans, who hurriedly retired into the wood. We then joined up with the Royal West Kents and finally found our way back to the company after going through a hot bombardment. All the eight men of my party got back safely.

It gave Rogers a good deal of satisfaction to know that he had had the last laugh and wiped out the ignominy of being captured.

In the ominous shape of a spearhead, three major roads drove across the seventeen miles that lay between the Royal Scots at Albert and the 30th Division at Bouchoir further south. At the tip of the spear was Amiens, on which the enemy had set his sights. If any one of the roads were to go, if the troops astride and between them were to give way, the Germans would be in Amiens in no time.[1] The roads were straight and unobstructed and, behind the thin screen of troops in front, there would be almost no one to stop them. Clear passage along the roads was vital if the Germans were to succeed in capturing Amiens. With the help of field artillery, a village could be captured by infantry and machine-guns, but the capture of a major objective, such as a town the size of Amiens, required back-up on a gargantuan scale – wagonloads of supplies, lorryloads of ammunition, enough water and rations to sustain thousands of men and horses, and, above all, motor-tractors to pull the heavy guns that would knock out the resistance and bowl the infantry through to victory.

The progress of the previous forty-eight hours had opened the most southerly road as far as Bouchoir along the road to Amiens and had given the Germans time to assemble supplies and vehicles ready to move up close behind their troops. In the early hours of 27 March a German transport column missed the left turning to the main road from Le Quesnoy, and

1. On modern maps these roads, from north to south, are the D 979, the N 29 and the D 934.

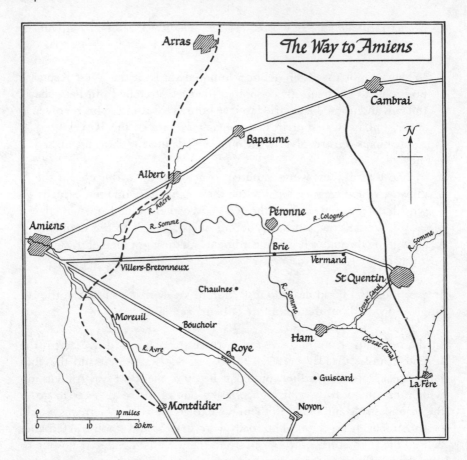

trundled on towards the village of Bouchoir directly ahead, just a rifle-shot across the fields. Le Quesnoy had been captured during the day, but Bouchoir had not, and Second Lieutenant Pat Hakewill-Smith (now reunited with the 30th Division after days of adventurous journeying) was holding the village with a scratch company. To be more precise, at that particular moment he was dozing in a comfortable armchair in front of a roaring wood fire. His new servant, whom Pat already regarded as a pearl beyond price, had found him an excellent billet in a well-appointed house, and he had also prepared a splendid meal, by courtesy of its absent owner, served on china plates on a table laid with a spotless white cloth and heavy silver cutlery. To complete this luxury, the cellar contained some excellent champagne, to which Pat and his servant (in the privacy of the kitchen) had both done full justice.

Before settling down to enjoy his stint off duty, Pat did the rounds of the company, established on the edge of the village in a makeshift trench that ran behind a lane leading to the Amiens road and swung round to form a barricade where the two roads met. It was not a particularly strong position, but they had been able to set up a line of protective wire on the far side of the lane, facing Le Quesnoy. Satisfied that all was in order, Pat returned to snooze by the fire in his splendid billet. It was three o'clock in the morning when he was abruptly wakened by the sound of rapid fire.

*Second Lieutenant E. ('Pat') Hakewill-Smith, 2nd Bn., Royal Scots Fusiliers, 30th Division*

I dashed out to see what was happening. The firing soon died down, and I found we had bagged some Boche transport. An enemy column had mistaken its way coming from Le Quesnoy and had turned down the Le Quesnoy–Bouchoir road. One of the listening posts came in and reported it, and the officer on duty gave orders that fire was not to be opened till the whole column was on the road between our trench and wire. (I've done a sketch of this and marked the position 'Y').

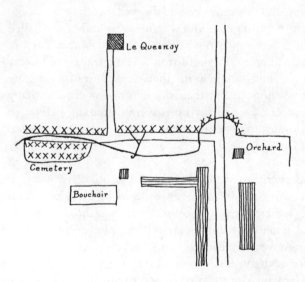

Unfortunately the men were too eager and they opened up too soon. Of course at that short range they did tremendous execution, and we found that we had made a bag of two field cookers, one water cart and five or six wagons and about sixteen prisoners. I quickly organized parties and got the wagons to the rear, but I'm afraid three or four must have escaped. One cooker contained most excellent hot soup and the other one good black coffee, but although the taste was good neither had much body. The harness of the horses was practically entirely composed of canvas, and the horses were in rather bad condition. We served the soup and coffee out to the men. It was the first hot food they had had that day, and it was quite chilly at the time. On another wagon we found three brand-new machine-guns and ammunition in belts complete. These were a godsend, and we immediately got them into position. The men were awfully pleased over the whole business and were tickled to death at the idea of having food at the expense of His Imperial Majesty. Personally I was more pleased with the machine-guns, and hoped they would shortly tickle some of the *enemy* to death. We got plenty of interesting documents for our intelligence staff, and they showed that we were once again up against our old friend who had attacked us in front of St Quentin.

Altogether it was quite a good night's work, and it put new spirit into the men. After six days' fighting like the devil, and retiring such a distance, I think they began to think the Boche were endowed with supernatural powers. But this little episode showed that they were only human. By the time we had got all the wagons away and camouflaged the dead men and horses so as not to be visible to hostile aircraft, dawn was breaking. There was a slight mist and there appeared every probability of an attack, as the wagons that escaped must have long ago reported our position. Just at that moment orders came to hang on at all costs, as several French divisions were detraining behind us and on no account must the enemy break through before the French had reached their battle station.

General Foch had every intention of being as good as his word, but, although some regiments had already been ordered by General Pétain to proceed north-west, sufficient troops could not be summoned up with a wave of the hand, and, while Foch did not entirely share Pétain's overcautious views, he could not remove men from the long French line without making adequate provision for its safety. All he could do was to gamble on his instinct that at present the Germans were too occupied to attempt another major attack, and to issue the orders that would shuffle his battalions and release troops for the move. He was also gambling on the goodwill of General

Pershing to supply American divisions to replace them. Foch was well aware that the British Fifth Army was in dire need of rest and relief after six days' ceaseless, and almost sleepless, fighting. But, in the short term, that simply could not be arranged. The front south of the Somme, where some elements were still inextricably mixed with the French Army, was equally weak, equally threatened, and, although a small force was sent post-haste to reinforce the British on its left, until the French front could be stabilized and strengthened the gap which divided the armies could not be finally closed and the way to Amiens be barred for good and all. With this object in view, the French troops now arriving, like those who would follow them, were ordered to concentrate behind the town of Montdidier, ready to move forward when a strong enough force was assembled.

In the ragged fighting line, which was still some distance east of Montdidier, Désiré Wavrin was having a good day – the first to give him a measure of satisfaction since the flight from Libermont. Near a farm at Canny-sur-Matz his company had been given the task of attacking an enemy position which was causing a considerable nuisance to the 307th Regiment in the line. It was a minor operation but it had to succeed, and Wavrin had taken his time and planned it carefully. It had not been his intention merely to lead his company, or to wave it on. Since his early days in the ranks he had been proud of his prowess as a bomber, and he had lost none of his skill. He had also been fired by a desire for revenge, for the enemy post was equipped with two light machine-guns which had accounted for several of his own men. Wavrin was too modest to claim that he had captured the post single-handed, but there was little doubt that the rifle grenades which he fired with unerring aim knocked out the machine-guns and so demoralized the Germans that, when the Company ran forward to the attack, they surrendered without firing another shot. The Company was in high spirits. Twenty-nine prisoners and two machine-guns captured was, he felt, a pretty good bag.

But it was not long before the enemy launched a counter-attack. Wavrin's company held on, but the troops on their left fell back and they were forced to retire. It was a bitter disappointment – and that was not the end of it.

*Capitaine Désiré Wavrin, 22nd Coy., 6th Bn., 307th Regt., 62nd [French] Division*

Colonel Montenon had been wounded and evacuated, and our new colonel, Colonel Tourlet, ordered us to retake the positions we had lost. By now, of course, the Boche had moved into them en masse. Yet again, I honestly believed that my last hour had come when the enemy brought up their awful *Flammenwerfers* and hosed us with liquid

fire. The flames were less than a metre from my face. I wondered if I
was going to be grilled like a piece of pork! I must admit that there
was some panic in the ranks.

Our attack failed completely. We were pushed back even further
than before, and yet again I was separated from my company, which
pulled back a little quicker than I did.

The whole line was swinging back north-west towards Montdidier, with
its right still swivelling on Noyon.

Paul Maze had ridden south to take a message from General Maxse's
headquarters to the headquarters of General Debeney on his right. Even on
his motorbike, it had taken him a long time to make the journey along the
congested roads, and by the time he arrived at Debeney's HQ messages
were coming in so thick and fast that it was some time before the General
could give Maze his attention. Charcoal in hand, he was standing in front
of a wall-map, marking the progress of the enemy on his front, and Maze
could see for himself that things were not going well. As Maze was leaving,
the General said, 'I would advise you not to go too far north of Montdidier,
for we are falling back.'

*Paul Maze*

Although I followed his advice, I was astounded when I reached the
heights just above Montdidier to see infantry deployed along the ditch
of the road ready to let the retreating troops come through them and
receive the enemy. There was no sound of artillery. The enemy had
advanced at least nine miles that afternoon – and quickly! I had to
make a large detour to reach Moreuil in safety, where General Maxse
had retired his headquarters. His corps had held its own throughout
the day and had hardly given any ground.

There was a good deal of confusion among the French troops as they
retired through Montdidier, and misunderstanding in the thin ranks of the
new troops who might have attempted to defend it. After nightfall the
Germans crept forward, cautiously and almost unmolested, to take possession
of the town. Their reserve divisions were moving up behind them.

*Leutnant Reinhold Spengler, 2nd Coy., 1st Bavarian Infantry Regt., 1st
Bavarian Division*

During the night of 27–28 March we marched to Lassigny, and on
the way we met French soldiers. They let us take them prisoner without

a struggle. When we questioned them, we found out that they were fresh recruits and had only been pushed into the line a short time before. The behaviour of these young Frenchmen was somewhat amusing. They constantly watched us and shook with fear. They emptied their haversacks and offered us chocolate and cookies, even their wallets and watches. We were very surprised. The Frenchmen seemed to believe we would shoot them or cut them to pieces. Finally, one of our men told them, 'Keep your stuff. You may need it later.'

The French poured a murderous artillery fire into our positions. We managed to hold on to Lassigny, but we were nearly exhausted. Our troops had come almost fifty kilometres since 21 March at the cost of a lot of blood. More than half of the 1st Bavarian Regiment was expended. On 21 March my company had attacked with 140 men. By the time we reached Lassigny it numbered only fifty-five. I was the only officer in the 2nd Company unwounded or still alive.

Pat Hakewill-Smith passed the night on a stretcher on the floor of a village church some distance behind the line. He neither knew nor cared where he was. The pain of his wounded leg made sleep impossible, but it did not prevent him from reflecting ruefully on the events of a disastrous day.

His company had been forced to relinquish Bouchoir – and, in his view, quite unnecessarily. It was true that the Germans had launched a fierce attack, pounding Bouchoir and beyond with a mighty fusillade of shells, but lying doggo in their position in front of the village his company had escaped most of the damage and were confident of holding on. But it was a nervy business. The German guns were so close that, through his field glasses, Hakewill-Smith could actually see the gunners putting shells into the breech and pulling the lanyard to fire. The one solitary howitzer behind their own line was firing at such long range that it did not seem to disturb the enemy, and Pat had been relieved when a message from the adjutant ordered him to 'conform to all movements of the division on the right'. He had naively assumed that they were intended to go forward and capture the enemy guns.

*Second Lieutenant E. ('Pat') Hakewill-Smith*

However, when I went to look at the division on our right, I found they were about a mile in our *rear*, and *still* retiring. My flank was now in the air, so I started to conform at once. We had not gone far when the CO came up. He had been round the line and hadn't heard about the order to 'conform', and so he ordered us to go back at once. We rushed back, and were just in time to stop the enemy from getting our trench. The machine-guns we had captured the night before did excellent work, and when the enemy started to develop his attack we stopped it easily enough. Then we got the order direct from the Commanding Officer to withdraw, which we did in quite good order. Of course the enemy followed us up and occupied the village. They also tried to rush our exposed flank, but they didn't succeed.

When we and the whole Brigade had retired about 1,200 yards, the Brigade Commander and his staff appeared on the scene and ordered us to counter-attack. I wondered what the deuce was happening, because the enemy was clearly through and was even *past* us on our right flank, and there was very heavy firing going on on our left. However, that was no business of ours. We had to retake Bouchoir!

As soon as we started off we came under terrible machine-gun and artillery fire, and I must say that the men were simply wonderful! In spite of the fact that they had been fighting for seven days and had had no sleep or food worth mentioning, and in spite of the terrific concentration of the enemy's fire, they *never* wavered, or even hesitated. They advanced over those ploughed fields as if they were going to work in the coal-pit or shipyard, under a hail of bullets whistling round their heads and kicking up little spurts of dust where they hit the ploughed ground. If you can imagine a pond in a hailstorm you will have some idea of what those fields looked like – and the whistling of bullets was mingled with the bursting of high-explosive shells and the cries of the wounded. It was bedlam!

We could only advance a platoon at a time, each platoon rushing as hard as it could about fifteen yards and then falling flat to open fire on the enemy while another platoon rushed forward. There were machine-guns posted at all the windows of the houses, and they must have got artillery observing officers in there too, because they put down a wonderful barrage of high-explosive shrapnel bursting close above our heads. By the time we reached a shallow trench a quarter of a mile from the village we had advanced over half a mile without a sniff of cover anywhere, and I was the only officer left in the front line. The fire had reached such a pitch that it was impossible to raise a little finger without getting a hail of bullets round it. The only thing to do was to scrape a hollow in the plough with your hand, get into it, and pray! The fire was so hot that we couldn't even fire back, and his guns had got our range to the inch and were fairly pumping shells into us. We were just lying there to be murdered, because it was impossible to advance, and equally impossible to retire.

I was wondering what to do, when the Boche settled the question for me. A machine-gun suddenly appeared on our left flank and started enfilading our line at close range, so I gave the order to withdraw. Six men and myself were the last to go. We had to run over absolutely open country, and, as we were now the only target, every gun in the place turned on us. How we were not hit fifty times I can't imagine! The rifle I was carrying was knocked out of my hand by a bullet, then I felt another go through my water-bottle, and *then* I was hit in the left leg, just above the ankle. I fell down, but I picked myself up again and somehow managed to run the rest of the distance and tumbled into a trench right on top of some stretcher-bearers, who cut away my boot and applied a field dressing to my leg.

Adrenalin, plus a healthy desire to get out of it, kept Hakewill-Smith going as he hobbled painfully back to the aid post, leaning on the arm of his loyal soldier servant. The man had only one arm to offer, for he had had a bullet through the other one, but he was in good spirits. 'Keep going, Sir, keep going,' he encouraged. 'Next stop Blighty!' Hakewill-Smith managed to keep going, and collapsed only when they reached the aid post.

Late in the evening, Alex Jamieson and his comrades of A Company were still huddled behind the railway embankment on the outskirts of Albert. The corporal had not moved from his position close to his Lewis-gun between the shattered rails, but he was no longer firing, for it was dark now, and the flashes from the muzzle would betray their position to the watching enemy. It was two nights since they had slept. For almost a week there had been neither relief nor rest, and they had almost given up hope of either. There was firing north and south of them, but on their immediate front it was almost quiet. There was no sign of B Company coming up to take over the position, and they had resigned themselves to another weary night. Jamieson was dozing fitfully, fighting the desire to succumb to sleep, when a tall figure loomed out of the darkness and jumped down beside him. The voice in his ear was low and laconic, but the twang of the accent was unmistakable. It said, 'Get the hell out of it, Jock.' With a thankful heart, Alex got the hell out of it, joined up with his platoon, and plodded back to rest.

The Aussies had arrived – and not a moment too soon.

It would have surprised some Allied soldiers on more harassed parts of the front had they known that General Ludendorff was dissatisfied with the progress of his offensive. But such was the case. After the first ecstatic breakthrough, mainly on the Fifth Army front, and the costly drive forward in the face of stout opposition, his armies were slowing down and making little headway. The men were tired and as much in need of rest and reinforcement as the Allies. Casualties had been far greater than expected, huge quantities of ammunition had been expended, and supplies could not be speedily replenished.[1] Amiens – Ludendorff's main objective – should have been captured days ago, and the juncture of the French and British armies irrevocably ruptured. But the Allied line was growing stronger and more obstinate, and the powerful sweep of the Germans' first massed assault had given way to scattered tactical attacks and insignificant gains, all but a few of them in places where the ground was weakly held by a mishmash of exhausted or unfledged troops.

But even the success of the drive against Montdidier was of small account in the Germans' overall scheme of things, for it was too far south to realize Ludendorff's original intention of smashing the British Army and capturing the Channel ports. If he now recognized his fatal error in changing his tactics, seduced as he had been by von Hutier's initial success, and if he now regretted his decision to exploit it, and having used up reserves in an area which needed to be held only as the southern pivot of a far wider offensive, Ludendorff gave no hint of his misgivings. But he did recognize that something had to be done.

The great drive westward had been code-named *Michael*. Ludendorff had always intended to widen the attack by launching a second assault on either side of the River Scarpe towards Arras and St Pol to open the way to the Channel ports. In an effort to give fresh impetus to the main assault, and as early as 23 March, he had taken the decision to go ahead with this second assault. Fresh troops had already been sent north to Prince Rupprecht's Army in preparation for the attack. It would be launched the following morning, 28 March.

This stage of Ludendorff's campaign was given the code-name *Mars* – and, with any luck, Mars, the god of war, would be on his side.

---

1. During their March offensive the Germans expended two and a half times the amount of ammunition they had fired during the whole of the Franco-Prussian War.

# Part 5

# The End of the Beginning

*Thus came the end of a beginning.*
*No poet-prince fought in Picardy,*
*No golden voice of immortality*
*Sang Crispin's day . . .*

LIEUTENANT J. R. T. ALDOUS
210 Field Coy., Royal Engineers
31st Division (1914–1918)

*Chapter 20*

The full moon brought a change in the weather. Clouds began to roll in from the west, and by morning the glowering sky was heavy with the threat of rain. But Prince Rupprecht did not regard this as an ill omen. Although it would be many hours before the first reports from the front could reach his headquarters, he had risen early in his impatience to begin the triumphant day. Already he could hear the rumble of guns massed along the Arras front, and he was perfectly confident of achieving the victory that might well finish the war. In the hours of waiting he wrote in his diary, 'We stand immediately before the success of the final breakthrough.'

Prince Rupprecht was far behind the lines, and the army group he commanded held the ground as far north as Ostend on the Belgian coast, but it was the Seventeenth Army of his left wing, under General von Below, which was to make the assault. North of Arras, on the extreme right of von Below's push, the front had been comparatively quiet and the British troops of the 56th Division were, at worst, still in the forward battle zone or even in the outpost line. Fourteen miles south of them, and eight miles beyond Arras, the 31st Division would be facing von Below's army on the extreme left of his attack.

The 31st Division had a chequered history. Most of its original members were from the north of England. They called them 'Kitchener's men', but in 1914 the majority were little more than boys who had enlisted on a wave of feverish patriotism, fired by the irresistible prospect of 'having a go at the Hun'. They were a tight-knit group. Friends and neighbours, brothers, workmates, whole troops of Rover Scouts, even local football teams with their attendant supporters, had rushed to join the Army. It was not for nothing that they were called 'The Pals Battalions'. To the horror of the country – and of the Army – the Pals had met with disaster on the first day of the Battle of the Somme and the old ranks were sadly diluted by fresh intakes of reinforcements. There was a small proportion of originals left, but many battalions had been amalgamated or disbanded in the recent shake-up, and a whole brigade had been removed and replaced by three battalions of the Guards. But, in the twenty-one months since its ordeal on the Somme, the 31st Division had earned its spurs, and the men were no longer innocents.

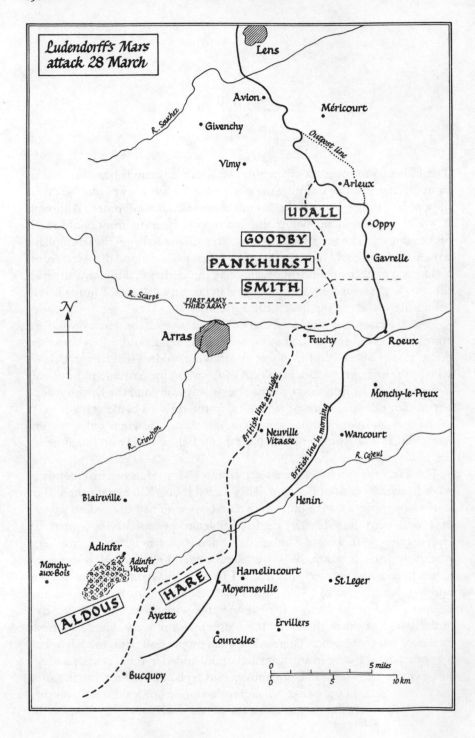

Ludendorff's Mars
attack 28 March

Lens

Avion

Méricourt

R. Souchez

Givenchy

Outpost line

Vimy

Arleux

UDALL

Oppy

GOODBY

PANKHURST

Gavrelle

SMITH

R. Scarpe

FIRST ARMY
THIRD ARMY

N

Arras

Feuchy

Roeux

Monchy-le-Preux

British line at night

R. Crinchon

Neuville
Vitasse

Wancourt

British line in morning

R. Cojeul

Blaireville

Henin

Adinfer

Monchy-
aux-Bois

Adinfer
Wood

HARE

Hamelincourt

St Leger

ALDOUS

Moyenneville

Ayette

Ervillers

Courcelles

0          5 miles

Bucquoy

0          5          10 km

It was barely a year since Walter Hare had joined the Division, after just five months' training, but he had learned a thing or two in the interval, even before he heard a shot fired in anger.

*37468 Private Walter Hare, 15th Bn., West Yorkshire Regt., 31st Division*

The sort of training we did wasn't a scrap of use to us when we got to France, because the only thing we learned was to slope arms and salute and things like that. You don't slope arms when you're in the trenches, and you don't salute officers when you're in the trenches. You've something else to do. I did fire five rounds from a rifle, but I never was told where the five shots went to. It was only when I got in France that I found out I was a good shot. I went on a draft, and on the way over I met a lad called Theaker, and he'd been out before so I thought he was a good lad to cotton on to. He would know the ropes. We landed at Boulogne, marched up St Martin's Hill to a transit camp, and Theaker said, 'Right, we'll find some place to kip for the night.' I said, 'There's some huts up here with some wire beds in them.' He said, 'No, we'll have a tent.' Well, it was December you know, so I said, 'Why a tent?' He said, 'Well, in France, if there's as much as a pile of empty sandbags they'll put a guard on it, and if I know the guard sergeant he'll go to the first hut he comes to and say, "You, you, you and you, for Guard." He'll not come trailing round tents looking for one here and one there.' So we settled down in this empty tent well down the lines. When it got to about half past nine, he said, 'Guard comes on about ten o'clock and they warn them in good time, so we're all right now.'

A few minutes later somebody opened the tent flap and said, 'How many in there?' Before I could answer, Theaker said, 'Four of us.' In came four packets of cigarettes – two packets of 'Oro' and two of 'Beeswing'. I'd never seen them before, and I've never seen them since either. So I said to him, 'Why did you shout "Four"? He said, 'Well, you're not grumbling, are you? You've got *two* packets of cigarettes where you'd only have had one. You've always got to be one jump ahead in France!'

Young Hare was a fast learner, and he had managed more or less successfully to keep one jump ahead of the Army ever since. He was soon to discover that keeping one jump ahead of the Germans was not so easy.

Although he was just nineteen and Private Hare's junior by two years, Jim Aldous occupied a more elevated position in the 31st Division. For one thing he was an officer – and a Regular officer to boot, having been commissioned direct from the Royal Military Academy, Woolwich, more than two years earlier, at the tender age of seventeen. He had been chafing to get to France ever since, and had finally made it just five months previously, on reaching his nineteenth birthday. Aldous was posted as a full lieutenant to the 210th Field Company, the Royal Engineers, and this he considered to be a great stroke of luck. Although a company of sappers was attached to each brigade of the Division, 210 Company belonged to the Brigade of Guards and privately considered themselves to be a cut above the rest.

For the past five days, ever since the 31st Division had been rushed to the front, the Guards Brigade had been in the thick of the fighting, and, as the right wing of the Third Army was forced back, they had not had an easy time. They had stabilized the shaky front and attacked and counter-attacked to recapture lost ground, but slowly, inevitably, they had been gradually forced back – gassed out of the trenches which Aldous and his sappers had so laboriously dug, shelled out of strongpoints which they had constructed further back, and obliged to retire further still when the line on their right was forced. Back, back, back: from St Leger to Hamelincourt, Hamelincourt to Moyenneville, and from Mory to Ervillers and Courcelles. The sappers were as exhausted as the infantry – indeed, two nights earlier, they had been sent post-haste to the line and forced to play the part of infantry themselves. There were no other reserves. Jim Aldous was of a naturally optimistic disposition, but this was his lowest point.

*Lieutenant Jim Aldous, MC, 210 Field Coy., Royal Engineers, 31st Division*

We were to dig a line just south of Hamelincourt and hold it as infantry until we were relieved by the 92nd Brigade, who are retreating from the front line to the new line. The reason is that the Boche has got through on the south and is round our right flank, and so we were told to hold our line if he continued to advance on our right. We got off within fifteen minutes and marched to the site with two other field companies, each man taking one tin of bully beef, three biscuits, and 150 rounds of ammunition. We dug the line in record time, and then manned the trench. I wonder what would have happened to us if the Boche had come through, because we had no Very lights and no SOS rockets. He could have come within twenty yards of us without our seeing him. I had one NCO and three men out in front as a standing patrol, but I fancy he would have finished them off before we knew it. It was very cold indeed, and standing-to for five hours nearly finished us off. A large fire started on our right front and burnt the whole night. At twelve midnight our guns pulled out past the line we had dug and went away to the rear. We waited till 2 a.m. the following day without anyone relieving us. We then got word that the enemy had attacked again and the 92nd Brigade could not retire, so we were to march back.

We arrived at Monchy-au-Bois at 6 a.m. on the 26th, dead beat, and no one could have moved another mile, as we'd had practically no sleep for two days before. I went to sleep in my clothes within two minutes of getting in, and slept till 4.30 p.m., when I awoke feeling absolutely starved. We were just picketed out in a field, of course, and I learned that the Boche had been shelling us most of the day. He was certainly doing it when I woke, but no one took any notice. A thing like that seems so trivial compared to what is happening. Today I hear that the Guards and 92nd Brigade are holding the line we dug last night and have evacuated all in front of it, so the retreat is in full swing. We are all praying for rain, which apparently is the only thing that can hold him up on our right. We *could* have held him, but he is round on our right flank and a retreat is imperative. The roads are a tangled mass of ammunition columns and transport going west – everything is very confused – and no one knows where the Boche is on our flanks. It is really open warfare. However, we know one thing and that is that we are retreating.

Even under shell-fire and in the open air, a few hours' sleep did a great deal to restore the sappers' spirits. They were even happier when they learned that they were not required to work that night, and there was a general rush to find sleeping quarters in the village. Monchy-au-Bois, where the Brigade transport lines now were, had been well back from the front when the battle erupted on 21 March – so far back that many of the inhabitants who had been forced to flee the fighting before the front moved east in 1917 had been able to return to till their fields, to retrieve what was left in their battered dwellings, and to take up residence in huts erected by the French Relief Committee. It had been a sad sight to see them take to the road for a second time, carrying what they could of their salvaged possessions, but the sappers were only too pleased to move into the vacated huts. The walls were corrugated iron, lined inside with wooden planks, but each one contained three rooms, they were warm and dry and, in the circumstances, they seemed the height of luxury. They were full of unimaginable treasures, and, since these were not required at present by their rightful owners, the men felt no compunction about plundering them. Aldous and his fellow officers more or less confined themselves to food, and collected five rabbits, four hens, a sack of potatoes and sixty pounds of flour. They also acquired a sack of cement (a valuable commodity to the Royal Engineers) and some voluminous nightgowns. These were donned with much mutual ribbing, but they enabled the officers to take off their stiff and grimy uniforms and slumber in blissful comfort during the night.

Other troops in the vicinity were even less particular in their acquisitions, and a battalion of the King's Own Yorkshire Light Infantry, enjoying a brief respite from the battle, were making the most of the unexpected windfall. In the morning, Jim Aldous was amused to see them passing in a long procession, wheeling barrows full of comestibles and domestic *objets d'art* for which they could have no conceivable use. Four men, making purposefully for the Koyli's mess, were actually carrying a four-poster bed, removed from heaven knew what salubrious dwelling, and another marched past with what Aldous delicately described as 'a most necessary article' in each hand and with a feather boa draped rakishly round his neck.

Despite the blatant thievery, the bizarre spectacle was a welcome diversion – but soon there were other matters to engage their interest. Orders came through that there must be no more retreating and that the present line must be maintained 'at all costs'. At 5.30 in the evening Aldous and his men set off to dig the Purple Line in front of Adinfer Wood – and the Purple Line was the line of last resort. In a few hours' time Ludendorff would launch the *Mars* attack, and already the shell-fire was becoming more intense. Again 210 Field Company was ordered to hold the trench as infantry and to defend it, if need be, to the last.

Two fields ahead, the Guards Brigade was holding the front line in the village of Ayette. Behind the Guards there was no defence but the sketchy line the Royal Engineers had dug in front of Adinfer Wood, and no other troops but the sappers to man it.

Adinfer Wood lay in front of Monchy-au-Bois and not far behind Ayette astride a minor road running south from Arras through Puisieux to Serre – the village where the unblooded troops of the 31st Division had been decimated in the Battle of the Somme. The engineers had dug a line of strongpoints on the eastern outskirts of Ayette, with a support line of scratch trenches on its western edge. There the Guards were standing when morning came and *Mars* was unleashed.[1]

Curving slightly eastward as it ran north, the line ran west of Moyenneville, which the Germans had occupied the previous night. But, as Walter Hare was shortly to discover, it was hard to tell exactly where it ran.

---

1. On modern maps the road to Puisieux is the D919. The track that now leads to the Chinese War Cemetery is roughly on the line of the strongpoints east of the village.

*Private Walter Hare*

We'd been up at Beuvry on rest, and when we'd first got there they gave us an extra bandolier of ammunition and another couple of grenades and said, 'Right! Move forward till you meet somebody – our own troops *or* the Germans.' So we went forward a couple of miles, and when we reached some British troops they told us, 'We've come back three or four miles and there's nobody in front of us but the Germans – but you'll soon find out!' And we did! We'd stuck it there about two days, and then we got orders to retire, because we couldn't hold the trenches any longer, and we came back and back as far as Moyenneville. Then the Jerries got into that and we had to shove out of there. We weren't far away from it on the morning of the 28th, and we were ordered to file up on to a sunken road and told we'd got to stay there. No more retreating. We'd got to hold that.

The shelling was terrible – an awful bombardment! – but we'd got quite good cover and I got myself dug into the embankment. And then the Germans got a machine-gun into a farmhouse on the left and they were shooting down the road at us. It was murder! There weren't too many of us left by then, and we were losing more chaps all the time. There were some battalions on our left and some on our right, but the Jerries burst through on our left and got behind us, and they were firing into our backs. The only chap left alive near me was our Company Sergeant-Major, a chap called Cousins. He was an ex-policeman, a good chap from Beasley. He said to me, 'Now, look, Walter, after the next burst of machine-gun fire we'll run for it. We can't stay here. We can't do any good.' So there was another burst of machine-gun fire down this road and the Sergeant-Major got up and ran, and he hadn't gone far when I saw him go down. So I thought, 'Well, that's no good. It's no use me going. I'd better stay here, and when it gets dark I'll go.' Suddenly I heard the Germans coming up, and the next thing I knew there was a chap going for me with his bayonet fixed, so I dropped my gun and put my hands up.

He shunted me out along the road, and when they got us together there were thirty-seven of us left out of the battalion. What was amazing to me was that my brother was there. I couldn't believe it! I'd been told he'd been killed two days before, but he was still there, and he waved his hand to me and we got together. He was in the same battalion, but a different company. I *was* glad to see him. We were both very fed up at being captured, but it made it a bit better that we were together.

Well, they moved us back into an old quarry and they lined us up.

I thought, 'This is it. They're going to shoot us now!' However, an officer came along who spoke a bit of English, and he told us we were to go and fetch their wounded out and bring them back to this post, where some men were looking after them. First of all they took our field dressings off us, because they didn't have any bandages except paper stuff. We spent the rest of the day doing that, and we didn't know *what* was happening. I thought we'd lost the war!

They had not lost the war. They had not even lost the fight. Between Ayette and Arras, although here and there the Germans managed to push forward to gain a tentative toehold, and although in some parts of the front the line was drawn back to a position of greater advantage, the enemy made small headway. His gains were insignificant, but his losses were inordinate. Every attempt to advance had been repulsed; many more were thwarted before they began by British guns bombarding the German troops as they massed behind their line.

Beyond Arras, at the northern extremity of the *Mars* assault, the 56th Division, which had not yet been attacked, was standing on the line it had held for many months. There had been ample time to strengthen it, and a line of strong outposts ran in front of the battle zone between Gavrelle and Arleux. The work had gone on until almost the last minute, and Harry Goodby of the London Scottish was heartily thankful that the Germans had not chosen to attack twenty-four hours earlier. Had they done so he would have been in trouble. The London Scottish were in the support line, but the night before last a working party had gone out to repair damaged wire at one of the strongpoints in the forefront of the line and, as stretcher-bearers, Goodby and a comrade had gone with them, in case of casualties.

*Private Harry Goodby, 14th (County of London) Bn. (London Scottish), The London Regt., 56th (London) Division*

We stretcher-bearers were told to stay in a disused trench about a hundred yards from the wire, and there was a small dugout built into the parapet with a tarpaulin curtain in front of it. It was big enough to hold two men, and we were told to stay there and that we would be called if we were wanted; otherwise we would be picked up by the wiring party on their way back to the support line when they'd finished. We got to the shelter about ten o'clock, and we should have got back to our lines about midnight. Of course there was nothing for us to do, and we dropped off to sleep.

I was suddenly wakened up by voices above our heads. Naturally I thought it was our party coming back, and then I realized that the voices were speaking German! I knew that we would be in trouble, because stretcher-bearers don't carry rifles, so we were quite helpless. My pal was still fast asleep, and he was snoring something awful, so I clapped my hands round his mouth and whispered to him to keep quiet. I just hoped and prayed the Germans wouldn't come down into the trench, but ten minutes passed – they seemed like hours! – and the voices stopped. After it had been quiet for a while, I pulled the ground-sheet aside to have a look, and I found to my amazement that it was nearly daylight. It was about four o'clock in the morning! Luckily we knew the way back to our lines, but we were only about 200 yards away from the German front line and we could easily have been spotted. There was a very shallow trench running back, so we crawled along it and eventually, and with a *lot* of difficulty, we got back. You can imagine how we felt when we heard that the wiring party had returned at midnight and they'd forgotten all about us! The lookouts had seen the German patrol very close to our wire and they thought we must have gone west – and we jolly nearly did!

That was a terrible part of the line, in front of Oppy Wood and Gavrelle. The Royal Naval Division had attacked there the year before, and their bodies were still hanging on the wire where they'd been caught up. The trench that was now our support line was called Naval Trench. That was their jumping-off point. It was most depressing to see these bodies everywhere.

*1498 Corporal Douglas Pankhurst, Stokes Mortar Section, 56th (London) Division*

When our Stokes-mortar section went up there we had to dig pits for our weapon, and we were digging through bodies. It was dreadful. There were bones and parts of bodies everywhere, but the awful thing was to see some still hanging on the German wire. Somehow it wasn't real. I don't know if it's because I was young, but I don't think at any time in the war I ever felt it was real. I suppose you blocked it out, because it was the only way you could do your job.

We were a small unit, only twenty-five strong, and we had one senior officer – a captain – two second lieutenants, one sergeant and four corporals. I seldom saw an officer or a sergeant in the line, and consequently I was my own kingpin. The Stokes was a sixty-pound mortar shaped like an aerial torpedo and they could only be flung a short distance, so we were always close up to the front line.

That day, 28 March, we'd been relieved the night before the attack.

Then the bombardment started at dawn, and the overriding impression that lasts with me today is the noise, the incessant bombardment that went on for hours. They had thousands of guns on that front, all firing away, and machine-guns rattling. The noise was terrific, and yet, you know, it still wasn't real. About nine o'clock in the morning the OC came to me and said, 'I want you to go up to the reserve pits. The Germans have attacked and run over our line.' I took my men up with me and we got to a sunken road, and a couple of wounded officers came along and said, 'You can't get through. He's got a machine-gun barrage on the sunken road.' They were also shelling badly, and the fellows began to get a bit extra windy, and I can remember doing a silly thing. I'm not boasting, because I never felt it was me walking around. I did my job, of course – in battle you do your job. When you're scared you do it automatically – partly through training, partly through discipline, but mostly, I think, through self-pride. It's difficult to describe. Anyway, I got on top and said, 'Look, it's not hurting me. Come on.' And we went and we got through. We were below the angle of fire, and I knew that the trajectory was such that they'd never get us.

Anyhow, we got into the reserve pit. I rolled back the camouflage, got the mortar ready, got the bombs ready, and then I got them to get hold of my heels and hold me up to the ramp so that I could see over the top of the pit. When I looked over I saw a sight which I'll never forget. It was the London Scottish advancing in open order with fixed bayonets, just as if they were going for a country walk. They were dropping and dropping as they went, the guns were firing, the shells were bursting, the machine-guns were going, and they just went on. It was the most wonderful thing I've ever seen, awe-inspiring, and yet it would nearly break your heart. I used to have *The Times* sent out to me, and I always remember the headline. It said, 'Hoch the London Territorials.' We were the only part that held the line. The Germans came over with spare boots and rations for a week. They took our front line. They might have taken the second line, but we held them.

The London Scottish were in support to the 4th Royal Fusiliers in the front line. When the attack broke and the outposts were overrun, Sergeant Frank Udall was a short distance behind them, at Advanced Company Headquarters. Before the war Udall had followed the undistinguished occupation of clerk to the Islington branch of the Conservative Association, and in 1914, when Germans were popularly supposed to be lurking behind every bush, he began his active service by guarding the railway station at Surbiton. Now he was a soldier to the backbone, a mainstay of the Battalion, a senior

NCO who had proved his worth in half a dozen battles and had won the Military Medal in the Battle of the Somme. Before the day was out he would have earned another.[1]

*Sergeant Frank Udall, MM and 2 bars, 4th Bn., Royal Fusiliers, 56th (London) Division*

We knew they were coming, because we'd made a raid the night before. Lieutenant Capley led it, and when he got in the German trench he went to fire his revolver and it wouldn't work, so he had a stand-up fight with the Jerry. He got a punch in the jaw and his teeth were all bashed in, but he got back, and they got a prisoner and all the information. So we knew it was coming and when. There was the front-line post and eighty yards behind it is *us*, and behind us is two or three Vickers machine-guns. So Jerry starts his bombardment with big trench mortars. Awful things they are! You think every one's going to hit you! But our artillery's opening up, I can tell you! Anyway, Jerry comes over. Well, there was nothing I could do but what I *had* done. I'd taken a load of bandoliers, and these bandoliers are divided into sections with about fifty rounds of ammo in them, five in each section, so I'd been taking the bullets out from every other section and laid them on the bandoliers on the fire-step ready for the men to man the trench. I also saw that all the grenades were fused up and ready.

Jerry didn't do much when he came over. He came on a bit, but he didn't do much. Of course the forward post went and we had to go back a bit, but only so as we could fight. The idea was to get at least eighty yards back from the line we were in, so that he can't reach that far with his own grenades, but to pick a straight trench if possible, so that you can easily hold it by a rifle. So we did that. I gathered a couple of snipers and got them to lie on top of the trench to cover us, and in this bit of trench I was on my own with a little chap, Lance-Corporal Taylor, who'd managed to get back from the post and attached himself to me.

We had a bag of grenades, so we put them down, and when I looked round there's two Jerries coming into the trench taking aim at us. How they missed us, God Almighty knows! I supposed they must have been just as bloody scared as we were. Just where we were in the trench – and this is a *good* trench remember, well built – there's a box

---

1. Frank Udall was one of the few soldiers to have been awarded two bars to the Military Medal: the first on 28 March 1918 and the second at Croisilles later the same year.

built into the parapet, with room enough for the bombers to take aim
and throw their bombs, and this is where training comes in. Neither
of us said a word. We just dived into the box together and from that
bit of shelter we started chucking bombs along the trench towards
these Jerries. Well, we got rid of the two in the trench, but from where
I was I could see a Jerry officer out in front pointing us out to his
machine-gun crew. The snipers on the top soon picked him off, but
I thought to myself, 'Now, he's in front over there, *and* he's in the
rear too, so it's about time we hopped back for safety.'

As I started getting back, I met Major Philips and he said, 'Retire,
and get your lads back to the Canadians.' (The Canadian line was just
on our left, because we were on the very left flank of our division.)
This is about eleven o'clock in the morning now, and by rights we
should have retired two or three hours before. We were completely
cut off. There were some poor buggers trying to get through to us,
but Jerry had got round the rear, and they were running into him
every time, so we had to hang on entirely on our own. We had no
gunfire, except the machine-guns. Of course the big guns were firing
ahead of us and, my God, they really done good work. They smashed
them up. *We* had to go back – we had no choice. But the Germans
only got three hundred yards. I honestly believe it was the turning
point of the war. I honestly do believe that.

When we got out of the trench, the Germans were firing heavy, so
we lay in a shell-hole for a time, and lying there was Captain Duffey
of C Company, badly wounded in the chest. Sergeant-Major James
asked me if I could get one of my sergeants to bring him back with
us, so I went and got a sergeant, and he gold hold of four men and a
duckboard to carry him to the trench we were making for. While we
were retiring across the open to the Canadians on our left, I looked
back and I saw a German who looked like an officer approaching the
sergeant and the four fellows carrying *our* officer on the duckboard, so
I thought that was the end for them, but a little while after we got
back to the trench, the sergeant arrived with the four men, officer,
duckboard and all! I saw him sent off to an aid post, and then I asked
the sergeant what had happened. I thought the sergeant must have
taken the German officer prisoner, but he said, 'No! The German
officer spoke English and he asked me what we were doing, and I said
we were stretcher-bearers. Then he pointed to the rifles I was carrying
– two on one shoulder and three on the other – and he laughed. But
he looked at the officer and he saw the DSO ribbon on his tunic, and
he said, "A brave officer! Is he badly wounded?" I told him he was
and we were taking him back to our line. Then he said, "Go ahead.

You can take him back. We will not fire on you." So here we are.' I
was impressed by that. I'll never forget it. That German officer was
certainly a good bloke.

Another chap who done good that day was Private Goodman. He
was a barman from Shoreditch, and he was the cook for our company
– one of the few who used to do the cooking in the front line on a
charcoal fire. Company HQ was going to have rabbit that day, and
when Goodman knew Jerry was coming he trod it all into the floor
of the dugout – trampled all the basins into the floor so Jerry wouldn't
get it. And when he *did* get there Goodman had a fight on top of the
trench. Fisticuffs – a real set-to! He was captured, but he made sure
they didn't get our rabbit. And they didn't get much else either! It was
the turning point of the war.

It was not precisely the turning point of the war, but the Germans had
suffered a serious setback. By late afternoon, after the gallant counter-attack
by the London Scottish, the fighting died down, but there was no guarantee
that it would not be renewed next day. Huge amounts of ammunition had
been used up, and more was urgently wanted. As soon as it was dark the
transport section of the London Rifle Brigade was ordered to take fresh
supplies to the line. For the men leading the mules it was an eerie journey.

*Rifleman A. Smith, 5th (City of London) Bn. (London Rifle Bde.), The
London Regt., 56th (London) Division*

Apart from various stretchers being brought down from the shambles
ahead of us, we had the track to ourselves. Presently the track led us
on to a road, where we halted beside some sandbagged dugouts, which
represented the Brigade bomb store. A sergeant in charge of our convoy
promptly roused the occupants of the dugouts for the purpose of
loading our ponies – much to the men's annoyance, for they had
obviously had a very trying day of it up here.

At long last we moved forward, threading our way among shell-holes.
What a deluge of shells this road had received! Fritz's enthusiasm for
the road had very luckily cooled down by nightfall, and no one could
complain of a few crumps. Jerry seemed to have spent himself that
day, and he must have had a nasty knock.

Our convoy turned up a little sunken lane, where quite a number
of our division were manning improvised fire-steps. The Germans had
got nearly as far as this during the day.

'It's the finest day in the history of the regiment,' said a sergeant.
'There's not many of 'em left, but we've killed simply thousands with

bombs and rifle fire and Lewis-guns. Fritz hasn't got a kick left in him.'

The few of them that were left (about ninety in all) were worn out with killing. Practically no one remained even in HQ to remind one even of 1916, let alone 1914. Among the rank and file, the transport section was now absolutely the last remnant of the old battalion.

But *Mars* North, like *Mars* South on the other side of Arras, had failed, and, despite Prince Rupprecht's desire to renew the battle, Ludendorff called it off. His gamble had failed, and he knew it. Years later he wrote:

The 17th Army had already attacked in the last days of March in the direction of Arras, making its principal effort on the north bank of the Scarpe. It was to capture the decisive heights east and north of Arras; the next day the 6th Army was to prolong the attack from about Lens and carry the high ground in that area. I attached the greatest importance to both these attacks. To have the high ground in our possession was bound to be decisive in any fighting in the plain of the Lys. In spite of employing extraordinary masses of artillery and ammunition, the attack of the 17th Army on both banks of the Scarpe was a failure; it fought under an unlucky star.

And, despite some small tactical gains further south, where the French and the British were proving to be so irritatingly obdurate, it was becoming apparent that the great sweeping victory on which he had staked so much would not be easily won.

Although it was against his own tactical judgement and appraisal of the situation, General Gough was anxious to comply with Foch's demand that his army should hold its ground come what may, but there had been another slight withdrawal during the previous night and some troops had come perilously close to being cut off. Even now the danger had not been wholly averted. Gough had spent the afternoon away from his headquarters, visiting his commanders in the field and making personal contact with General Mesple, in command of the newly arrived French force which was not yet fully organized. When he returned to Dury, a visitor was waiting in the mess, where the mess stewards were serving tea. It was General Ruggles-Brise, Haig's military secretary. He was a kindly unassuming man, whom Gough knew and liked, but, despite his bluff and genial welcome, Ruggles-Brise seemed preoccupied and ill at ease. He had an unpleasant message to deliver, and it was obvious that he did not relish the prospect. He asked to see General Gough alone, and Gough, still unsuspecting, led him into an ante-room. Ruggles-Brise spoke quietly. 'The Chief asked me to tell you that he thinks you and your staff are very tired after all these days of struggle, and he has decided to replace you by Rawlinson and his staff.'

Gough was more than surprised – he was dumbfounded. At face value the decision could be interpreted as a considerate act on the part of the Commander-in-Chief; but, although it was cloaked in kindly terms, General Gough was too wily a bird and too well versed in the gentlemanly etiquette of the military hierarchy not to realize its full import. He knew he was being sacked. Ruggles-Brise had no more to say, but as he took his leave he put all the sympathy he could muster into his handshake.

Schooled by long years of discipline and duty, Gough made a monumental effort to hide his feelings of dismay and soften the blow for his staff. But the shame of it was almost insupportable. The soldiering to which he had dedicated his life was bred in the bone. Both his father and his uncle had won the Victoria Cross, and his father had commanded a force in the Afghan War. In 1900, during the Boer War, Gough himself had led the force which relieved Ladysmith. By that time he was a seasoned soldier. At seventeen and a half he had been the youngest cadet at Sandhurst, and he was commissioned into the 16th Lancers on 5 March 1889. It was the anniversary of the Battle of Barossa, in which, seventy-eight years earlier to the very day, his great-grandfather, fighting under Wellington, had led the 87th Irish Fusiliers to victory. It was part of the Gough family legend, for Lord Gough had led them with the battle-cry '*Faugh-a-ballaugh!*' It meant '*Clear the way!*' The battle-cry had been proudly adopted by the troops as their motto – and no less proudly by the Gough family as theirs. Hubert Gough did not regard his dismissal as humiliation: to the scion of such a family as his it was little short of degradation – and he was stricken to the heart. As soldier to soldier, he did not blame Haig, who was well known for his exceptional loyalty to colleagues and subordinates. Gough could only guess at the pressures which had forced the Commander-in-Chief to remove him.

He stayed to welcome General Rawlinson and to formally hand over command, but he left as soon as he could decently get away. He had no idea where he was expected to eat or to sleep that night, but, as a homing pigeon returns to its loft, he made for the British GHQ, where the camp commandant found him a billet. Field-Marshal Haig was kind to him and did his best to mollify his old friend. 'I need you, Hubert,' he said. He explained that he wanted Gough and his staff out of the line so that they could reconnoitre the Somme valley from Amiens to the sea and prepare a system of defence – adding that, if the French did not hold on, it might be necessary for the British Army to retreat to it. 'I *must* have a Reserve Army staff,' he emphasized.

Gough had no choice but to acquiesce. Although he knew, in his heart of hearts, that the gesture was a sop to his pride, he was too sore and aggrieved to appreciate the consideration of the Commander-in-Chief. He was inwardly convinced that the only 'failure' which could be laid at his door was his failure to conform to the plans of the Germans. Had he obliged the Fifth Army to stand and fight until it was overwhelmed by the might of the enemy's attack, he would have played precisely the role Ludendorff intended. Its strength was horribly diminished, but the Fifth Army was still intact. It had checked the enemy at every stage of its slow retirement, gaining time for reinforcements to reach the line and seriously weakening the resources of the German Army. Ludendorff had undoubtedly been forced to use up quantities of men and munitions many times greater than those he would have expended had Gough chosen to stand his ground and thereby commit his army to heroic annihilation. In later years Ludendorff himself was of much the same opinion.

General Rawlinson's first act on taking over command of the Fifth Army was to send an urgent message to General Foch. It was timed at 6.30 p.m. on 28 March, and it was blunt and to the point:

The situation is serious, and unless fresh troops are sent here in the next two days, I doubt whether the remnants of the British XIX Corps which now hold the line to the east of Villers-Bretonneux can maintain their positions. The XVIII Corps has been pulled out; a few of its troops which were not relieved by the French are being transferred to the command of the XIX Corps. I feel some anxiety for the security of Amiens, and draw your attention to the danger in which this place will be if the enemy renews his attacks from the east before fresh troops are available . . .[1]

The long spell of fine weather had broken, and before dark the rain that had been falling intermittently for most of the day had become a steady downpour. It did nothing to raise the spirits of the troops as they settled down for a miserable night. Outside Adinfer Wood, Jim Aldous and his company were ordered to remain in the trench they had dug, in case the attack should be renewed.

1. XIX Corps was the only unit which was still serving exclusively under the banner of the Fifth Army. Of its three remaining corps, XVIII Corps had already been relieved; VII Corps, it may be remembered, had retired north of the dividing line of the Somme, away from the main force of the Fifth Army, and for this reason had been put under the orders of the Third Army; while on the south, the remnants of III Corps were still with the French around Montdidier and were only now being sent back piecemeal.

*Lieutenant Jim Aldous, MC (diary entry – 29 March 1918)*

The trenches were soon in a most atrocious condition! We spent the night in abject misery, as the rain could not be kept out. We placed wooden sleepers over the top of the trench to make a roof as best we could. The trench was three feet broad and three feet deep, and we sat in the bottom with our backs to the wall in mud about a foot deep. My revolver sank in the mud when I put it down and nodded off. When I woke up I was too exhausted to plunge my arm into the mud and grope for it. But the rain will have one good effect – it will tend to hold up the advance of the Boche. The luck he has had with offensives makes me really believe he is in league with Gott – or the Devil!

Close to Albert, where the 35th Division was on the right of the Australians, General Marandin made the rounds of his troops and hailed Major Harrison Johnston with surprising cheerfulness. 'Well, Johnston, still merry and bright?' Coming from a colleague of lower rank, these words might well have met with an unprintable reply, but Johnston answered politely, though with little enthusiasm, that they were all in good form and as merry and bright as the circumstances permitted. But, since the circumstances referred to had required him to occupy a sump-hole as Battalion Headquarters, he was not much amused by the General's greeting.

*Captain Harrison Johnston, 15th (Service) Bn., The Cheshire Regt., 35th Division*

Rain was coming through the riddled piece of old tarpaulin which served as a roof. If you leaned against the sides, earth came down your neck, and the civilian mattress meant for sleeping purposes was sodden. As soon as relief was complete I set off round the front line. The men were remarkably cheery, and asked me questions like, 'Are we winning, Sir?' 'Did you see old No. 7 Platoon get those six Boches trying to work round the flank?' 'Any chance of cigarettes in the next rations, Sir?' Ye gods! the guts of the British soldier are wonderful.

I found old Milne had put his men out all right. I went round his outposts with him, and they were mostly good. As we were returning we saw some small parties in front of our right flank moving towards the Hun line. Milne explained to me that these were Australians, who were pushing their line forward about 250 yards. They were shouting to each other as if there was no enemy for miles! The Boche outpost line was only three or four hundred yards away. Machine-guns opened on them and they got down, but they carried on a little later. Milne was highly amused and told me that the OC company on his right had been round to see him to inform him that he proposed to move his line forward during the night to shorten the joint frontage. He said, 'I don't have any of these red-hat fellows arranging where I sit. I go out and choose the sites, put the boys there, and *then* tell Brigade where we are.' The question of flanks did not seem to interest him much. He told the people on each side what he had done and said it was then up to them to conform or not, as they thought best. *He'd* looked after his bit. These Australians were a wonderful lot of fellows, and didn't care a row of pins for anything or anybody.

I went along the railway and found things OK. I then went to a little farmhouse, where the two forward companies there had their HQ. It was a topping place, though the CO of the Lancashire Fusiliers who we relieved thought it was too far forward for Battalion HQ. I decided to move in at once. I got back to the sump-hole about 3.30 a.m. and found old Binks sleeping peacefully in the mud and water. I told him of my find, and ten minutes later HQ were moving forward 1,000 yards.

Not far away across the rain-soaked battlefield the German soldiers were no better off, and they had not had a satisfactory day.

*Musketier Hans Schetter, 3rd Coy., 231st Reserve Infantry Regt., 50th [German] Reserve Division*

We are about one kilometre from Dernancourt when the English artillery starts to fire at us and shells continuously crash into the houses of the village. All day long 230th Regiment is engaged in heavy fighting for the bridge over the Ancre, and especially for a railroad spur on the Albert–Amiens–Paris line. But the Tommy defends his line tenaciously. Some of our wounded passing to the rear tell us about the terrific English machine-gun fire. Our divisional chaplain, a Lutheran pastor, helps to look after the badly wounded, and our regimental doctor puts on emergency bandages.

We put tarpaulins over a hole we have dug for ourselves in the chalk soil. It has started to rain again, and we creep together here to spend the night. Enemy shells crash down around us all night and we have little protection – just a tarpaulin.

It was exactly one week since the German boys had been exulting in the achievements of the first day's fighting and Schetter and his companions, replete with British rations, had been savouring the luxury of soft, new woollen socks. They had come a long way since then, but there was a new sense of anticlimax in the air. It was no doubt due to the unpleasant change in the weather, but, nevertheless, some German soldiers had an uneasy feeling that they might not get much further.

*Leutnant Rudolf Binding*

Today the advance of our infantry suddenly stopped near Albert. Nobody could understand why. Our way seemed entirely clear. When I asked the Brigade Commander why there was no movement forward, he shrugged his shoulders and said he did not know either. I turned round at once and took a sharp turn with the car into Albert. As soon as I got near the town I began to see curious sights. There were men driving cows before them, others who carried a hen under one arm and a box of notepaper under the other. Men carrying a bottle of wine under one arm and another one open in their hand. Men dressed up in comic disguise with top hats on their heads. Men staggering. Men who could hardly walk. The streets were running with wine. Out of a cellar came a lieutenant of the Second Marine Division, helpless and in despair. I asked him, 'What is going to happen?' He replied, 'I cannot get my men out of this cellar without bloodshed.'

I drove back to Divisional HQ with a fearful impression of the situation. The advance was held up, and there was no means of getting it going again for hours. When I considered what was happening up in front it seemed to me to be merely a magnified expression of the passion and craving which we were all experiencing. Yesterday an officer sitting beside me in the car suddenly called out to the driver to stop at once, without so much as asking my leave. When I asked him in astonishment what he meant by stopping the car when we were on an urgent mission, he answered, 'I must just pick up that English waterproof lying beside the road.' He jumped out, seized an English waterproof which lay on the bank, and then jumped joyfully back again.

If this lack of restraint seized an officer like that, one can imagine what effect it must have on the private soldier. In the case of the officer it was the waterproof which tempted him to forget his important duties. With the private soldiers it was the coloured picture-postcard, the silk curtain, the bottle of wine, the chicken or the cow – but in most cases the wine.

But there was one private soldier who had coveted a British overcoat. It belonged to the commanding officer of the 2nd West Yorks, and it was politely but insistently removed from his shoulders by one of the Germans who captured him that afternoon. Colonel Lowry was caught when his battalion was ordered to retire from the line at Moreuil, and it was a stroke of bad luck, because even under heavy shelling all the rest of the battalion had got safely away. The Colonel had sent them off in twos and threes until only he himself and two orderlies were left. Unfortunately, as they left the trench and prepared to make a dash for it, they came face to face with an enemy machine-gun team and were promptly taken prisoner.

In view of the weather, the German soldier who appropriated the Colonel's overcoat was kind enough to offer him his Army-issue rain-cape in exchange, and as the rain grew heavier Lowry was glad to put it on. There were many prisoners – perhaps too many for the Germans to handle – and at dusk the group which included Colonel Lowry was briefly left unguarded. Seizing his chance, he slipped across the road, hid behind a potato heap on the other side, and lurked there until the prisoners were herded on. He found that he was on the edge of a shell-pocked field, littered with battle debris. It included an abandoned German helmet, which the Colonel promptly grabbed. He stuck it on his head and waited. Presently an enemy transport column lumbered along the road and, relying on rain and poor light to make up for the deficiencies of his disguise, and hoping to give the impression that he had merely left the column to answer a call of nature, Lowry strode out from behind his shelter and tagged on to a contingent of men marching behind the wagons. They marched in silence, heads bent against the driving rain, but occasionally a man at his side uttered a remark which seemed to require an answer. Given the circumstances and the tone of voice, the Colonel assumed that his companion was not extolling the joys of a soldier's lot. His entire knowledge of German consisted of two words – 'Nicht wahr.' He was almost sure that this phrase implied agreement, but as he was not quite sure enough to take the risk he responded, when necessary, with a morose grunt, and depended on his confident bearing, the kindly darkness and the rain to get away with it.

He did get away with it as far as a crossroads near Villers-Bretonneux. Then, suspecting that German traffic-control police might not be so easily deceived by his disguise, he lagged behind, ambled to the side of the road as if nature was again insistent, and made his escape across the fields. It was almost dawn when Lowry reached the British lines, soaked, muddy and extremely tired, but delighted by his escapade.

He was probably the only man, British or German, who had been out all night in the streaming rain who was entirely happy.

## Chapter 21

Easter – and in normal times the working population of Great Britain might have railed against the vagaries of the weather as the spell of unseasonable warmth gave way to chill and damp on the eve of the first official holiday of the year. But the holiday spirit was largely absent. As a concession to the bank holiday, most theatres were putting on extra matinées on Easter Monday. Easter race meetings would be held as usual, but racegoers would have to make their way as best they could, without the benefit of special trains or charabancs to convey them. As if to give a foretaste of the dramatic exhortations which would loom large in a future war, Winston Churchill, now Minister of Munitions, had urged munition workers to carry on during the holiday and to speed up production to replace abandoned guns and the stock of ammunition, now dangerously depleted. Steelworks, engineering shops and shipyards also worked through the holidays to turn out the tanks, the aircraft, the ships that were more badly needed than ever, and even textile factories carried on non-stop, producing khaki uniforms for half a million new recruits.

For the first time, in view of the gravity of the situation, newspapers appeared on a Good Friday. They reported that the enemy was faltering and the Army was holding on, but no one could deny that all was far from well. On Good Friday and again on Easter Sunday, churches of all denominations were full and most services included special prayers and hymns appropriate to the circumstances. The poet John Oxenham had penned new lines 'For the Men at the Front' to be sung to the tune of the sailors' hymn 'For Those in Peril on the Sea'.

> Lord God of Hosts, whose mighty hand
> Dominion holds on sea and land,
> In Peace and War Thy Will we see
> Shaping the larger liberty.
> Nations may rise and nations fall,
> Thy changeless purpose rules them all.

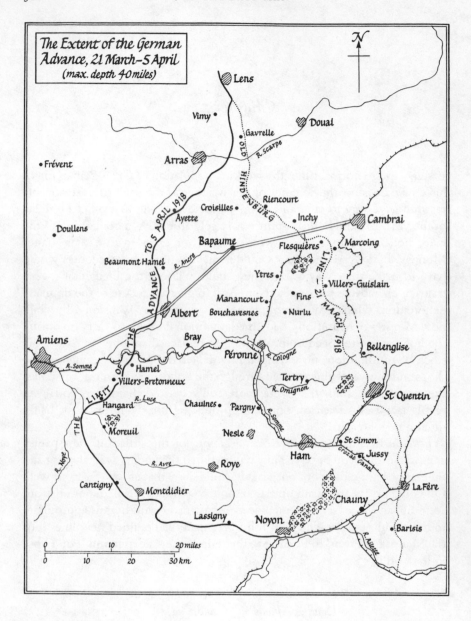

The Extent of the German
Advance, 21 March–5 April
(max. depth 40 miles)

N

Lens
Vimy
Gavrelle
Douai
R. Scarpe
Frévent
Arras
OLD HINDENBURG
Riencourt
Croisilles
Inchy
Cambrai
Ayette
ADVANCE TO 5 APRIL 1918
Doullens
Bapaume
Marcoing
Flesquières
Beaumont Hamel
R. Ancre
Ytres
Villers-Guislain
Manancourt
Fins
LINE – 21 MARCH 1918
Albert
Bouchavesnes
Nurlu
Bray
Péronne
R. Cologne
Bellenglise
Amiens
R. Somme
Hamel
Tertry
Villers-Bretonneux
R. Omignon
St Quentin
THE LIMIT OF THE
Hangard
R. Luce
Chaulnes
Pargny
R. Somme
Moreuil
Nesle
St Simon
Jussy
R. Avre
Roye
Ham
Crozat Canal
La Fère
Cantigny
Montdidier
Chauny
Lassigny
Noyon
Barisis
R. Noye
R. Oise

0        10        20 miles
0    10    20    30 km

*When death flies swift on wave or field,*
*Be Thou a sure defence and shield!*
*Console and succour those who fall,*
*And help and hearten each and all!*
*O, hear a people's prayers for those*
*Who fearless face their country's foes!*

*For those to whom the call shall come*
*We pray Thy tender welcome home.*
*The toil, the bitterness, all past,*
*We trust them to Thy Love at last.*
*O, hear a people's prayers for all*
*Who, nobly striving, nobly fall!*

*For those who minister and heal,*
*And spend themselves, their skill, their zeal –*
*Renew their hearts with Christ-like faith,*
*And guard them from disease and death.*
*And in Thine own good time, Lord, send*
*Thy Peace on earth till Time shall end!*

The prevailing mood was one of grim determination, and the headline 'Dogged Does It' summed it up.

In France, however, Easter brought a wave of near-hysteria, and anti-German sentiment climbed to new heights of rage and hatred. In Paris, and on Good Friday of all days, a shell from the long-range German gun fell on the church of St Gervais, packed with Easter worshippers, and struck a pillar which supported the roof of the nave. Seventy-five people were killed by falling debris, and ninety more were badly injured. It was a tragic mishap, for the shells fired by the gun over such a distance were not powerful and, until then, they had caused very little damage. It was not technically possible to range the gun on any specific target, and consequently the shelling was haphazard, but the 'Good Friday Massacre', as it would henceforth be known, was seen as a deliberate act of sacrilege. The news was wired around the world by Reuters, and in Great Britain, in America, in every neutral and allied country where the ghoulish details were reported, the Germans were denounced as barbarians. The Cardinal Archbishop of Paris arrived to view the damage while bodies were still being pulled from the wreckage. 'The wretches!' he cried. 'They have chosen the day and hour that Christ died on the cross to commit this crime!' President Poincaré also drove to the scene and expressed deep indignation, and the deliberations of the Chamber of Deputies were brought to a halt by the news. Even the most left-wing of the Socialist deputies, who was generally not much given to agreement with his colleagues, joined in the ringing denunciations. 'At the moment when these women, old men, and children were imploring heaven that the end which we all wish may be put to this horrible butchery, at this moment the ancient Gothic roof was rent open and a hail of iron drowned their prayers in blood . . .'

Near Montdidier, not many miles north-west of Paris, the French Army was under siege. Since the Germans had pushed forward, the line from Arras in the north to Chauny south of St Quentin ran in a wavering L shape, and the shorter, lower, leg ran westward from Chauny, passing south of Noyon to curve in a pocket round Montdidier. This front formed the southern flank of the German advance, and the French troops defending it were therefore facing due north. Capitaine Désiré Wavrin's company was still beating off heated attacks round Canny-sur-Matz, for the enemy was keeping up relentless pressure all along the flank, to pin the French down and prevent any chance of a counter-attack that would imperil the rear of the main German force as it pressed westward towards Amiens. Now that the Germans held the pocket where the front changed direction and swung north, a decisive breach in the line west of Montdidier might bring them to Amiens by the back door.

The Germans were well beyond Montdidier now, but they had not gone so far nor so fast as they had hoped, for the French soldiers who had shocked Paul Maze by appearing to relinquish Montdidier without a fight had stolidly contested every yard of ground beyond it. Nevertheless, by the morning of Easter Saturday, 30 March, the Germans had progressed north-west of Montdidier as far as Grivesnes and the village of Cantigny two miles south of it. These two sleepy villages were of small importance in themselves, but they were crucial to the fortunes of the French Army. At their backs, and only six miles away, was the main railway link between Paris and Amiens – the vital artery of communication which would bring French reinforcements from the east. If the enemy got through, and the railway was captured, Amiens would be lost.

Grivesnes was a seigneurial village, dominated by a handsome chateau and an imposing domed church, built fifty years earlier by the family of the present owner, the Comte de la Myre. The church was so large and so elaborate that anywhere other than in this tiny village it might easily have passed for a cathedral. A long, tree-lined avenue ran towards the chateau, straddling the road which ran past its gates and the church nearby. To the sides and rear of the chateau was an extensive wooded park, while a small square and a few streets of modest houses constituted the village itself. This Easter was the first time since the church had been consecrated in 1868 that

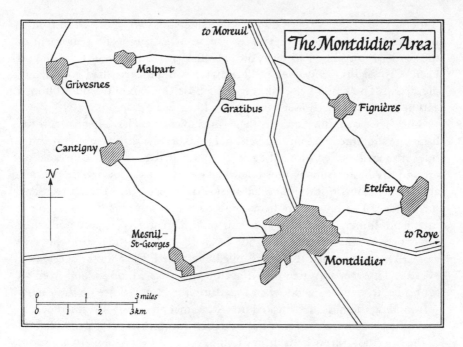

to Moreuil

**The Montdidier Area**

Malpart

Grivesnes

Gratibus

Fignières

Cantigny

N

Etelfay

to Roye

Mesnil—
St-Georges

Montdidier

0        1        3 miles
0    1    2    3km

its bells had not rung out to summon the faithful. The villagers had fled, and the 350th [French] Regiment of Infantry, which was holding the surrounding woods, had set up its command post in the abandoned chateau.

A long time earlier, when the fighting front was more than thirty-five miles away, French troops on rest or in reserve were billeted in Grivesnes. Knowing that the *poilus* would not be averse to poaching, and were partial to a pheasant or two, the Comte de la Myre had erected barriers to seal off the pathways through his woods. They were reinforced with wire mesh, and peremptory orders were nailed up to remind the troops that this was forbidden territory: 'It is expressly forbidden for troops to enter this property.' Now, as if in mockery of this stern warning, the dead bodies of French and German soldiers were sprawled around the barriers, and the trees which had once quivered to the crack of sporting rifles splintered and tumbled beneath the pounding of heavy cannon as the Germans prepared to storm the woods and advance on the village beyond. There were only two battalions of the 350th Regiment to defend it, and they were battalions in little more than name, for they had been fighting hard for days. One could account for only 250 men, and the other for not many more, and although there were also a company of engineers and a handful of chasseurs, the three full battalions ranged against them were the pick of the German Army – soldiers of the

Imperial Guard, the Kaiser's own troops. Since the start of the offensive the Imperial Guard had been kept in reserve, to await the decisive moment of the battle. Now they had been brought into it, and they were fresh and keen. Crown Prince Wilhelm, the Kaiser's son and heir, had confidently predicted, 'The Easter bells will ring out for victory', and Ludendorff hoped and believed that the Kaiser's troops would turn the tide.

Since dawn on Easter Saturday the French soldiers at Grivesnes had thrown back line after line of enemy soldiers, but, inexorably, as the troops on either side of them had been forced back, they too had been forced to give up ground. By Easter Sunday morning, the Germans had captured the woods, and the remnants of the *poilus* had been driven back into the chateau and surrounded. There were not many of them, and it must have seemed to the invincible Imperial Guard that it was only a matter of time before they surrendered. But the *poilus* did not mean to give up their stronghold so easily. They barricaded the doors, piled every bed, every desk, every sofa, every table, every movable object against the long windows, and from all four sides, from every window and aperture, they poured fire on the enemy surrounding them. Rifles cracked non-stop; machine-guns streamed deadly fire; rifle grenades and even a heavy trench mortar, laboriously hauled up to the first floor, threw lethal heavy bombs on every wave of German troops who attempted to move forward. From the low-level windows that lit the basement, from the long casements of the staterooms, from the bedrooms above them and from the windows of the attics, a relentless fusillade fell on successive waves of enemy soldiers as they tried to rush the chateau. Time and again the Germans retired and called on their guns to renew the bombardment and shell the chateau into submission.

It was unnerving for the men sheltering behind the walls that shook and crumbled beneath the explosions, but at the height of the bombardment a young lieutenant (who was never named) found a means to fire their courage. He rushed to a grand piano protruding from a barricade of piled-up furniture. The soldiers were crouched behind it, some were even sheltering underneath, but the keyboard was unobstructed and still undamaged. The lieutenant was not much of a musician, but he could play the tunes that mattered. He thumped out 'La Marseillaise', and then he thumped it out again. Then, mindful of the few chasseurs who were helping to defend the besieged chateau, he played the 'Sidi Brahim'.[1] It had a miraculous effect. Even

1. The march 'Sidi Brahim' was composed to commemorate the victory won by a regiment of chasseurs in Algeria on 24 September 1845, and the anniversary is still kept as a day of celebration by every regiment of French chasseurs. The chasseurs – originally scouts and marksmen – are the equivalent of the fast-marching British Light Infantry regiments.

before the bombardment stopped, the *poilus* surged forward to the windows, clambered up the barricades, and began to fire again. During the shelling the German infantry had retreated to a safe distance and the fusillade did them little harm, but it inspirited the *poilus* beyond belief.

At midday Colonel Lagarde sent a messenger to try to reach Divisional Headquarters, a mile away at Plessier, but he was far from sure that the man would get through the enemy line to reach it. The message he scribbled ended with the fatalistic words 'I am now in the chateau and shall hold on until death.' But, miraculously, the man did succeed in getting through. Reinforcements arrived. A counter-attack was launched. The men in the chateau were relieved, and the Germans were thrust back. All that the enemy managed to retain was the merest foothold on the far edge of the park. They never got any further. The advance stopped at Grivesnes. The line stayed intact.

During the course of Easter Sunday, Sir Douglas Haig received an unwelcome message from General Foch. It informed him that the French Army was still engaged in a critical struggle and that, for the moment, Foch could neither send more troops to Haig's assistance nor extend his own line further north than the road from Roye, the most southern of the roads that converged on Amiens. The British must hold on alone as best they could.

There was no denying that matters were serious in the French line beyond Montdidier, but reinforcements were already arriving, and soon the first trickle would burgeon to a tide which would sweep forward to secure the front. General Pershing had, at last, come up trumps. It had been one thing to attach his troops a few at a time to French and British units for training but, until now, he had jealously guarded against their being used merely as reinforcements. It was Pershing's heartfelt desire that when the Americans had gathered in sufficient strength they should fight under their own flag, as an American army. National pride no less than national honour required it. Now, however, when the fate of the Allies appeared to hang in the balance, the same sense of honour impelled Pershing to act.

Three days earlier he had personally visited General Foch and offered to throw his trained American divisions into the fight, and Foch had thankfully accepted. It was not Pershing's way to be emotional, and the meeting was confined to discussion of practical details, but General Bliss, America's representative on the Supreme War Council, called at Foch's headquarters hard on Pershing's heels and expressed himself more fulsomely. 'We have come over here to get ourselves killed,' he declared to Foch. 'If you want to use us, what are you waiting for?' Foch had wasted no time. It was speedily arranged that two American divisions should immediately take over part of the French line in places which were not immediately threatened, releasing many thousands of French soldiers to take part in the battle now raging in the west. In far-off Lorraine in eastern France the American 26th and 42nd Divisions had been standing by, and on Easter Sunday they were ordered to proceed to the line.

The 42nd Division was not unblooded. It had been in France for many months, its artillery had been in action, and, battalion by battalion, the infantry had served under French tutelage in this sector of the front. This had been comparatively quiet in recent months, but the Division had not escaped all the rigours of the war, and the training camps round Luneville were well within reach of enemy guns searching the back areas. Only two days ago a man of E Company had been killed when a shell burst near the ammunition depot. His name was Everett King, and he was the first casualty among the transport boys of the ammunition column. They were a close-knit bunch, and the officers clubbed together to purchase a fine French casket. Private King was buried on the afternoon of Easter Sunday, before the Division moved up towards the line. The funeral was an incongruous blend of elaborate French obsequies and traditional military ceremony, and Sergeant Earl Teagarden, who organized the firing party, never forgot it. The coffin was conveyed in a glass-sided hearse drawn by black-plumed horses; the officers marched alongside; Teagarden followed at the head of the firing party, and the rest of the company slow-marched behind them along the road to the civilian cemetery. There the chaplain said prayers at the graveside, the American flag was reverently removed from the coffin and handed to the senior officer, and Teagarden's squad fired a volley over the grave. That night they left to take over the Baccarat sector of the French front. Not many of the Doughboys who would die there in the days to come would be buried with such pomp and ceremony.

Every man who could possibly be moved was on his way to strengthen the weakened forces in the forefront of the battle. Setting off from Ypres on the Belgian front, Sergeant Hervey of the 24th Australian Infantry Battalion was struck by the emptiness of the back areas as their train lurched and rattled on its snail-like progress to the south.

*Sergeant Hervey, MM, 24th Infantry Bn., 2nd [Australian] Division, AIF*

In the reserve areas, where thousands of troops had always been encountered, not a single fighting unit remained. A few men on isolated duty here and there, a prison cage with a batch of defaulters, a workshop, or a small staff of soldiers at the baths, with nobody at their usually crowded ablution huts. That was all that marked the deserted camps.

The men couldn't help remarking, 'What if Fritz came at this front now?'

But there was little likelihood that 'Fritz' would attack, for he had his hands full elsewhere. The *Mars* attack on either side of the Scarpe had failed and fizzled out. A counter-attack, north of Arras, had advanced the British line 800 yards, and the Canadians who had taken it over from the 56th Division had moved into a field of dead. They were mostly dead Germans – scattered thick, in brutal testimony to the ferocity of the defence. There were token bombardments and some local skirmishing all along the front, but now it was becoming obvious that the bulk of the immediate German effort would be directed on the capture of Amiens, and as the fighting drew closer the population of Amiens was in flight.

For as long as the British Army had known it, Amiens had been a haven behind the lines. There were barbers where a man could enjoy the rare treat of a shave in hot, clean water, hotels where (if he had the means) he could wallow in the luxury of a bath, and, since most young Frenchmen were away at the front, and the female population had doubled with the influx of refugees and factory workers, there were plenty of friendly mademoiselles who were willing to solace a playful Tommy. There were also cafés and restaurants galore to provide sustenance and hours of uproarious jollity to men of all ranks, and modest *estaminets* where even the meagre pay of a private could stretch to a few beers or a feast of egg and chips. In the rue Cornu sans Tête was Chez Josephine, a favourite haunt of junior subalterns. It was presided over with astonishing speed and efficiency by the proprietress, Josephine herself, who had prospered mightily under their patronage. So many chickens were served at Josephine's that she was popularly supposed to run a poultry farm on the side. Her *pommes frites* were legendary, and her seafood was so delectable that, by the end of an evening, the floor was always several inches deep with the shells of oysters and langoustines which had been served up for the delectation of the officers. Fresh from a diet of Army food, they devoured them by the barrel.

Now, as the fighting approached and shells and bombs were raining on Amiens, even Josephine, businesswoman *extraordinaire*, was clearing out. But she was one of the last to go, and Paul Maze, a regular client of her restaurant, happened to be in Amiens that afternoon.

*Paul Maze*

The enemy had brought up his big guns. He concentrated his fire on all the roads leading to Amiens. At Longueau, an important railway junction just outside Amiens, a hush had fallen. Trains were running no more. The tracks were empty. Just on the outskirts of Amiens, in a network of waterways made by the Somme, where a section of the population cultivated their vegetables, shells were falling, shooting up high spouts of water and smashing the many cloches that were forcing melons and other vegetables for the spring market in Paris. I punted across to one of these small islets to get at some lettuces and fresh radishes, which were delicious after all these days without fresh food.

The bombardment of Amiens had begun. The station roof was already holed, and the town was empty. Some of the shops had been ransacked. The front of the patisserie had been torn open by a shell, and sweets were strewn all over the pavement and across the street. Military police were grimly patrolling the town, which was now out of bounds. The cathedral was being hurriedly protected by a wall of sandbags. Otherwise everybody had gone except Josephine, whom I found packing her cooking utensils into a cart. As I left she called out, '*Tiens, grand*', and threw me one of her last cooked chickens, which I caught like a rugby pass.

The bombardment was not yet inordinately heavy, and, although it was quite heavy enough to frighten its inhabitants, much of the town was still undamaged. On the evening of Good Friday, although the town was already being evacuated, Harold Howitt had succeeded in finding a dry and sheltered lodging in a deserted building. His brigade was still in the line near Villers-Bretonneux, but the new Brigadier who arrived that day had seen immediately that his Brigade-Major was dazed and disoriented by fatigue and lack of sleep after eight days' unremitting effort. He had ordered him back to Amiens for a night's rest, and Howitt had been only too thankful to obey. He had slept the sleep of the dead, and on the morning of Easter Saturday, reasonably refreshed and rested, he had even had time to write to his wife, Dorothy, before he went back to the line.

*Brigade-Major Harold Howitt, 183rd Bde., 61st Division*

30/3/18

My Dearest of All,

I am not going to say that I have not had a stiff time for you would not believe me and it would shake your faith in my reports – I will therefore confess to the worst week I remember, with the assurance that I am perfectly fit & cheery. Till last night I had not slept at all since 20th and have never before been so completely tired – I literally

slept while walking or riding. I have had 6 different Brigade Commanders, besides a long period when I was in command myself, and
yesterday we got our new General who saw I was a bit done and made
me turn in – so I had a perfect night & feel now as fit as a lark.

I could not hope to describe the events of the past 10 days – they
have been incessant battle of the fiercest kind & the details must just
come out by degrees round our own fireside. My little diary has of
course been impossible but I will try some time soon to collect a few
notes – the one I was keeping I tactfully discarded whilst a prisoner
for there were many things in it uncomplimentary to the Hun & they
would have gone against me – as it was they threatened to shoot me
for throwing away a note I had in my hand which they thought was
valuable information but turned out to be nothing.

Col. Wetherall got a nasty wound & I am going to boast that he
owes his life to me. An H.E. splinter got him in the throat whilst
talking to me and severed one of the main arteries & cut his throat –
he gushed all over me & it was a long time before I could stop it, but
he was a model of self-possession & I lay with him for over an hour
till a doctor could be found. All the time the Hun was attacking & I
had to keep one eye on him & the other on messages that were coming
in & yet not let Wetherall know. Finally the Hun was right round us
for he had taken Vesle on our left & there was nothing for it but to
make tracks at once – we had no stretcher so put the old Colonel on
a bike and pushed him along. I hear he is all right & you can look for
his name in the future as one of the soldiers of our day – I have never
met a finer fellow.

Our casualties have of course been terrific & we practically do not
exist as a Brigade – however we are hanging on & hope to do so. The
main Hun thrust is broken & if the weather does not let us down again
we may get our own back yet. However I hope I shan't shock you so
soon after confirmation if I say I am either an atheist or the Diety as
Ye Weather Committee wants the Hun to win – he has favoured him
hourly the whole time.

One of the most pathetic sights has been the evacuation of the
villages with all the refugees & their little Tonys.[1] I have felt ashamed
of myself to see them & yet I don't think we could have done more.
As to our own little Tony I hope he is well – I often think of him &

---

1. 'Little Tony' was the couple's name for the baby Dorothy was expecting.
They were hoping for a boy, but when he was born, in August, 'he' turned out to
be a girl, Mary. However, Tony Howitt (to whom the author is indebted for his
father's papers) did arrive two years later, in happier times.

of you – we will have an even happier time together hereafter because of all this trial & rest assured I have never been more contented in my life nor more sure I was in the right place. I have even felt at times that Providence is keeping me rather specially for you & him for else Heaven knows why I am still here. All is quiet now . . .

Love, love, love,
Harold.

Even by Easter Sunday morning, although most of the residents of Amiens had already quitted the town, isolated groups of refugees were still trudging by as the 13th Battalion, the Rifle Brigade, marched through on their way to reinforce the line. Since arriving at Doullens the previous day they had marched for many miles, they were dog-tired, and, for a fast-stepping rifle regiment, their progress was almost shambling. The battalion was at a low ebb.

*Rifleman C. Shepherd, 13th (Service) Bn., The Rifle Brigade, 37th Division*

Military law says you must have a break of ten minutes every hour. So when we got into Amiens we had a break. We just lay on the cobblestones in the main street. When we was lying there the chaplain came along. His name was the Reverend Pargiter-Owen, and when we got going again I remember he was carrying three men's rifles, the boys were so done in.

All these Froggies were passing us, poor little refugees, and the Padre got in front and he said, 'Sing! Sing any old thing. Let the Froggies see that we're not downhearted. Sing!' Well, we did sing. We marched through Amiens singing, and it brightened us up, made us step out, but I don't suppose the Padre much liked what we sang! It was Scruffy Wharton started it off. He knew fifty different verses to 'Mademoiselle from Armentieres', and every one was worse than the one before! Then, to cap it all, we sang 'One-Eyed Riley'. We sang all the way through Amiens. *Filthy* songs – but the Padre didn't seem to mind. At any rate, he kept us singing. It was Easter Sunday morning, but we didn't have no church parades nor nothing. Well, we couldn't, could we? All the Padre did was make us sing, and I don't suppose he was under the impression they was hymn tunes! He was a good bloke – always up front with us even in the trenches. 'Where my lads are, *I* am!' – that was the idea as far as he was concerned. He wasn't churchy for a padre. He thought more about us, he did.

The reinforcements were wanted not only to strengthen the line, but also to relieve the divisions who were reduced and worn out by a week or more of strenuous fighting. Twelve divisions of the Fifth Army which had been in action since the first day of the offensive were in action still, and part of Howitt's 61st Division, which should have been relieved on 30 March, was obliged to remain in the line in front of Amiens until well into Easter Sunday. But, like the 9th (Scottish) Division, the 36th Division had been relieved by the Australians. The 2nd Royal Irish Rifles had spent the previous night on a railway siding near Amiens.

*Second Lieutenant Tom Witherow, 2nd Bn., The Royal Irish Rifles, 36th (Ulster) Division*

With the dawn of Easter Sunday morning the train arrived and we embarked with joy at the prospect of at least a fortnight's rest in a pleasant part of the country where war and all its horrors were unknown. Our destination was a village called Masnières on the north-west coast of France, not far from Abbeville and the sea. We detrained at Gramaches and marched the remaining miles to Masnières, and how lovely it was to be away from war once again and to feel the joy of life this Easter morning! Here was a rich rural country without any signs of war whatsoever, and we might have been route-marching in Ireland. We arrived at the usual type of French village, billets were allocated, and we all settled down to have a good meal. The men were encamped in the grounds of the chateau, and I got a good bedroom above a small shop where we had our mess. I was exceedingly comfortable. I couldn't believe it. It was wonderful! Of course, when we had parades and took stock, there were horribly few of us, but drafts began to pour in almost immediately to bring us up to strength. They had come straight from England, and most of them were mere boys, just eighteen years of age.

Ted Organ did not see the dawn of that Easter Sunday morning, for he was incarcerated twenty feet underground in a sealed dugout with a bunch of Australians who were none too pleased to be stuck there. They could hardly be blamed, because there was no way out. Organ found it hard to believe that only three days earlier he had been at home in England, where he had enjoyed the enviable privilege of a month's time-expired leave. He had not served a full eight years in the Territorials but, as he had arrived in France in October 1914, and as each year of foreign service counted as the equivalent of two years served at home, his commitment to the Army was theoretically at an end. But in wartime there was no question of discharging

either Territorials or Regulars at the conclusion of their service. Instead they
received a cash bounty and a month's home leave.

On his return from this delightful interlude, Organ was disconcerted to
discover that during his absence the 4th Tank Battalion had been disbanded,
the remaining machines had been sent to replace lost tanks of other units,
and the redundant crews had been formed into a Lewis-gun company.
Organ's old boss, Major Watson, had gone home to Tank HQ at Bovington,
where there was a shortage of experienced officers to train the personnel of
the new and faster tanks, and his driver, now surplus to requirements, was
astonished to find that he had been lent to the Australians and attached to
the 4th Battalion of the Australian Imperial Force. It was something of a
comedown, for he had lost the big staff reconnaissance car which he had
come to regard as his own, but he was allocated a small Sunbeam and sent
off towards Dernancourt with vague instructions to find out the whereabouts
of the front line.

*1745 Corporal Ted Organ, A Sqdn., Queen's Own Oxfordshire Hussars and
Tank Corps*

I kept going until I came to a barbed-wire barricade across the road
and a battery of Australian eighteen-pounders was firing from the bank.
I drove up to the barricade and got out of the car and there was an
Australian sergeant there, and I said, 'How far is the front line from
here?' And he said, 'This *is* the bloody front line. What are you doing
up here?' I said, 'Well, I was told to come up as far as I could and wait
for an officer.' He said, 'Oh, you want to get out of it, mate. It's not
safe here.' Then he said, 'Hey, sport, could you do with a cuppa?' I
said, 'Yes, I certainly could do with a cuppa.' He said, 'Have you got
a mug?' So I went to the little glove compartment in the car, took out
the mug, went down into the dugout.

It should have been a good tea. The abandoned Edgehill Casualty Clearing
Station was just within the Australians' line. It was several days since it had
been evacuated and the patients and staff removed to safety, along with as
many beds and medical supplies as could be packed into lorries. But quantities
of stores and 'comforts' had been left behind, and, although they had been
in position for a very short time, the Aussies, with their notorious instinct
for scrounging, even under fire, had already acquired a quantity of dainties,
with unlimited fresh supplies available for the taking. They had enough tea
to fill their billycans with a brew that was good and strong, lavishly sweetened
with plenty of sugar, and they had jars of delicious extract of malt, which
they spread thick as treacle on their bread. A few men were enjoying these

luxuries as Organ entered their dugout, but he was fated not to share them. The Germans had doubtless observed the arrival of the motor car, and Ted was only halfway down the steps when the explosion of a high-velocity shell blew him the rest of the way. The dugout caved in and the entrance was blocked.

*Corporal Ted Organ*

I didn't get my tea! There was about forty or fifty railway sleepers all collapsed, and there were five or six chaps underneath there. We were there all day. Anyway, it was pitch dark when we got dug out, and when the daylight came we looked out and there was my car upside down on a telegraph pole. It was a touring car, and it was upside down, with the body and the windscreen at an angle on *top* of the telegraph pole.

The 4th Australian Division was in the line just behind the village of Dernancourt, and not far away, on the German side of the line, Hans Schetter was not enjoying the Easter holidays. His observation section had been stuck in the same place since Good Friday.

*Musketier Hans Schetter, 3rd Coy., 231st Reserve Infantry Regt., 50th [German] Division*

This pause is used to bring up more ammunition and other supplies. The railroad system has to be rebuilt behind the front. We don't know how long we will be halted. Many of our troops live in tents which the English left behind. They offer better protection from the rain than our German tarpaulins. Our lieutenant's orderly goes at noon to fetch our daily rations from the kitchen, and we are getting hungry waiting for his return. We finally decide to look for him, but we find him dead. Our aluminium mess tins, half-filled with food, are still in his hands. A large shell splinter had killed him instantly. We spend the afternoon in low spirits in our tent. Our cigarette smoke drifts away slowly into the damp air, and we put our heads down on our knapsacks. The English shells are crashing down endlessly, and the steel fragments fly through the air for hundreds of metres. One hears them cutting the air and landing in the soft earth around us, and the explosions are so close that we decide to move. We retire about 500 metres with others of our company and get orders to entrench here, so we dig in again.

We have dug a hole one metre deep in a French farmer's rye field. We fill the bottom with rye-grass and make a roof from boards and an English tarpaulin. Near us we have some Navy personnel with small ships' cannons to help repulse English tank attacks. These Navy men have been especially successful in finding alcohol – as we can see from the many empty bottles near their position. They also sing happily until late into the night. Our field kitchen has only sparse supplies for us, and the kitchen personnel go into the villages to requisition flour and other provisions. The weather is miserable – cold and rainy – but we are happy that the shooting has diminished. Daily we await the order to attack. So, through the Easter holidays of 1918, we live in low spirits, sitting in the rain in a rye field with tobacco as our only diversion.

Stuck in the dreary fields outside Albert, the German soldiers who were not close enough to a village to forage for foodstuff were having a miserable time. They had advanced so far that they had long ago outrun their supply lines, and rations were short. The Tommies and the Diggers on the other side were well off by comparison – so well off that they could afford to turn up their noses at the rations supplied by the Army: there were better pickings to be had. This pleasant region, which just a week ago was miles behind the battlefront, had been so recently evacuated that it was a veritable land of milk and honey, where, as close to the front as the support line, a soldier could live like a lord. On Easter Sunday morning Major Harrison Johnston's battalion was moved back into reserve at La Houssoye.

*Major Harrison Johnston, 15th (Service) Bn., The Cheshire Regt., 35th Division*

During our stay in this bit of the line we had certain unusual luxuries, such as rabbits (out of hutches), pigeons (shot off roofs) and chickens – all of which might have starved or been killed by shell-fire had we not have saved them! Champagne also was greatly enjoyed (the bottles would certainly have been broken). A certain amount of drinkable red wine and a good supply of vegetables of all kinds were also available. I saw some very funny sights in that village. A very senior officer walking down the main street with a twelve-bore shotgun (salved from the chateau) shooting pigeons! He told me that he'd had champagne for his breakfast for the first time in his life. The men's stew, for *one* meal, had fifty-seven chickens and umpteen fresh vegetables in it, and they also enjoyed pigeons etc. cooked in the most weird ways and always with potatoes. Cattle were collected and driven back, but I saw very many that were killed or maimed by shells.

It went without saying that such animals were butchered and cooked without compunction. It was no longer necessary to rely on abandoned canteens and dumps to replace rations or to forage as they had been obliged to during the retreat, though some men still had sizeable hoards of chocolate and cigarettes which they had managed to carry back. The gunners, with their wheeled transport, came off best of all, but Sergeant Alex Dunbar had a nasty moment during one rearguard action. On lifting the lid of the gun limber, expecting to find twenty-four rounds of ammunition, which were instantly and urgently required, he was appalled to find that it contained several dozen tins of condensed milk. He scrounged a few rounds from the other guns, but, seized by devilment, and 'just for luck', he placed one of the tins in front of the first shell he fired – and wondered ever afterwards if some hapless German soldier had died for Kaiser and Fatherland through a random blow from a tin of milk descending at high velocity. The idea amused him, and yet he was strangely disturbed. It seemed so much more personal than the firing of a mere shell. For years afterwards the memory resurfaced from time to time and continued to worry him.

Throughout the Easter weekend the lost sheep had been gradually returning to the fold as the troops who had been fighting alongside the French were slowly being pulled out and sent back to the Fifth Army. The 10th Essex arrived at midnight on Good Friday in a procession of jolting buses that had brought them from Vic-sur-Aisne, roughly forty miles south-west of Amiens as the crow flies. But a crow could fly over enemy territory, and the distance measured across a long circuitous route behind the Allied lines was several times as great. The journey had lasted twenty bruising hours – the last in the chain of eventful moves since they had retired from Ly-Fontaine. This time at least they had not had to fight along the way as they had been fighting for the past week.

It had not required many buses to transport the Essex, for there were not very many of them left. On his return to France after his interrupted leave, Colonel Frizell had experienced some difficulty in tracking down his battalion before he eventually found them at the village of Autrèches, a long way south of Noyon and quite near the forest of Compiègne. It had been his intention to congratulate his men on their excellent performance, but, as he stood facing the Battalion when it paraded, the CO was incapable of uttering a word. The men were hollow-eyed, bedraggled, exhausted, and there were hardly enough to make up a decent-sized company. After a long and awkward silence, the Colonel managed to speak. 'Well done, men. Dismiss.' It was not much of a eulogy, but it was the best he could do.

Colonel Frizell had hoped that the men might at least have one good night's rest, but the Army had ordered otherwise. Shortly after midnight the 10th Essex had set off on a slog of three miles to Vic-sur-Aisne, to board the buses that would carry them north. Their destination was the village of Gentelles, in the support line of the battlefield in front of Amiens.

*Captain R. Chell, MC, 10th Bn., The Essex Regt., 18th Division*

In the thick darkness we had no idea where we were, but all was very quiet, and the whitewashed houses of the village looked comfortable and inviting. It did not take long to allot the village for billets, for we found it completely evacuated. We were the sole inhabitants, with every comfort to gladden our tired senses. There were cockerels crowing, hens cackling, and pigs snorting, alarmed at the unusual tramp of feet. Hunger had been hard to bear, but here was the reward. Next day we gorged on fowl and pig. So lavishly did we feed on these that for long afterwards the sight of feathered fowl and bristled beast awakened the feelings of a sea voyage! With mouths full of fowl, and with cooks working at high pressure feathering and roasting more, we were moved out on 30 March, Easter Saturday, about a thousand yards east of the village, and dug another defensive line. Instead of finding ourselves going back to Gentelles that evening to renew the interrupted feast, we were ordered to concentrate near the village of Hangard, and to take over the line from the Australians.

They moved into the line on sloping ground between the hamlet of Hangard and Lancer Wood. Until two days earlier this unimpressive strip of woodland had been referred to when necessary as 'the nameless wood', to distinguish it from its larger neighbour, Hangard Wood, a short distance behind it. It was the Australians who had suggested it should be renamed in honour of the 12th Lancers, who had galloped forward squadron after squadron in a classic cavalry charge and, fighting at close quarters, swept the enemy back and cleared the way so that the 33rd Australian Infantry could advance. Australians were not usually left breathless in admiration of the exploits of their British colleagues, but this time they were, and the change of name which their commander graciously proposed was now adopted.

After years of static warfare and ignominious service as dismounted troops, the cavalry had at last come into their own, and their appearance at the battlefront, like that of the Australians, had done wonders for the morale of the battle-worn troops. All weekend the cavalry had been heavily engaged as the fighting swayed back and forth around Moreuil at the junction of the French and British armies. Six miles north-east of Grivesnes and halfway between Montdidier and Amiens, the small town of Moreuil stands on the banks of the River Avre as it pursues a meandering course to swell the waters

of the Somme. The importance of this place lay in the high ground behind
it, which gave an uninterrupted view of all the ground to the west of Moreuil
Wood on the crest of the slopes. If the Germans held this, as they seemed
determined to do, it would give them a dangerous advantage. If they thrust
out beyond it, the tenuous link between the thinly spread French and British
troops might well be snapped, the line to the north rolled up, and Amiens
captured.

During Easter weekend, as cavalry and infantry fought the enemy for
possession, the wood and the town in the Avre valley beneath it changed
hands many times. By nightfall on the 31st, after the mighty German effort
along the line between Montdidier and Amiens, and beyond to Albert and
the Ancre, only a sliver of Moreuil Wood remained in British hands. The
enemy had also captured Rifle Wood, lying a short way to the north, almost
on the roadside of the highway into Amiens. The cavalry were ordered up
to counter-attack and retrieve the situation. They attacked on the morning
of Easter Monday.

*Trooper H. Ward, A Sqdn., Queen's Own Oxfordshire Hussars*

April the first, we went into action about nine o'clock in the morning.
(I remember thinking it was April Fool's Day.) The guns fired a
bombardment – quite a short one it was – and then we went over the
top dismounted. Not that there was a top to go over, as such! We
were near a road that went up a slight incline to the top. Funnily
enough we took the pack-horses up with us that time. I was No. 1
on the machine-gun, and we had a pack-horse with the gun and
ammunition. The officer was in front of me, just a few yards, and he
was shouting, 'Come on! Come on!' And there was a machine-gun
firing at us just at the side of the road, about thirty or forty yards in
front, and of course the horses were scared. You could hear the *pwhht
pwhht* of these bullets going past and the horses were hanging back, so
I went behind the horse and gave it a smack to make it go forward.
The officer was killed by that machine-gun: Second Lieutenant Dove
he was – hadn't been with us very long, and down he went. So we
carried on, myself and my other gunner, Stanmore, and we made it.
The Germans had got this high ridge to look over Amiens, and the
infantry had tried several times to take it and they couldn't, so the
cavalry was called in to take it, and we did.

We went in with the Canadians – good riders them. But out of our
machine-gun section Stanmore and myself were the only two that got
right up to the top of the wood. There were eight guns and all the
others were knocked out. The officers had all gone. So we just stayed

there and kept firing until they came up to consolidate the line and
we went back to the horses and were relieved.

Rifle Wood, at all events, had been recaptured, though the attack had
been less fortunate at Moreuil. But the situation was reasonably secure,
and General Rawlinson was quick to send messages of congratulation to
encourage the troops. They might have been even more encouraged had
they known that General Ludendorff had called a temporary halt. After the
near-debacle of the abortive *Mars* offensive on the 30th, he had hoped to
pound his way towards Amiens on the 31st through a series of strong assaults
along the rest of the Allied line. But the defence had been infuriatingly
obdurate. Late in the evening of 31 March, even before the full extent of
German losses was known, Ludendorff was forced to a reluctant decision.
In view of 'the disappointing results' of the day's fighting, it was useless to
continue until he had restored his supply lines and relieved or reinforced
the weariest of his troops. Some of his staff were in favour of calling a halt
entirely, but Ludendorff made it clear that he had no intention of giving up.
He was adamant that the next bid to secure Amiens must succeed, and he
decreed that preparations should continue.

He also set a date for the renewal of the assault. It would take place four
days hence – on 4 April.

# Chapter 22

North and south of Amiens, not every soldier on the Allied front was aware that the Germans had slackened their offensive, for General Ludendorff had ordered his divisional commanders to keep up the pressure. They were to attack wherever possible, to keep the enemy busy while he brought up troops and guns, and to improve the line where it was awkwardly situated, to give them a good start on the race to Amiens.

But the fighting was isolated and intermittent, and in some places there was a noticeable lull. It encouraged an aged pair of civilians to climb out of a cellar near Dernancourt beneath the astonished gaze of a patrol of Australians. Private Stanley Sutcliffe's company had just moved up to the front line, and they regarded it as a pleasant change after their stint in reserve trenches directly in front of the guns. The firing in support of the fighting at Dernancourt had never seemed to stop, and, although the Aussies of the 12th Brigade relished abundant feeds of roast pork, chickens, and even geese, their stay in the reserve line had been far from peaceful. They were thankful to escape from the constant din, and their comrades of the 13th Brigade were equally thankful to quit the front line when the 12th came up to relieve them. They had undoubtedly had the worst of it, but by the time Sutcliffe and his companions took over the line the fighting had temporarily died down.

*Private Stanley Sutcliffe, 51st Bn., 4th [Australian] Division, AIF*

Things were so quiet we hardly knew the Germans were there at all. At night we would go up to the outposts with rations and come back to Edgehill Clearing Station, which had been evacuated. Here we salvaged cases of surgical instruments and plenty of clothing and blankets, and we also got a lot of tinned food of different kinds and big jars of extract of malt. We had nothing to do, only a little bombing in the streets of Dernancourt. Then this old Frenchman and his wife came wandering into our lines. They were both about sixty years old and, from what they told us, they had taken cover in their cellar immediately the first bombardment opened up and had been there for

six days without any food. All that time the 12th Brigade had been
fighting like fury, and their house was being blown to bits above their
heads. They could hardly walk! We gave them a good feed and the
old man got some cigarettes, and then they were escorted back behind
the line and taken out of it altogether.

No matter how humble his abode, how meagre his plot of land, a French
countryman was not willingly parted from his property, and not many miles
away another French civilian who had been clinging tenaciously to his roots
had also been 'escorted back and taken out of it'. But he had been taken by
the Germans and escorted back behind the enemy line. Émile Goulieux was
particularly unhappy, for it was the second time he had been uprooted and
sent far into the hinterland of occupied France, where life was not easy
under the restrictive rule of the Germans. It was hard enough for the local
population trying to sustain normal life, but it was a thousand times worse
for the incomers evacuated from places close to the fighting fronts and
dumped willy-nilly in districts far from home. Deprived of their means of
livelihood, billeted on reluctant local landlords, they had to shift for themselves as best they could, working in the fields when there was work to be
had and depending on the charity of the Germans when there was not.

Jean Dignoire, who had been the stationmaster at Bapaume, had been
evacuated with his wife and daughter in the early summer of 1916, when
the Allies had launched their offensive on the Somme, and Émile Goulieux
had been in the same batch of evacuees. They had been sent to the village
of Vertain, twelve miles east of Cambrai and some thirty miles from home.
It was no great distance measured on the map, but it seemed so far away
from France that it had become almost a matter of course to call it 'Germany'.
Then, as the war tightened its grip, as food grew scarce, the Germans
themselves began to feel the pinch and were anxious to rid themselves of
the burden of feeding useless mouths.

*Mme Flora Verdel (née Dignoire)*

Early in 1917 the authorities in the village of Vertain offered to allow
a certain category of refugee – the oldest and the youngest – to be
repatriated to unoccupied France via Switzerland, which was neutral
of course. So a lot of them decided to go, including this little old chap,
Monsieur Goulieux, whom we had got to know well. Quite a number
of people went, and we waved them off a little enviously when they
started for the east. I remember seeing Monsieur Goulieux carrying
his belongings in a small suitcase. He was very happy to go!

After a long journey, which took him through Belgium and Germany to Switzerland, and then back into France to Lyons, on to Paris and then eventually to the north, he managed to get back to his own district, which had been liberated by the British in March 1917, because it was given up by the Germans when they went back to the Hindenburg Line. It took him many, many months. It was the end of 1917 before he got there, and even then civilians were not encouraged to go back. But he had managed it, and he settled down not far from his village. It had been completely destroyed (I have an idea that it was somewhere round Suzanne, or Bray-sur-Somme), but he built himself a hut from material he recovered from the debris, and he even started to lay out a little garden. He was there only one or two weeks when the Germans advanced again, and they advanced so rapidly that the poor man didn't have time to get away. He was caught *again*, poor Monsieur Goulieux!

One day, just about the beginning of April, we saw a new batch of refugees trailing into the village, and we were amazed to see Monsieur Goulieux carrying the same little suitcase – just as we had seen him leaving nearly a year before! He was actually sent back to Vertain – the very same village! We were in the street at the time, and he saw us and called out to us. He had to travel at least fifteen hundred kilometres to get away, but he only had to go a few dozen kilometres to get back. He called out to us, 'Next time I go to France, I'm telling you, I'd rather go by tram-car!'

Fritz Nagel was also on a leisurely journey through 'Germany', but it was leisurely by his own choice. To Nagel's delight, he had been ordered back to attend a course at the German Artillery School at Lille, and he was taking his time about getting there. It was a justifiable indulgence, for the course was not due to start until 6 April and he felt that he had earned a holiday. The last few days at the front had not been pleasant and, with the change in the weather and few aeroplanes to be seen, Nagel's anti-aircraft gun crew had had nothing to do but stay put and shelter from the insistent shelling of British guns.

*Leutnant Fritz Nagel, Anti-Aircraft Gun Bty. K Flak 82*

Albert was crumbling under heavy bombardment, so we tried to find some reasonably safe position in the fields. It was cold, rainy, wet and misty, we were in little slit trenches, hastily dug for protection, and the idea of remaining there made us shiver. Everything was peaceful – no small-arms fire could be heard anywhere. Then out of the fog came a major, all wrapped up in a cloak, and he stalked towards us through the mud, swinging his cane as one would at a trespasser. He

began shouting, telling me to go away. What could we do with that
silly little gun? His men had suffered enough, and when the fog lifted
the enemy would zero in on us and hit his men in the trench. He
threatened that they would take pot-shots at us if we didn't disappear
right away. I tried to reason with him, but the man was hysterical. We
left.

I saw a tidy-looking dugout about forty metres away from us, so I
went over to take a look. I had entered many of these enemy dugouts
and they were poorly constructed compared to ours, but this one
looked good – and it even had a small window in the rear. Although
the light was so dim, I was shocked to see two English officers at a
table, one sleeping with his head on his arm and the other sitting
straight up, both with their caps on. This stupefied me, and I stood
there wondering if they would say 'Hello.' Then I realized they were
dead. To see those men so motionless and rigid made my heart pound.

After his initial shock, Nagel had been sorely tempted to rifle the contents
of the dugout, and even the bodies, for he coveted the dead officers' leather
boots, but, remembering rumours of booby traps, he had refrained. There
was nothing for it but to remain in the open and shiver in the rain. It had
been some comfort when he received a message signed, to his astonishment,
by a full general.

Command of 23rd. Reserve Corps
Headquarters April 1, 1918

In the name of His Majesty the Emperor and King I am decorating
Leutnant der Reserve Nagel of K Flak 82 with the Iron Cross 1st
Class.

Nagel had been delighted by the honour, but he was even happier when,
shortly afterwards, he was ordered to leave his battery and proceed to the
Artillery School at Lille.

Hans Schetter was also informed that he was to receive the Iron Cross (in
his case second class). As long as the inclement weather lasted, Schetter's
observation section had as little to do as Nagel's anti-aircraft crew, but they
were not lucky enough to be relieved. Two had been wounded by shrapnel
and evacuated, and the others were still crouched in their wet bivouac in
the rye field, waiting for the rain to go off, for the shelling to abate, and for
notice of the next attack.

Now that the German offensive appeared to have been checked, the
question of the next attack was also uppermost in the minds of the Allied

commanders. It was clear that Ludendorff would make another strike, but no one could be sure where or when. Sir Douglas Haig was convinced that the new thrust would come somewhere on the British front, and, in the front's present state, he was doubtful if he could withstand a second major blow. He was pressing General Foch to launch an offensive from some part of the French front south of Amiens to pre-empt the enemy strike and draw Ludendorff's forces away from his own dangerously thinned and weakened line. Foch had promised to do so 'as soon as possible', but, although his strength was steadily increasing with the arrival of reinforcements, there were as yet no concrete plans.

Foch was far from reluctant to fight but he was dissatisfied with his own position, which he regarded as ambivalent, for, while he had been given the overall task of co-ordinating Allied operations, he did not have the power of command that would enable him to control them or to orchestrate the strategy of future Allied initiatives. Without such power he could not count on the wholehearted co-operation of General Pétain, his equal in rank and seniority. Foch complained to Clemenceau that the authority he had been given by the delegates at Doullens was insufficient, and Clemenceau agreed to call another Allied conference with a view to appointing Foch to the *de facto* position of generalissimo of the Allied armies on the Western Front. It was hastily arranged to take place at Beauvais on Wednesday 3 April.

The British representatives left London late on Tuesday evening, spent the night at Folkestone, and sailed for France at 8.30 the following morning. They did not enjoy the crossing. Instead of travelling in the relative comfort of a destroyer, the British Prime Minister Lloyd George, Chief of the Imperial General Staff Sir Henry Wilson, Secretary to the War Cabinet Sir Maurice Hankey and a clutch of accompanying officials were squeezed into the narrow confines of a 'P boat'. This pursuit craft was not much more than a glorified motor-launch, with little enough accommodation for a maximum crew of eight, and none at all for passengers. But no other craft was available, for every destroyer, every steamer, every escort ship, was engaged in ferrying reinforcements across the Channel to the front.

A convoy of staff cars was waiting on the quayside at Boulogne to convey the Prime Minister's party on the four-hour journey to Beauvais. Sir Henry Wilson and Lloyd George entered the leading vehicle, and, although there had been no chance to stretch their legs, its spacious comfort was a welcome relief after the spartan conditions of the crossing.

At Montreuil, where they stopped to pick up Sir Douglas Haig with his Chief of Staff, Sir Henry Lawrence, Wilson gave up his place in the first car and invited Lawrence to join him in the second, while Lloyd George, with a show of geniality, ushered the Commander-in-Chief to the vacant seat in his own car. On the face of it this was a chance arrangement, but it had been carefully planned in advance. Lloyd George, ever manipulative, was not driven by the desire for convivial companionship on the journey, nor would he have found it in Sir Douglas Haig, whose icy courtesy did not mask the fact that he disliked and despised the talkative Welshman, so different in his views and in his personality to Haig himself. His dislike was reciprocated, and the two men had been at odds too many times in the past to have any mutual sympathy, but, as Prime Minister, Lloyd George had had the upper hand. He now wished to have a private conversation with Sir Douglas Haig on a topic which had none of the cosy connotations usually associated with a tête-à-tête. It concerned General Gough, and he launched into the attack as soon as they drove off. Gough must not be employed again. On Gough's shoulders lay the entire responsibility for the present crisis. Gough was unworthy to command, and he must be sent home immediately. Gough must be disgraced, and seen to be disgraced. Public opinion demanded it, the Prime Minister alleged, and wounded soldiers of the Fifth Army, now at home, were wild in imprecation of their commander – or so he claimed. He ranted and raved. He wanted Gough's head on a charger, and he ordered Haig to get rid of him for good and all.

Haig resisted furiously.

I pointed out that 'fewer men, extended front, and increased hostile forces' were the main causes to which the retreat may be attributed. He was much down upon Gough. I championed the latter's case. 'He had very few reserves, a very big front entirely without defensive works, recently taken over from the French, and the weight of the enemy's attack fell on him,' I said. Also that, in spite of a most difficult situation, he had never really lost his head. L. G. said he had not held the Somme bridges, nor destroyed them, and that G. must not be employed. To this I said I could not condemn an officer unheard and that if L. G. wishes him suspended he must send me an order to that effect. L. G. seems a 'cur' and when I am with him I cannot resist a feeling of distrust of him and his intentions.

The Prime Minister was unmoved by Haig's defence. He hardly listened. By the time they reached Abbeville there was no more to be said and each man was too incensed to suffer the company of the other any longer. When the cavalcade halted briefly and Haig and Wilson changed places in their respective cars it was noticed that the face of the Commander-in-Chief, normally so imperturbable, was white with anger. But by the time they reached Beauvais and joined their French hosts for a late lunch Haig had recovered his composure.

Later, at the formal conference, at which General Pershing represented the USA, it was agreed that General Foch's powers should be extended to enable him to exercise control over future Allied operations, and with only one proviso – if any Allied commander believed that his army was endangered by a decision of General Foch he would have the right to appeal to his own Government.[1]

No one was more supportive of Foch or more fulsome in declaring his acceptance of the proposal than Lloyd George, and he was as voluble in his insistence that the British public were united in their desire that Foch should be given real power as he had been in declaring their supposed condemnation of General Gough. Haig said little except to acquiesce with grace to the proposals put forward at the meeting. He was not looking forward to his interview with General Gough.

In accordance with Haig's most recent instructions, Gough had already begun to set up a Reserve Army headquarters at Crécy, not far from Montreuil, but out of consideration for his Commander-in-Chief, and well aware of his discomfiture, Gough reacted with tight-lipped dignity to the news of his final dismissal. Haig made it clear that it was none of his doing. 'I am sorry to lose you, Hubert,' he said, adding that there would undoubtedly be an inquiry, at which Gough would certainly be vindicated. With this crumb of comfort, Sir Hubert Gough made his sad departure and left immediately for home.[2]

1. Although Foch acted from then on as General-in-Chief of the Allies, it was not until 14 May that his position was formalized and he was given that official title.

2. Despite pressure from General Gough and his friends, every request for a formal inquiry was subsequently refused. It was believed by many, not without reason, that an impartial inquiry into the circumstances which led to the retirement of the Fifth Army under General Gough might, in vindicating him, have laid the ultimate responsibility on the shoulders of the Government, which, for political reasons, had insisted on the extension of the British line and denied the reinforcements which might have enabled the Fifth Army to repel a major assault. As long as three months after General Gough's dismissal, a member of the Army Council, Sir Sam Fay, made a significant entry in his diary: 'July 3rd. Army Council Meeting. Question of Gough and retreat of March 21st discussed. No report from Haig. Considered that any report would lead to higher game than Haig, viz: War Cabinet and thinning of the line.' As Duff Cooper was to put it succinctly in his biography of Haig (Faber and Faber, 1935), '. . . the Government would not dare to institute an inquiry which might so easily have ended by the prosecutor finding himself in the dock'. General Gough, alone of the Army Commanders, was not invited to the victory celebrations, nor did he receive the decorations awarded to the others. Not until 1937 was he awarded the GCB by King George VI. At the King's own wish, he was invited to Buckingham Palace for a private ceremony weeks in advance of the official investiture. 'After all,' said the King, 'he's had to wait a long time, poor man. I don't see why he should be kept waiting any longer.' Handing the order to General Gough, the

Haig had also hinted that his own fate was in the balance and that he himself quite expected to be sent home within the week. He had indeed offered his resignation over the Gough affair, and Lloyd George, who would have liked nothing better than to be shot of him, was sorely tempted to accept it. But Sir Henry Wilson dissuaded the Prime Minister from acting hastily. Haig was too popular. To replace him might shake the confidence of the Army and reflect badly on the Government. And, besides, there was no officer of sufficient rank more qualified to take his place – at least, at the moment. No one could fight a defensive battle better than Haig, and Wilson's advice to Lloyd George was to wait a while. The time to 'get rid of Haig', as he put it, would be when the present crisis was over and the situation had calmed down.

It was after nine o'clock in the evening before Lloyd George's party arrived back at Boulogne. As they paced the quayside waiting to board the 'P boat' for the return crossing to Folkestone, soldiers were streaming down the gangways of a Channel steamer, wallowing low in the water under the weight of a multitude of men. Sir Maurice Hankey was not much cheered by the sight, for in his eyes they were hardly men at all. They were 'lads of 18 or 19 for the most part. They belonged to some Scottish regiment and in the glimmer of the dimmed arc lights looked pale and pathetically young.' The scene, he admitted, 'remains graven in my memory'.[1]

The Prime Minister's party eventually reached London at 2.30 a.m. and, having been on the go for more than twenty hours, thankfully retired to bed. Long before they woke again, Ludendorff's armies were moving to the assault in a final bid to capture Amiens. It was 4 April.

In the early hours of the morning the heavens opened and it began to teem with rain. By half past four, when the guns began to bombard the Allied lines, the Germans were already wringing wet, for they were working flat out to keep to the prearranged timetable and rain-capes would have hindered them. It was worst for the men who loaded the shells and slammed them home with wet hands, chilled red-raw, while their feet, shod in insubstantial boots, sank ever deeper into the wet ground. The earth, already drenched by two days of rain, rapidly became a quagmire, and with every shell and every recoil the trails of the guns in their ill-prepared positions drove further into the mud. But the firing continued, and the sound of the bombardment

---

King remarked, 'I suppose you can take this as a recognition of the gratitude of your country.' (Quoted in *Goughie: The Life of General Sir Hubert Gough*, by Anthony Farrar-Hockley (Hart-Davis, MacGibbon, 1975).)

1. Lord Hankey, *The Supreme Command 1914–1918*, Vol. II (George Allen & Unwin, 1961).

gave encouragement to the German infantrymen assembling for the attack beneath the streaming skies. But it was a far cry from the prelude to the battle just two weeks ago, with its certainty of victory. This time there was no stirring message from the Kaiser to spur them on, and the shallow trenches, rapidly filling with water as the hours dragged on, were no substitute for the fine shelters and trenches where they had assembled two weeks earlier to launch the Kaiser's Battle. The weather then had been different too. Soaked and sleepless, the German soldiers now crouched beneath the rain, doing their best to cover the rifles that would save their bacon in the morning. Equally cold and wet and miserable, the Allied soldiers opposite, alerted by the bombardment, took what cover they could, and waited to meet the attack. SOS signals soaring above the Allied lines flared against glistening curtains of rain that streamed down without remission. The murky dawn was slow to break, and when the light began to crawl across the battlefield there was again a thick mist.

The 15th Bavarian Infantry Regiment were at Moreuil, and it was past four o'clock in the morning before their orders arrived. In four hours' time they were to attack Génoville Farm. There was no time to brief the men, and hardly time to inform company leaders of anything except their bare instructions – nor was there time to give the men a meal before they went into action. There was nothing for it but to go ahead and do the best they could. It was ten past eight in the morning when they set off.

Inevitably, without detailed orders and the customary meticulous planning, things went awry from the start. It was true that they managed to burst beyond the borders of the small town of Moreuil, pushing back the thin line of French troops who had clung on to them, but the reserves, who should have awaited the signal to go forward to reinforce and exploit the advance, set off early and followed so closely that they were drawn too soon into the fight. French machine-guns, ripping through the clustered ranks, caused mayhem. The German machine-gun teams, moving across the fields to support the assault, were bogged down in the claggy earth. The infantry scattered and tried to shelter behind the trusses of straw that littered the farmland, but these gave little protection from the punishing fire. Leutnant Joseph Kübler was horrified. 'This hillside of corpses and wounded,' he said, 'was one of the most horrible sights that I saw in this war.'

Those who survived pressed on. They pressed on towards the village of Rouvrel, but Rouvrel was a stronghold now. There were machine-guns in the houses and in the tower of the church, and they spewed such merciless fire that the Germans could make no headway.

*Leutnant Joseph Kübler, 15th Bavarian Infantry Regt., 2nd Bavarian Division*

Our own losses became ever greater, the battlelines ever thinner. One could detect enemy reserves moving up to the front at a distance of about eighteen hundred yards. The enemy's artillery fire intensified. Our own was silent. At the front all was chaos and confusion – scrambled companies, scrambled regiments, even some people from another division.

They had advanced their line a little – a very little – but the cost had been enormous and the advantage was insignificant.

Ludendorff's plan on the first day of the assault was to attack across the front which ran south from the River Somme as far as Grivesnes and to capture ground from which his heavy guns could fire northward to bombard Amiens. The line at Grivesnes did not budge, and the advance at Moreuil, such as it was, was not nearly enough to achieve his object. North of Moreuil, where the British joined hands with the French at Hangard, the attack fell across the front where Villers-Bretonneux stood on the Roman road that led directly to Amiens.

Although it was now destined to enter the history books with a certain aura of glory, Villers-Bretonneux had no previous claim to fame. It was a small manufacturing town, prosperous enough, and not unimportant to the peacetime economy of the region. It had nine cotton mills, three brickworks and a hat factory, which provided ample employment for its 5,000 inhabitants. Now the inhabitants had fled – except for one household, and the fact that this lady and her brood of children had remained was entirely due to a single, anonymous Australian soldier, who happened to pass as she was loading her household goods on to a wooden cart. He stopped and looked her straight in the eye. 'You needn't go, Ma,' he said. 'The Aussies are here. Best stay where you are.' He even helped her to unload the cart and carry her possessions back into her house. She may or may not have understood the words, but his friendly grin and his stalwart frame must have been sufficient reassurance. For better or worse, and almost alone of the townspeople, she stayed. She perhaps had reason to regret her decision in the days that followed.

The towers of Amiens, less than ten miles distant, were clearly visible from Villers-Bretonneux on its shoulder of flat land astride the Roman road. The ground fell away on either side, to the banks of the Somme north of the plateau and to the River Luce to the south of it, and the dead ground – the clefts and gullies in the valleys – could only give advantage to an enemy creeping forward to fight for the high ground above. It was a commanding position. The battlefront ran across it, and across both valleys, and the British

Army was disposed in depth behind it. But this was not an army as the military would once have understood it, for there was a brigade here and a brigade there, and divisions that were divisions only in name, reinforced by battalions, even companies, thrust haphazardly into the line – a conglomeration of units, growing all the time as troops arrived from the north and men who had retreated south with the French Army were brought back.

The fighting raged all day as the rain continued to pour down, and, although the line was pushed back in certain places, nowhere did it give way. The gunners did as much as anyone to repulse the attacks and hold the enemy back.

*Lance-Bombardier Robert Ford, C 157 Bty., Royal Field Artillery*

It was literally all hands on deck, so to speak. I mean, I wasn't a gunner. I was with the ammunition column, a driver. To be honest, I don't know where we got the ammunition from, but we were taking it up to the guns and they were firing for the best part of the day. We had no signals, of course, no telephone lines or anything. About midday I was ordered to go on one of the guns as relief to one of the gunners. I'd never been on a gun in my life, and I had to take what they call No. 2. They all have numbers, you see. On a field gun you sit on the gun that's firing – there's a seat each side of the breech. Well, I had to sit on the right-hand side, and my job was to line up the range drum so that it registered 1,000 yards, and the bombardier in charge of the gun was on the left-hand side, and he did the gun laying, which was the actual aiming. When the gun fires it recoils, and, as the recoil recovers, the No. 2 puts his hand out, gets hold of the handle of the breech, swings the breech open, and out comes the old shell-case. The gunner standing there pops a new shell in and it's ready to fire again. No. 1 does the firing as well, of course.

Well, I roughly knew what to do, but the first shell that went off nearly killed me. The noise! I thought someone had cut my throat! I got partly accustomed to it, but after about two hours my right ear was completely deaf, so I asked for permission to come off, and they let me go and put someone else on. That's the first and last time I ever actually worked a gun. How those chaps can stand it for hours I don't know at all! I was only too glad to get back to carting shells. I was completely deaf. My left ear came back after two days, but my right ear never recovered. Whether I did any good on that gun, whether I got the range right and they managed to hit anyone, I have no idea!

It was inky-dark night when the fighting died down. The rain abated and a watery moon appeared behind the scudding clouds, but it was a miserable night on the battlefield. The troops of both sides laboured through the mud, hauling up fresh supplies of ammunition for the guns and food for the men in front, carrying off the wounded, floundering back and forth with messages and orders, slogging through darkness and mud to take up new positions, or working to consolidate and strengthen the positions they now held. Two battalions of the 9th Australian Brigade, who were dissatisfied with their position and more than a little put out by the fact that they had been pushed back during the day, at one o'clock in the morning crept forward in the dark and took back the trench they had lost in the afternoon. The night was noisy with guns, but on the German side the firing was haphazard and desultory. The gunners were saving their efforts for the morning, when Ludendorff would play his last card.

Behind the German line the troops were already moving into position for the assault. In the early hours of the morning Hubert Schroeter marched through Albert and down the road where Fritz Nagel and the men of K Flak 82 had had their thrilling escapade as they had tried to help forward the last abortive attack. The Jägers moved into position behind the railway embankment and in front of the post which Alex Jamieson had so thankfully quitted a few nights before. The post was stronger now, for the Australians were there in force, and the German boys were well aware that, with new reserves and new defensive positions, the line was strongly held. In the morning, when the barrage lifted, it would be their job to storm it.

Ludendorff's plan on the second day was to widen the attack to the north. After the lamentable results of the previous day it was apparent that there was nothing to be gained by pressing on south of Hangard on the French front. The full force of the attack was to fall on both sides of the road to Amiens and beyond the River Somme, up the valley of the Ancre where the line ran through Aveluy Wood, and over the Auchonvillers Ridge to Puisieux and Bucquoy.

George McKay and the Lewis-gun team were still in the line. In the absence of his corporal, who had been mildly shell-shocked, George had been in charge of the team moving to different parts of the New Zealanders' front and helping to beat off local attacks as the Germans nibbled and probed at their line. Yesterday the corporal had returned, and George had handed over the gun with mixed feelings.

*Private George McKay, 1st Bn., NZ Rifle Brigade*

If they had put that gun completely in my charge quite a while before they did, it would have been a much better team. The corporal we had, he was not only half-pai, shell-shock, he was practically a nervous wreck before we finished.[1] When he came back after his rest and I made him take charge of the gun, which I did against his will, I told him I wasn't going to be in a position where they could say I had legs on my belly, crawling for promotion.

Well, here was a hill, La Signy Farm, and some fellows had dug a front-line trench there, and we had to keep men in it. We'd been up to the outposts for a week, and we came back for one night there on 4 April – that was the night before the big attack. I told this corporal, 'I watched the shelling today and there was a German battery got the range of that sap that runs across the hill. They've got it lined up quite well and, if anything starts, *that*'s where the shelling will be.' All right. When the attack started and the SOS went up I scrambled out of this front-line trench and looked back, and here was this corporal not making a move to come. So I went to grab the Lewis-gun, but when he saw me going for it *he* grabbed a hold of it and started off. Of course he was the wrong man to be shooting in his panic like that. He wouldn't know whether he was hitting the mark or not, would he? No good in the firing line – just a menace. He would be just the wrong bugger in every way. Well, he'd just got up, and the bullets were flying, and a salvo of bullets whistled past and he ran back into the trench again. Well, that's not the place for a Lewis-gun! I thought, 'I'm going to take it off him.' So I jumped back into the trench just as Major O'Shaughnessey came through. 'McKay, take that gun out.' Well, as soon as he said that, the corporal grabbed the gun and ran forward again.

You could see Huns everywhere! Best bit of shooting you ever saw. Would have been lovely! There were paddocks *full* of them, in threes and fours everywhere, just the idea for Lewis-gun work. They were coming forward, because they meant to take our trenches, but as soon as this silly bugger got a look at the field of Huns he ran back and put the gun in that sap again.

Well, I felt my blooming adrenalin boiling in my blood. The anger I had that he'd sacrificed everything just because his nerve was buggered! Then came bang, bang. Two shells. I said to McArthur, 'We're getting the next one, Steve!' And with that up we went, up into the bloody air. I was standing in the middle of three – McArthur and the corporal, with myself in the middle, just shoulder to shoulder you might say. The shell must have landed right behind me, and I was blown straight over the top of the trench. As I turned over I saw first one and then

1. 'Half-pai' means half-good – a corruption of *ka pai*, which means 'good' in the Maori language.

the other in the air – we were all three of us in the air together. The other two were killed, but I was blown straight forward.

I tried to stand up, got up on the left leg, and then fell over as soon as I tried the right leg. There was no feeling in it. It could have been absent for all the good it was. I tried that twice, and then I went back into the front line on one knee and two hands, trailing the leg. I think what prevented me from getting shell-shock was that I was so angry with that bugger putting the gun where he did, because it was a sure target for the Hun. They registered on it.

One of the men who was in the first bay of the trench had been a Lewis-gunner – he was Sergeant Norris – and he took charge after I went. He said that our gun was the only one working at the finish. The others all had stoppages, but our gun kept on firing. Well, I know why that would be. I made every man clean his ammunition so there was no dust or mud on it. No mud or dust. The German attack stopped! Never got into our lines.

Not much more than a rifle shot away, the Jägers charging on the outskirts of Albert were equally unsuccessful, and Hubert Schroeter had not got far.

*Jäger Hubert Schroeter, 3rd Jäger Bn., 3rd [German] Marine Division*

At 8 a.m. we started. After a few hundred metres, when we crossed a road that led to Amiens, we were met by a terrific explosion of machine-gun fire. In the middle of the road I was hit by a machine-gun bullet which shattered my left upper arm. Both my legs were also hit slightly, just below the knees. Next to me my good comrade and friend Ludwig Krause was shot dead with a gaping wound in his chest. The other comrades of my section stormed forward and, as I found out later, all of them fell before they reached the English position.

I crawled into a deep furrow at the side of the road, seeking cover from the continuous machine-gun fire. I thought I was going to bleed to death, and I tried to bind my upper arm with a rifle sling. To do this I had to move about, and every time my helmet jutted up above the lip of the furrow the English fired their machine-guns at me. Due to a heavy loss of blood, I lost consciousness many times.

Outside Dernancourt, a little way to Schroeter's left, the German attack at first had greater success as they stormed through to capture the village. After the comparative quiet of the previous day it was a rude awakening for the Australians.

*Private Stanley Sutcliffe*

At seven o'clock in the morning such a barrage started as I have never seen before or since. Jerry had his guns registered on all our batteries, and was even knocking guns out miles behind the line at Warloy. It was a very foggy morning and we couldn't see much. He started this barrage on our front line and gradually lengthened his range until he got back on our artillery, and then he would shorten it gradually until he got on the front line again.

He did this three times until eleven o'clock, with the idea of killing every living thing in its way. He put three heavy shells within thirty yards of our post, but did no more damage than covering us with mud and giving us a good shaking up. Then he came over in full marching order, evidently with the idea of reaching Amiens without a stop. They say he had four divisions against only two of our brigades.

The first wave of Germans came in massed formation, and they were cut down by machine-gun fire just like a scythe cuts grass. But his second wave appeared, so the 52nd Battalion and our 12th Brigade hopped up and met it. That was the first time I experienced hand-to-hand fighting with the bayonet, and it was heavy! But the Germans kept being reinforced, with the result that we were pushed back about 1,000 yards.

The Australians did not take kindly to being pushed back, and, but for a direct order, they would not have relinquished their positions willingly, for, despite the bitter hand-to-hand combat, it seemed even to the fighting men that, although the shelling was more intense, the German infantry lacked spirit. That was not surprising, for, although some fresh troops had reached the line, the soldiers who were up against the tough Australians of the 12th Brigade had sustained two weeks of campaigning.

Unfortunately, the position of the 12th Brigade, along the curve of the railway, was a bad one, and the Corps Commander himself had admitted that it would be untenable if it were strongly attacked. Hand-to-hand fighting was one thing, but standing fast against heavy bombs was another, and trench mortars were soon firing from the village at close range. They were aimed at the railway embankment, and the very curve of the line enabled the Germans to break in on the right flank and fire into the backs of the men defending it. It was fortunate that this situation had been partly envisaged and that a new line of posts and trenches had been set up on the hill behind. It was to this line that the 12th Brigade was ordered to retire. It hardly gave them a breathing space, for they were not intended to remain there for long.

*Private Stanley Sutcliffe*

In the afternoon we were ordered to move up to a jumping-off point.
We came under some heavy machine-gun fire going over some hills.
The 49th Battalion were all in extended order behind a hill, and my
company was a little on their right, ready to make a counter-attack.
Evidently Jerry knew we were there, and he shelled us heavy with
instantaneous-fuse shells. They burst as soon as they touch the ground
and the pieces fly level with the ground, with the result that they are
very deadly. Our job was to start off with the 49th and move half-right
to reinforce the 52nd Battalion in a cutting alongside the railway
leading from Buire to Dernancourt. It seemed a strange thing that we
should be fighting on the very same hill on which a year before we
used to practise attacks in making ready for Bullecourt.

We started off, and the 49th went over just as calm as though they
were on parade. As soon as they got on the skyline the machine-guns
began to open up on them. We also started off, and we crossed one
gully that was being swept by machine-gun fire and got up near a
bank. We followed that for a way, but Jerry evidently knew we were
there and he followed us up with shrapnel until he got us in full view
on a hillside going down towards the railway. The machine-guns
opened up from Edgehill Clearing Station, which was on our flank,
and he was also firing point-blank at us with his artillery. The bullets
were whistling past you in all directions and chipping the earth up all
round you, whilst shells were bursting just in front of us all the way.

Through making it in rushes of a few men at a time and taking
advantage of cover so that we had very few casualties, we at last got
to where the 52nd were in the cutting. What a sight met us there!
Men were lying dead all over the place, and the Germans seemed to
be all around us. If you got up on the railway line they would fire into
you from behind from Edgehill Clearing Station. Then if you got up
facing the clearing station they would still fire into you from behind,
from the other side of the railway. We soon found out which side the
heaviest fire was coming from, so we settled down facing the CCS
and blazed away at all the windows we could see in the huts. We
hadn't been there long when word came that the 49th could not
connect up with the 52nd owing to casualties, so my company again
had another little job of going out just after dark to clear them out of
the clearing station and to dig in in front of it to establish a connection
between the 49th and 52nd Battalions. We did this with nothing more
than a bit of rifle fire.

There was also furious fighting in front of Villers-Bretonneux, where more Australian troops had moved up during the night to strengthen the line. The German troops attacking there were fresh; it was the guns that beat them back for most of the day. But the German guns were busy too. Late in the afternoon they launched a hurricane bombardment and, despite the rain, which had started to pour again, the Germans beat back the 55th Brigade more than a mile, and recaptured part of Lancer Wood.

Brigadier-General Wood did not take kindly to his brigade being scored over by the Germans. He was not a Regular officer, but pre-war service with the Brtitish South Africa Police had earned him a temporary commission with the rank of Captain at the start of the war. He had helped to train a new battalion of the King's Own Shropshire Light Infantry and had gone with it to France. In the course of three years' fighting and rapid promotion, Captain Wood rose to command the battalion, and eventually to command the brigade to which it belonged. He was as proud of it as he was of his original battalion, and he was not content to order its affairs at one remove from Brigade Headquarters – or certainly not today. Even as a Brigadier-General, Wood was first and foremost a soldier of the line, and, when a single battalion of his Brigade was ordered to attack with the Australians to recover the lost ground, nothing would deter him from leading the 7th Queen's into the attack. He led it from the front, cheering on the men, regardless of the consequences. They recovered the ground, although they suffered many losses, but the Brigadier emerged victorious and unscathed.

All along the front the fighting continued well into the evening and after it grew dark. In front of the railway embankment where he had been wounded early in the day, Hubert Schroeter recovered consciousness.

*Jäger Hubert Schroeter*

When I finally came to it was night. I had lain there all day, and now I saw death before my eyes. I was in pain, and I started to call for help. I hoped that perhaps the English would come after me, since I was not able to help myself. But then the first miracle happened. A soldier of my company, Gefreiter Fehlau, had fallen back to the railroad embankment after our unsuccessful attack. He heard my cries and sneaked from tree to tree along the road until he reached me. Then he carried me back to the railroad, where he dressed my wounds by the light of the moon with his own first-aid dressing. Throwing me over his back, Fehlau carried me through Albert. The English artillery were shelling the town, and we were in great danger of being hit by falling debris. When we crossed a street to find shelter in a doorway,

Fehlau told me he had noticed a light shining from a basement window. He was nearly at the end of his strength from carrying me.

Now the second miracle occurred. Fehlau left me in the doorway while he searched for the entrance to the basement, and there he found a doctor, several orderlies, and the equipment for a complete field hospital which was to have been built if our attack had been successful. An orderly helped him to carry me to the basement, and there I was treated. I was young and athletic, so, with great anxiety, I asked the doctor whether I would lose my arm. 'Dear friend,' he said, 'that is possible. But at least you will stay alive.'[1]

George McKay had also been carried out of the line, but he was far less happy than Schroeter, because his present situation seemed to him to be a good deal more dangerous than in the forefront of the fighting. His wounded leg had stiffened up, he was weak from loss of blood, and, helpless as he was, there was nothing he could do about it.

*Private George McKay*

I went back on a stretcher to Mailly-Maillet, and the first place they put me in was in the *estaminet*. Well, with every terrific crash of a shell bursting in the village there would be a whole lot of bottles falling down. Then they came and picked our stretchers up and took us into a church. So I'm lying there in the church, looking at a wall of bricks forty or fifty feet high. Can you believe how I would feel under those bricks? Of all the bloody places to put a wounded man! One smack from a shell and there would be tons of them down on us. So I was very happy when they moved us out of there. The church didn't agree with me. Too many bricks about. Well, one brick would have done it. Wouldn't have needed a thousand, and *that*'s what would have come down.

Through the days and across the miles of the retirement, the medical services had made almost superhuman efforts to rescue the wounded. Stretcher-bearers risked death or capture rather than leave the wounded behind; orderlies in regimental aid posts and doctors in field dressing stations chose to be captured with the wounded rather than abandon them. Ambulances drove forward through hair-raising bombardments to pick up casualties

1. Schroeter was eventually sent to the Empress Augusta Hospital in Breslau, where he remained for three years. The doctors saved his arm. It remained paralysed but, as he later philosophically remarked, 'At least I still had it.'

and carry them back to safety. At the Casualty Clearing Stations, when every bed in every tent was occupied, when stretchers had been laid in every possible space, all that could be done was to lay the overflow of wounded men on tarpaulins in the open and to cover them with blankets to wait their turn for the operating tent, for a bed in a marquee ward or, at worst, for a place in a convoy of lorries when the clearing station itself was forced to evacuate. If a wounded man was lucky he was carried on board an ambulance train. Twelve trains a day shuttled non-stop on ever-shorter journeys to hospitals at the base.

The base hospitals stretched for miles across the hills above the sea between Étaples and Boulogne, but they were also swamped, and their frantic staffs were working day and night as convoy upon convoy of casualties poured in.

*Sister Helen Boylston, No. 22 General Hospital, (Harvard Unit)*

Nearly every case should have been a stretcher-case. Ragged and dirty; tin hats still on; wounds patched together any way; some not even covered. They came direct from the line and their faces were white and drawn and their eyes glassy from lack of sleep. Matron sent us to the D lines, and she asked if my friend Ruth, myself and Topsy Stone could clean up 500 walkers. We thought we could, though heaven knows how we thought we were going to do it. We made a small table for the medical officer, and then a large table piled with bandages, splints, boric ointment, sponges and a basinful of Dakins solution for wet dressings. There were two smoky lanterns and an enfeebled primus stove. Ruth, armed with a pair of scissors, stood in the doorway and beckoned the boys in, two or three at a time. Because there was so much to do it was impossible to try to take the stiff, dried bandages off carefully. The only thing to do was to snatch them off with one desperate tug. Poor Ruth! She could hardly stand it. She'd cut the dressing down the middle, the poor lad looking on with set jaw and imploring eyes. There would be a quick jerk, a sharp scream from the lad, a sob from Ruth, and he was passed on to the medical officer, and Ruth began on the next. They came much too fast for us, and within fifteen minutes were standing twenty deep around the dressings table. As the hours went by we ceased to think. We worked through the night until dawn.[1]

1. Quoted from *The Roses of No Man's Land* by Lyn Macdonald (Michael Joseph, London, 1980; Penguin, London, 1993).

It was possible to keep only the most severely of the wounded at the base, and every man who could stand the journey – including those fortunate soldiers whose wound would not otherwise have been regarded as a Blighty – was sent directly to England by hospital ship, or even squeezed as a sitting case into an ordinary steamer bound for home. Charles Ruck was now a stretcher-case, although when he was first wounded as his company went forward to counter-attack at Aveluy Wood he had managed to crawl out of action.

*304723 Rifleman Charles Ruck, 1/28th (County of London) Bn. (The Artists' Rifles), The London Regt., 63rd Division*

The machine-gun fire caught me as I was making my dash, and I went down out of action, hit through the right knee. There was no point in exposing myself to further wounding, so it was time to evacuate – a painful procedure! That completed my military experience. There was nothing I could do about it. All that expensive training and endeavour, to end like this, without honour or glory – just a casualty! I hadn't even got into the attack with my section. Then it was dressing station, Doullens, Calais, Dover, where I lay on one of many stretchers on the Marine Station waiting to be shipped home. I knew I had a Blighty one, but I didn't feel grateful that I'd been spared a worse fate. All the old magic had suddenly gone.

At General Ludendorff's headquarters on the evening of 5 April the gloom deepened with the arrival of each fresh report from the front. They were bleak and disappointing. At the end of the day's fighting the German gains were so paltry that they merely amounted to an adjustment of the lines that was barely visible on the largest of large-scale maps. The gamble had not come off. There had been no final breakthrough, and the glorious beginning of the great advance on which Ludendorff had staked so much had ended in failure. He was forced to face the fact and to report that 'The enemy's resistance was beyond our powers.'

Late that evening, Ludendorff called off the offensive. It had failed in its ultimate objective. The Allied line was holding. Amiens was out of reach, and the game was no longer worth the candle.

It was exactly 1,340 days since the start of the war that was meant to be 'over by Christmas'. But as weeks became months, and months became years, as the roll of dead and wounded mounted, the names of the battles and campaigns that marked the course of the war rang ever more hollow in British ears. Mons. Ypres. Gallipoli. Loos. Somme. Arras. Passchendaele.

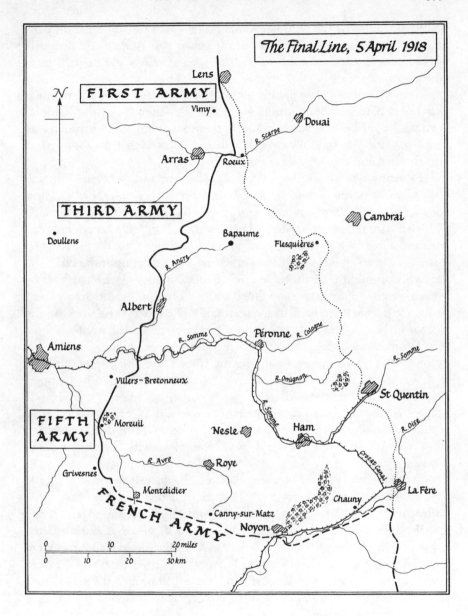

The Final Line, 5 April 1918

FIRST ARMY

N

Lens

Vimy

Douai

R. Scarpe

Arras

Roeux

THIRD ARMY

Cambrai

Doullens

Bapaume

Flesquières

R. Ancre

Albert

R. Somme

Péronne

R. Cologne

Amiens

R. Somme

Villers-Bretonneux

R. Omignon

St Quentin

FIFTH
ARMY

Moreuil

Nesle

R. Somme

Ham

R. Oise

Grivesnes

R. Avre

Roye

Crozat Canal

Montdidier

La Fère

FRENCH ARMY

Canny-sur-Matz

Chauny

Noyon

0        10              20 miles
0    10       20       30 km

Cambrai. And now the Battle of Amiens – or so it was later termed by the Battle Nomenclature Committee, whose job it was to date and designate every important action of the war for the sake of clarity and the benefit of historians.

But the Tommies were indifferent to historical niceties. To them, just as the Third Battle of Ypres would always be 'Passchendaele', the Battle of Amiens would be for ever 'the March Retreat'. They were hardly aware that the battle was officially over, but they did know that the long retreat had finished and that they were fighting back.

The Army was weary. Its ranks had multiplied and, weakened though they were, at home or abroad there were more than twenty men in khaki for every one of the gallant men of 1914 who had fought their way through the legendary retreat from Mons. There were a very few officers and men now at the front who had been there since the beginning, for the old Regular Army had been all but wiped out in the first three months of the war. The survivors of the first Territorial and Kitchener battalions – the 1915 men – were now the 'old sweats', and those who had fought on the Somme and at Passchendaele were hardened veterans. They had left their mark on the face of France, where a forest of graves ran thick along the front among a trail of towns and villages hammered into ruins by the guns.

The air of glum acceptance among the troops, the philosophy of taking each day as it came, was summed up by a cartoon published in a troops' magazine. Two battle-stained veterans are contemplating a shattered landscape. 'Do you remember halting here on the retreat, George?' asks the first. 'Can't call it to mind somehow,' replies the other. 'Was it that little village in the wood down by the river, or was it the place with the cathedral and all them factories?'

But the fact was that the deadlock had been broken. It was the end of the long beginning, of the campaigns and battles launched with high hopes that so frequently foundered in stalemate; the end of grinding drudgery in the trenches; the end of minuscule advances hailed as victories and of partial successes which were also semi-failures. The last people to realize this were the soldiers in the field, and they could hardly be blamed, for it was apparent only with hindsight that Ludendorff's offensive had broken the mould and, in a sense, pointed the way to eventual victory. It would come a good deal sooner than most people expected.

The end was still a long way off, and there were critical days ahead – but the last lap would soon be in sight.

# Epilogue

The British soldiers who were still face to face with the enemy in the line were slow to realize that the battle had ended, still less that, in one sense, they had won it. It did not feel much like a victory to the jaded men who had fought day by day, almost yard by yard, across the wearisome miles of the retreat. But they had done their job and stuck it out.

It was clear to both sides that their casualties had been considerable, although it was some time before the total losses of the British Army could be accurately assessed, for it had been almost impossible to record them day by day. They could be calculated approximately from routine battalion returns, but, given the nature of the fighting in the early stages of the retreat, such returns were invariably rough and ready. It could hardly have been otherwise. There were too few cases where a man was positively seen to have been killed, and too many where the lists of hard-hit battalions, made up after scratch roll-calls, were miserably inconclusive. *Missing. Missing. Missing.* A fair proportion of the men who were reported missing in the confusion of the retreat found their way back to rejoin their units, but many who were not accounted for were dead – and thousands had been captured.[1]

It was by no means easy for the Germans to deal with such numbers. The first unfortunates, like Ted Gale, Burt Eccles and Jim Brady, who were captured at the start of the offensive, were already on their reluctant way to Germany. After days of tramping round, it was almost a relief.

*3774 Corporal Ted Gale, 7th Bn., The Rifle Brigade, 14th Division*

We had nothing to eat for three days, and we was all worn out. Marching, marching, marching to God knows where. They kept us on the go all the time. Several times a French farmer who saw us going

---

1. The official final figures for British casualties between 21 March and 5 April 1918 were 160,000 killed, wounded and missing. Of this total, some 22,000 had been killed and approximately 72,000 had been captured by the enemy. German numbers of killed and wounded were roughly similar, with a much smaller number of prisoners.

along would throw us a carrot or a turnip. The women would leave pails of water along the side of the road, and if the Jerry guard was agreeable – and they weren't always! – they'd let us scoop it up with our hands. After three days they gave us a basin of soup. It was that thin that if you'd had a newspaper you could have read it through the stuff. Vegetable soup it was supposed to be. The vegetables were missing!

*203694 Rifleman Burt Eccles, 7th Bn., The Rifle Brigade, 14th Division*

They used to put us in a field at night. Just an open field – no shelter. My, but it was cold! Eventually we got to this railhead, and they loaded us in cattle trucks. We were in there twenty-four hours. It was an awful journey that! If only there'd been room to lie down, but there wasn't. Packed like sardines we were! We ended up at this place, Langensalze, and we had to turn out and strip, and they shaved all the hair off our bodies and gave us a cold shower. No soap. It was a shocking place. When you went on parade you hadn't to move a muscle or they slapped you. They were a rotten lot at that place! I got a bad impression of the Germans there. Not fighting soldiers at all. The dregs of their army. At least when we landed there we got a bit of food, if you can call it that. It was just about enough to keep body and soul together.

*37468 Private Walter Hare, 15th Bn., West Yorkshire Regt., 31st Division*

They didn't knock us about, but a lot of our chaps died of cold and starvation after we were taken. We were just lying out on the ground. It was cold and it was raining, and there you were. You'd be trying to get a bit of sleep, and then you found you were lying in a pool of water and you had to get up again.

The first few days they made us carry ammunition to their troops – boxes of small-arms ammunition. Prisoners weren't supposed to do that, but there's nothing you could do about it – they wouldn't take the slightest notice of you. We were prisoners, and we were treated as prisoners. Then we had to work on a railway line they were building, and we were starving hungry. After five days we got some soup and a bit of bread. Nothing else.

I remember one morning we were walking down to Rommecourt, where this railway was – it was two miles away – and I noticed at the roadside there was a little stream and there was some watercress growing. So I thought, 'Right, I'll get to that side as we come back, and I'll have some of that watercress.' So I got to the left-hand side of the

column. We didn't have to march as such, we were just trailing along.
So we got to where this stream was. I got down and I was just getting
a bunch of watercress when the butt of a rifle came into my back and
this German knocked me right into the stream. I was absolutely wet
through – and I got no watercress. All I got was a bruise as big as a
dinner plate on my back – so I didn't do that any more! We were glad
to get away from there and get sent back into Germany. It wasn't too
bad there – not as bad as that, anyway!

But it was depressing to be in limbo, deprived of any news but rumour
and propaganda passed on by their captors, and the guards in camps where
there were prisoners of long standing were only too pleased to inform their
captives that the Kaiser had trounced the British Army, and to gloat over
their dismay. Fred White, who had been captured at Cambrai in November,
had been incarcerated ever since in a prison work camp in Belgium, and his
particular *bête noire* was an unfriendly guard who was especially disdainful of
the British and never missed an opportunity of rubbing it in.

*8529 Rifleman Fred White, 10th (Service) Bn., The King's Royal Rifle
Corps, 20th Division*

The food we got was terrible – well, it wasn't food that you could call
food. Naturally we had to eat this blooming muck, but of course we
used to grumble about it. Whenever we did, this Jerry *Posten* always
came out with the saying '*Englander nicht essen*' – as if to say that we'd
never had any decent grub and didn't recognize good German food
when we got it. Good food! It was a bit of rotten cabbage leaf floating
in dishwater most of the time. Well, one day he turned up smoking
Gold Flake cigarettes, flashing the packet, and flashing packets of
chocolate and I don't know what all. His brother had brought a load
of things back from France, and this fellow was going on about how
the Germans had advanced and captured food and stuff galore. Done
down the British, he was saying – '*England kaput*' sort of thing – and
boasting about all the stuff they'd got off us. So I just looked at him,
and I said, 'So? *Englander nicht essen?*' And he waved his arms about
and said, '*Nie, nie, nie, nie! Englander essen.*' At least he had the decency
to admit it! Not that he offered me any of the stuff. Oh no!

The great *Michael* offensive had cost the Germans dear in manpower and
materials. Much blood had been spilled. It was true that they had advanced
as much as forty miles, but where they had travelled furthest and gained
most ground their position in a mishmash of abandoned trenches and

rudimentary emplacements was far from favourable. Their supply lines were now dangerously stretched – stretched, moreover, across the shattered terrain of the old Somme battlefield and beyond it across the twenty-five miles of devastated country which the Germans themselves had deliberately laid waste in their tactical retirement the previous spring.

If anyone had been tempted to say 'I told you so', it might have been Colonel Georg Wetzell, Ludendorff's Operations Officer on the German General Staff. Wetzell had envisaged this very situation, and emphasized its difficulties in a thoughtful strategical study drawn up as long ago as the previous December.

> It must not be forgotten that in a successful offensive the attacker will be forced to cross a difficult and shot-to-pieces battle area and will get gradually further away from his railheads and depots, and that, having to bring forward his masses of artillery and ammunition columns, he will be compelled to make pauses which will give time to the defender to organize resistance. Too optimistic hopes should not be conceived, therefore, as regards the rapidity of a breakthrough attack on the Western Front.

The plan which Wetzell had gone on to propose certainly did include a breakthrough on the St Quentin front, but only as the first of a series of blows struck swiftly at different points along the British line. He had never suggested that it should progress beyond a certain point, nor that it should continue longer than was necessary to draw away reserves from the northern areas and weaken those parts of the front on which fresh powerful assaults would fall. This plan, strategically sound though it was, had been rejected in favour of a massive blow from St Quentin. Now, having failed in his ultimate objective, and although his manpower and resources were seriously diminished, Ludendorff turned back to Wetzell's original scheme. Arrangements had already been put in hand for a fresh attack – although, of necessity, it would have to be scaled down.

Even before Ludendorff made his final bid for Amiens on 5 April, British intelligence had reported that the enemy was moving troops and guns to the north. He would surely strike again, and the Allied commanders were fully aware of it. Precisely where or when the attack would be launched was still not clear, but they braced themselves to meet it when it came.

At the end of the Kaiser's Battle, the Allies were out of breath – but they were not at their last gasp. Nor had Ludendorff given up hope of victory. He had played his last trump card and had finally thrown in his hand. But the Germans had not thrown in the towel.

Many more battles would be waged and many more months would pass before they did.

# Bibliography

*History of the Great War, Military Operations – France and Belgium, 1918, Vols. I and II*, compiled by Brigadier-General Sir James E. Edmonds (Macmillan, 1935 and 1937)

*The Official History of New Zealand's Effort in the Great War, Vol. II: The New Zealand Division 1916–1919*, Colonel H. Stewart, CMG, DSO, MC (Whitcombe & Tombs, 1921)

*Official History of Australia in the War of 1914–1918, Vol. VI*, C. E. W. Bean (Angus & Robertson, 1942)

*The Eighth Division in War 1914–1918*, Lieutenant-Colonel J. H. Boraston and Captain Cyril E. O. Bax (Medici Society, 1926)

*The History of the 9th (Scottish) Division: 1914–1919*, Major John Ewing, MC (John Murray, 1921)

*The Fifteenth (Scottish) Division 1914–1919*, Lieutenant-Colonel J. Stewart, DSO, and John Buchan (William Blackwood, 1926)

*History of the 17th (Northern) Division*, A. Hilliard Atteridge (Robert Maclehose, 1929)

*The 18th Division in the Great War*, Captain G. H. F. Nichols (William Blackwood, 1922)

*The History of the Twentieth (Light) Division*, Captain V. E. Inglefield (Nisbet, 1921)

*The 47th (London) Division 1914–1919*, ed. Alan H. Maude (Amalgamated Press, 1922)

*History of the Royal Regiment of Artillery*, General Sir Martin Farndale, KCB (Henry Ling, 1986)

*Historical Records of the Buffs (East Kent Regt.) 3rd Foot, 1914–1919*, Colonel R. S. H. Moody (Medici Society, 1922)

*A Short History of the 55th Infantry Brigade in the War of 1914–18* (privately published, n.d.)

*The Rifle Brigade 1914–1918, Vol. II*, Brigadier-General William Seymour (The Rifle Brigade Club, 1936)

*The History of the London Rifle Brigade 1859–1919* (Constable, 1921)

*The Royal Scots 1914–1919*, Major John Ewing, MC (Oliver & Boyd, 1925)

*The Oxfordshire Hussars in the Great War*, A. Keith-Falconer (John Murray, 1927)

*The Worcestershire Regiment in the Great War*, Captain H. FitzM. Stacke, MC (G. T. Cheshire & Sons, 1928)

*The London Scottish in the Great War*, ed. Lieutenant-Colonel J. H. Lindsay, DSO (London Scottish Regimental HQ, 1925)

*The History of the Prince of Wales's Own Civil Service Rifles* (Wyman & Sons, 1921)

*The History of the 1/4th Battalion Duke of Wellington's (West Riding) Regiment, 1914–1919*, Captain P. G. Bales, MC (Edward Mortimer, 1920)

*Sir Douglas Haig's Despatches*, ed. Lieutenant-Colonel J. H. Boraston, CB, OBE (J. M. Dent & Sons, 1919)

*The Private Papers of Douglas Haig 1914–1919*, ed. Robert Blake (Eyre & Spottiswoode, 1952)

*Douglas Haig – The Educated Soldier*, John Terraine (Hutchinson, 1963)

*Haig*, Duff Cooper (Faber and Faber, 1935)

*Field-Marshal Sir Henry Wilson, GCB, DSO – His Life and Diaries, Vol. II*, ed. Major-General Sir C. E. Callwell, KCB (Cassell, 1927)

*The Fifth Army*, General Sir Hubert Gough, GCMG, KCB, KCVO (Hodder & Stoughton, 1931)

*The March Retreat*, General Sir Hubert Gough, GCMG, KCB, KCVO (Cassell, 1934)

*Soldiering On*, General Sir Hubert Gough, GCB, GCMG, KCVO (Arthur Barker, 1954)

*Goughie: The Life of General Sir Hubert Gough*, Anthony Farrar-Hockley (Hart-Davis, MacGibbon, 1975)

*Tempestuous Journey – Lloyd George, his Life and Times*, Frank Owen (Hutchinson, 1954)

*The Supreme Command 1914–1918, Vol. II*, Lord Hankey (George Allen & Unwin, 1961)

*The First World War 1914–1918*, Lieutenant-Colonel Repington, CMG (Constable, 1920)

*The Sword-Bearers*, Correlli Barnett (Eyre & Spottiswoode, 1963)

*My War Memories 1914–1918, Vol. II*, General Ludendorff (Hutchinson, n.d.)

*My Memoirs: 1878–1918*, Ex-Kaiser William II (Cassell, 1922)

*The Last Kaiser*, Tyler Whittle (William Heinemann, 1977)

*A Fatalist at War*, Rudolf Binding (George Allen & Unwin, 1933)

*The Storm of Steel*, Ernst Jünger (Chatto & Windus, 1929)

*Victory Must be Ours – Germany in the Great War – 1914–1918*, Laurence V. Moyer (Leo Cooper, 1995)

*The First World War – Germany and Austria-Hungary 1914–1918*, Holger H. Herwig (Arnold, 1997)

*The Memoirs of Marshal Foch*, trans. Col. T. Bentley Mott (William Heinemann, 1931)

*At the Heart of a Tiger – Clemenceau and his World*, Gregor Dallas (Macmillan,
1993)

*French Headquarters, 1915–1918*, Jean de Pierrefeu, trans. Major C. J. C. Street,
OBE, MC (Geoffrey Bles, 1926)

*La Grande Guerre – par les combattants*, ed. M. Christian-Frogé (Librairie
Aristide Quillet, 1933)

*The War Office at War*, Sir Sam Fay (EP Publishing, 1973)

*The Red and White Diamond*, Sergeant W. J. Harvey, MM (Alexander
McCubbin, n.d.)

*With the 10th Essex in France*, Lieutenant-Colonel T. M. Banks, DSO, MC,
and Captain R. A. Chell, DSO, MC (Burt & Sons, 1921)

*A Company of Tanks*, Major W. H. L. Watson, DSO, DCM (William
Blackwood, 1920)

*A Frenchman in Khaki*, Paul Maze, DCM, MM, C. de G. (William Heinemann, 1934)

*Extracts from an Officer's Diary 1914–1918*, Lieutenant-Colonel Harrison Johnston, DSO (G. Falkner & Sons, 1919)

*War is War*, A. McLelland-Burrage (Victor Gollancz, 1930)

*Four Years on the Western Front*, Aubrey Smith (Odhams, 1922)

*War Letters to a Wife*, Lieutenant-Colonel Rowland Feilding (Medici Society,
1929)

*The Great War . . . 'I Was There'*, Vol. III, ed. Sir John Hammerton (Amalgamated Press, n.d.)

*The Doughboys*, Laurence Stallings (Harper & Row, 1963)

*The Home Fronts – Britain, France and Germany – 1914–1918*, John Williams
(Constable, 1972)

# Author's Note

I wish to acknowledge my debt to all of the following, without whose valuable assistance this book could never have been written.

Private F. J. Ahlquist, 2/1st Battalion, Cambridgeshire Regiment
Guardsman J. Alderman, 4th Battalion, Grenadier Guards
Lieutenant J. R. T. Aldous, MC, 210 Field Company, Royal Engineers
Corporal R. H. Allan, OBE, 14th Battalion, Argyll and Sutherland Highlanders
Second Lieutenant William Allbeury, MC, C. de G. (Belg.), 18th Battalion, Durham Light Infantry
Lance-Corporal John Alpe, 13th Battalion, The Rifle Brigade
Private H. Atherton, 28th Field Ambulance, Royal Army Medical Corps
Lieutenant-Colonel M. F. T. Baines, OBE, Royal Artillery
Rifleman J. Baker, 13th Battalion, The Rifle Brigade
Private L. Baldwin, MM, 8th Battalion, East Surrey Regiment
Driver W. Ballard, MBE, 290 Brigade, Royal Field Artillery
Corporal G. Barnes, 8th Battalion, Oxfordshire and Buckinghamshire Light Infantry
Sergeant H. Bartlett, 115 Brigade, Royal Field Artillery
Rifleman J. Bassett, 11th Battalion, The Rifle Brigade
Colonel H. A. Bazley, 3rd Field Squadron, Royal Engineers
Lance-Corporal J. Belsey, 9th (County of London) Battalion, The London Regiment
Corporal T. Benson, 20th Battalion, The King's (Liverpool Regiment)
Second Lieutenant R. Best, 53 Squadron, Royal Flying Corps
Sergeant Major H. Blizard, 2/16th (County of London) Battalion (Queen's Westminster Rifles), The London Regiment
Private J. Brady, 43rd Field Ambulance, Royal Army Medical Corps
Captain G. Brett, MC, 23rd (County of London) Battalion, The London Regiment
First Lieutenant A. Brewer, 1st Battalion, 101st Infantry Regiment, 26th (Yankee) Division

Corporal A. B. Brown, 3rd (City of London) Battalion (Royal Fusiliers),
The London Regiment

Private J. Bryant, MM, 8th Battalion, Australian Imperial Force

Private R. Buckley, MM, 9th Battalion, Royal Irish Fusiliers

Private A. J. Bull, 2/5th Battalion, West Yorkshire Regiment

Private W. Callow, 13th Battalion, Royal Welch Fusiliers

Private W. R. Carter, 7th Battalion, Leicestershire Regiment

Gunner W. P. Castel, MM, 2/20th (County of London) Battalion, The
London Regiment

Sergeant C. Caulton, 9th Battalion, Leicestershire Regiment

Private F. Caulton, 2nd (City of London) Battalion (Royal Fusiliers), The
London Regiment

Private E. S. Cecil, 15th Battalion, The Hampshire Regiment

Lieutenant L. Chamberlen, MC, 2nd Battalion, The Rifle Brigade

Private W. Chambers, 1st Battalion, The Sherwood Foresters (Nottinghamshire and Derbyshire Regiment)

Lieutenant H. M. Chaundy, MC, 4th Battalion, The Duke of Cambridge's
Own (Middlesex Regiment)

Pioneer G. T. H. Cheeseman, 7th Signal Troop, Royal Engineers (Signals),
7th Cavalry Brigade

Captain R. Chell, DSO, MC, 10th Battalion, The Essex Regiment

Private F. Christianson, Royal Canadian Dragoons

Lance-Corporal F. B. J. Cleary, 1st (City of London) Battalion (London
Rifle Brigade), The London Regiment

Sergeant H. B. Coates, 14th (County of London) Battalion (London Scottish),
The London Regiment

Sapper J. Cobb, 39 Brigade, Royal Engineers (Signals)

Rifleman W. F. Coldrick, 13th Battalion, The Rifle Brigade

Private P. M. Cook, 6th Battalion, Royal West Kent Regiment

Driver C. W. Coombe, Royal Army Service Corps

Private G. Copping, 2/20th (County of London) Battalion, The London
Regiment

Private J. B. Coventry, 1st Battalion, The Royal Warwickshire Regiment

Private E. Cowles, 3rd Battalion, The Worcestershire Regiment

Trooper J. Cowling, B Squadron, 18th Hussars

Private T. Coy, 6th Battalion, The Northamptonshire Regiment

Sergeant J. C. Craddock, 2nd Battalion, The Royal Irish Rifles

Lieutenant Marsden Crawshaw, MC, The Loyal North Lancashire
Regiment

Lieutenant K. Crewes, MC, 27th Battalion, 2nd [Australian] Division,
Australian Imperial Force

Rifleman D. Cronk, 11th Battalion, The Rifle Brigade

Sergeant W. Darlington, 18th Battalion, The Manchester Regiment

Sergeant E. J. Davidson, MM, Royal Engineers

Corporal J. W. Davies, 18th Brigade, Field Ambulance, Royal Army Medical Corps

Private J. A. Davison, 6th Battalion, The Northumberland Fusiliers

Rifleman J. W. Dicker, 13th Battalion, The Rifle Brigade

Corporal G. Douglas, 7th Battalion, Seaforth Highlanders

Sergeant A. Dunbar, 236 Artillery Brigade, Royal Field Artillery

Sergeant Pilot G. F. Duncan, Royal Flying Corps

Captain F. E. Dunsmuir, MC, 2nd Battalion, The Highland Light Infantry

Sergeant H. J. Dykes, Tank Corps

Rifleman B. Eccles, 7th Battalion, The Rifle Brigade

Sergeant S. E. Elford, NZ Rifle Brigade

Gunner A. E. Ellingford, MM, 28 Brigade, Royal Field Artillery

Sergeant R. Elwis, 12th Siege Battery, Royal Garrison Artillery

Lance-Corporal G. England, 3rd Battalion, Grenadier Guards

Rifleman J. R. Finch, 2nd Battalion, The King's Royal Rifle Corps

Corporal R. Findlater, 9th Battalion, The Highland Light Infantry

Sergeant G. W. Fisher, MM, 1st Battalion, The Hertfordshire Regiment

Private E. Foote, 10th Battalion, The Royal Warwickshire Regiment

Rifleman J. Forbes, 5th Battalion, The Rifle Brigade

Private E. Ford, 10th Battalion, The Queen's (Royal West Surrey Regiment)

Corporal R. A. Ford, 157 Brigade, Royal Field Artillery

Lance-Corporal H. Forrest, 9th Battalion, Argyll and Sutherland Highlanders

Signaller F. Foster, Royal Field Artillery

Corporal J. Francis, The Middlesex Regiment

Corporal F. Franklin, 5th (City of London) Battalion (Royal Fusiliers), The London Regiment

Sapper G. A. Franklin, Royal Engineers Signal Company

Private S. Fraser, MM, 2nd Battalion, Honourable Artillery Company

Corporal E. Gale, 7th Battalion, The Rifle Brigade

Second Lieutenant J. R. Gammell, 1/7th Battalion, The Black Watch (Royal Highlanders)

Signaller C. Gardner, 15th Battalion, The Rifle Brigade

Private A. Garrison, 6th Battalion, The York and Lancaster Regiment

Private H. Goodby, 1/14th (County of London) Battalion (London Scottish), The London Regiment

Sergeant W. Haddleton, 1/6th Battalion, The Royal Warwickshire Regiment

Private J. Hain, 9th Battalion, Royal Irish Fusiliers

Sapper A. Halestrap, MBE, Royal Engineers (Signals)

Captain Eric Hall, MC, 1st Battalion, The Buffs (East Kent Regiment)

Sapper J. Hamill, 36 Signal Company, Royal Engineers

Second Lieutenant J. Phelps Harding, 3rd Battalion, 154th Infantry, 42nd [US] Division

Private J. Hardy, 1/7th (Robin Hood) Battalion, The Sherwood Foresters (Nottinghamshire and Derbyshire Regiment)

Private W. Hare, 15th Battalion, West Yorkshire Regiment

Corporal A. Harris, 27th Battalion, Australian Imperial Force

Lance-Corporal A. Hartland, 1/6th Battalion, The South Staffordshire Regiment

Private H. Haynes, 2/6th Battalion, The Royal Warwickshire Regiment

Rifleman D. Haywood, 15th (County of London) Battalion (Prince of Wales' Own Civil Service Rifles), The London Regiment

Lieutenant C. W. Healey, MC, 9th Battalion, The Lancashire Fusiliers

Brigadier T. E. H. Helby, Royal Garrison Artillery

A. B. E. Henderson, 63rd Royal Naval Division

Sergeant Hervey, MM, 24th Infantry Battalion, 2nd [Australian] Division, Australian Imperial Force

Signaller L. Hill, 16th Battalion, The Cheshire Regiment

Sergeant T. S. Hogg, 12th Battalion, The York and Lancaster Regiment

Private R. Holmes, 2/5th Battalion, The South Staffordshire Regiment

Corporal R. Houghton, 20th (County of London) Battalion, The London Regiment

Rifleman A. Howard, 9th (County of London) Battalion (Queen Victoria's Rifles), The London Regiment

Lieutenant J. Hudson, 10th Battalion (Kent County), The Queen's Own (Royal West Kent Regiment)

Lieutenant R. Hudson, MC, 9th Battalion, The Royal Sussex Regiment

Private G. Hull, The Queen's (Royal West Surrey Regiment)

Private H. Hurst, 1/5th Battalion, South Lancashire Regiment

Private H. Innis, 7th Battalion, The Northumberland Fusiliers

Rifleman R. Ison, 9th Battalion, The Rifle Brigade

Private H. R. James, 2/7th Battalion, The Manchester Regiment

Lieutenant G. B. Jameson, MC, Royal Field Artillery

Private A. J. Jamieson, MM, 11th Battalion, The Royal Scots

Private H. N. Jeary, 1st Battalion, The Queen's (Royal West Surrey Regiment)

Second Lieutenant A. B. Jeffries, 2nd Battalion, Royal Berkshire Regiment

Sergeant G. Johnson, DCM, 16th Battalion, The Royal Sussex Regiment

Lieutenant R. C. B. Jones, MC, 15th Battalion, The Lancashire Fusiliers

First-Class Air Mechanic G. Joyce, Royal Flying Corps

Private F. Julian, 2/14th (County of London) Battalion (London Scottish), The London Regiment

Lance-Corporal G. Labdon, Machine Gun Corps

Captain G. Lawrence, 1st South African Battalion, 9th (Scottish) Division

Private R. F. Lawrence, 1st Battalion, South African Infantry

Rifleman S. E. Lawrence, 13th Battalion, The Rifle Brigade

Private H. Leak, 1/5th Battalion, West Yorkshire Regiment

Lieutenant-Colonel W. F. Lean, DSO, C. de G., Inns of Court Officers Training Corps, West Yorkshire Regiment

Driver E. Ledger, 159 Brigade, Royal Field Artillery

Sergeant E. Lincoln, 13th (County of London) Princess Louise's Kensington Battalion, The London Regiment

Rifleman H. E. Lister, MM, 12th Battalion, The Rifle Brigade

Signaller C. Littlewood, 1/14th (County of London) Battalion (London Scottish), The London Regiment

Second Lieutenant R. Lloyd, A Battery, Royal Horse Artillery

Private W. Lockey, 1st Battalion, The Sherwood Foresters (Nottinghamshire and Derbyshire Regiment)

Corporal L. Longhurst, 16th (County of London) Battalion, The London Regiment

Private W. Luff, 1st Battalion, The Queen's (Royal West Surrey Regiment)

Private C. H. Luffman, 7th Battalion, The King's (Shropshire Light Infantry)

Gunner W. Lugg, MM, 83 Brigade, Royal Field Artillery

Gunner Lynch-Staunton, 5th Brigade, 2nd Canadian Division, Canadian Field Artillery

Private G. McKay, 1st Battalion, NZ Rifle Brigade

Colonel A. E. MacNicol, 103 Brigade, Royal Field Artillery

Private H. de Maine, 1/6th Battalion, The Duke of Wellington's (West Riding Regiment)

Signaller N. Maltby, MM, 291 Brigade, Royal Field Artillery

Driver W. Mann, Royal Field Artillery

Lieutenant F. Mansfield, 8th Siege Battery, Royal Garrison Artillery

Gunner D. Marchant, Royal Field Artillery

Lance-Corporal H. E. Marden, 13th Battalion, The Royal Sussex Regiment

Private H. Marshall, 7th Battalion, The Border Regiment

General Sir James Marshall-Cornwall, KCB, CBE, DSO, MC, Royal Artillery

Private N. Mellor, 4th Battalion, The Bedfordshire Regiment

Corporal H. Merrett, MM, Royal Engineers

Private J. Mortimer, MM, 10th Battalion, The York and Lancaster Regiment

Corporal E. Organ, A Squadron, Queen's Own Oxfordshire Hussars and Tank Corps

Brigadier E. K. Page, MC, 40 Brigade, Royal Field Artillery

Private G. Palmer, 7th Battalion, The Queen's Own (Royal West Kent Regiment)

Corporal A. D. Pankhurst, Stokes Mortar Section, 56th (London) Division

Rifleman C. Ruck, 1/28th (County of London) Battalion (The Artists' Rifles), The London Regiment

Rifleman C. Shepherd, 13th (Service) Battalion, The Rifle Brigade

Private W. Shepstone, 4th Battalion, The Queen's Own (Royal West Kent Regiment)

Signaller V. Simpson, 9th Battalion, The Duke of Wellington's (West Riding Regiment)

Rifleman A. Smith, 5th (City of London) Battalion (London Rifle Brigade), The London Regiment

Private R. Smith, 16th (County of London) Battalion (Queen's Westminster Rifles), The London Regiment

Corporal R. Tate, 3rd Battalion, Tank Corps

Private F. A. J. Taylor, 2nd Battalion, The Worcestershire Regiment

Sergeant E. H. Teagarden, 117th Ammunition Train, 42nd [US] Division

Private J. H. Tottey, 1/7th Battalion, The Lancashire Fusiliers

Sergeant F. Udall, MM and 2 bars, 4th (City of London) Battalion (Royal Fusiliers), 56th (London) Division

Trooper H. Ward, A Squadron, Queen's Own Oxfordshire Hussars

Rifleman F. White, 10th (Service) Battalion, The King's Royal Rifle Corps

Private E. G. Williams, 19th Battalion, The King's (Liverpool Regiment)

Lieutenant A. Wilson, MC, 7 Squadron, Royal Flying Corps

Lieutenant T. Witherow, 2nd Battalion, The Royal Irish Rifles

Guardsman J. H. Worker, 1st Battalion, Scots Guards

# Index